ARLENE FELTMAN SAILHAC'S
De GUSTIBUS PRESENTS

Great Recipes of the Great Cooks

ARLENE FELTMAN SAILHAC'S
De GUSTIBUS PRESENTS

Great Recipes
of the
Great Cooks

DESIGN BY MARTIN LUBIN

BLACK DOG
& LEVENTHAL
PUBLISHERS
NEW YORK

Published by

Black Dog & Leventhal Publishers
151 West 19th Street
New York, NY 10011

Distributed by

Workman Publishing Company
708 Broadway
New York, NY 10003

Typesetting by Angela Taormina

Manufactured in the United States of America

ISBN 1-884822-85-1

h g f e d c b a

Catalan Tomato Bread; Swordfish with Pine Nuts and Raisins adapted from *Catalan Cuisine* by Colman Andrews. Copyright © 1988 Colman Andrews. Used by permission of Atheneum Publishers, New York.

Thanks to Lidia Bastianich for permission to publish her recipes. Potato Gnocchi with Fresh Sage Sauce appears in *La Cucina di Lidia* by Lidia Bastianich and Jay Jacobs. Copyright © 1990 by Lidia Bastianich and Jay Jacobs. Published by Bantam Doubleday Dell Publishing Group, Inc., New York.

Stuffed Cornish Game Hens with Crumb and Sausage Stuffing adapted from *A Family Christmas*, a Reader's Digest Publication. Special thanks to Edwin O. McFarlane at Reed College, Portland, Oregon, for use of this recipe. All of James Beard's recipes used by permission of John Ferrone.

Eggplant and Crab Garbure with Cumin and Tomato Confit; Broiled Pompano with Pickles and Vegetables from *Cooking with Daniel Boulud* by Daniel Boulud. Copyright © 1993 Daniel Boulud. Reprinted by permission of Random House, Inc., New York.

Sweet Green Tomato Pie adapted from Tomato Tourte in *Antoine Bouterin's Desserts from Le Périgord* with Ruth Gardner. Copyright ©1989 by Antoine Bouterin. Used by permission of G.P. Putnam's Sons, New York.

Tirami-sù by Biba Caggiano to be published in *Love Cookbook* used by permission of Slack Publishing.

Julia Child's recipes are reprinted by permission of Julia Child. Artichoke Bottoms Filled with Poached Oysters appears in *Julia Child: The Way to Cook* by Julia Child. Copyright © 1989 by Julia Child. Published by Alfred A. Knopf, New York.

All of Craig Claiborne's recipes adapted from *Craig Claiborne's: A Feast Made for Laughter* by Craig Claiborne. Copyright © 1982 by Craig Claiborne. Used by permission of Doubleday, a division of Bantam Doubleday Dell Publishing Group, Inc., New York.

Warm Lobster Taco with Yellow Tomato Salsa and Jícama Salad; Grilled Swordfish with Pineapple-Red Chile Salsa; and Brown Butter Berry Tart adapted from *The Mansion on Turtle Creek Cookbook* by Dean Fearing. Copyright © 1987 by Rosewood Hotels, Inc. Used by Permission of Grove Press, New York.

Grilled Tuna Tostada with Black Bean-Mango Salsa and Avocado Vinaigrette; Spicy Chicken, Eggplant, and Grilled Red Onion Quesadilla with Tomatillo Salsa; Roast Leg of Lamb with Red Chile Crust and Jalapeño Preserves; Sweet Potato Gratin with Chiles; Red Pepper-Crusted Tenderloin of Beef with Wild Mushroom-Ancho Chile Sauce and Black Bean-Goat Cheese Torta; and Blue Corn Biscotti reprinted by permission of Warner Books/New York from *Bold American Food* Copyright © 1993 by Bobby Flay.

Fillet of Beef with Horseradish Sauce from *Cuisine Rapide* by Pierre Franey and Bryan Miller. Copyright © 1989 by Pierre Franey and Bryan Miller. Adapted by permission of Times Books, a division of Random House, Inc., New York.

Spanakopita; Almond Skordalia; White Beans with Garlic; Fillet of Snapper with Tomato, Onion, and Garlic; and Baklava adapted from *The Periyali Cookbook—New Classic Greek Cooking* by Holly Garrison with Nicola Kotsoni and Steve Tzolis. Copyright © 1992 Holly Garrison, Nicola Katsoni, and Steve Tzolis. Used by permission of Villard Books.

Spaghetti with Saffroned Onions, Greens, Sun-Dried Tomatoes, and Currants; Gateau Rolla adapted from *Back to Square One: Old World Food in a New World Kitchen* by Joyce Goldstein. Copyright © 1992 Joyce Goldstein. Used by permission of William Morrow & Co., Inc., New York.

Clams "Al Forno"; Shells "Al Forno" with Mushrooms and Radicchio; and Cranberry-Walnut Tart from *Cucina Simpatica* by Johanne Killeen and George Germon. Copyright © 1991 by Johanne Killeen and George Germon. Reprinted by permission of Harper-Collins Publishers, Inc., New York.

Big Easy Seafood-Okra Gumbo from *Emeril's New Orleans Cooking* by Emeril Lagasse and Jessie Tirsch. Copyright © 1993 Emeril Lagasse. Reprinted by permission of William Morrow and Company, Inc., New York.

Penne with Asparagus; Trout Cooked in Vernaccia di Oristano; and Walnut Tart adapted from *The Food of Southern Italy* by Carlo Middione. Copyright © 1987 by Carlo Middione. Used by permission of William Morrow & Company, Inc., New York.

All of Bradley Ogden's recipes adapted from *Breakfast, Lunch and Dinner* by Bradley Ogden. Copyright © 1991 by Bradley Ogden. Used by permission of Random House, Inc., New York.

Lettuce Soup; Scallopine of Turkey Breast with Morel and Cognac Sauce; and Fricassee of Turkey and Brown Rice adapted from *Cuisine Economique* by Jacques Pépin. Copyright © 1992 by Jacques Pépin. By permission of William Morrow & Company, Inc., New York.

Apple Bonne Femme adapted from *Everyday Cooking with Jacques Pépin* by Jacques Pépin. Copyright © 1982 by Jacques Pépin. By permission of Harper & Row, New York.

Grilled Salmon with Black Pepper and Ginger from *Adventures in the Kitchen* by Wolfgang Puck. Copyright © 1991 by Wolfgang Puck. Adapted by permission of Random House, Inc., New York.

Fresh Tuna with Maui Onions and Avocado, and Pecan Pie from *The Wolfgang Puck Cookbook* by Wolfgang Puck. Copyright © 1986 by Wolfgang Puck. Adapted by permission of Random House, Inc., New York.

Marta Pulini's Gelato di Parmigiano to be published in *The Taste of Memory*. Used with permission of Sterling Publishing Co., Inc., 387 Park Avenue South, New York, N.Y., 10016 from *The Art of Italian Regional Cooking* by Francesco Antonucci, Marta Pulini, and Gianni Salvaterra. Copyright © 1993 by Edizioni Il Fenicottero, English Edition Text © 1995.

Jícama-Melon Relish; Creamed Corn Pudding; and Cranberry-Mango Cobbler with Cinnamon-Pecan Cream adapted from *The New Texas Cuisine* by Stephan Pyles. Copyright © 1993 by Stephan Pyles. Used by permission of Doubleday, a division of Bantam Doubleday Dell Publishing Group, Inc., New York.

Thanks to Anne Rosenzweig for permission to reprint Chocolate Bread Pudding, adapted from *The Arcadia Seasonal Mural and Cookbook* by Anne Rosenzweig. Copyright © 1986 Anne Rosenzweig. Published by Harry N. Abrams, Inc., New York.

Sweet Pepper and Yellow Pepper Soup from *The New Basics Cookbook* by Julie Russo and Sheila Lukins. Copyright © 1989 Julie Russo and Sheila Lukins. Reprinted by permission of Workman Publishing, New York.

Jamaican Jerk Chicken with Banana-Guava Ketchup from *The Thrill of the Grill: Techniques, Recipes & Down-Home Barbecue* by Chris Schlesinger and John Willoughby. Copyright © 1990 Chris Schlesinger and John Willoughby. Reprinted by permission of William Morrow and Company, Inc., New York.

London Broil "Smoke Gets in Your House" Style with Lime-Marinated Red Onions and Chunky Pineapple Catsup; Parsley Salad with Bulgur, Mint, and Tomatoes; and Grilled Peaches with Blue Cheese and Sweet Balsamic Glaze adapted from *Big Flavors of the Hot Sun: Hot Recipes and Cool Tips from the Spice Zone* by Chris Schlesinger and John Willoughby. Copyright © 1994 Chris Schlesinger and John Willoughby. Reprinted by permission of William Morrow and Company, Inc., New York.

Chanterelles with Blue Corn Chips; Escalope of Salmon with Pepper-Ginger Medley; and Passion Fruit Ice Cream with Raspberry Purée and White Chocolate Sauce adapted with the permission of Macmillan Publishing Company from *Cooking For All Seasons* by Jimmy Schmidt. Copyright © 1991 by Jimmy Schmidt.

Apricot and Cherry Tart adapted from *Chez Panisse Desserts* by Lindsey Remolif Shere. Copyright © 1985 Lindsey Remolif Shere. Used by permission of Random House, Inc., New York.

Napoléon of Roquefort and Boursin; and Wild Mushroom Gateau from *Simple Cuisine: The Easy, New Approach to Four-Star Cooking* by Jean-Georges Vongerichten. Copyright © 1990 Jean-Georges Vongerichten. Used by permission of Prentice Hall Press/ A Division of Simon & Schuster, New York.

Smoked Salmon, Salmon Roe, and Pasta Salad; and Fusilli with Tomatoes and Bread Crumbs, adapted from *Chez Panisse Pasta, Pizza and Calzone* by Alice Waters, Patricia Curtan, and Martine Labro. Copyright © 1984 by Alice Waters, Patricia Curtan, and Martine Labro. Used by permission of Random House, Inc., New York.

Hot and Sweet Red Pepper Dip with Walnuts and Pomegranate; Couscous with Greens; Mussels "Saganaki" adapted from *The Cooking of the Eastern Mediterranean: 215 Healthy, Vibrant, and Inspired Recipes* by Paula Wolfert. Copyright © 1994 Paula Wolfert. Used by permission of HarperCollins Publishers, Inc., New York.

Flaked Parsley Salad with Black Olives and Pecorino Cheese; Sweet and Sour Pumpkin or Butternut Squash; Walnut Roll used by permission of Paula Wolfert and adapted from *Paula Wolfert's World of Food: A Collection of Recipes From Her Kitchen, Travels and Friends* by Paula Wolfert. Copyright © 1988 Paula Wolfert, published by Harper & Row Publishers, New York.

ACKNOWLEDGMENTS

During the sixteen-year existence of De Gustibus at Macy's, many people have given their support and encouragment.

First, my profound thanks to all the wonderful chefs and cooks who have taught at De Gustibus at Macy's.

Thanks to my priceless assistants who are always there for me in a million ways: Jane Asche, Barbara Bjorn, Pam Carey, Corrine Gherardi, Yonina Jacobs, Nancy Robbins, and Betti Zucker.

Thanks to Barbara Teplitz for all her help and support throughout the years, and to Gertrud Yampierre for holding the office together.

Thanks to Ruth Schwartz for believing in the concept of De Gustibus and helping to orchestrate its initiation at Macy's.

Thanks to J. P. Leventhal and Pamela Horn of Black Dog & Leventhal Publishers for providing the vehicle to put our cooking classes into book form and for being so encouraging.

Thanks to Marty Lubin for his wonderful design.

Thanks to my agent Judith Weber for her help and advice.

Special thanks to Judith Choate, who shaped all my words into meaningful prose and never ceased to amaze me with her knowledge of food and her patience and calm, and to Steve Pool for getting these words into the computer with smiles and enthusiasm.

Finally, thanks to all the faithful De Gustibus customers who have made all our classes spring to life.

Contents

Strategies for Cooking from Our Great Chefs and Cooks

MISE EN PLACE

Before beginning to prepare any meal, regardless of how simple or how complicated, take the following steps to heart:

1 Read through the entire recipe in advance.

2 Place all the ingredients for a particular recipe on, or in, individual trays, plates, or bowls, according to the specific steps in the recipe. Each item should be washed, chopped, measured, separated—or whatever is called for. The organizational technique, known as the mise en place (from the French, it literally means "putting into place"), is the most valuable lesson we at De Gustibus have learned from the pros. We strongly urge you to cook this way.

A WORD ABOUT THE NUTRITIONAL ANALYSIS

Great Recipes of the Great Cooks combines all six books from the De Gustibus cookbook series. One of those books is *Low-Fat Cooking*. Therefore, fifty recipes in this collection are accompanied by a nutritional analysis that includes grams of total fat, saturated fat, total calories, and percentage of calories from fat.

Introduction

Great Recipes of the Great Cooks compiles all six books in the De Gustibus series into one—*Southwest Cooking, French Cooking for the Home, The Art of New American Cooking, Rustic Italian Cooking, Mediterranean Cooking* and *Low-Fat Cooking*. We have created this book to be a complete kitchen compendium. Organized according to courses, it provides hundreds of suggestions for apppetizers, soups, entrées, and desserts; and rounds out your cooking needs with chapters on sauces, dressings, salsas, sides, salads, and pastas.

Great Recipes of the Great Cooks gives the home cook a vast repertoire from which to create the most basic stocks, flavored oils, and breads, to choosing an interesting vinaigrette to toss on a salad, or a bold side dish for your tried-and-true roast chicken. This book offers answers to every cooks' questions about what to serve for a small cocktail party, a Thanksgiving feast, or a light mid-week dinner.

When we started De Gustibus in 1980, we had no inkling of the variety of cuisines that would become an integral part of American cooking. As American and international cuisines have changed and our tastes have broadened, De Gustibus has stayed on the cutting edge of the culinary experience. We have invited teachers, cooks, and chefs to De Gustibus both because of their recognition in the American cooking scene, and because of their challenging, unique, current, and above all, noteworthy cooking styles.

The goal of the cooking demonstrations at De Gustibus is to make the art of the grand master chefs and cooks accessible and practical for the home kitchen. In these recipes, each chef leads the way and holds out a helping hand to the home cook. New and unfamiliar ingredients, untried techniques, and even a little dazzle all find a place in the amateur's kitchen.

ARLENE FELTMAN SAILHAC
1996

Cooks and Chefs

COLMAN ANDREWS Food writer; Executive Editor, *Saveur Magazine,* New York, New York. Author: *Everything on the Table*

FRANCESCO ANTONUCCI Chef/Owner, Remi, New York, New York; Santa Monica, California; Mexico City, Mexico; and Tel Aviv, Israel. Author: *Venetian Taste*

PAUL BARTOLOTTA Chef, Spiaggia, Chicago, Illinois

LIDIA BASTIANICH Chef/Owner, Felidia *and* Becco, New York, New York. Author: *La Cucina di Lidia*

MARIO BATALI Chef/Owner, Pó; television personality, New York, New York

JAMES BEARD Late dean of New American Cooking, cookbook author, New York, New York

JEAN-MICHEL BERGOUGNOUX Chef, L'Absinthe, New York, New York

DAVID BOULEY Chef/Owner, Bouley, New York, New York

DANIEL BOULUD Chef/Owner, Restaurant Daniel, New York, New York. Author: *Cooking with Daniel Boulud*

ANTOINE BOUTERIN Chef/Owner, Bouterin, New York, New York. Author: *Cooking Provence*

CHARLES BOWMAN Chef, Peryali, New York, New York. Author: *The Periyali Cookbook*

TERRANCE BRENNAN Chef/Owner, Picholine, New York, New York

JANE BRODY Personal Health columnist, the *New York Times;* cookbook author, New York, New York

ED BROWN Chef, Sea Grill, New York, New York. Author: *Modern Seafood Cooking*

GIULIANO BUGIALLI Noted cookbook author, New York, New York

DAVID BURKE Executive Chef, Park Avenue Cafe, New York, New York; Chicago, Illinois. Author: *Cooking with David Burke Of the Park Avenue Cafe*

BIBA CAGGIANO Chef/Owner, Biba, Sacramento, California. Author: *Biba's Italian Kitchen, Trattoria Cooking*

DOMINICK CERRONE Chef/Owner, Solera, New York, New York

JULIA CHILD Grande Dame of French Cooking, cookbook author, and television personality, Cambridge, Massachusetts

CRAIG CLAIBORNE Cookbook author and former *New York Times* food writer, New York, New York

PATRICK CLARK Executive Chef, Tavern on the Green, New York, New York

ANDREW D'AMICO Executive Chef/Owner, The Sign of the Dove, New York, New York

GARY DANKO Executive Chef, The Dining Room at the Ritz-Carlton Hotel, San Francisco, California

ROBERT DEL GRANDE Chef/Owner, Cafe Annie, Cafe Express, and Rio Ranch, Houston, Texas

CHRISTIAN DELOUVRIER Executive Chef, Les Célébrités, Essex House Hotel, New York, New York

JEAN-MICHEL DIOT Chef/Owner, Park Bistro *and* Park Avenue Gourmandise, New York, New York

ROBERTO DONNA Chef/Owner, Galileo *and* I Matti, Washington, D.C.

TODD ENGLISH Chef/Owner, Olives *and* Figs, Charleston, Massachusetts

DEAN FEARING Executive Chef, The Mansion on Turtle Creek Restaurant, Dallas, Texas

BOBBY FLAY Executive Chef/Owner, Mesa Grill, Bolo, *and* Mesa City, New York, New York. Author: *Bold American Food*

PIERRE FRANEY Chef, cookbook author, and television personality, New York, New York

MARILYN FROBUCCINO Formerly Executive Chef, Arizona 206 *and* Cafe Mimosa, New York, New York

JOYCE GOLDSTEIN Chef/Owner, Square One, San Francisco, California. Author: *Mediterranean the Beautiful, Back to Square One, The Mediterranean Kitchen*

VINCENT GUERITHAULT Chef/Owner, Vincent Guerithault on Camelback, Phoenix, Arizona. Author: *Vincent's*

GORDON HAMERSLEY Chef/Owner, Hamersley's Bistro, Boston, Massachusetts

RON HOOK Chef, Canyon Ranch, Berkshire Hills, Massachusetts

PATRICIA JAMIESON Kitchen director for *Eating Well Magazine,* New York, New York. Author: *The Eating Well Cookbooks*

MATTHEW KENNEY Chef/Owner, Matthew's Restaurant *and* Mezze, New York, New York

JOHANNE KILLEEN AND GEORGE GERMON Chefs/Owners, Al Forno, Providence, Rhode Island. Authors: *Cucina Simpatica*

GRAY KUNZ Executive Chef, Lespinasse Restaurant, The St. Regis Hotel, New York, New York

EMERIL LAGASSE Chef/Owner, Emeril's *and* Nola, New Orleans, Louisiana. Author: *Emeril's New New Orleans Cooking*

MICHAEL LOMONACO Former Executive Chef, '21' Club, New York, New York. Author: *The '21' Cookbook: Recipes and Lore From New York's Fabled Restaurant*

SHEILA LUKINS Cookbook author; food editor *Parade Magazine,* New York, New York. Co-author: *The Silver Palate Cookbook, The Silver Palate Good Times Cookbook, The New Basics Cookbook.* Author: *Sheila Lukins' All Around the World Cookbook*

CARLO MIDDIONE Chef/Owner, Vivande, San Francisco, California. Author: *The Food of Southern Italy*

MARK MILITELLO Executive Chef/Owner, Mark's Place, Miami Beach; Mark's Los Olas, Fort Lauderdale, Florida

WAYNE NISH Chef/Owner, March, New York, New York

BRADLEY OGDEN Chef/Owner, Lark Creek Inn, Larkspur, California. Author: *Bradley Ogden's Breakfast, Lunch & Dinner*

CHARLES PALMER Chef/Owner, Aureole, Alva, *and* Lenox Room, New York, New York

JAQUES PÉPIN Cookbook author, television personality, Dean of Special Programs at The French Culinary Institute, New York, New York

GEORGES PERRIER Chef/Owner, Le Bec-Fin, Philadelphia, Pennsylvania

DEBRA PONZEK Formerly Executive Chef, Montrachet, New York, New York; Chef/Owner gourmet food store, Connecticut

ALFRED PORTALE Chef/Owner, Gotham Bar & Grill, New York, New York

WOLFGANG PUCK Chef/Owner, Spago, Chinois on Main, Granita, Los Angeles; Postrio, San Francisco, California. Author: *The Wolfgang Puck Cookbook*

MARTA PULINI Executive Chef, mad.61, New York, New York

STEPHAN PYLES Chef/Owner, Star Canyon, Dallas, Texas. Author: *New Texas Cuisine*

DOUGLAS RODRIGUEZ Chef/Owner, Patria, New York, New York. Author: *Nuevo Latino*

ANNE ROSENZWEIG Chef/Owner, Arcadia *and* Lobster Club, New York, New York

ALAIN SAILHAC Dean of Culinary Arts at The French Culinary Institute; Former Executive Chef, Le Cirque, New York, New York

CLAUDIO SCADUTTO Executive Chef, Trattoria dell'Arte, New York, New York

CHRIS SCHLESINGER Chef/Owner, East Coast Bar and Grill, Jake and Earl's, The Blue Room; Cookbook author, Boston, Massachusetts

JIMMY SCHMIDT Chef/Owner, The Rattlesnake Club, Detroit, Michigan

SALLY SCHNEIDER Noted cookbook author, New York, New York

NANCY SILVERTON & MARK PEEL Chefs/Owners, Campanile *and* La Brea Bakery, Los Angeles, California. Authors: *Mark Peel and Nancy Silverton at Home—Two Chefs Cook for Family and Friends* and *Desserts* (Nancy Silverton)

MARIE SIMMONS Noted cookbook author, New York, New York. Author: *The Light Touch, Italian Light Cooking,* and *Rice, the Amazing Grain.* Co-author: *Lighter, Quicker, Better*

ANDRÉ SOLTNER Formerly Executive Chef/Owner, Lutèce, New York, New York. Author: *The Lutèce Cookbook*

TOM VALENTI Executive Chef/Owner, Cascabel, New York, New York

JEAN-GEORGES VONGERICHTREN Chef/Owner, JoJo *and* Vong, New York, New York

BRENDAN WALSH Chef/Owner, North Street Grill, Great Neck, New York

DAVID WALZOG Chef, Tapika, New York, New York

ALICE WATERS Chef/Owner, Chez Panise, Berkeley, California. Author: *Chez Panise Cooking, Chez Panise Menu Cookbook, Chez Panise Pizza, Pasta & Calzone*

PAULA WOLFERT Noted food writer and cookbook author, San Francisco, California. Author: *The Cooking of the Eastern Mediterranean, Paula Wolfert's World of Food, The Cooking of Southwest France, Couscous and Other Good Foods from Morocco*

Techniques

CUTTING VEGETABLES

Into julienne: Using a small, very sharp knife, a mandoline, or an inexpensive vegetable slicer, cut vegetables into thin, uniform sticks, usually about ¼-inch thick and 1 to 2 inches long. This process is easiest when each vegetable is first cut into uniform pieces. For instance, trim a bell pepper into two or three evenly shaped pieces and then proceed to cut into a julienne.

Into dice: Trim vegetables into uniform rectangles. Using a very sharp knife, cut into strips ranging in width from ⅛ to ¼ inch, depending upon the size dice you require. Lay the strips together and cut into an even dice by cross cutting into squares ⅛ to ¼ inch across. When dicing bell peppers, it is particularly important to trim all the membranes and ridges so that you have an absolutely smooth rectangle.

Tourner: This French term literally means "to turn." When used to describe the preparation of vegetables, it means to trim them into small, uniform shapes (generally oval or olive-shaped) using a very sharp knife or parer. The vegetable to be turned is usually cut into quarters and then each piece is made uniform by trimming the flesh as you turn it in your fingers. The vegetable should have seven sides. This preparation facilitates the uniform cooking of the vegetables.

BLANCHING VEGETABLES

Place trimmed vegetables (or fruit) into rapidly boiling water for a brief period, often no more than 30 seconds, then immediately drain and plunge into ice cold water to stop the cooking process. Blanching serves to set color and flavor, firm up the flesh, and/or loosen the skin.

ROASTING VEGETABLES

Preheat the oven to 350 degrees F.

For root vegetables, trim and peel if desired. If small, cut in half lengthwise; if large, cut into quarters. Toss with a small amount of olive oil and salt and pepper to taste. For tomatoes, cut in half, and seed if desired. For onions, peel if desired. If large, cut in half. Rub with olive oil, salt, and pepper.

Place the vegetables on a heavy-duty baking sheet and bake until tender when pierced with a fork.

NOTE: To slow-roast tomatoes, cut as above, and bake at 200 degrees F for about 3 hours, or until they are almost dried. Alternatively, if you have a gas oven with a pilot light, lay cut-side down on a baking sheet and place in the oven with the pilot light on for at least 12 hours, or until almost dry.

PREPARING CHILES

The intense heat of the chile is mainly found in the seeds, the placenta (the fleshy part near the stem end), and the white veins that run down the inside of the chile. When removing these parts, some cooks prefer to use rubber gloves. Whether you choose to wear gloves or not, be sure to wash your hands well after working with chiles. Also, keep your hands away from your eyes and mouth until your hands are clean and the chile oil has completely dissipated. Both fresh and dried chiles can be stemmed, seeded, and deveined before use. Dried chiles are frequently reconstituted by soaking them in hot water or broth for about 30 minutes, or until softened.

Three Methods for Roasting Chiles and Bell Peppers

Using a fork with a heatproof handle, hold the chile or pepper close to the flame of a gas burner, without actually placing it in the flame, until the skin puffs and is charred black on all sides. Turn to ensure that the entire chile or pepper is charred. Immediately place the charred chile or pepper in a plastic bag and seal. Allow to steam for about 10 minutes.

Remove the chile or pepper from the bag and pull off the charred skin. Stem and seed. Dice, chop, or puree as required.

If using an electric stove, place the entire chile or pepper in a large, dry cast-iron skillet over medium heat. Cook slowly, turning frequently, until completely charred. Proceed as above.

To roast several chiles or peppers at a time, place on a baking sheet under a preheated broiler as close to the heat as possible without touching the flame. Roast until the skin puffs and is charred black, turning as necessary to char the entire chile or pepper. Then proceed as above.

When roasting chiles, remember that their oils are very potent. As the skin blackens, you may feel burning in your throat and eyes, which may cause some momentary discomfort. When roasting a large number of

chiles, it is best to do so under a broiler to contain the potency.

Toasting Chiles

Dried red chiles are often toasted before using. This is done to heighten their aroma, flavor, and, according to some experts, digestibility.

Remove the stem and, using a sharp knife, slit the chile open lengthwise. Remove the seeds and veins and flatten the chile out. Heat a griddle over medium heat until hot. Add the flattened chile, skin-side up, and toast for 4 seconds. Turn over and toast for 3 seconds more, being careful not to burn the chile. The chile should just darken slightly and begin to release its aroma; if it burns, it will turn bitter.

Making Chile Powder

Using the method described above in "Toasting Chiles," toast the chiles over very low heat for about 1 minute per side, or until completely moisture-free and crisp. Do not burn!

Tear the toasted chiles into small pieces and process in an electric coffee grinder, spice grinder or mini food processor to a very fine powder. Cover tightly and store in the freezer.

Making Chile Puree

For fresh chiles: Stem, seed, and remove the membranes. Place in a food processor fitted with the metal blade and process until smooth. You may need to add a drop or two of water to create a puree. Use immediately.

For dried chiles: Toast as directed above. Tear into pieces and place in hot water to cover for 15 to 30 minutes (depending upon the age and the chile as well as the toughness of the skin), or until the chile is completely reconstituted. Drain well and place in a blender. Process until smooth. Strain through a fine sieve to remove any bits of tough skin. Cover and refrigerate for up to 3 days or freeze for up to 6 months.

TOASTING SPICES AND SEEDS

Toast spices and seeds in a heavy cast-iron skillet over medium heat, stirring or shaking the pan frequently. Toast for 2 to 5 minutes, depending on the ingredient, or until it turns a shade darker and is fragrant.

TOASTING AND SKINNING NUTS

Preheat oven to 400 degrees F. Lay the nuts in a single layer on a baking sheet or pie tin. Using a spray bottle such as those used to mist plants, lightly spray the nuts with cool water. Roast for 5 to 10 minutes, depending on the nut's size and oil content, or until golden. Remember, since nuts have a high oil content, they can burn very quickly. Immediately remove from oven and transfer to a cool plate or tray to cool. If you leave them on the baking sheet, they will continue to cook. If the nuts have skins, immediately spread them on a clean kitchen towel. Let them cool slightly and then wrap them in the towel and rub the nuts back and forth to remove the skins.

If you do not need to toast nuts but want to skin them, put them in boiling water for 1 minute. Drain well. Place in a clean kitchen towel and rub the nuts to remove the skins.

PITTING OLIVES

Place olives between two kitchen towels and pound gently with a mallet or the broad side of a cleaver. Unwrap and remove the pits from the flesh.

COOKING PASTA

Pasta, whether fresh or dried, should be cooked in ample boiling, salted water just until it is *al dente,* or still firm to the bite. Usually 2 gallons of water is enough to cook 1 pound of pasta.

To ensure the best possible taste and texture, the chefs always add salt just at the point when the water comes to a boil before adding pasta.

MAKING BREAD CRUMBS

One slice of fresh bread yields approximately ½ cup fresh bread crumbs.

One slice dried (or toasted) bread yields approximately ⅓ cup dried bread crumbs.

Trim crusts from slices of firm, good-quality fresh or dried white bread. Cut the bread into cubes and place in a food processor fitted with the metal blade. Pulse until crumbs are formed.

Store fresh bread crumbs in a tightly covered container in the refrigerator for up to 3 days.

Store dried bread crumbs in a tightly covered container at room temperature for up to 1 month.

GRATING CHEESE

Italian hard cheeses, such as Parmigiano-Reggiano, should be purchased in chunks and grated as needed. You can purchase a grater made especially for Parmesan cheese in Italian markets or kitchen equipment shops. Alternatively, you can use the traditional 4-sided kitchen grater or even a small Mouli grater. Do not use a food processor—the speed of the blade creates heat, which will change the taste and texture of the cheese.

RENDERING DUCK FAT

Place pieces of duck fat in a non-stick sauté pan and cook over very low heat, stirring occasionally, until the fat has melted and all the skin and connective tissue has turned brown and crisp. Remove the "cracklings" from the fat. (Reserve for a salad garnish, if desired.) Strain the fat through a paper coffee filter or a triple layer of cheesecloth to remove any remaining cooked particles. Store, tightly covered and refrigerated, for up to 1 month. Use as you would any animal fat to pan fry potatoes or other foods.

ZESTING CITRUS FRUITS

For strips of zest or chopped zest, using a vegetable peeler, a sharp paring knife, or a zester, remove *only* the thin layer of oily colored outer skin of any citrus fruit (the white pith beneath the colored skin tastes bitter). Then cut into thinner strips or chop as required. For grated zest, carefully remove the colored outer skin using the smallest holes of a metal grater.

MAKING CHOCOLATE CURLS

For ease of handling, you will need at least a 4-ounce solid block of cool, room-temperature chocolate. Using a paper towel, grasp one end of the chocolate block, holding it so that the paper protects it from the heat of your hand. Using a very sharp potato peeler, gradually peel off a thin sheet of chocolate from the top to the bottom, moving the peeler toward you. The chocolate will curl as it peels off the block. The lighter the pressure, the tighter the curls will be. If the chocolate is too warm, it will not curl; if it is too cold, it will break into slivers.

GRATING CHOCOLATE

Small amounts of solid, room temperature chocolate may be grated on a nutmeg grater. Larger amounts can be processed in a food processor fitted with the metal blade. Grate only as much as you need, since if stored, grated chocolate tends to melt back together.

USING AN ICE WATER BATH

Place the container of hot cooked food in a larger container (or a plugged sink) filled with enough ice and cold water to come at least halfway up the sides of the hot container. Stir the food from time to time to speed cooling. An ice water bath is used to cool foods quickly in order to halt cooking and prevent bacteria formation. Foods cooled in this fashion are often further chilled with refrigeration or freezing.

USING A MORTAR AND PESTLE

The ingredients to be ground or pulverized are placed in the mortar, a bowl-shaped container. The pestle, an easily gripped hand-sized club with a rounded or pointed end, is rotated, pressing the ingredient against the bottom and sides of the mortar, until the desired consistency is reached. A mortar and pestle, one of the world's most ancient kitchen devices, may be made of hardwood, marble, or glazed stone.

Pantry Recipes

CHICKEN, DUCK, OR TURKEY STOCK

MAKES ABOUT 4 CUPS

PREPARATION TIME: ABOUT 40 MINUTES

COOKING TIME: ABOUT 2 HOURS AND 30 MINUTES

2 quarts (8 cups) water

2 chicken carcasses or duck carcasses or 5 pounds turkey bones, cut in small pieces

3 onions, chopped

1 carrot, chopped

2 ribs celery, chopped

3 sprigs fresh thyme

3 sprigs fresh parsley

1 bay leaf

1 tablespoon white peppercorns

We supply standard stock recipes for chicken, duck or turkey, and beef, lamb or veal stock used in the recipes. Homemade stock adds a depth of flavor to a dish not possible with canned broth. However, if time is a factor, use canned chicken (or beef) broth, buying those brands that are labeled "low-sodium." Do not use diluted bouillon cubes; they are excessively salty.

1 In a large saucepan or stockpot, combine the water and chopped carcasses. Bring to a simmer over medium heat and skim the surface of any foam.

2 Add the onions, carrots, celery, thyme, parsley, bay leaf, and peppercorns. Bring to a boil, reduce the heat, and simmer for 1½ to 2 hours, skimming fat and foam from the surface as necessary, until reduced to 4 cups.

4 Pour the stock into a fine sieve and strain, extracting as much liquid as possible. Discard the solids. Cool to tepid (this can be done by plunging the stockpot into a sinkful of ice), cover, and refrigerate for 6 hours or until all fat particles have risen to the top. Spoon off solidified fat and discard. Heat the stock over medium-high heat for about 30 minutes. Adjust the seasonings and use as directed in recipe.

5 To store, cool to tepid (this can be done by plunging the stockpot into a sinkful of ice), cover, and refrigerate for 2 to 3 days or freeze in 1-cup quantities (for ease of use) for up to 3 months.

BEEF, LAMB, OR VEAL STOCK

MAKES ABOUT 3 QUARTS
PREPARATION TIME: ABOUT 40 MINUTES
COOKING TIME: ABOUT 7 HOURS

¼ cup plus 2 tablespoons vegetable oil

4 pounds beef, lamb, or veal marrow bones, cut into 2-inch pieces

3 onions, peeled and quartered

1 carrot, peeled and chopped

1 rib celery, chopped

1 tomato, quartered

1 bay leaf

1 tablespoon black peppercorns

2 sprigs fresh thyme

3 cloves garlic, crushed

Approximately 1 gallon (16 cups) water

1 Preheat the oven to 450 degrees F.

2 Using ¼ cup of oil, lightly oil the bones. Spread the bones in a single layer in a large roasting pan. Roast the bones, turning occasionally, for 20 minutes, or until bones are dark golden-brown on all sides.

3 Transfer the bones to a large saucepan or stockpot. Add the remaining oil to roasting pan and stir in the onions, carrot, celery, and tomato. Cook on top of the stove for about 15 minutes over medium-high heat until brown, stirring frequently.

4 With a slotted spoon, transfer the vegetables to the stockpot. Add the bay leaf, peppercorns, thyme, and garlic.

5 Pour off the fat from the roasting pan and discard. Return the pan to moderate heat and deglaze it with 2 cups of water, scraping up any particles sticking to the bottom. Remove from the heat and add this liquid to the stockpot. Pour enough of the remaining water into the stockpot to cover the bones by 2 inches. Bring to a boil, reduce the heat, and let the stock barely simmer, uncovered, for 6 hours, skimming fat and foam from the surface as necessary. Remove from the heat. Cool slightly and chill in the refrigerator for 12 hours or overnight.

6 Pour the stock into a fine sieve into a clean pan. Discard the solids. Spoon off any trace of fat. Place stockpot over high heat and bring stock to a rolling boil. Lower heat and simmer for 30 minutes or until flavor is full-bodied and liquid has slightly reduced. Use as directed in the recipe.

7 To store, cool to tepid (this can be done by plunging the stockpot into a sinkful of ice), cover, and refrigerate for 2 to 3 days or freeze in 1-cup quantities (for ease of use) for up to 3 months.

FISH STOCK

MAKES ABOUT 3 CUPS

PREPARATION TIME: ABOUT 20 MINUTES

COOKING TIME: ABOUT 25 MINUTES

2 sprigs fresh parsley

2 sprigs fresh thyme

1 small bay leaf

2 pounds fish bones (saltwater fish such as sole, John Dory, turbot, halibut, or other very fresh, non-oily fish), cut into pieces

2 tablespoons canola or other flavorless oil

1 small onion, chopped

1 small rib celery, chopped

1 cup dry white wine

*M*aking fish stock is easier and faster than making chicken or beef stock. Substituting a canned broth is tricky in recipes calling for fish stock, but if you have no time to make stock, substitute low-sodium canned chicken broth for fish stock.

1 Make a bouquet garni by tying together with kitchen twine the parsley, thyme, and bay leaf. Set aside.

2 Clean the fish bones under cold running water.

3 Heat the oil in a large saucepan or stockpot over medium heat. Add the fish bones and vegetables. Lower the heat and lay a piece of wax paper directly on bones and vegetables in the pan. Cook for 10 minutes, stirring once or twice to prevent browning. Be careful not to push the paper into the pan.

4 Remove the wax paper. Add the wine and enough water to cover the bones and vegetables by 2 inches. Add the bouquet garni. Increase the heat to high and bring to a boil. Skim the surface of all foam. Lower the heat and simmer for 20 to 25 minutes.

5 Strain the stock through an extra-fine sieve. Discard the solids. Use as directed in recipe or cool to tepid (this can be done by plunging the stockpot into a sinkful of ice), cover tightly, and refrigerate for 2 to 3 days or freeze in 1-cup quantities (for ease of use) for up to 3 weeks.

VEGETABLE STOCK

MAKES ABOUT 3 CUPS
PREPARATION TIME: ABOUT 20 MINUTES
COOKING TIME: ABOUT 2 HOURS

---

3 quarts cold water

1 carrot, peeled and chopped

1 potato, peeled and chopped

1 large onion, chopped

3 ribs celery, chopped

½ leek, white part only, chopped

1 small tomato, chopped

1 tablespoon salt or to taste

2 cloves garlic, peeled

1 teaspoon chopped fresh parsley

½ teaspoon black peppercorns

Making vegetable stock is easy and fast. Substituting a canned broth is difficult, as finding a good one can be a problem. Low-sodium vegetable bouillon cubes, sold in health food stores, are a good substitute. Low-sodium canned chicken broth can also be used in recipes calling for vegetable stock.

---

1 In a 5-quart saucepan, bring 1 cup of the water to a boil over medium-high heat. Add the carrot, potato, onions, celery, leeks, tomato, and salt. Cook for 5 minutes, stirring occasionally.

2 Add the remaining 11 cups of water to the pan, along with the garlic, parsley, and peppercorns. Bring to a simmer, reduce the heat to low, and simmer gently for 2 hours.

3 Strain the liquid through a fine sieve into a bowl. Discard the vegetables. Let cool for 1 hour and then pour the stock through a fine sieve again. Use as directed in the recipe.

4 To store, cover and refrigerate for up to 3 days or freeze in 1-cup quantities (for ease of use) for up to 3 months.

Cooked Beans

Makes about 2½ cups cooked beans
Preparation time: about 10 minutes
Cooking time: 1 to 2 hours
Soaking time: at least 4 hours

1 cup dried black, white, fava, or other beans

Cooking dried beans is simply a matter of reconstituting them by soaking, followed by long, slow cooking. You can double or triple the recipe. Cooked beans keep in the freezer for up to one month. Lentils and black-eyed peas do not require soaking before cooking.

1 Check the beans for pebbles and other debris. Rinse them in a colander. Put the beans in a large pot and add about 10 cups of water (or 10 times the amount of the beans). Cover and let soak at room temperature for at least 4 hours. Change the water 3 or 4 times during soaking. If the beans are particularly old, let them soak for 8 hours or overnight.

2 Drain the beans, rinse with cold water, and return to the pot. Add fresh cold water to cover the beans by about 2 inches. Bring to a boil over high heat, skim the foam that rises to the surface, and reduce the heat to a simmer. Cover and cook for 1 to 2 hours, until tender, adding more water to the pot as necessary. The beans are done when they are fork-tender. Drain and proceed with the specific recipe.

NOTE: To prepare the beans by the "quick-soak method," put the beans in a large pot and add enough water to cover by 3 inches. Bring to a boil and boil for 5 minutes. Remove from the heat, cover, and soak for no less than 1 hour and no longer than 2 hours. Drain and discard the soaking water. Rinse well. Proceed with the cooking instructions above.

ROASTED GARLIC

1 or more whole garlic heads (bulbs) or 1 or more cloves garlic

You may roast whole heads of garlic (bulbs) or you may cut each head in half, crosswise, or separate each one into individual cloves.

1 Preheat the oven to 200 degress F.

2 Lightly wrap the garlic in aluminum foil. Place on a pie plate or small baking sheet. Bake for 1 hour for a whole head, 15 minutes for individual cloves, or until the pulp is very soft. Remove from the oven. Unwrap and allow to cool.

For whole heads: Cut in half crosswise, and working from the closed end, gently push the soft roasted garlic from the skin. Discard the skin.

For individual cloves: Slit the skin using a sharp knife point. Gently push the soft roasted garlic from the skin. Discard the skin.

CLARIFIED BUTTER

MAKES ABOUT 3 CUPS

2 pounds unsalted butter, cut into pieces

Clarified butter burns less easily than other butter because during the clarifying process, the milk particles are removed. For the same reason it stores longer.

1 Melt the butter in a medium-sized saucepan over very low heat. Skim off the foam that rises to the top using a ladle, taking care to remove as little of the clear, yellow fat as possible.

2 Let the butter cool slightly and settle. Carefully strain the butter through a fine sieve into a clean, glass container, leaving the milky residue on the bottom of the saucepan. Discard the residue.

3 Cover and refrigerate for up to 2 weeks or freeze for up to 1 month.

FLOUR TORTILLAS

---

2 cups sifted all-purpose flour, plus additional for dusting

1 teaspoon baking powder

½ teaspoon salt

½ teaspoon granulated sugar

1 tablespoon solid vegetable shortening

Approximately ½ cup warm water

This simple tortilla recipe from Dean Fearing does not require any unusual ingredients or even a tortilla press.

---

1 Assemble the *mise en place* trays for this recipe (see page 00).

2 Sift the dry ingredients together into a bowl. Cut in the shortening with a fork or pastry blender until the mixture resembles coarse meal. Add just enough warm water to make a soft dough.

3 Turn the dough out onto a well-floured surface and knead for 3 to 5 minutes. Cover the dough and let it rest for 30 minutes in a warm, draft-free area.

4 Form the dough into 2-inch balls between the palms of your hands. On a lightly floured surface, roll out each ball into a circle about 7 inches in diameter and ¼ inch thick.

5 Heat a cast-iron griddle or skillet over medium-high heat. Place a tortilla on the ungreased griddle and cook for about 2 minutes, or until lightly browned around the edges. Turn over and cook for about 1 minute longer, or until the edges are brown.

6 Wrap tightly in foil to keep warm, and repeat with the remaining tortillas. If cooking in advance, wrap in foil and store at cool room temperature for an hour or so, or in the refrigerator for longer, until needed. Reheat, still wrapped in foil, in a 300 degree F. oven for 10 to 15 minutes, or until heated through.

⤳ If these are for chips, undercook the tortillas slightly.

CORN TORTILLAS

MAKES 8 TORTILLAS

PREPARATION TIME: ABOUT 10 MINUTES

COOKING TIME: ABOUT 35 MINUTES

¾ cup stone-ground yellow or blue cornmeal or masa harina

1 tablespoon plus 1 teaspoon corn oil

⅛ teaspoon salt

About 2 tablespoons hot water

- Special Equipment: tortilla press, optional

1 Preheat the oven to 175 degrees F. or 200 degrees F. if that is the lowest setting. Assemble the *mise en place* trays for this dish (see page 00).

2 In a small bowl, combine the cornmeal, 1 tablespoon of the oil, and the salt until just blended. Add just enough water to form the dough into a ball.

3 Divide the dough into 8 even, small balls. Place each ball between 2 sheets of wax paper and flatten in a tortilla press. Alternatively, using a rolling pin, roll out each ball into a circle ⅛-inch thick.

4 Heat a cast-iron griddle or skillet over medium-high heat. Lightly brush with the remaining 1 teaspoon of the oil. Peel off one sheet of wax paper from a tortilla and place it, dough side down, on the griddle. Cook for 2 minutes. Remove the other sheet of wax paper, turn the tortilla over, and cook for 2 minutes more, or until slightly browned and firm.

5 Wrap in a kitchen towel and keep warm in the oven, and repeat with the remaining tortillas.

❧ If the dough crumbles or cracks around edges while rolling, add a bit more water and reform.

❧ If these are for chips, undercook the tortillas slightly.

❧ Tortillas may be made early in the day. Store, covered and refrigerated in the towel or in aluminum foil.

Tortilla Chips

PREPARATION TIME: ABOUT 5 MINUTES
COOKING TIME: ABOUT 3 MINUTES PER CHIP

Corn or Flour Tortillas (page 00)

Oil for deep frying

■ Special Equipment: deep-fry thermometer

1 Cut the tortillas into quarters or sixths, depending upon the size you want.

2 Heat the oil in a deep fat fryer or deep skillet to 325 degrees F. Add the tortilla pieces, a few at a time, and fry, stirring continuously, for 3 minutes, or until crisp. Using a slotted spoon, remove the chips from the oil and drain on paper towels.

❧ If you don't have a deep-fry thermometer, you can check for proper oil temperature by dropping a ½-inch bread cube into the oil. When small bubbles begin to surround the cube and it starts to turn golden, the oil is the correct temperature. Remove the bread cube with tongs or chopsticks.

Tostadas

PREPARATION TIME: ABOUT 5 MINUTES
COOKING TIME: ABOUT 3 MINUTES PER TOSTADA

Corn Tortillas (recipe page 00)

Oil for shallow-frying

Heat ¼ inch of oil in a large, heavy skillet over high heat to 325 degrees F. Cook the tortillas, one at a time, for about 3 minutes, or until crisp and golden. Do not deep-fry. Tostadas are best eaten as they are fried. If this is not possible, drain well and place on a baking sheet lined with paper towels. Reheat in in a preheated 350 degree F. oven for 2 to 3 minutes, or until hot.

ACHIOTE PASTE

MAKES ABOUT ½ CUP

PREPARATION TIME: ABOUT 15 MINUTES

STANDING TIME: AT LEAST SEVERAL HOURS

---

1 tablespoon achiote seeds

1 teaspoon black peppercorns

1 teaspoon dried oregano

4 whole cloves

½ teaspoon cumin seeds

1 one-inch piece of cinnamon stick

1 teaspoon coriander seeds

1 teaspoon salt

5 cloves garlic, minced

2 tablespoons cider vinegar

1½ teaspoons all-purpose flour

1 Assemble the *mise en place* trays for this recipe (see page 00).

2 Put the achiote, peppercorns, oregano, cloves, cumin, cinnamon, and coriander into an electric coffee grinder, spice grinder, or mini food processor and process until fine. Transfer to a small bowl and stir in the salt.

3 Place the garlic in another small bowl and sprinkle with 2 teaspoons of the ground spices. Using the back of a spoon, mash the garlic and spice mixture into a smooth paste. Blend in the remaining spice mixture, the vinegar, and flour. Scrape into a glass or ceramic container with a lid. Let stand at room temperature for several hours, or overnight, before using. Store tightly covered in the refrigerator for up to 3 months.

CHILE-FLAVORED VINEGAR

MAKES ABOUT 2 CUPS

PREPARATION TIME: ABOUT 5 MINUTES

STANDING TIME: ABOUT 1 WEEK

---

2 cups good-quality white wine vinegar

2 green chiles, halved lengthwise

1 small dried red chile

1 clove garlic

To make this vinegar, select a dried red chile with the amount of "heat" you prefer. There is no need to remove the seeds from the chiles unless you want to. Likewise, there is no need to remove the chiles from the vinegar after they have soaked in it.

Combine all the ingredients in a glass jar with a tight-fitting lid. Let sit in a cool dark place for 1 week before using. Store in the refrigerator for up to 6 months.

Appetizers

Catalan Tomato Bread ❧ Fried Parmesan Cups ❧ Asparagus and Morel Bruschetta ❧ Tomato Tart ❧ Spanakopita ❧ Almond Skordalia ❧ White Beans with Garlic ❧ Toasted Couscous Risotto ❧ Intercontinental Chickpea Spread ❧ Red Potato and Goat Cheese Tart ❧ Onion and Zucchini Frittata ❧ Seared Scallops in Gazpacho-Thyme Sauce ❧ Artichoke Bottoms Filled with Poached Oysters ❧ Buffalo Chicken Wings ❧ Baba Ganoush ❧ Asparagus with Red Onion Vinaigrette ❧ Cream Biscuits with Barbecued Crabmeat ❧ Burger of Fresh Foie Gras ❧ Fig and Prosciutto Tart ❧ Warm Lobster Taco ❧ Grilled Tuna Tostada ❧ Spicy Chicken, Eggplant, and Grilled Red Onion Quesadilla ❧ Baked Eggplant and Manchego Salad ❧ Flatbread with Spicy Hummus, Goat Cheese, and Roasted Vegetables ❧ Chipotle-Garbanzo Bean Dip ❧ Seafood Seviche with Summer Greens ❧ Smoked Salmon Quesadillas ❧ Sea Scallops with Potato Cakes ❧ Braised Wild Mushrooms with Roasted Garlic Toasts ❧ Asparagus Salad with Littleneck Clams ❧ Caramelized Onion Pizza ❧ Ahi Tuna Tartare with Fennel, Caraway Toast, and Green Olive Tapenade ❧ Clams "Al Forno" ❧ Smoked Trout Mousse on Pumpernickel ❧ Provençal Vegetable Tart with Seared Tuna ❧ Potato Crêpes ❧ Tuna Tartare and Herb Salad ❧ Fresh Tuna with Maui Onions and Avocado ❧ Parmesan Ice Cream ❧ Spinach Tart ❧ Red Snapper with Mexican Oregano Pesto Sauce ❧ Shrimp Ceviche ❧ Roasted Eggplant Roulade ❧ Antipasto ❧ White Pizza with Arugula ❧ Chanterelles with Blue Corn Chips ❧ Escalope of Salmon with Pepper-Ginger Medley ❧ Wild Mushroom Ragout with Roasted Polenta ❧ Smothered Escarole on Whole Wheat Crostini ❧ Onion Tart ❧ Baked Cod with Bulgur ❧ Napoléon of Roquefort and Boursin ❧ Hot and Sweet Red Pepper Dip

Catalan Tomato Bread ❧ Colman Andrews

SERVES 6

PREPARATION TIME: ABOUT 15 MINUTES

SOAKING TIME (ANCHOVIES ONLY): ABOUT 1 HOUR

TOASTING TIME: ABOUT 4 MINUTES

———————

24 large anchovy fillets

Six 1½-inch-thick slices country-style French or Italian bread (see Note)

3 medium-sized very ripe tomatoes, halved

About ½ cup mild Spanish extra-virgin olive oil (preferably a Catalan brand, such as Siurana, Verge de Borges, or Lerida)

Salt to taste

This simple combination of country-style bread and lush, ripe tomatoes is a fantastic introduction to casual Mediterranean dining. For a relaxed meal al fresco, you might want to place all the ingredients on the table and let your guests assemble their own plates. Colman told us that ham, sardines, herring, or sausage are all welcome additions.

———————

1 Assemble *mise en place* trays for this recipe (see page 6).

2 Place the anchovy fillets in a small bowl and add enough cool water to cover. Allow to soak for 1 hour. Drain and pat dry.

3 Prepare a charcoal or gas grill or preheat the broiler.

4 Lightly toast the bread on both sides over the fire or under the broiler.

5 Squeezing gently, rub the tomatoes over both sides of each slice of toast, leaving a thin film of tomato flesh and seeds on the surfaces. Drizzle olive oil to taste evenly over both sides of each toast. Sprinkle both sides with salt to taste. Place 1 toast slice on each plate. Arrange 4 anchovy fillets on top of each toast and serve immediately.

NOTE: You will need a large round or oval dense hearty bread. Do not use a baguette, as it will not be of the right consistency to absorb the tomato juices and oil properly.

Fried Parmesan Cups and
Prosciutto ❧ Francesco Antonucci

SERVES 6

PREPARATION TIME: ABOUT 5 MINUTES

COOKING TIME: ABOUT 10 MINUTES

---

3 cups (about ¾ pound) freshly grated Parmigiano-Reggiano cheese

18 two-and-a-half-inch-by-two-and-a-half-inch, very thin slices prosciutto (from about 6 whole slices)

6 sprigs fresh herb, such as oregano, parsley, or rosemary

■ Special Equipment: 8-to-10-inch nonstick skillet or griddle; 3 to 6 custard cups

Once you get the knack of these cups, you'll make them regularly. The rich cheese taste is completely unadulterated and quite addictive! For success in creating these gems, start with a perfectly smooth, nonstick pan and the best imported Parmigiano-Reggiano you can find.

---

1 Assemble *mise en place* trays for this recipe (see page 6). Position 3 to 6 six-ounce custard cups upside down on a work surface. The diameter of the upturned cups should be no greater than 2 to 3 inches.

2 Heat an 8- or 10-inch nonstick skillet or small, smooth griddle over medium heat for about 5 minutes, until very hot. Sprinkle 2 tablespoons of the grated cheese into the center of the pan and, gently shaking the pan in a back-and-forth motion or spreading the cheese with a spatula, evenly distribute it to form a thin, lacy circle. Cook for 30 seconds, or until the cheese has melted and turned pale golden. (Do not turn the cheese circles over.) Using a spatula, carefully lift the cheese circle and place onto an inverted cup, letting it bend down over the sides of the cup. Allow to cool completely and harden before gently lifting the cheese cup off the custard cup. Continue making cheese circles until you have at least 18 cups.

3 Arrange 3 Parmesan cups on each serving plate, rounded side up. Drape a square of prosciutto over the top of each one. Garnish the plates with the fresh herb sprigs, and serve immediately.

❧ Three measured cups of cheese should make as many as 24 cooked Parmesan Cups. This amount allows for a couple of "practice" cups, breakage, and nibbling.

❧ If the air is humid, the cups may collapse if made in advance and left at room temperature. Even slight humidity will make them chewy.

Asparagus and Morel Bruschetta ❧ Mario Batali

SERVES 6

PREPARATION TIME: ABOUT 15 MINUTES

COOKING TIME: ABOUT 10 MINUTES

FAT PER SERVING: 5.5 GRAMS

SATURATED FAT: 0.8 GRAM

CALORIES PER SERVING: 195

CALORIES FROM FAT: 25%

2 teaspoons olive oil

3 shallots, minced

6 ounces fresh morels, trimmed

10 medium-sized spears asparagus (about ½ pound), trimmed, blanched, and cut into ¼-inch pieces

Juice of 1 small lemon

3 tablespoons fresh thyme leaves

1 tablespoon extra-virgin olive oil

1 tablespoon white truffle oil (optional)

Coarse salt and freshly ground black pepper to taste

Twenty-four ¼-inch-thick slices French bread, toasted

The flavors of spring absolutely sing through this aromatic mixture. It could also be served on a bed of wild greens for a first-course salad. Tossed with pasta, it's a delicious main course.

1 Assemble *mise en place* trays for this recipe (see page 6).

2 In a medium-sized sauté pan, heat the 2 teaspoons olive oil over medium heat. Add the shallots and cook for 1 minute. Add the morels and sauté for about 5 minutes, or until tender. Remove from the heat. Add the asparagus, lemon juice, thyme, extra-virgin olive oil, and the truffle oil if desired. Toss gently and season to taste with coarse salt and pepper.

3 Place 3 slices of toast on each warm plate. Spoon the morel mixture onto the toast and serve immediately.

NOTE: You can replace the morels, which are very expensive, with any other aromatic wild mushrooms, such as cremini, shiitakes, or chanterelles.

❧ White truffle oil is available at specialty food markets.

Tomato Tart with Lime Butter ❧ Antoine Bouterin

SERVES 6

PREPARATION TIME: ABOUT 35 MINUTES

BAKING TIME: ABOUT 30 MINUTES

TART:

½ pound frozen puff pastry, thawed

2 pounds ripe tomatoes, cored, peeled, seeded, and finely chopped

Juice of 1 large lemon

2 shallots, minced

2 cloves garlic, minced

½ teaspoon minced fresh parsley

¼ teaspoon minced fresh basil

¼ teaspoon minced fresh thyme

Salt and freshly ground black pepper to taste

2 tablespoons olive oil

LIME BUTTER:

Juice of 1 large lime

8 tablespoons unsalted butter, cut into tablespoon-size pieces

2 tablespoons heavy cream

Salt and freshly ground black pepper to taste

½ cup peeled, seeded, and diced ripe tomatoes, for garnish

■ Special Equipment: six 4-inch tartlet pans (not with removable bottoms); pastry weights, dried beans, or rice

This tart is not only a sensational first course, but would also be a wonderful brunch or light lunch entrée.

---

1 Preheat the oven to 400 degrees F. Assemble *mise en place* trays for this recipe (see page 6).

2 On a floured surface, roll out the pastry to approximately a 15-inch square. Using a sharp knife, cut the pastry into six 5¼-inch squares. Gently fit each square into a 4-inch tartlet pan. Trim the excess dough from the edges. Prick the bottom of the pastry shelves all over with a fork. Line the pastry shells with aluminum foil cut about 2 inches larger than the pan so that there is no overhang. Spread pastry weights, dried beans, or rice over the foil. Set the tartlet pan on a baking sheet and bake for about 15 minutes, until the pastry is lightly browned. Lift out the foil and weights. Gently lift the baked shells from the tartlet pans and set the pastry shells on a wire rack to cool. Do not turn off the oven.

3 Meanwhile, put the tomatoes in a colander and let drain for about 15 minutes. Pat dry with paper towels.

4 In a glass or ceramic bowl, combine the tomatoes, lemon juice, shallots, garlic, parsley, basil, thyme, and salt and pepper to taste. Stir in the olive oil.

5 Put the baking sheet back in the oven for about 5 minutes. Lift the hot sheet from the oven and position the tartlet shells on it. Spoon approximately 2 tablespoons of the tomato mixture into each shell. Do not overfill. Bake for about 15 minutes, or until centers are firm. As the tartlets bake, pat the filling with paper towel 2 or 3 times to absorb excess liquid. Grind a light coating of pepper over the top of each tartlet. Let cool for 5 minutes before serving.

6 Meanwhile, make the lime butter: In a small non-reactive saucepan, combine the lime juice with an equal amount of water (about ⅓ cup). Bring to a boil over high heat, and boil for about 3 minutes, or until reduced by half. Whisk in the butter, a tablespoon at a time, until well incorporated. Stir in the cream and season to taste with salt and pepper. Pour into the top half of a double boiler and place over hot water to keep warm.

7 Spoon the lime butter onto plates. Set the tartlets on top, and garnish with the diced tomatoes. Serve immediately.

❧ It's important to let the tomatoes drain to remove excess moisture and then to blot them during baking. Have the paper towels ready—folded two or three thick—before opening the oven door. Work quickly so as not to let too much heat escape.

Spanakopita ❧ Charles Bowman

MAKES 48 PIECES
PREPARATION TIME: ABOUT 45 MINUTES
CHILLING TIME: ABOUT 1 HOUR
COOKING TIME: ABOUT 35 MINUTES

½ cup plus 1 tablespoon extra-virgin olive oil

½ cup shredded onions

½ cup shredded leeks

Three 10-ounce packages frozen chopped spinach, thawed, drained, and squeezed of all excess liquid

2 tablespoons chopped fresh dill

1 teaspoon salt, or to taste

This crispy spinach-filled appetizer can be made well in advance, frozen, and then reheated.

---

1 Assemble *mise en place* trays for this recipe (see page 6).

2 In a large skillet, heat 1 tablespoon of the oil over medium heat. Add the onions and leeks and sauté for about 5 minutes, or until lightly browned. Stir in the spinach and the remaining ½ cup oil and cook, stirring constantly, for about 4 minutes. Add the dill, salt, and white pepper and stir to blend. Transfer to a large bowl. Cover and refrigerate for 1 hour, or until well chilled.

3 Preheat the oven to 400 degrees F.

¼ teaspoon freshly ground white pepper

2 large eggs

¾ cup crumbled feta cheese

¼ cup small-curd cottage cheese

1 tablespoon freshly grated Parmesan cheese

1 tablespoon dry bread crumbs

20 sheets phyllo dough, thawed according to the package directions

2 cups Clarified Butter (see page 20), melted

■ Special Equipment: Pizza cutter (optional)

4 Stir the eggs, cheeses, and bread crumbs into the spinach mixture. Set aside.

5 Lay the phyllo sheets on a dry work surface with a long side toward you. Using a ruler and a pizza cutter or a very sharp knife, cut the sheets crosswise into three 5½-inch-wide strips. Lift off 12 strips and fold crosswise in half. Cut at the fold to make 24 pieces. Again fold the strips in half and cut to make 48 pieces in all. Set aside, covered with a well-wrung-out damp kitchen towel. These will be used as patches to reinforce the phyllo under the filling.

6 Lay 2 strips of dough side by side on the work surface. (Keep the strips that you are not actually working with covered with a well-wrung-out damp kitchen towel so that the pastry doesn't dry out.) Using a pastry brush, lightly and completely coat both strips with clarified butter, starting at the center and working out toward the ends. Position a phyllo patch lengthwise about an inch up from the bottom and in the center of each strip. Butter the patches.

7 Working quickly, place 1 rounded measuring teaspoon of the filling in the center of 1 patch. Fold the sides of the strip over the filling. Brush the folds with clarified butter. Fold the bottom of the strip up over the filling to form a triangular point, then continue folding, making sure that with each fold you align the bottom edge with the alternate side of the pastry strip, as if you were folding a flag. Lightly coat the finished triangle with butter and place on an ungreased baking sheet. Repeat with the second strip, then continue until all of the phyllo is used.

8 Bake in the top third of the oven for 10 minutes. Brush the triangles with butter again and continue to bake for 10 to 15 minutes longer, or until golden brown. Cool slightly on wire racks and serve warm or at room temperature.

ALTERNATIVE TECHNIQUE: To create Spanakopita rolls, complete the instructions through step 6. Then place 1 rounded measuring teaspoon of the filling in the center of 1 patch. Beginning at the short end, roll the phyllo into a roll to encase the filling. Brush the end of the strip with clarified butter and press to seal the roll. Continue with the instructions in step 7. Instead of folding the strip, roll it up to encase the filling, lightly coating the finished rolls and placing on the baking sheet. Proceed with step 8.

NOTE: If the triangles will be eaten within an hour or so, you can reheat them in a 375-degree-F oven for 10 minutes, or microwave on high for 30 seconds. The triangles can be baked ahead of time and refrigerated in a single layer, covered, until ready to serve. Allow them to reach room temperature before reheating. They can also be frozen in a tightly covered container—take care to stack them carefully. Reheat them, unthawed, in a 375-degree-F oven for about 15 minutes.

Almond Skordalia ❧ Charles Bowman

MAKES ABOUT 1½ CUPS
DRYING TIME (BREAD ONLY): 24 HOURS
COOKING TIME: 10 MINUTES
PREPARATION TIME: ABOUT 25 MINUTES
CHILLING TIME: AT LEAST 4 HOURS

6 ounces (about 6 slices) firm home-style white bread

1 small all-purpose potato (about 3 ounces), peeled and quartered

½ cup coarsely chopped blanched almonds

5 large cloves garlic, minced

Nutty yet light and refreshing, this unusual almond dip is a real treat.

1 Assemble *mise en place* trays for this recipe (see page 6).

2 Trim the crusts from the bread. If not sliced, cut into slices. Lay the slices in a single layer on a baking sheet and let air-dry for 24 hours, turning from time to time.

3 In a small saucepan, cover the potatoes with cool water and bring to a boil over medium heat. Reduce the heat and simmer for about 6 minutes, or until very soft. Remove from the heat, drain, and set aside to cool.

3 tablespoons extra-virgin olive oil

2 tablespoons white wine vinegar

1 tablespoon plus 1 teaspoon fresh lemon juice, or more to taste

½ teaspoon sugar

¾ teaspoon salt, or more to taste

Pinch of freshly ground white pepper, or more to taste

Transfer the potatoes to a food processor fitted with the metal blade. Add the almonds and garlic and process until smooth.

4 In a small bowl, combine the oil, vinegar, lemon juice, sugar, salt, and white pepper. Set aside.

5 Fill a large bowl with cool water. One at a time, drop in the dry bread slices. When well soaked, remove and squeeze out most of the water from each slice. The bread should still be moist. With the food processor running, alternately add the bread and the oil mixture to the almond mixture, and process until very smooth. Taste and adjust the seasonings with additional lemon juice, salt, and/or pepper. Transfer to a nonreactive container, cover, and refrigerate for about 4 hours, or until well chilled. If the mixture seems too stiff, beat in a little water. Serve chilled, with pita chips if desired.

White Beans with Garlic ❧ Charles Bowman

MAKES ABOUT 4½ CUPS

SOAKING TIME (BEANS ONLY): 12 HOURS

COOKING TIME: ABOUT 1 HOUR AND 40 MINUTES

PREPARATION TIME: ABOUT 10 MINUTES

CHILLING TIME: AT LEAST 4 HOURS

1 pound dried gigandes (giant white lima beans)

1½ teaspoons salt

½ cup extra-virgin olive oil

¼ teaspoon freshly ground white pepper

1 tablespoon chopped fresh flat-leaf parsley

6 to 8 sprigs fresh flat-leaf parsley

These huge lima beans have a buttery flavor and creamy texture, which make a fabulous amalgam on the appetizer table. For a perfect match, serve with Skordalia.

1 Assemble *mise en place* trays for this recipe (see page 6).

2 Check through the beans and remove any damaged ones or foreign matter. Place in a large bowl and add enough cold water to cover. Discard any beans or skins that float to the surface. Drain in a colander, rinse under cold running water, and return the beans to the bowl. Cover with cold water and soak for 12 hours, or overnight.

3 Drain the beans and transfer to a large heavy saucepan. Add enough cold water to cover by about 1 inch and bring to a boil over high heat. Boil for about 10 minutes, skimming off any foam as it rises to the surface. Add 1 teaspoon salt, reduce the heat, cover, and simmer, stirring occasionally, for 1½ hours, or until the beans are fork-tender. Drain, transfer to a bowl, and cool for about 15 minutes, or until the beans stop steaming but are still very warm.

4 In a small bowl, whisk together the oil, the remaining ½ teaspoon salt, the white pepper, and chopped parsley. Pour over the warm beans and toss gently to coat. Cover and refrigerate for at least 4 hours, or until well chilled and the flavors have blended. Serve at room temperature, garnished with the parsley sprigs.

Toasted Couscous Risotto ❧ **Terrance Brennan**

SERVES 6

PREPARATION TIME: ABOUT 30 MINUTES

COOKING TIME: ABOUT 20 MINUTES

2½ cups Chicken Stock (see page 14)

½ cup dry white wine

2 tablespoons olive oil

½ cup chopped onions

1 tablespoon minced garlic

Pinch of salt, plus more to taste

2 cups toasted Israeli couscous

5 ounces fresh morels, cooked (about 1½ cups cooked; see Note)

18 medium-sized spears asparagus, trimmed, cut into 1-inch lengths, and blanched

18 ramps or baby leeks, trimmed and blanched

*T*his is an absolutely delicious play on classic Italian risotto. And it requires much less stirring time at the stove.

1 Assemble *mise en place* trays for this recipe (see page 6).

2 In a bowl or large glass measuring cup, combine the stock and wine. Set aside.

3 In a medium-sized saucepan, heat the oil over medium heat. Add the onions, garlic, and a pinch of salt and cook for about 4 minutes, or until just softened. Add the couscous and 2 cups of the stock mixture and cook, stirring occasionally, for about 15 minutes, or until all the liquid has been absorbed. Add the remaining stock mixture and cook for about 4 minutes, beating rapidly with a wooden spoon until the couscous softens and plumps. Stir in the morels, asparagus, ramps, and fava beans and cook for 1 minute.

4 Remove the pan from the heat and stir in the grated cheese, truffle oil, butter, parsley, and chives. Season to taste with salt and white pepper.

1 cup shelled fresh fava beans or peas, blanched

½ cup freshly grated Parmesan cheese

3 tablespoons white truffle oil

3 tablespoons unsalted butter, at room temperature

¼ cup chopped fresh flat-leaf parsley

¼ cup snipped fresh chives

Freshly ground white pepper to taste

Parmesan cheese, for shaving

5 Spoon into warm shallow soup bowls and garnish with shavings of Parmesan. Serve immediately.

NOTE: Cook the morels by sautéing them in a small amount of olive oil or butter until just tender. If you can't find morels, use any type of small, earthy mushrooms of equal size or use common button mushrooms.

―――――

❧ Large-grained Israeli couscous does not require the constant stirring rice does when making traditional risotto; stir it only enough to keep it from sticking.

Intercontinental Chickpea Spread ❧ Jane Brody

SERVES 6

PREPARATION TIME: ABOUT 30 MINUTES

CHILLING TIME: ABOUT 1 HOUR

FAT PER SERVING: 9 GRAMS

SATURATED FAT: 2.8 GRAMS

CALORIES PER SERVING: 237

CALORIES FROM FAT: 35%

―――――

One 20-ounce can chickpeas, rinsed and drained

¼ cup plain nonfat yogurt

1 large clove garlic, chopped

½ teaspoon salt, or to taste

⅓ cup store-bought salsa, preferably hot

1 small zucchini, shredded and squeezed almost dry (about ½ cup before squeezing)

3 ripe plum tomatoes, peeled, seeded, drained, and cut into small dice

2 tablespoons diced red onion

2 tablespoons shredded Parmigiano-Reggiano cheese

1 tablespoon chopped fresh cilantro

*A*ll the ingredients in this recipe can be prepared ahead of time but, if the spread is prepared more than an hour or so before serving, it may get runny. The percentage of fat is relatively high, but the saturated fat is quite low. The spread can be scooped up with toasted pita wedges, baked tortilla chips, or crisp raw vegetables.

1 Assemble *mise en place* trays for this recipe (see page 6).

2 Combine the chickpeas, yogurt, garlic, and salt in a food processor fitted with the metal blade and process to a smooth paste. Transfer to a container, cover, and refrigerate for about 1 hour, or until well chilled.

3 Just before serving, put the chickpea spread on a chilled plate and pour the salsa over it. Sprinkle with the zucchini, tomatoes, onions, cheese, and cilantro and serve immediately.

―――――

❧ Although this recipe calls for prepared salsa, if you have the time, by all means make it fresh.

Red Potato and Goat Cheese Tart with Frisée and Bacon Salad ❧ David Burke

SERVES 6

PREPARATION TIME: ABOUT 1 HOUR AND
10 MINUTES

COOKING TIME: ABOUT 1 HOUR

RESTING TIME (BASIL OIL ONLY): AT LEAST
24 HOURS

---

10 medium Red Bliss potatoes,
washed and dried

½ cup plus 2 tablespoons olive oil

2 tablespoons ground cumin

1 teaspoon chopped fresh rosemary

Kosher salt and freshly ground black
pepper to taste

12 strips bacon, diced

½ pound semisoft goat cheese

6 store-bought flour tortillas

½ cup chopped fresh chives

6 tablespoons mustard oil (see note)

3 tablespoons tarragon vinegar

1 large head frisée, trimmed, rinsed,
and dried

1 cup baby spinach leaves, trimmed,
rinsed, and dried

Goat Cheese Fondue (see page 273)

½ cup olivada (see note)

½ cup cored, peeled, seeded, and
diced tomatoes

3 tablespoons Basil Oil (see
page 263)

Many flavors are magnificently combined to make these tasty tarts. Hints of the flavors of Mexico, the Middle East, and France are pulled together in a totally American fashion.

---

1 Preheat the oven to 350 degrees F. Assemble the *mise en place* trays for this recipe (see page 6).

2 In a shallow roasting pan, combine the potatoes with ¼ cup of the olive oil, the cumin, rosemary, and salt and pepper to taste, and toss to coat. Roast for about 30 minutes, or until the potatoes are tender when pierced with a fork. Set aside to cool.

3 Meanwhile, in a medium-sized sauté pan, cook the diced bacon over medium-low heat for 6 to 8 minutes, or until crisp. Lift the bacon from the pan with a slotted spoon and drain on paper towels. Pour off all but 3 tablespoons of the bacon fat, and set the pan aside to use for the vinaigrette.

4 In a small bowl, combine the goat cheese with 2 table-spoons of the olive oil and salt and pepper to taste. Beat with a wooden spoon until smooth.

5 Cut the tortillas into 4½-inch rounds. Generously coat each one with the goat cheese mixture.

6 Slice the cooked potatoes crosswise into thin slices. Arrange them overlapping slightly, around the edges of the tortillas. Sprinkle with the chives, and season to taste with salt and pepper. Set aside.

7 Set the pan with the bacon fat over low heat. Stir in the mustard oil and vinegar. Cook, stirring, for about 1 minute, or until the vinaigrette is well blended and warm. Remove from the heat and cover to keep warm.

8 Divide the remaining ¼ cup olive oil between 2 large skillets and heat over medium-high heat. When the oil is hot, lay 3 tortilla tarts, potato side down, in each pan. Cook for 3 minutes, or until the potatoes are crisp. Carefully turn and cook for 1 additional minute longer, or until the tortillas are crisp. Remove from the skillets and drain on paper towels.

9 In a large bowl, combine the frisée and spinach with the cooked bacon. Pour the warm vinaigrette over the top, and toss to coat. Arrange the salad on 6 plates. Lay the warm tarts on top and spoon some Goat Cheese Fondue, olivada, and diced tomatoes on top of the tarts. Drizzle with Basil Oil. Serve immediately.

❧ NOTE: Mustard oil and olivada (black olive purée) are available from specialty food stores. Mustard oil is also sold in Asian markets, and olivada in good Italian delicatessens. Both can be used as pungent accents in salads, stir fries, sauces, and dressings.

❧ Make sure the oil is good and hot before cooking.

Onion and Zucchini Frittata with Balsamic Vinegar ❧ Biba Caggiano

SERVES 6

PREPARATION TIME: ABOUT 20 MINUTES

COOKING TIME: ABOUT 25 MINUTES

---

9 large eggs

¾ cup freshly grated Parmigiano-Reggiano cheese

1½ tablespoons chopped fresh parsley

A frittata is an easy-to-make Italian omelet in which the flavors are mixed into the eggs. This frittata is incredibly versatile. Try serving it at brunch or lunch as a light entrée by making individual frittatas in a nonstick five- or six-inch crêpe pan; prepare it for a picnic; or slice and serve it as an hors d'oeuvre.

---

1 Assemble *mise en place* trays for this recipe (see page 6).

8 fresh basil leaves, finely shredded

Salt to taste

3 tablespoons olive oil

1 large onion, thinly sliced

2 medium zucchini, trimmed and thinly sliced

2 tablespoons balsamic vinegar

2 In a medium-sized bowl, lightly beat the eggs. Stir in the Parmigiano, parsley, and basil. Season to taste with salt.

3 In a 12-inch, nonstick skillet, heat the oil over medium heat. Add the onion and cook, stirring continuously, for 3 to 5 minutes. Add the zucchini and cook, stirring, for 5 to 8 minutes, until both vegetables are lightly golden. Stir in 1½ tablespoons of the balsamic vinegar and immediately remove from the heat. Using a slotted spoon, transfer the vegetables to the egg mixture, draining them against the side of the skillet and leaving what liquid there is in the pan. Mix vegetable and egg mixture well.

4 Return the skillet to medium heat and add the vegetable-egg mixture. Cook for about 6 minutes, or until the bottom of the frittata is set and lightly browned.

5 Invert a large, flat plate over the skillet and invert the frittata onto it. Slide the frittata back into the skillet and cook for 3 to 4 minutes more, until set in the center and lightly browned on the bottom. Slide the frittata onto a warm serving dish. Immediately drizzle the remaining ½ tablespoon balsamic vinegar over the top. Serve warm or at room temperature, cut into 6 wedges.

❧ The amount of balsamic vinegar required really depends on the strength of the vinegar. The stronger the vinegar, the less you need to use. It's worth it to taste different brands of balsamic vinegar and choose those that you particularly like. Not all taste the same.

Seared Scallops in Gazpacho-Thyme Sauce ❧ Dominick Cerrone

SERVES 6

PREPARATION TIME: ABOUT 1 HOUR

COOKING TIME: ABOUT 7 MINUTES

SAUCE:

1 red bell pepper, cored, seeded, and chopped

½ green bell pepper, cored, seeded, and chopped

½ yellow bell pepper, cored, seeded, and chopped

1 large ripe tomato, cored and chopped

1 rib celery, chopped

½ hothouse cucumber, chopped

¼ small onion, chopped

1 clove garlic, chopped

6 fresh basil leaves, chopped

2 cups plus 1 tablespoon tomato juice

2 tablespoons plus 1 teaspoon sherry wine vinegar

1 tablespoon extra-virgin olive oil

Fine sea salt and freshly ground white pepper to taste

Pinch of cayenne pepper, or to taste

1 large sprig fresh thyme

SCALLOPS:

½ hothouse cucumber, cut into fine julienne (avoid the seedy center)

The ubiquitous gazpacho reaches a totally new dimension when it's served as a sauce for sea scallops. The zesty flavors intermingle with the sweet, firm-fleshed shellfish, giving new meaning to the opening of a fine meal.

1 Assemble *mise en place* trays for this recipe (see page 6).

2 To make the sauce, in a food processor fitted with the metal blade, combine the chopped bell peppers, tomatoes, celery, cucumbers, onions, garlic, basil, tomato juice, vinegar, and oil. Process until smooth. (For a more refined sauce, strain through a fine sieve.) Transfer to a nonreactive container and season to taste with salt and white pepper and cayenne. Add the thyme sprig and set aside.

3 To prepare the scallops, in a colander, combine the cucumber, zucchini, and yellow squash. Lightly salt and toss well. Set the colander on a plate and drain for about 15 minutes. Rinse the vegetables under cold running water, pat dry, and lay on paper towels.

4 In a large saucepan of boiling water, blanch the bell peppers for 10 seconds. Drain, rinse under cold running water, and pat dry. Set aside.

5 Wash the scallops and pat dry with paper towels. Season to taste with salt and white pepper. In a large non-stick skillet, heat the oil over high heat. Add the scallops and sear for about 3 minutes, or until golden on the bottom. Turn and sear for 2 minutes longer, or until the scallops are golden on both sides and firm to the touch. Transfer to a warm baking sheet and cover to keep warm.

6 In the same skillet, sauté the julienned vegetables for 1 minute, or just until they absorb some scallop flavor and soften slightly. Do not overcook.

1 small zucchini, trimmed and cut into fine julienne (avoid the seedy center)

1 small yellow squash, trimmed and cut into fine julienne (avoid the seedy center)

Fine sea salt to taste

1 red bell pepper, cored, seeded, and finely diced

½ green bell pepper, cored, seeded, and finely diced

½ yellow bell pepper, cored, seeded, and finely diced

30 sea scallops

Freshly ground white pepper to taste

2 tablespoons extra-virgin olive oil

1 tablespoon fresh thyme leaves

6 small sprigs fresh thyme

7 Pour about ¼ cup of the sauce onto the center of each plate and allow to spread to cover the plate. Sprinkle the diced peppers over the sauce. Pile equal portions of julienned vegetables in the center of each plate and surround with an equal number of scallops (or create a balanced design of your choice with the julienned vegetables and scallops). Sprinkle with the fresh thyme leaves and garnish each plate with a thyme sprig. Serve immediately.

NOTE: The julienned vegetables are salted and drained to reduce their moisture content so that they do not release liquid into the sauté pan.

_____

❧ Chef Cerrone suggests canned Sacramento-brand tomato juice and either a spicy green Lerida olive oil or a sweet yellow oil from southern Spain.

❧ You will have lots of extra sauce, which you can use to garnish other fish dishes or chicken or as a salad or vegetable dressing. The sauce may also be frozen for up to 1 month.

Artichoke Bottoms Filled with Poached Oysters ❧ Julia Child

SERVES 6
PREPARATION TIME: ABOUT 25 MINUTES
COOKING TIME: ABOUT 50 MINUTES

_____

¼ cup all-purpose flour

6 cups cold water

¼ cup fresh lemon juice

½ teaspoon salt, or to taste

6 large artichokes with 3-inch bases

1 lemon, halved

This most traditional French dish is so typically Julia you will love it just as you do all her food. Cream, butter, succulent oysters, and tender artichokes are put together beautifully and served with her trademark, a merry "Bon Appétit!"

_____

1 Assemble *mise en place* trays for this recipe (see page 6).

2 In a medium-sized saucepan, whisk the flour into 3 cups of the water. Stir in the remaining 3 cups of water, the lemon juice, and salt. Bring to a boil over medium-

2 tablespoons unsalted butter, melted

Freshly ground black pepper to taste

4 tablespoons unsalted butter

1 tablespoon minced shallots

1 pint large fresh shucked oysters in their liquor

½ cup dry white wine or vermouth

1 large egg yolk

½ cup heavy cream

2 tablespoons minced fresh parsley

high heat. Remove from the heat and set aside. (This mixture, known as a blanc, will be used to cook the artichokes to insure that they will not discolor.)

3 Cut off the stems of one of the artichokes. Bend the outer leaves back and snap them off, leaving the edible leaf bottoms attached to the base. Continue to remove the leaves, leaving the edible bottoms, until you reach the soft crown of leaves in the center. Cut off this crown of leaves. Using a small sharp knife, trim the base evenly to remove all the greenish parts and create a perfect round. To keep the artichoke from discoloring, frequently rub the cut surfaces with the lemon halves as you work. Drop the artichoke into the blanc, and repeat with the remaining artichokes. If the liquid does not cover the artichokes, add additional water as necessary.

4 When all the artichokes are trimmed, place the pan over medium-high heat and bring to a boil. Reduce the heat and simmer for 30 minutes, or until the artichoke bottoms are tender when pierced with a knife.

5 Meanwhile, preheat the oven to 300 degrees F.

6 Drain the artichokes well, and reserve ½ cup of the cooking liquid. Rinse the artichokes under cold running water and dry with paper towels. Scoop out the chokes (fuzzy interior) with a teaspoon and discard. Brush the artichokes with the melted butter and sprinkle with salt and pepper. Place in a shallow baking pan, cover with aluminum foil, and bake for 15 minutes.

7 Meanwhile, in a medium-sized sauté pan, melt the butter over medium heat. Add the shallots and sauté for about 3 minutes, or until just soft. Drain the oysters, reserving the liquor, and cut in half any that are especially large. Add to the pan and cook for 1 minute, or until plumped. Using a slotted spoon, transfer the oysters to a bowl.

8 Add the reserved oyster liquor to the pan. Stir in the wine and the ½ cup of reserved artichoke cooking liquid. Bring to a boil, and cook, stirring frequently, for about 2 minutes, until just thickened.

9 In a medium-sized bowl, whisk the egg yolk and cream together. Add a little of the thickened sauce, whisking continuously. Continue to add the sauce, whisking, until it is all incorporated. Return the sauce to the pan and bring to a simmer over medium heat. Season to taste with salt and pepper.

10 Carefully fold the oysters into the sauce, and remove from the heat.

11 Arrange the artichoke bottoms on a serving platter. Spoon the oysters and sauce into the cavities of the artichokes. Sprinkle with the parsley and serve immediately.

Janice Okun's Buffalo Chicken Wings with Blue Cheese Dressing ❧ Craig Claiborne

SERVES 6
PREPARATION TIME: ABOUT 25 MINUTES
COOKING TIME: ABOUT 35 MINUTES

———————

Blue Cheese Dressing (see page 272)

CHICKEN WINGS:

4 pounds chicken wings

Salt and freshly ground black pepper to taste

About 4 cups peanut, vegetable, or corn oil, for deep-frying

4 tablespoons salted butter

2 tablespoons hot red pepper sauce

1 tablespoon white vinegar

24 to 30 four-inch celery sticks

*H*ere's a great recipe for one of America's all-time favorite bar foods. Craig Claiborne brings chicken wings into the dining room as an appetizer, but you could easily increase the amount for a big bowl of tasty party fare.

———————

1 Preheat the oven to 250 degrees F. Assemble *mise en place* trays for this recipe (see page 6).

2 Prepare the dressing.

3 To prepare the chicken, wash the wings and dry well. Cut off and discard the small tip of each wing. Cut apart the wings at the joint. Sprinkle with salt and pepper to taste.

4 In a deep-fat fryer or a large, deep saucepan, heat the oil over medium-high heat until almost smoking. Add half of the wings and cook for about 10 minutes, stirring occasionally or turning with tongs, until golden brown and crisp. Drain well on paper towels or a brown paper bag. Put the drained wings on a baking sheet and keep warm in the oven while you cook the remaining wings. Drain well and place on the baking sheet in the oven.

5 In a small saucepan, melt the butter over low heat. Stir in the hot sauce and vinegar.

6 Put the chicken wings on a warm serving platter and pour the butter mixture over them. Serve with the Blue Cheese Dressing and celery sticks.

❧ Buffalo chicken wings originated in a bar in Buffalo, New York. The cool blue cheese dressing offsets the heat of the wings. The crunchy celery is for dipping into the dressing.

Baba Ganoush ❧ **Andrew D'Amico**

MAKES ABOUT 2 CUPS
PREPARATION TIME: ABOUT 30 MINUTES
COOKING TIME: ABOUT 20 MINUTES
CHILLING TIME: AT LEAST 30 MINUTES

---

1 large eggplant, about 1 pound

2 cloves garlic

¼ to ⅓ cup fresh lemon juice

Salt to taste

2 to 4 tablespoons tahini

2 tablespoons olive oil

Ground cumin to taste

Freshly ground black pepper to taste

*A*ndy's tangy version of the famous Lebanese dip has the added flavor of smoky eggplant. For a stunning visual effect, complete the dish with the traditional pomegranate seed garnish. Serve this with pita bread, crackers, or toasted country-style bread rubbed with garlic.

---

1 Assemble *mise en place* trays for this recipe (see page 6).

2 Prepare a charcoal or gas grill or preheat the broiler.

3 Using a fork, puncture the eggplant in several places. Roast the eggplant on the grill or under the broiler for about 20 minutes, turning occasionally, until the skin is completely charred and the eggplant is soft. Cool until cool enough to handle. Halve and scrape out the pulp, put it in a fine sieve, and hold under gently running cold water to wash away any bitterness. Shake dry and use your hands to squeeze out as much liquid as possible.

3 tablespoons pomegranate seeds, or 1 tablespoon chopped fresh flat-leaf parsley, or ⅛ teaspoon ground sumac, or 1 tablespoon extra-virgin olive oil

4 In a food processor fitted with the metal blade, combine the eggplant pulp, garlic, ¼ cup lemon juice, and salt to taste. Process until smooth. Add 2 tablespoons tahini and process just to incorporate. Taste and, if necessary, adjust the flavors with additional lemon juice and tahini. With the processor running, add the oil. Season to taste with cumin, salt, and pepper. Transfer to a small serving bowl, cover, and chill for at least 30 minutes, or up to 2 days.

5 Garnish with pomegranate seeds, parsley, sumac, or a drizzle of olive oil if desired, and serve.

NOTE: To retrieve pomegranate seeds neatly, barely cut into the tough skin and then peel it back as you would peel an orange. The seeds will fall out without staining your hands with the intense red juice.

Asparagus with Red Onion Vinaigrette ∾ Gary Danko

SERVES 6

PREPARATION TIME: ABOUT 15 MINUTES

COOKING TIME: ABOUT 2 MINUTES

---

2 pounds pencil-thin asparagus, trimmed to equal lengths

Red Onion Vinaigrette (see page 275)

2 roasted red or yellow bell peppers, peeled, seeded, and cut lengthwise into ¼-inch-wide strips

¼ cup plus 2 tablespoons freshly grated Parmigiano-Reggiano cheese

12 oil-cured black olives

Parmigiano-Reggiano shavings

A delicious salad that could stand on its own as a main-course lunch dish, this enticing combination has its roots in Italy. Light and easy to prepare, with many components made in advance, it is a perfect addition to any entertaining menu.

---

1 Assemble *mise en place* trays for this recipe (see page 6).

2 In a large pot of boiling water, blanch the asparagus for about 2 minutes, or until tender and bright green. Immediately drain and place in an ice water bath. When chilled, drain and pat dry.

3 Prepare Red Onion Vinaigrette.

4 Place equal portions of asparagus on each plate, all facing in the same direction with the bases together and the stalks fanning out. Make a lattice of pepper strips covering the base of each fan. Drizzle the vinaigrette over the asparagus and sprinkle with the grated cheese. Garnish each plate with 2 olives and Parmigiano-Reggiano shavings and serve immediately.

❧ Pencil-thin asparagus do not usually require much peeling or trimming. However, if you can only find medium or large stalks, they must be trimmed to the tender point and the outer skin peeled off with a vegetable peeler or sharp knife.

❧ To eliminate problems with digestion, wrap raw onions in a clean kitchen towel and twist to squeeze out the liquid. Chef Danko feels that it is the onion juice that causes unpleasant reactions.

Cream Biscuits with Barbecued Crabmeat and Buttermilk Dressing ❧ Robert Del Grande

SERVES 6
PREPARATION TIME: ABOUT 30 MINUTES
COOKING TIME: ABOUT 15 MINUTES

½ pound fresh lump crabmeat

2 tablespoons plus 1½ teaspoons Barbecue Spice (see page 265)

2 tablespoons unsalted butter

1 bunch arugula, washed, trimmed, and dried

1 tablespoon olive oil

Salt and freshly ground black pepper to taste

6 Cream Biscuits, freshly baked (recipe follows)

"Imagine this: A petite cream biscuit, hot from the oven, its heady aroma of toasted butter and flour startling those quiescent memories of youth. Still hot to the touch, gingerly split equatorially. On the bottom half of such a tender pastry, centered on a huge white plate, is placed some peppery arugula (glistening from a deft treatment with olive oil) and nestled on this, pan-seared crabmeat redolent of barbecued spice and fresh lime. Ah ha ... is the picture becoming clearer ... le petite biscuit farci? ... "

---

1 Assemble *mise en place* trays for this recipe (see page 6).

2 Pick over the crabmeat to remove any shell and cartilage. Set aside 1 tablespoon of the Barbecue Spice for garnish.

Buttermilk Dressing (see page 273)

Tabasco to taste

6 sprigs fresh cilantro

6 lime wedges

3 In a bowl, combine the crabmeat with the remaining 1 tablespoon plus 1½ teaspoons Barbecue Spice and toss to mix. In a medium-sized skillet melt the butter over medium heat. Add the seasoned crabmeat and sauté for 1 minute, or until just heated through. Remove from the heat.

4 In a bowl, toss the arugula leaves with the olive oil. Season to taste with salt and pepper.

5 Split the freshly baked biscuits in half crosswise. Place the bottom halves in the centers of warm plates. Place a few leaves of arugula on each biscuit. Spoon equal portions of the crabmeat on top of the arugula. Drizzle with a little of the Buttermilk Dressing. Place the biscuit tops over the crabmeat. Lightly dust a little of the reserved Barbecue Spice on each plate. Garnish each biscuit with a drizzle of Tabasco, a sprig of cilantro, and a wedge of lime. Serve immediately.

~ **Do not dress the arugula more than 5 minutes before serving or it will begin to wilt.**

CREAM BISCUITS

MAKES 10 TO 12 BISCUITS

2 cups all-purpose flour

1 tablespoon baking powder

½ teaspoon baking soda

1 tablespoon granulated sugar

½ teaspoon salt

3 tablespoons unsalted butter, chilled and cut into ½-inch cubes

½ cup buttermilk, or more as needed

½ cup heavy cream

1 Preheat the oven to 425 degrees F.

2 In a medium-sized bowl combine the flour, baking powder, baking soda, sugar, and salt. With your fingertips or a pastry blender, blend in the butter until the mixture resembles coarse crumbs.

3 Make a well in the center of the flour mixture and add the buttermilk and cream, mixing just enough to form a soft dough. If the dough seems sticky, add a tablespoon or two more flour. If it is dry and crumbly, add a little more buttermilk. Knead the dough for no more than 2 minutes. Press it out with your hands to a circle about ½ inch thick and 8 inches in diameter. Allow the dough to rest for 5 minutes.

2 tablespoons unsalted butter, melted

4 Using a 2-inch biscuit-cutter or a glass, cut the dough into circles. Gather the scraps together, press out the dough again and cut out more biscuits. Put the biscuits on an ungreased baking sheet and brush with the melted butter.

5 Bake for 10 to 12 minutes or until puffed and lightly browned. Remove from the oven and place on a wire rack to cool for about 2 minutes. You need 6 biscuits for the crabmeat recipe. Serve the others on the side, or save for breakfast.

Burger of Fresh Foie Gras and Frisée Salad with Cider Vinaigrette ~ Christian Delouvrier

SERVES 6

PREPARATION TIME: ABOUT 25 MINUTES

COOKING TIME: ABOUT 45 MINUTES

Cider Vinaigrette (see page 274)

FOIE GRAS BURGERS:

2 cups chicken stock (see page 15)

6 small, tart apples, such as Granny Smith

2 tablespoons granulated sugar

2 to 3 tablespoons duck fat (see Note)

⅔ cup finely sliced fresh porcini mushrooms

3 ounces fresh foie gras, diced

2 tablespoons cider vinegar

6 slices fresh foie gras (about 2 ounces each), 3 to 4 inches wide and ½ inch thick

The traditional French combination of foie gras and apples is given a new twist. This very rich appetizer adds a festive note with its luxurious taste. This is Chef Delouvrier's tribute to "The Big Apple"!

1 Assemble *mise en place* trays for this recipe (see page 6).

2 Prepare the vinaigrette.

3 To make the foie gras burgers, in a small saucepan, bring the chicken stock to a boil over medium-high heat. Reduce the heat and simmer for about 20 minutes, or until reduced to ⅔ cup. Remove from the heat and set aside.

4 Peel the apples. Trim each end, cutting crosswise through the center. Cut 2 large slices from each apple the same thickness as the foie gras slices. Core the slices and sprinkle with the sugar. Keep the slices together as pairs. Chop enough of the trimmings to equal 1 cup.

5 Preheat the oven to 400 degrees F.

1 head frisée, trimmed, washed, and dried

6 In a medium-sized, nonstick sauté pan, heat 1 tablespoon of the duck fat over medium heat. Keeping the apple pairs together, carefully lay them in the fat and sauté for 8 to 10 minutes, turning once, until tender and glazed. Remove from the pan and set aside.

7 Add another tablespoon of duck fat to the pan. Add the porcini and sauté for 5 minutes, or until crisp. Remove from the pan and set aside.

8 Add the diced foie gras to the pan. Sauté for 3 minutes, or until golden. Using a slotted spoon, transfer the foie gras to paper towels to drain.

9 If the pan seems dry, add 1 more tablespoon of duck fat and heat until hot. Add the reserved chopped apple trimmings and cook, stirring frequently, for about 4 minutes, until the apples begin to soften and release liquid. Stir in the vinegar and deglaze the pan, scraping up all the brown bits. Cook for 2 to 3 minutes, until the vinegar has evaporated. Stir in the reserved chicken stock. Strain the sauce through a chinois or other fine sieve into a small saucepan, pressing on the apples to extract all the liquid. Taste and season with salt and pepper. Cover and keep warm.

10 Place 1 slice of foie gras on the bottom half of each apple slice. Place an equal portion of porcini on top of the foie gras and top with the matching apple slice. Place on a nonstick, rimmed baking sheet and bake for about 3 min-utes, until the foie gras is just heated through. Remove from the oven.

11 In a bowl, toss the frisée with the vinaigrette. Arrange equal portions of frisée on one side of each serving plate. Spoon the diced foie gras over the salad. Place the foie gras burger next to the salad, drizzle the sauce over the burger, and serve.

NOTE: The duck fat gives the sauce and foie gras a wonderful flavor. If you cannot find it at your butcher or a gourmet shop, substitute chicken fat or vegetable or olive oil.

_____

✎ Frisée is also called curly endive. A head is about 3 ounces.

✎ Buy the best grade of foie gras available. The flavors are very intense in this appetizer.

Fig and Prosciutto Tart ✎ Todd English

SERVES 6
PREPARATION TIME: ABOUT 30 MINUTES
COOKING TIME: ABOUT 1 HOUR
BAKING TIME: ABOUT 15 MINUTES

_____

½ cup red wine

1 cup balsamic vinegar

⅔ cup granulated sugar

1 cup roughly chopped dried figs, preferably Turkish

3 sprigs fresh rosemary, leaves only, chopped

Pizza Dough (recipe follows)

3 tablespoons olive oil

¼ cup crumbled Gorgonzola cheese

12 to 18 thin slices prosciutto

■ Special Equipment: Pizza stone or baking tiles

*T*odd told us that the combination of fresh figs and prosciutto was one of his most favorite childhood treats. Memories of his Italian boyhood helped create this unusual tart, combining the always-available sweet, dried figs with salty prosciutto, slightly pungent Gorgonzola, and rich pizza dough.

_____

1 Assemble *mise en place* trays for this recipe (see page 6).

2 In a medium-sized nonreactive saucepan, bring the wine to a boil over high heat. Reduce the heat and simmer gently for about 7 minutes, or until reduced by half. Raise the heat, add the vinegar, and bring to a boil. Reduce the heat and simmer for about 15 minutes, or until reduced by half. Stir in the sugar, adjust the heat so that the mixture just barely simmers, and cook, stirring frequently, for 5 minutes. Add the figs and half the rosemary and cook, stirring frequently, for about 20 minutes, or until the figs are plump and the jam has thickened. Allow to cool to room temperature.

3 Set a pizza stone or baking tiles on the bottom rack and preheat the oven to 450 degrees F.

4 Divide the dough into 6 equal portions. Working with one piece at a time, on a lightly floured surface,

roll out each portion into a ½-inch-thick circle about 8 inches in diameter. Drizzle each circle with 10½ teaspoons oil, sprinkle with the remaining rosemary, and spread a thin layer of fig jam over each. Sprinkle the Gorgonzola over the jam. Crimp the edges of the tarts by folding small pinches of dough in toward the center.

5 Place the tarts on the hot stone and bake for about 15 minutes, or until the crust is lightly browned and crisp and the cheese has melted. Remove from the oven and lay 2 to 3 pieces of prosciutto on top of each. Serve immediately.

NOTE: If your baking stone and oven are large enough, bake all the pizzas at once. Otherwise, bake 2 to 3 at a time and serve immediately, or cover to keep warm until all are baked.

❧ If fresh figs are in season, Chef English recommends placing a few slices on top of the prosciutto for garnish.

❧ The fig jam also makes a rich condiment for grilled or roasted pork or duck.

PIZZA DOUGH

MAKES SIX 8-INCH ROUND PIZZAS OR 2 MEDIUM-SIZED PIZZAS

1½ teaspoons active dry yeast

1½ teaspoons honey

2 cups lukewarm water

2 tablespoons olive oil

2 cups all-purpose flour

½ teaspoon salt

8 tablespoons (1 stick) unsalted butter, softened

1 In a large bowl, combine the yeast, honey, and ½ cup of the water. Let stand for 5 minutes, or until the mixture bubbles and swells. Stir in the oil and the remaining 1½ cups water with a wooden spoon. Stir in the flour and salt until well combined.

2 Turn the dough out onto a lightly floured surface and knead for about 10 minutes, or until elastic and smooth. Form into a ball and place in a lightly oiled bowl, turning the dough to coat it with oil. Cover loosely and place in a warm spot for about 1 hour, or until doubled in size.

3 Turn the dough out onto a lightly floured surface and flatten it into a smooth, even rectangle about 6 inches wide and 10 inches long. Using a spatula, spread the butter over one half of the rectangle. Fold the dough in half, like a book, to cover the butter and flatten with a rolling pin into a rectangle about 6 inches wide and 10 inches long. Fold and roll out three more times, turning the folded dough a quarter turn between each rolling. Wrap in plastic wrap and refrigerate for 1 hour.

7 Divide the dough into 6 pieces and follow the recipe for the tart, beginning with step 4.

NOTE: To freeze the dough, divide it into the desired number of pieces, roll out to pizza shapes, and wrap tightly in plastic wrap and foil. It is not necessary to thaw the dough before topping and baking, but it may require a longer baking time.

◆ This recipe can be used to make larger pizzas than called for in the tart recipe.

Warm Lobster Taco with Yellow Tomato Salsa and Jícama Salad ◆ Dean Fearing

SERVES 6

PREPARATION TIME: ABOUT 35 MINUTES

COOKING TIME: ABOUT 25 MINUTES

CHILLING TIME (SALSA ONLY): AT LEAST 2 HOURS

---

4 one-pound live lobsters

6 seven-inch fresh flour tortillas (see page 21) or store-bought flour tortillas

3 tablespoons corn oil

1 cup grated Monterey Jack cheese with jalapeños

In the off-season, one-pound lobsters may not yield enough meat, so buy one-and-a-quarter-pound lobsters. The recipe calls only for the tail meat and so you will have left-over claw meat. Because the salsa needs to chill, make it before making the taco. The salsa can be made up to 8 hours in advance.

---

1 Preheat the oven to 200 degrees F. Assemble mise en place trays for this recipe (see page 6).

2 Fill a large stockpot with lightly salted water and bring to a boil over high heat. Plunge the lobsters head-

1 cup shredded spinach leaves
Yellow Tomato Salsa (see page 283)
Jícama Salad (see page 122)

first into the boiling water, cover, and cook for about 8 minutes, or until the shells turn red. Drain and let the lobsters cool slightly.

3 Stack the tortillas and wrap them tightly in aluminum foil. Warm in the oven for 15 minutes, or until heated through. Wrap the hot, foil-wrapped stack in a thick terry towel to keep warm until ready to use.

4 Meanwhile, remove the meat from the lobster tails and try to keep it intact. Reserve the remaining meat (from the claws, etc.) for another use. Cut the lobster tail meat into thin medallions or chop in ¼-inch pieces if it falls apart.

5 In a medium-sized skillet, heat the oil over medium heat. When hot, add the lobster meat and sauté for about 2 minutes, or until just heated through. Remove from the heat.

6 Unwrap the tortillas and lay them out on a work surface. Lift the lobster meat from the pan using a slotted spoon and divide it among the warm tortillas. Sprinkle with grated cheese and shredded spinach. Roll the tortillas into cylinders and place each one on a warm serving plate, seam side down. Surround the soft tacos with the Yellow Tomato Salsa and spoon a small mound of Jícama Salad on either side.

~ If wrapped in wet newspaper, lobsters (and crabs and crayfish) can be kept alive in the refrigerator for up to 4 days. Do not allow the newspaper to dry out.

~ The lobsters can be cooked, cooled, and the tail meat cut up early in the day. Refrigerate until ready to use.

Grilled Tuna Tostada with Black Bean-Mango Salsa and Avocado Vinaigrette ～ Bobby Flay

SERVES 8

PREPARATION TIME: ABOUT 30 MINUTES

COOKING TIME: ABOUT 8 MINUTES

This is one of Bobby's signature dishes that offers his exciting execution of contrasts in taste, texture, and color. This vibrant dish makes a terrific appetizer.

2 one- to 1¼-pound tuna steaks, trimmed (about 2¼ pounds)

2 tablespoons vegetable oil

Salt to taste

12 four-inch freshly fried Flour Tostadas (see page 23) or store-bought tostadas

Black Bean-Mango Salsa (see page 290)

Avocado Vinaigrette (see page 274)

½ cup diced red bell pepper, for garnish

½ cup snipped fresh chives, for garnish

1 Prepare a charcoal or gas grill or preheat the broiler. Preheat the oven to 350 degrees F. Assemble *mise en place* trays for this recipe (see page 6).

2 Brush the tuna with the oil and season to taste with salt.

3 Lay the fish on the grill or under the broiler and cook for 1½ to 2 minutes, or just long enough to lightly color the side facing the heat. If using a grill, this should be long enough to mark that side with grill marks. Turn the fish over and cook for 2 minutes more or until the flesh is firm and opaque. (To prevent overcooking and keep the fish moist, allow no more than 5 minutes total cooking time for each ½ inch of thickness at the thickest part.) Cut the tuna into 12 equal slices.

4 Meanwhile, spread the freshly fried tostadas on paper towel-lined baking sheets. Heat them in the oven for 2 to 3 minutes.

5 Arrange the tostadas on a large serving platter. Lightly coat each one with the Black Bean Salsa. Lay a grilled tuna slice in the center. Drizzle the top of each tostada with the Avocado Vinaigrette and then drizzle it in a decorative pattern around the edge of the platter.

6 Sprinkle the bell pepper and chives around the edge of the platter. Serve immediately.

Spicy Chicken, Eggplant, and Grilled Red Onion Quesadilla with Tomatillo Salsa ~ Bobby Flay

SERVES 8

PREPARATION TIME: ABOUT 30 MINUTES

COOKING TIME: ABOUT 20 MINUTES

MARINATING TIME: ABOUT 4 HOURS

1½ cups Chicken Stock (see page 15)

⅓ cup fresh lime juice

⅓ cup olive oil

3 jalapeño chiles, seeded and sliced

¼ cup chopped fresh cilantro

1 pound boneless, skinless chicken breast (1 whole breast) sliced on the diagonal into strips about 3 inches long and ¼-inch wide

12 ¼-inch-thick slices red onion

12 ¼-inch thick slices peeled eggplant

9 six- or seven-inch Flour Tortillas (see page 21) or storebought flour tortillas

¾ cup grated Monterey Jack cheese

¾ cup grated white Cheddar cheese

Salt and freshly ground white pepper to taste

4 tablespoons sour cream

Tomatillo Salsa (see page 287)

This quesadilla can be served as a zesty appetizer, a main course for brunch or lunch, or a Sunday night supper. Its greatest appeal is that it can be prepared totally in advance and baked at the last minute.

1 Assemble *mise en place* trays for this recipe (see page 6).

2 In a blender or food processor fitted with the metal blade, combine the stock, lime juice, olive oil, chiles, and cilantro. Blend until smooth.

3 Put the sliced chicken in a glass or ceramic dish and pour the chicken stock mixture over it. Cover and refrigerate for 4 hours.

4 Prepare a charcoal or gas grill or preheat the broiler. Lightly oil the grid.

5 Remove the chicken from the marinade and discard the marinade. Grill or broil the chicken for 1½ to 2 minutes per side or until cooked through. Remove from the heat and set aside.

6 Grill or broil the onion slices for 2 to 3 minutes on each side. Remove from the heat and set aside. Then grill or broil the eggplant slices for 1½ to 2 minutes on each side. Remove from the heat and set aside.

7 Preheat the oven to 350 degrees F.

8 Place 6 of the tortillas on an ungreased baking sheet and sprinkle with the cheeses. Top each one with an equal portion of chicken, 2 slices of eggplant, and 2 slices of onion. Season to taste with salt and white pepper. Stack one layered tortillas to make 3 stacks of 2 tortillas each. Top each stack with a plain tortilla.

9 Bake for 8 to 12 minutes or until the tortillas are slightly crisp and the cheeses have melted. Remove from the oven and let rest for about 2 minutes. Cut into quarters, and place a dollop of sour cream on the top of each quarter. Serve hot with the Tomatillo Salsa.

Baked Eggplant and Manchego Salad with Oregano and Balsamic Vinegar Glaze ❧ Bobby Flay

SERVES 6

PREPARATION TIME: ABOUT 1 HOUR

COOKING TIME: ABOUT 30 MINUTES

8 medium-sized eggplants, peeled and sliced crosswise ⅛ inch thick (5 to 6 pounds total; see Note)

¼ cup olive oil

2 cups balsamic vinegar

½ pound Manchego cheese, sliced paper-thin

1 cup loosely packed fresh oregano leaves

Salt and freshly ground black pepper to taste

About 1 teaspoon ancho chile powder or Spanish paprika

Although this dish is an inspired first course, it would also make a terrific vegetarian main course. The meltingly mellow sheep's milk cheese adds an authentic taste of Spain.

1 Assemble *mise en place* trays for this recipe (see page 6).

2 Preheat the oven to 425 degrees F.

3 Lay the eggplant slices in a single layer on ungreased baking sheets. Using a pastry brush, lightly coat both sides with oil. Bake for about 8 minutes, or until slightly softened but not mushy. Allow to cool on the baking sheets. (Do not turn the oven off.)

4 In a small nonreactive saucepan, bring the vinegar to a boil over high heat. Reduce the heat slightly and simmer for about 10 minutes, or until the vinegar turns syrupy. Cool slightly, transfer to a plastic squeeze bottle with a fine tip, and set aside.

5 Lay a slice of cheese on a slice of eggplant, sprinkle with a few oregano leaves, and season to taste with salt and pepper. Continue making layers in this manner, using 6 slices of eggplant in all. Sprinkle the top slice with chile powder. Transfer to a nonstick baking sheet. Make 5 more identical stacks. Bake for about 10 minutes.

6 Cut each eggplant stack in half on the diagonal and set one stack on each plate, separating the halves slightly. Drizzle each with the balsamic glaze and sprinkle with a few oregano leaves. Serve immediately.

NOTE: As many as 8 eggplants are needed to get 36 uniformly sized slices. Discard the tapered ends, or use them for another dish.

Flatbread with Spicy Hummus, Goat Cheese, and Roasted Vegetables ∿ Bobby Flay

SERVES 6

PREPARATION TIME: ABOUT 2 HOURS

BAKING TIME: ABOUT 35 MINUTES

BAKING TIME: ABOUT 5 MINUTES

2 medium-sized eggplants, trimmed and quartered

2 red bell peppers, cored, seeded, and quartered

2 yellow bell peppers, cored, seeded, and quartered

1 large red onion, quartered

8 spears asparagus, trimmed

¼ cup plus 1 tablespoon olive oil

Salt and freshly ground black pepper to taste

3 cups drained cooked chickpeas

¼ cup tahini

¼ cup chopped fresh flat-leaf parsley

2 tablespoons chopped garlic

The flavors absolutely blossom on this multileveled pizza-like appetizer. I could easily eat it as light lunch or supper.

1 Assemble *mise en place* trays for this recipe (see page 6).

2 Preheat the oven to 400 degrees F.

3 Toss the eggplant, peppers, onions, and asparagus with 3 tablespoons of the olive oil and season with salt and pepper to taste. Arrange on nonstick baking sheets, keeping the vegetables separate, and bake until just tender and slightly crisp, turning occasionally, about 10 minutes for the asparagus, 15 minutes for the eggplant, 20 minutes for the peppers, and 25 minutes for the onions. Set aside. When the peppers are cool, peel off the skin with a sharp knife. Increase the oven temperature to 450 degrees F and place a pizza stone or baking tiles on the bottom rack.

4 In a food processor fitted with the metal blade, combine the chickpeas, tahini, parsley, garlic, chile, lemon juice, the remaining 2 tablespoons olive oil, the honey, cumin, and salt and pepper to taste. Process until the

2 teaspoons minced green *chile de árbol* or other hot green chile

¼ cup fresh lemon juice

1 tablespoon honey

1 tablespoon ground cumin

Flatbread (recipe follows)

¼ cup crumbled fresh goat cheese

¼ cup pitted black olives

¼ cup Basil Oil (see page 263; optional)

■ Special Equipment: Pizza stone or baking tiles

chickpeas are finely chopped but the mixture is not smoothly puréed.

5 Spread the hummus on the flatbread and top with an assortment of roasted vegetables. Sprinkle with the goat cheese. Place on the pizza stone and bake for about 5 minutes, or until the cheese is melting and the flatbread is hot. Garnish with olives and, if desired, drizzle Basil Oil over the top. Serve immediately.

NOTE: If your baking stone is large enough, bake all the flatbreads at once. Otherwise, bake 2 to 3 at a time and serve immediately, or cover to keep warm until all are baked.

FLATBREAD

MAKES 6

1¼ cups lukewarm water

3 tablespoons olive oil

1½ teaspoons granulated sugar

½ ounce fresh yeast or 1 package (¼ ounce) active dry yeast

¾ cup buckwheat flour

1½ tablespoons salt

About 3 cups sifted bread flour

■ Special Equipment: Electric mixer with dough hook

1 In the bowl of an electric mixer fitted with a dough hook, combine the water, 2 tablespoons of the oil, the sugar, and yeast. Mix on low speed for about 1 minute, or until the sugar and yeast are dissolved. Add the buckwheat flour and salt. Add the bread flour ¼ cup at a time, mixing until the dough forms a cohesive mass. Turn the dough out onto a lightly floured surface and divide into 6 pieces. Form each piece into a ball, place the balls on a nonstick baking sheet, and lightly brush with the remaining 1 tablespoon oil. Cover loosely and set aside in a warm place to rise for 2 hours, until nearly doubled in volume.

2 Preheat the oven to 450 degrees F and place a pizza stone or baking tiles on the lower rack.

3 Pat the balls into discs. On a lightly floured surface, sprinkle each disc with flour and roll out to a circle about ⅛ inch thick. Prick the circles all over with a fork, place on the pizza stone, and bake for about 5 minutes, or until crisp and browned around the edges. Serve warm or cool.

NOTE: You can make the dough ahead of time, form it into balls, and let them rise in the refrigerator for up to 12 hours.

Chipotle-Garbanzo Bean Dip with Blue Corn Tortilla Chips and Salsa Cruda ❧ Marilyn Frobuccino

SERVES 6

PREPARATION TIME: ABOUT 25 MINUTES

COOKING TIME: ABOUT 1 HOUR

MARINATING TIME (SALSA ONLY): 1 HOUR

2 heads roasted garlic (see page 20)

2 sixteen-ounce cans garbanzo beans (chick peas), drained, liquid reserved

1 tablespoon canned chipotle chiles in adobo sauce (see Glossary), or more to taste

½ cup olive oil

2 tablespoons fresh lime juice

3 tablespoons ground toasted sesame seeds (see page 13)

1 tablespoon ground toasted cumin seeds (see page 13)

2 large radicchio leaves, washed and dried

1 tablespoon salt, or to taste

Salsa Cruda (see page 289)

Freshly fried Blue Corn Tortilla Chips (see page 23) or storebought, unsalted chips

*M*arilyn's healthful bean dip is perfect for today's entertaining—quick and inexpensive to prepare and low in fat.

1 Preheat the oven to 400 degrees F. Assemble *mise en place* trays for this recipe (see page 6).

2 Place the roasted garlic, garbanzo beans, chipotle and sauce, olive oil, and ½ cup of the reserved bean liquid in a blender or food processor fitted with the metal blade. Blend or process for 30 seconds or until smooth, adding additional bean liquid (or water) if the mixture seems too thick. Add the lime juice, ground sesame seeds, ground cumin, and salt. Blend or process until combined.

3 Taste and adjust the seasoning with additional chipotle purée, if desired. Scrape into the radicchio leaves and serve with the Salsa Cruda and Blue Corn Tortilla Chips.

❧ The bean dip can be made up to 3 days ahead of time. Cover and refrigerate. Allow it to sit at room temperature for at least 1 hour before serving.

Seafood Seviche with Summer Greens ❧ Marilyn Frobuccino

SERVES 6

PREPARATION TIME: ABOUT 30 MINUTES

CHILLING TIME: ABOUT 3 HOURS

½ pound sea scallops, each sliced into 3 equal-sized discs

½ pound red snapper fillet, skinned and sliced, 3 inches long and ¼-inch wide

½ pound mackerel or bluefish fillet, skinned, sliced into strips, 3 inches long and ¼-inch wide

½ pound Atlantic or Norwegian salmon fillet, skinned and sliced, 3 inches long and ¼-inch wide

1 white onion, thinly sliced, halved crosswise

3 cloves garlic, thinly sliced, halved crosswise

1 large red bell pepper, seeded and julienned

1 large yellow bell pepper, seeded and julienned

2 to 3 pickled jalapeño chiles, seeded and julienned

1 tablespoon minced fresh cilantro

1 tablespoon coarse salt

¼ teaspoon red chile flakes

2 cups fresh lime juice (16–20 limes)

½ cup extra-virgin olive oil

1 head frisée (curly endive), washed, trimmed, and dried

1 bunch arugula, washed, trimmed, and dried

*S*ince the acid in the lime juice "cooks" the fish just as effectively as heat does, seviche is a wonderful addition to the home cook's summer-meal repertoire. Feel free to experiment with other types of fish, or use only one or two of the types listed here if you cannot find them all. A reliable fishmonger will be able to suggest substitutes for the perch or mackerel. Be sure to use the freshest fish available.

1 Assemble *mise en place* trays for this recipe (see page 6).

2 In a large glass or ceramic bowl, combine the scallops, perch, mackerel, and salmon. Add the onion, garlic, bell peppers, and jalapeño and toss gently. Stir in the cilantro, salt, and chile flakes. Add the lime juice and olive oil and toss gently to coat. Cover and refrigerate, stirring occasionally, for about 3 hours until the scallops and fish become opaque.

3 Arrange the frisée and arugula on serving plates or, for a pretty presentation, in parfait or martini glasses. Using tongs or a slotted spoon, place equal portions of the seviche on top of the greens. Serve immediately.

❧ It takes 8 to 10 limes to make 1 cup of juice. You will extract more juice from the limes if you roll them on a countertop, exerting pressure with your palm, before squeezing. Alternatively, place the limes in a microwave oven for 5 seconds on high before juicing. Do not microwave them for any longer—just long enough to warm them a little and release the juice. If you are squeezing the limes by hand, consider wearing rubber gloves, as the 16 to 20 limes you will need produce a lot of juice that can sting small cuts and abrasions.

Smoked Salmon Quesadillas ❧ Vincent Guerithault

SERVES 6

PREPARATION TIME: ABOUT 10 MINUTES

COOKING TIME: ABOUT 6 MINUTES

2 ounces mild goat cheese

1 tablespoon grated fresh horse-radish or well-drained prepared horseradish

1 tablespoon sour cream

1 tablespoon plus 1 teaspoon chopped fresh dill

Salt to taste (optional)

Freshly ground white pepper to taste

3 tablespoons extra-virgin olive oil

3 seven- or eight-inch fresh flour tortillas (see page 21) or store-bought flour tortillas

6 thin slices smoked salmon (about 4 ounces)

1 tablespoon fresh lemon juice

This is Vincent's innovative way of pairing succulent yet conventional smoked salmon with the bread of the Southwest. This recipe can easily be doubled or tripled. Traditionally, quesadillas are folded tortillas. Vincent plays with the concept by serving them unfolded.

1 Assemble *mise en place* trays for this recipe (see page 6).

2 In a small bowl, combine the goat cheese, horseradish, sour cream, 1 teaspoon of the chopped dill, salt, if desired, and white pepper to taste. Beat with a wooden spoon until smooth and well blended. Set aside.

3 In a small skillet, heat the oil over medium-high heat for 1 minute. Fry the tortillas, one at a time, turning once, for 2 minutes, or until lightly browned. Drain on paper towels.

4 Spread about 2 generous teaspoons of the horseradish cream on each tortilla. Arrange the smoked salmon over the cheese. Sprinkle with the remaining chopped dill and drizzle with the lemon juice.

5 Cut each tortilla into 6 wedges and serve immediately.

Sea Scallops with Potato Cakes and Sherry-Vinegar Dressing ~ Vincent Guerithault

SERVES 6

PREPARATION TIME: ABOUT 20 MINUTES

COOKING TIME: ABOUT 45 MINUTES

DRESSING:

3 teaspoons sherry vinegar

1½ teaspoons honey

3 tablespoons extra-virgin olive oil

POTATO CAKES:

3 baking potatoes, peeled and cut into ½-inch chunks

1½ tablespoons unsalted butter

2 tablespoons plus 2 teaspoons extra-virgin olive oil

2 tablespoons chopped fresh cilantro

Salt and freshly ground black pepper to taste

SEA SCALLOPS:

6 large sea scallops, about 2 inches in diameter

1 tablespoon olive oil

1 head frisée (curly endive), trimmed, washed, and dried

On its own, this appetizer can become a quick midweek supper for two or three when served with a crisp green salad.

1 Assemble *mise en place* trays for this recipe (see page 6).

2 To make the dressing, whisk the vinegar and honey together in a glass or ceramic bowl. Slowly add the olive oil, whisking until thick and emulsified. Set aside.

3 Preheat the oven to 350 degrees F.

4 To make the potato cakes, in a large saucepan, cover the potatoes by several inches with salted, cold water and bring to a boil over high heat. Boil for 20 minutes, or until tender when pierced with a fork. Drain well. Put the potatoes in a medium-sized bowl and add the butter and 2 tablespoons of the olive oil. Mash with a fork or potato masher until smooth. Stir in cilantro, salt and pepper to taste, and mix well. Divide the mixture into 12 equal portions and form each into a patty about 3 inches in diameter.

5 Heat a nonstick griddle over medium-high heat. Brush the griddle with 1 teaspoon of oil. Place 4 to 6 of the potato patties on the griddle and cook, turning once, for 6 minutes, or until golden brown. Transfer to a wire rack set on a baking sheet and keep warm in the oven. Cook the remaining potato patties in the same way, brushing the griddle with a teaspoon of the oil before cooking the next batch. Keep warm.

6 To prepare the scallops, brush them with the olive oil. Heat a nonstick skillet over medium-high heat. Add the scallops and sauté, turning once, for 3 to 5 minutes, or until firm and opaque. Drain on paper towels.

7 Arrange the frisée on serving plates. Arrange 2 potato cakes so that they overlap slightly in the center of each plate. Place a scallop on top, drizzle with the Sherry-Vinegar Dressing and serve immediately.

❧ Keep olive oil in a spray bottle and use it to spray skillets when sautéing. You will use much less oil than when you pour it directly into or even brush it onto the pan.

❧ If holding the potato cakes for longer than 1 hour, reduce the oven temperature to 300 degrees F. to prevent them from drying out.

Braised Wild Mushrooms with Roasted Garlic Toasts ❧ Gordon Hamersley

SERVES 6

PREPARATION TIME: ABOUT 15 MINUTES

COOKING TIME: ABOUT 18 MINUTES

FAT PER SERVING: 3.5 GRAMS

SATURATED FAT: 0.9 GRAM

CALORIES PER SERVING: 147

CALORIES FROM FAT: 20%

---

1 pound fresh wild mushrooms in any combination (shiitakes, chanterelles, cremini, pleurottes, porcinis, morels, and/or oysters)

2½ teaspoons olive oil

3 shallots, minced

2 cloves garlic, minced

Pinch of dried thyme or marjoram

¼ cup dry white wine

Coarse salt and freshly ground black pepper to taste

So simple, light, and easy to prepare, yet this quick braise is full of robust flavor. Having roasted garlic on hand turns this into a meal in a minute! Double the recipe for a terrific brunch or late-night supper dish.

---

1 Assemble *mise en place* trays for this recipe (see page 6). Preheat the oven to 350 degrees F.

2 Using a damp cloth, wipe the mushrooms clean. Trim off any tough stems and cut the larger mushrooms in half. In a large sauté pan, heat 1½ teaspoons of the oil over medium-high heat. Add the mushrooms and sauté for about 3 minutes, or until the mushrooms begin to exude their juices. Stir in the shallots, garlic, and herbs. Add the wine and coarse salt and pepper to taste and bring to a simmer. Lower the heat and simmer gently for about 5 minutes, or until the mushrooms are tender and the juices have thickened slightly. Stir in the butter, if desired, until smooth and melted.

1 teaspoon unsalted butter (optional)

Six ¼-inch-thick slices French bread

¼ cup plus 2 tablespoons Roasted Garlic pulp (see page 20)

6 sprigs watercress, for garnish

3 Brush the bread on one side with the remaining 1 teaspoon oil and sprinkle with coarse salt and pepper to taste. Lay on a baking sheet and bake for about 5 minutes, or until lightly toasted. Spread 1 tablespoon garlic pulp on each slice and bake for about 3 more minutes, until the croutons are browned.

4 Place 1 hot crouton on each of 6 warm plates or in each of 6 shallow soup bowls. Top with the mushroom ragout and garnish with the watercress.

Asparagus Salad with Littleneck Clams and Thyme ～ Gordon Hamersley

SERVES 6

PREPARATION TIME: ABOUT 30 MINUTES

COOKING TIME: ABOUT 15 MINUTES

FAT PER SERVING: 5.5 GRAMS

SATURATED FAT: 0.7 GRAM

CALORIES PER SERVING: 159

CALORIES FROM FAT: 35%

2 tablespoons plus 2 teaspoons olive oil, or more if desired

2 shallots, minced

2 cloves garlic, sliced

18 littleneck clams, scrubbed

1 cup dry white wine

½ teaspoon chopped fresh thyme

Pinch of fennel seeds

Pinch of red pepper flakes

Juice of 1 lemon

1 teaspoon Dijon mustard

Coarse salt and freshly ground black pepper to taste

Elegant, but so light and easy to prepare, this salad makes an excellent dinner party first course, or double the recipe for a beautiful luncheon main course. The percentage of fat looks high here, but note that there are only 159 calories and 5.5 grams of fat per serving.

1 Assemble *mise en place* trays for this recipe (see page 6).

2 Set a sauté pan large enough to hold the clams in a single layer over medium heat and heat 1 teaspoon of the oil. When hot but not smoking, add the shallots and garlic and sauté for 1 minute. Stir in the clams, wine, thyme, fennel seeds, and red pepper flakes. Cover and cook for about 5 minutes, or just until the clams start to open. Using a slotted spoon, remove the clams to a bowl, cover, and refrigerate; discard any that have not opened. Simmer the liquid for about 5 minutes longer, or until reduced by half. Allow to cool to room temperature.

3 Whisk the lemon juice and mustard into the cooled liquid. Add 2 tablespoons olive oil in a slow, steady stream, whisking constantly until well emulsified. Add

24 spears asparagus, trimmed and blanched

6 sprigs watercress, for garnish

Six ½-inch-thick slices French bread, toasted

additional oil if desired to make a thick vinaigrette. Season to taste with coarse salt and pepper. Set aside.

4 Divide the remaining 1 teaspoon oil between 2 sauté pans and heat over medium heat. Add the clams to one pan and the asparagus to the other. Using tongs, gently rotate the clams and asparagus just until heated through.

5 Place a piece of toast on each warm plate. Crisscross 4 asparagus spears on top of each and top with the clams. Drizzle the dressing over the clams, garnish each plate with a sprig of watercress, and serve immediately.

NOTE: Any shellfish could replace the clams in this recipe. If you prefer, remove the clams from their shells before reheating them.

Caramelized Onion Pizza ❧ **Patricia Jamieson**

SERVES 6

PREPARATION TIME: ABOUT 1 HOUR

COOKING TIME: ABOUT 1 HOUR AND 5 MINUTES

FAT PER SERVING: 12 GRAMS

SATURATED FAT: 2.9 GRAMS

CALORIES PER PIZZA: 295

CALORIES FROM FAT: 23%

1½ teaspoons olive oil

4 cups sliced onions (about 4 medium-sized onions)

Coarse salt and freshly ground black pepper to taste

1 tablespoon balsamic vinegar

1 recipe Quick-Rising Pizza Dough (recipe follows)

¾ cup (about ¼ pound) Kalamata or Gaeta olives, pitted and chopped

The rosemary and olives in the dough give these pizzas an earthy flavor, while the onions add rich sweetness. Cut into wedges, these make great appetizers. Left whole, they are an excellent lunch or late-night snack. The dough recipe makes enough for eight pizzas, which means you can freeze some for another time.

---

1 Assemble *mise en place* trays for this recipe (see page 6).

2 In a large nonstick sauté pan, heat the oil over medium-low heat. Add the onions, season to taste with coarse salt and pepper, and cook, stirring frequently, for about 20 minutes, or until lightly browned and soft. Stir in the vinegar. Taste and adjust the seasoning with salt and pepper. Set aside to cool.

3 Place a pizza stone, baking tiles, or an inverted heavy-duty baking sheet on the lowest rack of the oven. Preheat the oven to 500 degrees F (or the highest setting).

1 tablespoon chopped fresh rosemary or 1 teaspoon crumbled dried

About 1 cup yellow or white cornmeal

¾ cup grated part-skim-milk mozzarella cheese (about 3 ounces)

■ Special Equipment: Pizza stone or baking tiles; pizza peel

4 Place the dough on a lightly floured surface and knead in the olives and rosemary. When evenly incorporated, divide the dough into 8 equal pieces. Wrap 2 pieces in wax paper and then in plastic wrap and freeze for a later use.

5 Using your fists, stretch 2 pieces of the dough into 6-inch circles. As you work, keep the remaining dough covered with a kitchen towel or plastic wrap. Put the rounds side by side on a cornmeal-dusted pizza peel or inverted baking sheet, using enough cornmeal so that the dough will slide easily off the peel. Working with 2 pieces of dough at a time, continue to make circles as described above. (Alternatively, use a rolling pin to roll out, on a lightly floured surface, into 6-inch circles.)

6 Sprinkle 2 tablespoons of mozzarella over each dough circle and arrange about ¼ cup of the onions on top of each. Carefully slide the pizzas onto the hot stone in the oven and bake for about 14 minutes, or until the bottoms are crisp and well browned. Serve hot or at room temperature.

NOTE: If you have more than one oven, you can bake 4 pizzas at the same time. Do not bake more than 2 at a time in each oven, as the pizzas must bake on the hot tiles.

QUICK-RISING PIZZA DOUGH

MAKES ENOUGH FOR EIGHT 6-INCH PIZZAS

1¾ cups water

2 teaspoons olive oil

4 to 4½ cups all-purpose flour

Two ¼-ounce packages rapid-rise yeast

1 In a small saucepan, heat the water and oil over low heat until the mixture reaches a temperature of 125 degrees F on a candy thermometer. Remove from the heat.

2 In a large bowl, stir together 3 cups flour, the yeast, salt, and sugar. Using a wooden spoon, gradually stir in the water mixture until well mixed. Slowly add enough of the remaining flour to make a firm, soft dough. Turn

2 teaspoons salt

1 teaspoon granulated sugar

- Special Equipment: Candy thermometer

out onto a lightly floured surface and knead for 8 to 10 minutes, until smooth and elastic. Cover with plastic wrap and let rest for 10 minutes, then roll out as directed in the recipe.

NOTE: Alternatively, in a large-capacity food processor fitted with the metal blade, combine 4 cups flour, the yeast, salt, and sugar. With the motor running, gradually pour 1½ cups warm water (125 degrees F) and 2 teaspoons olive oil through the feed tube. Process, adding up to 2 tablespoons cold water if necessary, until the dough forms a ball, then process for 1 minute to knead. Turn out onto a lightly floured surface, cover with plastic wrap, and let rest for 10 minutes.

_____

➤ Rapid-rise is a strain of yeast that does not need to be dissolved separately in liquid. It requires only a 10-minute resting time instead of the traditional 1- to 2-hour rise. Look for Fleishmann's Rapid-Rise Yeast in the supermarket.

➤ The dough can be made ahead, enclosed in a large plastic bag, and stored in the refrigerator overnight. Bring to room temperature before using.

Ahi Tuna Tartare with Fennel, Caraway Toast, and Green Olive Tapenade ➤ Matthew Kenney

SERVES 6

PREPARATION TIME: ABOUT 1 HOUR

TOASTING TIME: ABOUT 2 MINUTES

_____

¾ pound very fresh sushi-grade tuna, cut into ⅛-inch dice

1 tablespoon plus 1½ teaspoons grated lemon zest

For this dish to be perfection, you must use sushi-grade tuna. If it is unavailable, substitute very fresh salmon. For a different take on this aromatic recipe, you could also marinate tuna fillets for about an hour in the tartare ingredients and then grill them.

_____

1 Assemble *mise en place* trays for this recipe (see page 6).

1 tablespoon plus 1½ teaspoons olive oil

1½ teaspoons light soy sauce

¼ cup plus 1 tablespoon minced fresh chives, flat-leaf parsley, or cilantro

Tabasco sauce to taste

Salt and freshly ground black pepper to taste

Fennel Salad (see page 124)

Green Olive Tapenade (see page 272)

Caraway Toast (recipe follows)

¼ cup sliced pitted Picholine olives

2 tablespoons minced fresh fennel fronds (fennel tops)

Cracked black pepper to taste

2 In a medium-sized bowl, combine the tuna, lemon zest, oil, soy sauce, and chives. Toss gently. Add the Tabasco and salt and pepper to taste.

3 Place equal portions of the salad on 6 plates and spoon the tuna mixture on top. Spoon some tapenade around the edge and put a small amount on top of each portion of tuna. Arrange 4 toast quarters next to each salad and garnish the plates with the sliced olives and fennel fronds. Sprinkle with cracked pepper and serve.

❧ To prevent sticking when cutting tuna (or other fish), rub the knife with a lightly oiled paper towel.

CARAWAY TOASTS

MAKES 6 SLICES

2 tablespoons unsalted butter, at room temperature

1½ teaspoons freshly ground toasted caraway seeds

Pinch of salt

Six ¼-inch-thick slices slightly stale brioche, challah, or other egg-rich bread

1 Preheat the broiler.

2 Combine the butter, caraway, and salt. Spread on 1 side of each slice of brioche.

3 Toast under the broiler, butter side up, until lightly browned. Turn and toast the other side until lightly browned. Cut into quarters and serve warm.

NOTE: The bread can also be toasted on a charcoal or gas grill.

Clams "Al Forno" ~ Johanne Killeen and George Germon

SERVES 6

PREPARATION TIME: ABOUT 15 MINUTES

COOKING TIME: ABOUT 25 MINUTES

42 littleneck clams

1½ cups cored, peeled, seeded, and chopped ripe plum tomatoes

2 onions, halved and thinly sliced

2 tablespoons minced garlic

1 tablespoon minced jalapeño, or to taste

½ teaspoon red pepper flakes

¾ cup dry white Italian wine, such as Pinot Grigio

½ cup water

8 tablespoons unsalted butter, cut into pieces

3 scallions, trimmed and cut into 1-inch julienne

6 lemon wedges

This aromatic appetizer could easily be served as a main course in larger portions, with crusty bread and a tossed salad.

1 Preheat the oven to 450 degrees F. Assemble *mise en place* trays for this recipe (see page 6).

2 Wash the clams under cold running water, scrubbing them with a stiff brush. Lay in a single layer in 2 nine-by-twelve-inch shallow baking dishes. Cover with the tomatoes, onions, garlic, jalapeño, pepper flakes, wine, water, and butter.

3 Bake the clams for 6 to 7 minutes. Turn the clams and stir them to move those in the center to the sides of the pans. Bake for 10 to 15 minutes longer, or until the clams open. Discard any unopened clams.

7 Spoon the clams into shallow soup bowls. Using tongs, distribute the tomatoes and onions evenly among the bowls. Pour the broth into the bowls, sprinkle with the scallions, and garnish with the lemon wedges. Serve immediately.

~ Although we call for more clams than you will need, to allow for any that do not open, if none stay closed, serve them all.

~ You can use canned imported Italian plum tomatoes in place of the fresh tomatoes.

Smoked Trout Mousse on Pumpernickel ∾ Michael Lomonaco

SERVES 6

PREPARATION TIME: ABOUT 20 MINUTES

---

1 tomato, cored, peeled, seeded, and diced

6 ounces boned, skinned, smoked trout fillets

3 tablespoons heavy cream

6 tablespoons unsalted butter, softened

6 slices pumpernickel bread

24 small, fresh dill sprigs

You can use any fine smoked fish for this mousse. Since it multiplies easily, you could also serve it in an attractive bowl, with crackers, pita crisps, or toast points for an easy hors d'oeuvre for a large party.

---

1 Assemble *mise en place* trays for this recipe (see page 6).

2 Put the tomato in a strainer set over a plate to catch the juices. Set aside.

3 In a blender or a food processor fitted with the metal blade, combine the fish fillets and cream and process to a thick paste. Add the butter and pulse to combine. Scrape the mixture into a small bowl. Cover and refrigerate for 15 minutes.

4 Trim the crusts from the bread, and cut each slice into 4 triangles. Spoon the trout mousse into a pastry bag fitted with a star tip. Pipe an equal portion of mousse onto each bread triangle. Garnish each one with a sprig of dill and a few cubes of drained tomato.

Provençal Vegetable Tart with Seared Tuna ❧ Wayne Nish

SERVES 6

PREPARATION TIME: ABOUT 1 HOUR AND 30 MINUTES

COOKING TIME: ABOUT 30 MINUTES

CHILLING TIME (PASTRY ONLY): 1 HOUR AND 30 MINUTES

TART PASTRY:

¾ cup unsalted butter

½ cup solid vegetable shortening

1½ cups sifted all-purpose flour

½ teaspoon kosher salt

½ cup ice water

TOPPING:

3 baby artichokes, trimmed, or artichoke hearts (not marinated)

1 large ripe tomato, cored, peeled, seeded, and cut into strips 1 to 1½ inches long

2 teaspoons chopped fresh thyme

Salt and freshly ground black pepper to taste

1 clove garlic, sliced

½ lemon, quartered

1 cup plus 3 tablespoons extra-virgin olive oil

1 large zucchini, trimmed, cored, and cut into 2-inch long bâtonnets

½ cup fresh peas or fava beans

½ cup tomato juice

The simple tastes of Provence combine in an unusual fashion to make this a very contemporary dish. Since all of the components can be prepared in advance, it is an especially appealing appetizer for the busy cook.

---

1 Assemble *mise en place* trays for this recipe (see page 6).

2 To make the tart pastry, cut the butter and shortening into tablespoon-sized pieces. Wrap the butter and shortening separately in plastic wrap and freeze for 30 minutes.

3 Combine the flour and salt in the bowl of a food processor fitted with the metal blade. Add the chilled butter and pulse until the mixture is the consistency of coarse meal. Add the shortening and pulse for 3 to 4 seconds longer.

4 With the motor running, slowly add the ice water and process until the dough comes together in a smooth, sticky ball. Wrap in plastic wrap and refrigerate for 1 hour.

5 Roll out the dough between 2 sheets of plastic wrap to a rectangle about ¼ inch thick. Place on a baking sheet and freeze for about 30 minutes.

6 Preheat the oven to 350 degrees F.

7 Using a 3-inch round cookie cutter, cut the dough into 6 circles. Place on an ungreased baking sheet. Cover the circles with parchment paper, waxed paper, or foil, and set another baking sheet on top of pastry circles. Bake for 7 minutes. Remove the top baking sheet and the paper and bake for 3 or 4 minutes longer. Turn the pastries over and bake for another 3 to 4 minutes or until the pastry is golden. Remove to a wire rack to cool. Reduce the oven temperature to 300 degrees F.

12 ounces sashimi-quality tuna, about 1 inch thick, cut into slices, 2-inches by 2-inches

SALAD:

2 cups mesclun or other baby salad greens, rinsed and dried

1 tablespoon chopped fresh basil leaves

1 tablespoon chopped fresh tarragon leaves

1 tablespoon chopped fresh parsley leaves

1 tablespoon chopped fresh chives

1 tablespoon chopped fresh chervil sprigs

■ Special Equipment: 3-inch round cookie cutter

8 To prepare the topping, cook the artichokes in boiling salted water for 10 minutes, or until tender. Drain well and let cool.

9 In a small bowl, combine the tomato strips, 1 teaspoon of the thyme, and salt and pepper to taste. Set aside.

10 Cut the artichokes in half lengthwise. Place in a small, ovenproof dish and add the garlic, the remaining 1 teaspoon thyme, the lemon quarters, and salt and pepper to taste. Cover tightly with aluminum foil and bake for 10 minutes. Uncover and let cool.

11 Meanwhile, in small sauté pan, heat 1 teaspoon of the olive oil over medium heat. Add the zucchini, season to taste with salt and pepper, and sauté for 2 minutes, or until just beginning to color. Remove from the heat and set aside.

12 Blanch the peas or fava beans in boiling salted water for 30 seconds. Drain and refresh under cold running water. Set aside. (If using fava beans, peel them after blanching.)

13 Place the tomato juice in a blender with the motor running, and add 1 cup of olive oil in a slow, steady stream until fully emulsified. Season to taste with salt and pepper. Set aside.

14 In a large, heavy sauté pan, heat 1 tablespoon of the oil over medium heat. Sear the tuna for 15 to 20 seconds on all sides; it should be rare in the middle. Transfer to a cutting board and allow to cool.

15 Cut the tuna into long, thin slices about ¼ to ⅛ inch thick. Season the slices lightly with the remaining 1 tablespoon plus 2 teaspoons olive oil and salt.

16 To make the salad, toss the salad greens with the fresh herbs.

17 Place a pastry disk in the center of each appetizer plate. Arrange the tomato, artichokes, peas or beans, and zucchini on the disks and top each one with a small mound of the herb salad. Drape the sliced tuna over the salad, and drizzle with the tomato and oil dressing. Serve at once.

――――――――――

❧ Freshness is always important when purchasing fish. Sashimi-quality tuna refers to the freshest, highest-quality tuna available, because it is the tuna used for Japanese sashimi, fish served raw. For this recipe, buy the very best tuna you can find.

Potato Crêpes with Dried Tomatoes, Goat Cheese, and Basil ❧ Debra Ponzek

SERVES 6
PREPARATION TIME: ABOUT 35 MINUTES
COOKING TIME: ABOUT 30 MINUTES
DRYING TIME (TOMATOES ONLY): 8 TO 24 HOURS

――――――――――

DRIED TOMATOES:

6 very ripe but firm plum tomatoes, cut into ⅛-inch thick slices

¼ cup olive oil

2 tablespoons chopped fresh parsley

2 tablespoons chopped fresh thyme

2 tablespoons chopped fresh savory

POTATO CRÊPES:

3 large baking potatoes

2 tablespoons clarified butter (see page 20)

This simple first course should only be made with very ripe tomatoes so that their flavor, when dried, is sweet, intense and a perfect balance for the potatoes and goat cheese. You can, if you choose, place the crêpes on top of a mesclun salad.

――――――――――

1 Assemble the *mise en place* trays for the dried tomatoes (see page 6). Line a baking sheet with parchment paper.

2 To prepare the tomatoes, place the slices on the prepared baking sheet. Sprinkle with a few drops of olive oil and the chopped herbs. Allow to dry at room temperature, uncovered, for at least 8 hours or up to 24 hours.

3 Assemble the *mise en place* trays for the rest of this recipe (see page 6).

4 To prepare the potato crêpes, peel the potatoes and cut, crosswise, into ¹⁄₁₆-inch thick slices or as thin as possible. Brush a nonstick skillet with about 1 teaspoon of the clarified butter, and place over medium heat. When

About 3 ounces fresh soft goat cheese, cut into 1/8-inch thick slices

Salt and freshly ground black pepper to taste

2 tablespoons chiffonade of fresh basil leaves

the skillet is hot, lay 8 potato slices, slightly overlapping, to form a circle in the center of the skillet. Cook for 2 to 3 minutes, until golden brown on the bottom. Turn carefully with a wide spatula and cook for 2 to 3 minutes longer. Transfer to paper towels to drain. Cover with aluminum foil and keep warm. Continue making potato crêpes until you have 6.

5 Preheat the broiler.

6 Place a slice of goat cheese in the center of each crêpe. Cover the cheese with the dried tomatoes. Season with salt and pepper.

7 Place the crêpes on an ungreased baking sheet and broil for about 1 minute. Place on 6 warm serving plates, sprinkle with the basil chiffonade and drizzle with the remaining olive oil. Serve immediately.

❧ Peel and slice the potatoes just before making the crêpes, or they will discolor. Do not place the potatoes in water, or they will be too wet to crisp quickly.

❧ A mandoline or other vegetable slicer is the best tool for slicing the tomatoes and potatoes.

❧ If the weather is very humid, dry the tomatoes in a 200 degree F. oven for about 2½ hours.

Tuna Tartare and Herb Salad ~ Alfred Portale

SERVES 6

PREPARATION TIME: ABOUT 40 MINUTES

Ginger Vinaigrette (see page 275)

TUNA:

1 Japanese or hot-house cucumber, washed and dried

1½ pounds sashimi-grade yellowfin tuna

2 scallions, trimmed and minced

Salt and freshly ground black pepper to taste

CROUTONS:

1 long, thin baguette

3 tablespoons extra-virgin olive oil

HERB SALAD:

2 cups mesclun salad, washed and dried

¼ cup flat-leaf parsley leaves

¼ cup inch-long chive stalks

2 tablespoons fresh mint leaves

2 tablespoons fresh cilantro leaves

2 tablespoons fresh chervil leaves

The tuna must be absolutely pristine for this refreshing first course. Complex in presentation, it surprises by being quite easy to put together. However, it requires last-minute preparation and assembly.

---

1 Preheat the oven to 375 degrees F. Assemble *mise en place* trays for this recipe (see page 6).

2 Prepare the Ginger Vinaigrette.

3 Using the tines of a fork, make long, deep cuts down the length of the cucumber. Slice crosswise into very thin slices. Cover and refrigerate.

4 To prepare the tartare, cut the tuna into ¼-inch dice. Place in a glass or ceramic bowl and add ¾ cup of the Ginger Vinaigrette and the minced scallions and toss to mix. Season to taste with salt and pepper and set aside at room temperature.

5 To make the croutons, slice the baguette diagonally into ¼-inch slices so that you have at least 18 slices. (Cut a few extra slices in case guests want more croutons.) Lay the bread slices on a baking sheet and bake for 5 minutes or until golden, turning once. Drizzle with the olive oil and set aside.

6 To make the salad, toss the salad and herbs in a bowl. Add the remaining Ginger Vinaigrette and toss to coat.

7 Place a 3-inch round ring mold or pastry cutter in the center of a chilled serving plate. Make a circle of overlapping cucumber slices around the outside circumference of the mold. Lightly pack one portion of the tuna mixture into the mold and lift off the mold. Stand 3 or 4 croutons around the tuna, leaning them slightly outward. Arrange about ½ cup of the herb salad on top of the tuna, in between the croutons. Working quickly,

assemble the remaining plates. Serve immediately with extra croutons on the side.

_____

❧ You can marinate the tuna in the vinaigrette for as long as 45 minutes ahead of time, but any longer will render the fish soft. Cover and refrigerate the fish during marinating, if making ahead.

❧ To replicate Chef Portale's presentation of this recipe exactly, put hoisin sauce in a squeeze bottle and dot each cucumber slice with a little sauce for extra garnish.

Fresh Tuna with Maui Onions and Avocado ❧ Wolfgang Puck

SERVES 6

PREPARATION TIME: ABOUT 25 MINUTES

_____

VINAIGRETTE:

Juice of 3 limes

¼ cup plus 1 tablespoon soy sauce

⅓ cup extra-virgin olive oil

1½ teaspoons minced fresh ginger

Freshly ground black pepper to taste

TUNA:

¾ pound sashimi-grade yellowfin tuna, about 1 inch thick

3 cups radish sprouts, rinsed and dried

2 ripe avocados

1 cup diced Maui or other sweet onion

1 tablespoon golden caviar

Simple yet sublime. Increase the portion sizes and you have a perfect summer's luncheon.

_____

1 Assemble *mise en place* trays for this recipe (see page 6).

2 To make the vinaigrette, whisk together the lime juice, soy sauce, olive oil, and ginger in a glass or ceramic bowl. Season to taste with pepper. Set aside.

3 To prepare the tuna, slice the fish into ¼-inch thick slices. Cut each slice into 3-inch triangles.

4 Place equal portions of the sprouts on one side of 6 chilled plates.

5 Peel, halve, and pit the avocados. Cut lengthwise into very thin slices. Fan an equal number of avocado slices around the other side of the plates from the sprouts. Arrange the tuna slices in the center of the plates. Sprinkle the onions on top of the tuna and place ½ teaspoon of caviar on top of the onions on each plate. Whisk the

vinaigrette, and spoon over the tuna and avocado. Serve immediately.

─────────────

↝ Use ripe California avocados (black-skinned Haas) that give when held in the palm of the hand and pressed gently with your fingers. Underripe avocados will ripen at room temperature in a few days.

↝ Maui onions are sweet onions similar to Vidalia and Walla Walla. Any sweet onion works well in this recipe.

↝ Radish sprouts are easy to find, but you can substitute any sprout, or to maintain the peppery flavor use arugula or watercress greens.

Parmesan Ice Cream ↝ Marta Pulini

SERVES 6

PREPARATION TIME: ABOUT 15 MINUTES

COOKING TIME: ABOUT 40 MINUTES

CHILLING TIME (CHEESE AND CREAM ONLY): AT LEAST 12 HOURS

─────────────

3½ cups freshly grated Parmigiano-Reggiano cheese

2 cups plus 2 tablespoons heavy cream

⅛ teaspoon freshly ground white pepper

1 loaf Italian bread

3 firm pears, such as Bosc or Anjou

6 very small bunches of grapes, washed and dried

1 tablespoon balsamic vinegar, or to taste

This gelato is heavenly. The taste is so smooth and rich that nobody can guess exactly how it is made. And certainly your guests will never suspect how easy it has been to "wow" them! This is wonderful, too, as a cheese course or as an hors d'oeuvre at a cocktail party.

─────────────

1 In the top of a double boiler set over boiling water, combine the grated cheese, cream, and pepper. Cook, stirring continuously, for 5 minutes, or until the cheese is completely melted and the mixture is smooth. Remove from the heat and pour through a fine strainer into a shallow pan. Cool slightly and then cover and refrigerate for at least 12 hours.

2 Preheat the oven to 300 degrees F. Assemble the *mise en place* trays for the remaining ingredients (see page 6).

3 Slice the bread on the diagonal into at least 18 pieces about ¼ inch thick. Place on a baking sheet on the bottom rack of the oven and bake, turning several times, for

25 to 35 minutes, or until dry and golden brown. Set aside.

4 To serve, peel the pears. Cut in half lengthwise and remove the core. Slice each pear half lengthwise into thin slices, and fan out one pear half on each chilled serving plate. Scoop a heaping spoonful of gelato at the base of the pear fan. Add a bunch of grapes and 3 slices of bread. Drizzle a few drops of balsamic vinegar over the gelato and serve immediately. Pass any remaining bread.

Spinach Tart ❧ Marta Pulini

SERVES 6

PREPARATION TIME: ABOUT 1 HOUR AND 20 MINUTES

COOKING TIME: ABOUT 45 MINUTES

CHILLING TIME (DOUGH ONLY): ABOUT 30 MINUTES

COOLING TIME (FILLING ONLY): ABOUT 15 MINUTES

DOUGH:

2¾ cup plus 2 tablespoons unbleached, all-purpose flour

½ teaspoon salt, or to taste

1 cup (16 tablespoons) unsalted butter, cut into small pieces, chilled

4 to 6 tablespoons ice water

FILLING:

3 pounds fresh spinach, washed and tough stems removed

¼ pound pancetta, diced

1 clove garlic, minced

This tart can be served warm or at room temperature, and as either an appetizer or a main course. What more could any home cook ask?

1 Assemble *mise en place* trays for this recipe (see page 6).

2 To make the dough, mound the flour and salt on a work surface and make a well in the center. Add the butter and, using your fingertips, rub into the flour until the mixture resembles small peas. Stir in the ice water a little at a time, until the dough just holds together. Form into a ball, wrap in plastic wrap and refrigerate for at least 30 minutes.

3 Preheat the oven to 350 degrees F. Generously butter a 12-inch fluted tart pan with a removable bottom.

4 To make the filling, blanch the spinach in a large pot of boiling water for 10 seconds. (Depending on the size of the pot, you may have to do this in two batches.) Drain well and refresh under cold running water. Drain again and let cool slightly. Squeeze out all the excess water from the spinach and chop it. Place it in a colan-

About 2 tablespoons olive oil, if necessary

1 bunch scallions, trimmed and sliced

1 bunch fresh flat-leaf parsley, stems discarded and leaves chopped

2 cups freshly grated Parmigiano-Reggiano cheese

Freshly ground black pepper to taste

2 large eggs

4 cups fresh bread crumbs

1 large egg yolk beaten with 1 tablespoon milk, for egg wash

■ Special Equipment: 12-inch fluted tart pan with removable bottom

der placed over a plate so that it can continue to drain, and set aside.

5 In a large sauté pan, cook the pancetta over medium heat for 4 to 5 minutes, to render the fat. Add the garlic and cook for 2 to 3 minutes, or just until the garlic starts to brown. Add 1 to 2 tablespoons of olive oil if the pan seems dry. Stir in the spinach and scallions and cook for 3 to 5 minutes, until the spinach has wilted. Transfer to a large bowl and stir in the parsley and cheese. Season to taste with pepper. Allow to cool for about 15 minutes.

6 Add the eggs and bread crumbs to the spinach mixture and stir to combine.

7 Divide the dough into 2 pieces, one slightly larger than the other. On a well-floured surface, roll out the larger piece to a 14-inch circle. Carefully fit into the prepared tart pan. Spoon the spinach filling into the tart shell, spreading it evenly and smoothing the top.

8 Roll out the remaining dough to a thin, 12-inch circle. Lay the circle on top of the filling and pull the overhanging dough up over it. Press the edges of dough together and pinch them to make a raised edge, using your thumb and index finger to flute the edge. Prick the top with a fork. Using a pastry brush, coat the top of the tart with the egg wash.

9 Bake the tart for 30 minutes, or until the top is golden. Remove from the oven and let rest for 5 minutes. Remove the tart ring, cut into wedges, and serve.

◆ If time is an issue, substitute 1¾ pounds (3 ten-ounce boxes) frozen chopped spinach. Thaw it and squeeze as much moisture as possible from it before proceeding with the recipe. (This eliminates at least 30 minutes of preparation time, as cleaning and stemming fresh spinach is tedious work.)

◆ The tart dough is fragile. Take care when working with it, but if it rips, simply smooth it together again. The dense filling does not require a flawless crust.

Red Snapper with Mexican Oregano Pesto Sauce and Jicama-Melon Relish ~ Stephan Pyles

SERVES 6

PREPARATION TIME: ABOUT 45 MINUTES

COOKING TIME: ABOUT 30 MINUTES

Jícama-Melon Relish (see page 269)

1 tablespoon Mexican Oregano Pesto (see page 271)

SAUCE:

⅔ cup Fish Stock (see page 14)

⅓ cup dry white wine

2 tablespoons white wine vinegar

1 tablespoon minced shallots

1 sprig fresh parsley

½ cup heavy cream

1 cup (2 sticks) unsalted butter, softened

1 teaspoon fresh lime juice

Salt and freshly ground white pepper to taste

SNAPPER:

6 seven-to-eight-ounce red snapper fillets, rinsed and patted dry

Salt and freshly ground black pepper to taste

1 cup all-purpose flour

Vegetable oil for shallow frying

Mexican oregano (found in Hispanic markets), with a somewhat sharper flavor than the traditional Mediterranean oregano, perfectly complements the mild fish.

1 Assemble mise en place trays for this recipe (see page 6).

2 Make the Jícama-Melon Relish and Mexican Oregano Pesto.

3 To make the sauce, in a medium-sized saucepan, combine the stock, wine, vinegar, shallots, and parsley. Bring to a boil over medium heat and cook for about 10 minutes or until the liquid is reduced to 2 tablespoons. Add the cream and boil for 4 to 5 minutes longer, until reduced by one third.

4 Remove the pan from the heat and whisk in 2 tablespoons of the butter. Return the pan to very low heat and whisk in the remaining butter, a tablespoon at a time. Do not add the next tablespoon of butter until the one before it is incorporated. If drops of melted butter appear on the surface, remove the pan from the heat and whisk to reincorporate the butter. Then return to the heat and continue adding the butter.

5 Strain the sauce through a fine sieve into the top half of a double boiler. Whisk in the pesto and lime juice. Season to taste with salt and white pepper. Set over gently simmering water and keep warm until ready to serve. (You should have about 1½ cups of sauce.)

6 To prepare the fish, season the fillets with salt and pepper to taste. Place the flour in a shallow bowl and lay the fillets in it, one at a time, turning to coat on both sides. Shake off the excess flour.

7 Heat about ½ inch of vegetable oil in a large skillet over medium heat. When the oil is hot, add the fish

fillets and cook, turning once, for about 5 minutes, or until golden. Do not crowd the pan; fry the fish in batches if necessary.

8 Drain the fish fillets on paper towels. Place on plates, spoon a little of the sauce around the fish and garnish with Jícama-Melon Relish. Serve immediately.

Shrimp Ceviche ❧ Douglas Rodriguez

SERVES 6

PREPARATION TIME: ABOUT 30 MINUTES

COOKING TIME: ABOUT 2 MINUTES

CHILLING TIME: AT LEAST 1 HOUR

FAT PER SERVING: 1.4 GRAMS

SATURATED FAT: 0.2 GRAM

CALORIES PER SERVING: 113

CALORIES FROM FAT: 11%

1½ pounds medium shrimp, peeled and deveined

2 red bell peppers, roasted, peeled, cored, and seeded (see page 12)

2 jalapeño chiles, roasted, peeled, cored, and seeded (see page 12)

1 large tomato, roasted, peeled, cored, and seeded (see page 11)

1 small onion, roasted and chopped (see page 11)

¾ cup fresh lime juice (5 to 6 limes)

½ cup fresh orange juice

¼ cup tomato juice

1 scant tablespoon granulated sugar

Tabasco sauce to taste

Salt to taste

1 small red onion, sliced

This recipe is Doug Rodriguez at his best. He is well known for light, refreshing, perfectly flavored ceviches finished with absolutely wild garnishes. This one will not disappoint.

---

1 Assemble *mise en place* trays for this recipe (see page 6).

2 Bring a large saucepan of water to a boil. Add the shrimp and cook for 2 minutes, or just until pink and opaque throughout. Drain and place in an ice water bath to stop the cooking. Drain, pat dry, and put in a nonreactive container.

3 In a blender, combine the roasted vegetables, the lime, orange and tomato juices, the sugar, and Tabasco and salt to taste. Process until smooth and pour over the shrimp. Cover and refrigerate for at least 1 hour, or until chilled.

4 When ready to serve, toss the shrimp mixture with the sliced onion, chopped tomato, scallions, chives, and cilantro. Mound on chilled plates, sprinkle with the popcorn and corn nuts, and serve immediately.

1 large tomato, peeled, cored, seeded, and finely diced

2 tablespoons chopped scallions, white part only

2 tablespoons chopped fresh chives

About 15 fresh cilantro leaves

1 cup unsalted popcorn

½ cup corn nuts

Roasted Eggplant Roulade with Oregano and Marinated Goat Cheese ✒ Alain Sailhac

SERVES 6

PREPARATION TIME: ABOUT 45 MINUTES

COOKING TIME: ABOUT 15 MINUTES

MARINATING TIME: ABOUT 1 HOUR

CHILLING TIME: AT LEAST 8 HOURS

---

1 ten-ounce goat cheese log, sliced into 5 equal portions

1 tablespoon plus ½ teaspoon minced garlic

3 tablespoons chopped fresh oregano

½ cup plus 1 teaspoon olive oil

Freshly ground black pepper to taste

1 large eggplant (about 1½ pounds), trimmed and cut lengthwise into ⅛-inch-thick slices

Salt to taste

1 pound fresh spinach leaves, washed and dried

1 roasted red bell pepper, peeled (see page 12), seeded, and diced

This recipe has lots of components, but each one is easy to prepare. Without the radicchio and tomato garnish, it would also make a terrific, simple hors d'oeuvre.

---

1 Assemble *mise en place* trays for this recipe (see page 6).

2 In a bowl, combine 2 tablespoons of the olive oil, 1 teaspoon of the garlic, and the oregano. Season to taste with pepper. Add the goat cheese and let marinate for 1 hour at room temperature.

3 Preheat the oven to 450 degrees F.

4 Lay the eggplant slices in a large colander so that they overlap slightly. Sprinkle them with a little salt. Set aside for 10 minutes. Rinse and immediately pat dry.

5 Brush a baking sheet with 1 tablespoon of the olive oil. Lay the eggplant slices on the baking sheet. Brush with 2 tablespoons of the olive oil. Bake for 5 to 10 minutes, until the eggplant begins to brown. Set aside.

6 In a medium-sized sauté pan, heat 2 tablespoons of the olive oil over medium heat. Add the spinach, 1 teaspoon of the garlic and salt and pepper to taste. Cook,

6 ripe plum tomatoes

3 tablespoons chopped fresh basil

Juice of ½ lemon

12 small radicchio leaves, washed and dried

12 small celery leaves, washed and dried

stirring, for about 5 to 6 minutes, until wilted, tossing the spinach. Remove from the heat.

7 In a medium bowl, combine the diced red pepper, 1 tablespoon of the olive oil, and 1 teaspoon of the garlic. Season to taste with salt and pepper. Stir in the spinach.

8 Drain the goat cheese well. Add to the red pepper mixture and mash to make a smooth, spreadable mixture. Check the seasoning.

9 Line a 12 x 18-inch baking sheet with plastic wrap. Arrange the eggplant slices, overlapping, to cover the plastic, leaving a 1-inch border all around. Spread the spinach and cheese mixture evenly over the eggplant. Lift the plastic wrap along the long side nearest you and gently roll the eggplant into a roulade. Twist plastic wrap at each end to tighten, forming an even jelly-roll shape. Leaving the roulade on the baking sheet, chill for at least 8 hours.

10 Blanch the tomatoes in boiling water for 10 seconds. Drain and refresh in ice water. Peel and seed the tomatoes and cut into small dice.

11 About an hour before serving, in a medium bowl, combine the diced tomatoes, the remaining 1 teaspoon of olive oil, and the remaining ½ teaspoon of garlic. Add the chopped basil, lemon juice, and salt and pepper to taste. Set aside.

12 Remove the roulade from the refrigerator. Do not remove the plastic. Using a sharp knife dipped in hot water for 1 second and then wiped dry, cut 18 half-inch slices from the roulade, dipping the knife in the hot water and drying it between each slice. Arrange 3 slices in a triangle pattern on each of 6 chilled serving plates, removing the plastic.

13 Place 2 radicchio leaves in the center of each triangle. Spoon about 2 tablespoons of the tomato mixture onto the radicchio leaves, and arrange 2 celery leaves on top of the tomatoes. Serve immediately.

Antipasto ❧ **Claudio Scadutto**

SERVES 6

PREPARATION TIME (ALL 3 ANTIPASTI): ABOUT 40 MINUTES

COOKING TIME (ALL 3 ANTIPASTI): ABOUT 40 MINUTES

This selection is only the beginning. Use your imagination and let your creativity fly. An antipasto platter can be filled with any variety of cold meats, vegetables, and condiments.

The following recipes are designed to serve 6 people. If one recipe particularly appeals to you, the ingredients can easily be doubled to increase your antipasto bounty.

BROCCOLI RABE, GARLIC, AND PIGNOLI NUTS

2 pounds broccoli rabe (about 2 bunches)

4 cloves garlic, minced

¼ cup toasted pignoli nuts (pine nuts; see page 13)

¼ cup extra-virgin olive oil

Salt to taste

1 Assemble *mise en place* trays for this recipe (see page 6).

2 Soak the broccoli rabe in cold water to cover for about 15 minutes. Drain well. Trim off any large leaves and the tough stem ends. Using a small sharp knife, cut slashes into the stalks. Using the kitchen twine, tie the broccoli rabe into bunches.

3 In a large deep saucepan of boiling, salted water, cook the broccoli rabe, standing it upright so that the heads are covered by about 1 inch of water for 4 to 5 minutes, until just tender and bright green. Drain well and remove the twine.

4 Arrange the broccoli rabe on a serving platter or in a shallow bowl. Gently toss with the garlic, nuts, olive oil, and salt to taste. Serve at room temperature.

❧ This is also delicious served over pasta for a quick dinner.

Roasted Carrots, Oregano, Rosemary, and Fontina Cheese

8 carrots, peeled and sliced diagonally into ½-inch thick slices

3 tablespoons extra-virgin olive oil

Salt and freshly ground black pepper to taste

2 teaspoons minced fresh oregano

2 teaspoons minced fresh rosemary

½ cup freshly shredded Fontina cheese

1 Preheat the oven to 350 degrees F. Assemble *mise en place* trays for this recipe (see page 6).

2 In a shallow baking dish, combine the carrots with the olive oil and salt and pepper to taste, and toss lightly to coat. Roast for 35 minutes, or until just slightly crisp.

3 Transfer the carrots to a serving platter. Sprinkle with the minced herbs and cheese. Serve at room temperature.

Roasted Fennel, Thyme, and Parmigiano

3 small fennel bulbs, washed, trimmed, cored, and quartered lengthwise

¼ cup extra-virgin olive oil

Salt and freshly ground black pepper to taste

2 teaspoons minced fresh thyme

1 three-ounce piece Parmigiano-Reggiano cheese

1 Preheat the oven to 350 degrees F. Assemble *mise en place* trays for this recipe (see page 6).

2 In a shallow baking dish, combine the fennel with the olive oil and salt and pepper to taste, and toss lightly to coat. Roast for 30 to 35 minutes, or until light golden brown.

3 Transfer the fennel to a serving platter. Sprinkle with the thyme. Using a vegetable peeler or cheese slicer, shave the Parmigiano over the top. Serve at room temperature.

White Pizza with Arugula ❧ Claudio Scadutto

SERVES 6

PREPARATION TIME: ABOUT 30 MINUTES

COOKING TIME (FOR ALL 6 PIZZAS AT 15 MINUTES PER INDIVIDUAL PIZZA): 1 HOUR AND 30 MINUTES

RESTING TIME (DOUGH ONLY): ABOUT 2 HOURS

PIZZA DOUGH:

3 cups water

¼ cup sugar

One ¼-ounce package active dry yeast

¼ cup vegetable oil

1 tablespoon salt

1½ cups plus 3 tablespoons bread flour

1½ cups plus 3 tablespoons semolina flour

TOPPING:

3 cups packed finely shredded arugula

¼ cup finely chopped garlic

¾ to 1 cup extra-virgin olive oil

■ Special Equipment: Pizza stone

These delightfully crisp pizzas bear no resemblance to the soggy, fast-food variety. They are wonderfully fresh-tasting, with no tomato sauce or cheese. These little pizzas are best eaten directly from the oven. Serving them this way turns your party into an informal affair, as you continue to cook pizzas while others are being happily devoured.

1 Assemble *mise en place* trays for this recipe (see page 6).

2 In a large, warm bowl, combine the water, sugar, and yeast. Stir to dissolve. Let rest for 15 minutes.

3 Stir the vegetable oil and salt into the yeast mixture. Add both the flours and mix with a wooden spoon or your hands to combine. Put the dough in a bowl, cover with a kitchen towel, and let stand for 20 minutes in a warm, draft-free place.

4 Turn the dough a few times in the bowl. Let stand 20 minutes longer.

5 Again, turn the dough and let stand 20 minutes.

6 Turn the dough out onto a lightly floured surface and knead dough for about 3 minutes, until smooth and elastic. Divide into 6 pieces and shape into balls. Leaving the balls on the floured surface, cover them with kitchen towels, and let rest for about 1 hour.

7 Put a pizza stone on the center rack of the oven and preheat the oven to 450 degrees F.

8 Flatten each piece of dough into a round, pushing it into a 6-inch circle with your fingertips. Place 1 pizza on the hot pizza stone and bake for about 15 minutes, or until golden. Remove from the oven and sprinkle with ½ cup of the arugula and 2 teaspoons of the garlic. Drizzle with olive oil and serve. Continue baking the remaining pizzas, serving each one as soon as it is assembled.

❧ If you have 2 pizza stones, raise the oven temperature to 500 degrees F. and bake 2 pizzas at a time. If you don't have a pizza stone, you can bake the pizzas on a preheated heavy baking sheet, but the crusts will not be as crispy. Pizza stones are sold in kitchenware shops. You can also use unglazed ceramic tiles, found in kitchenware shops, instead of a pizza stone.

❧ You can make 2 large pizzas with the dough and the same amount of topping and serve them cut into wedges.

Chanterelles with Blue Corn Chips ❧ Jimmy Schmidt

SERVES 6

PREPARATION TIME: ABOUT 10 MINUTES

COOKING TIME: ABOUT 7 MINUTES

½ cup sour cream

¼ cup mild goat cheese, such as a Bucheron

Tabasco to taste

4 tablespoons unsalted butter

2 cups trimmed and cleaned chanterelles

24 fresh blue corn tortilla chips (see page 23) or store-bought, unsalted blue corn chips

¼ cup chopped fresh mint

¼ cup snipped fresh chives

These have got to be the world's most elegant nachos! With these as hors d'oeuvres and a glass of bubbly, you are on your way to a great party.

---

1 Preheat the oven to 400 degrees F. Assemble *mise en place* trays for this recipe (see page 6).

2 In a bowl, beat the sour cream and goat cheese until smooth. Season to taste with Tabasco. Set aside.

3 In a large skillet, melt the butter over high heat. Add the chanterelles and sauté for about 3 minutes, or until golden. Drain on paper towels and keep warm.

4 Spread the corn chips on an ungreased baking sheet. Generously spread the sour cream mixture on each chip. Bake on the lower rack of the oven for about 4 minutes, or until hot.

5 Sprinkle the chips with the mint and chives. Top with the chanterelles and serve immediately.

_____

❧ Always cook chanterelles quickly over high heat, or they will toughen. Substitute any cultivated "wild" mushrooms for the chanterelles if you cannot find them in the market.

Escalope of Salmon with Pepper-Ginger Medley ❧ Jimmy Schmidt

SERVES 6

PREPARATION TIME: ABOUT 25 MINUTES

COOKING TIME: ABOUT 1 HOUR

_____

1½ cups chopped fresh ginger

½ cup fresh lemon juice

2 tablespoons granulated sugar

2 cups water

12 three-ounce salmon fillets, trimmed of dark flesh

⅓ cup Achiote Paste (see page 24)

2 tablespoons olive oil

½ cup finely julienned chayote squash (about ½ chayote)

1½ cups fish stock (see page 17)

1½ cups Chardonnay or other dry white wine

1½ cups heavy cream

1 red bell pepper, seeds and membranes removed, cut into fine julienne

*T*he mildly spicy, marinated salmon resting on a bed of crisp greens, with its slightly acidic sauce, is a zinging rendition of the traditionally sedate fish course.

_____

1 Assemble *mise en place* trays for this recipe (see page 6).

2 In a small saucepan, combine the ginger, lemon juice, sugar, and water. Bring to a boil over high heat. Reduce the heat and simmer, partially covered, for about 30 minutes, until slightly thickened. Transfer the mixture to a blender or food processor fitted with the metal blade. Blend or process until smooth. Strain through a fine sieve into a glass or ceramic bowl and discard the solids. Set aside.

3 Rinse the salmon under cold, running water and pat dry on paper towels.

4 In a small bowl, combine 2 tablespoons of the ginger purée, the Achiote Paste, and the olive oil. Lay the salmon in a shallow container. Generously rub the ginger mixture over the salmon. Cover and refrigerate until ready to grill, but for no longer than 2 hours.

1 yellow bell pepper, seeds and membranes removed, cut into fine julienne

Salt and freshly ground black pepper to taste

Juice of 1 lime

1 poblano chile, roasted (see page 12), peeled, seeded and diced

2 heads frisée (curly endive), trimmed, washed and dried

⅓ cup chopped fresh Italian parsley

5 Blanch the chayote in a small saucepan of boiling water for 30 seconds. Refresh under cold, running water and set aside.

6 Prepare a charcoal or gas grill or preheat the broiler.

7 Meanwhile, in the top half of a double boiler, combine the stock and wine. Set over medium-high heat and bring to a simmer. Simmer for 20 to 25 minutes, or until reduced to ¼ cup. Add the cream and remaining ginger purée and simmer for 10 to 12 minutes more, or until the sauce is thick enough to coat the back of a spoon. Remove from the heat and set the top of the double boiler over very hot water. Cover to keep warm.

8 In a lightly oiled, nonstick skillet, sauté the red pepper over medium-high heat for 2 minutes. Add the yellow pepper and chayote and sauté for 1 minute more, or until hot. Season to taste with salt and pepper. Remove from the heat and set aside.

9 Grill the salmon for 2 minutes. Turn it over and cook for 4 minutes more, or until medium rare. Do not overcook.

10 Meanwhile, test the sauce. If it is not hot, reheat the sauce in the double broiler over medium-high heat. Stir in the lime juice and diced poblano. Taste and adjust seasoning with salt and pepper, if necessary.

11 Arrange equal portions of the frisée and parsley leaves in the center of each plate. Sprinkle with the sautéed vegetables. Position salmon on top of peppers. Spoon the sauce over the salmon and serve immediately.

***

❧ The recipe is delicious made with skinless, boneless chicken breasts.

❧ If you don't have Achiote Paste on hand, you can substitute a mixture of 3 tablespoons mild Hungarian paprika, 3 tablespoons red bell pepper purée, and 1 tablespoon red wine vinegar.

Wild Mushroom Ragout with Roasted Polenta ～ **Sally Schneider**

SERVES 6

PREPARATION TIME: ABOUT 20 MINUTES

COOKING TIME: ABOUT 50 MINUTES

CHILLING TIME: ABOUT 10 MINUTES

FAT PER SERVING: 3 GRAMS

SATURATED FAT: 0.3 GRAM

CALORIES PER SERVING: 225

CALORIES FROM FAT: 14%

¾ ounce dried wild mushrooms (such as porcini or morels)

6 dry-packed sun-dried tomato halves

¾ cup boiling water

1½ pounds fresh wild mushrooms in any combination (shiitakes, chanterelles, cremini, pleurottes, porcini, morels, and/or oysters)

2 teaspoons olive oil

2 large onions, chopped

4 cloves garlic, minced

¾ cup red wine

3 sprigs fresh thyme or ⅜ teaspoon dried

5¼ cups canned Italian plum tomatoes, seeded and chopped, juices reserved

1 teaspoon granulated sugar

½ teaspoon salt, or to taste

Freshly ground black pepper to taste

Roasted Polenta (recipe follows)

Rich, earthy flavor masks the low calorie content of this rustic stew. Paired with Roasted Polenta, it is a sublime first course, or even a light entrée. This can also be used as a sauce for pasta, grilled meat, or poultry. If you serve it as a sauce, to keep calories low, serve no more than one and a half cups of pasta or three and a half ounces of poultry or meat per person.

---

1 Assemble *mise en place* trays for this recipe (see page 6).

2 In a small heat-proof bowl, combine the dried mushrooms, sun-dried tomatoes, and boiling water. Cover and allow to steep for at least 15 minutes.

3 Using a damp cloth, wipe the fresh mushrooms clean. Trim off any tough stems and cut large mushrooms into ¼-inch-thick slices. Leave small (under 1 inch in diameter) mushrooms whole. Set aside.

4 In a medium-sized saucepan, combine the oil, onions, and garlic, cover, and cook over medium heat for about 3 minutes, or until the onions begin to wilt. Uncover and sauté for about 3 minutes, or until the onions begin to brown. Remove the pan from the heat.

5 Using a slotted spoon, scoop the sun-dried tomatoes and mushrooms from the soaking liquid into a strainer. Reserve the soaking liquid. Rinse the tomatoes and mushrooms under cold running water and press against the strainer to squeeze out all the water. Coarsely chop.

6 Without disturbing the sediment on the bottom of the bowl, spoon 7 tablespoons of the soaking liquid into the onion mixture. Add the red wine and thyme and return the pan to the heat. Bring to a boil over medium-high heat and boil for 1 minute. Stir in the fresh mushrooms. Stir in the canned tomatoes with their liquid, the chopped dried mushrooms and tomatoes, the sugar, salt, and pepper to taste. Partially cover, bring to a simmer, and cook, stirring occasionally and breaking up the tomatoes with the back of a spoon if necessary, for about 20 minutes, or until the mushrooms are tender and the ragout has thickened. Taste and season generously with more pepper.

7 Place 4 Roasted Polenta triangles in the center of each plate. Spoon the ragout over them and serve immediately.

NOTE: If the fresh mushrooms are exceedingly gritty, wash them under cool running water. Dry them thoroughly immediately after washing. The ragout can be made up to 4 days ahead. Cover and refrigerate or, for longer storage, freeze. If the ragout is too thick, thin it with a touch of red wine, bring to a boil over medium heat, and boil for 1 minute to allow the alcohol to evaporate.

Most dry-packed sun-dried tomatoes are packed as halves. If you can only find sun-dried tomatoes packed in oil, rinse them under hot running water and pat dry.

ROASTED POLENTA

SERVES 6
FAT PER SERVING: 2.8 GRAMS
SATURATED FAT: 0.4 GRAM
CALORIES PER SERVING: 148
CALORIES FROM FAT: 17%

1½ cups coarsely ground cornmeal

1 teaspoon salt, or to taste

5¼ cups cold water

1 In a large heavy saucepan, combine the cornmeal, salt, and cold water and bring to a boil over high heat, stirring constantly with a wooden spoon. Lower the heat to medium-high and cook, stirring constantly to prevent scorching, for about 10 minutes, or until the polenta pulls away from the sides and bottom of the pan.

2 Scrape the polenta onto a nonstick rimmed baking sheet and, using a spatula, pat it out into a ½-inch-thick rectangle or square. Cover with plastic wrap and refrigerate for about 10 minutes, or until firm.

2 cloves garlic, sliced

1 tablespoon extra-virgin olive oil

4 sprigs fresh rosemary, leaves only

Freshly ground black pepper to taste

3 Preheat the oven to 500 degrees F.

4 In a small bowl, combine the garlic and oil. Set aside for about 15 minutes to allow the garlic to infuse the oil.

5 When the polenta is firm, cut it into 6 rectangles or squares of equal size. Slice each shape diagonally into 4 triangles. Brush each triangle very lightly with the garlic-infused oil and lay on a nonstick baking sheet. Sprinkle the rosemary leaves on top and push a few underneath each triangle. Gently push down on the rosemary so that the leaves adhere to the polenta. Season with pepper to taste.

6 Bake in the top half of the oven for 7 to 10 minutes, or until very crisp on the outside but still soft in the center. Serve hot.

NOTE: Sally recommends that you use the traditional coarsely milled cornmeal available in Italian markets or specialty food shops for polenta, as it has a more interesting texture and a more robust flavor than finely grained polenta flours.

Smothered Escarole on Whole Wheat Crostini ~ Marie Simmons

SERVES 6

PREPARATION TIME: ABOUT 20 MINUTES

COOKING TIME: ABOUT 10 MINUTES

FAT PER SERVING: 3 GRAMS

SATURATED FAT: 0.4 GRAM

CALORIES PER SERVING: 83

CALORIES FROM FAT: 32%

Rich in vitamins and slightly bitter, escarole makes a crunchy, easy-to-prepare appetizer. You could use other greens in its place, but try to use whole wheat bread: Its sweetness offsets the greens beautifully.

1 Assemble *mise en place* trays for this recipe (see page 6).

2 Bring a large saucepan of water to a boil over high heat. Add the escarole and cook, stirring constantly with

2 pounds escarole, washed, trimmed, and torn into 2-inch pieces

1 tablespoon extra-virgin olive oil

1 clove garlic, crushed

Pinch of red pepper flakes

Coarse salt and freshly ground black pepper to taste

Twelve ¼-inch-thick slices whole wheat Italian bread, toasted

a wooden spoon, for about 4 minutes, or until just tender. Drain in a colander, pressing on the escarole with the back of the spoon to remove all moisture. Set aside.

3 In a large sauté pan, combine the oil, garlic, and red pepper flakes and cook over medium-low heat for about 3 minutes, or until the garlic begins to sizzle. Immediately add the escarole and stir to coat. Cook, stirring constantly, for about 2 minutes, or until the pan juices begin to evaporate. Season to taste with coarse salt and pepper.

4 Place 2 slices of toast on each warm plate. Spoon the escarole over the toast and serve immediately.

~ Whole wheat Italian bread makes especially delicious crostini, or toasts. Use a grill, broiler, or toaster oven. Brush the bread with olive oil and toast until golden on both sides. To prepare crostini in the oven, brush the bread very lightly on one side with olive oil and lay on a baking sheet. Bake in a preheated 350-degree-F oven for about 15 minutes, or until the edges are golden. If desired, rub the toasted bread very lightly with the cut side of a halved garlic clove. You can also bake split pita-bread crostini in the same fashion.

~ Escarole prepared this way is also a delicious side dish served with chicken, veal, or fish.

Onion Tart ~ André Soltner

SERVES 6

PREPARATION TIME: ABOUT 25 MINUTES

COOKING TIME: ABOUT 45 MINUTES

CHILLING TIME (PASTRY ONLY): AT LEAST 1 HOUR

---

2 cups all-purpose flour

Salt

This is a classic French recipe and one that has remained on the menu at Lutèce since the day the restaurant opened. Proof that one can never get too much of a good thing.

---

1 Assemble *mise en place* trays for this recipe (see page 6).

2 In a medium-sized bowl, combine the flour and 1 teaspoon of salt. With your fingertips or a pastry blender,

4 tablespoons chilled, unsalted butter

½ cup cold water

2 tablespons lard

3 large yellow onions, chopped

½ cup heavy cream

1 large egg

Freshly ground black pepper to taste

Freshly grated nutmeg to taste

■ Special Equipment: 8-inch tart pan with removable bottom

quickly blend in the butter until the mixture resembles coarse meal. Stir in the water and quickly mix to form a soft dough. Do not overmix, or the pastry will be tough. Shape the pastry into a ball and flatten slightly. Wrap in plastic and chill for at least 1 hour.

3 Preheat the oven to 375 degrees F.

4 In a large sauté pan, melt the lard over medium heat. Add the onions and sauté for 10 to 15 minutes, or until lightly browned. Transfer to a bowl.

5 In a small bowl, beat cream and egg together. Add to the onions, stirring to combine. Season to taste with salt, pepper, and nutmeg. Set aside.

6 On a lightly floured surface, roll out the pastry to a circle about 10 inches in diameter. Transfer the pastry to an 8-inch tart pan with a removable bottom. Gently fit the pastry into the pan, and trim off any excess pastry.

7 Spoon the onion filling into the pastry shell. Bake for 25 to 35 minutes, or until well browned. Cut into wedges and serve hot.

❧ Lard imparts a distinct flavor to the onions, and Chef Soltner recommends using it. However, you can substitute olive oil or butter.

❧ Served at room temperature, the tart makes a great hors d'oeuvre for a cocktail party.

Baked Cod with Bulgur ~ Tom Valenti

SERVES 6

PREPARATION TIME: ABOUT 30 MINUTES

SOAKING TIME (BULGUR ONLY): ABOUT 15 MINUTES

BAKING TIME: ABOUT 15 MINUTES

---

15 Sicilian or other large green olives, pitted and sliced

9 shallots, thinly sliced

3 tomatoes, cored, seeded, and chopped

3 cloves garlic, sliced

1 lemon, peeled and sectioned

1 teaspoon minced fresh tarragon

1 teaspoon minced fresh oregano

¾ cup dry white wine

½ cup water

Salt and freshly ground black pepper to taste

Six 6-ounce pieces skinless cod fillet

1½ cups bulgur

2½ cups plus 2 tablespoons boiling salted water

¾ cup extra-virgin olive oil

Cod is not often on the De Gustibus menu, but after tasting Tom's version, we decided it should be a regular item. Although he served it as a first course, I think it makes a terrific, easy-to-put-together entrée.

---

1 Assemble mise en place trays for this recipe (see page 6).

2 Preheat the oven to 450 degrees F. Lightly oil a baking dish large enough to hold the fish easily.

3 In a medium-sized bowl, combine the olives, shallots, tomatoes, garlic, lemon, tarragon, oregano, wine, water, and salt and pepper to taste. Pour into the baking dish and lay the fish on top. Cover tightly with aluminum foil. Reduce the oven temperature to 400 degrees F and bake for about 15 minutes, or until the fish is firm to the touch. Set aside uncovered to cool slightly.

4 Meanwhile, put the bulgur in a heat-proof bowl. Add the boiling water, cover tightly with plastic wrap, and set aside for about 15 minutes, or until all the water has been absorbed.

5 Carefully pour the cooking liquid from the baking pan into a blender and process until smooth. With the motor running, slowly add the oil, blending until the mixture is emulsified and smooth.

6 Spoon an equal portion of bulgur onto each plate. Place a fish fillet on top, arrange the vegetables on top of the fish and the bulgur, and drizzle with the sauce. Serve immediately.

Napoléon of Roquefort and Boursin ❧ Jean-Georges Vongerichten

SERVES 6
PREPARATION TIME: ABOUT 35 MINUTES
COOKING TIME: ABOUT 10 MINUTES
CHILLING TIME: AT LEAST 1 HOUR

3 sheets phyllo dough, thawed

4 tablespoons unsalted butter, melted

4 ounces Roquefort cheese

4 ounces Boursin cheese

½ cup heavy cream, softly whipped

1 tablespoon chopped fresh chives

½ teaspoon Cognac

Salt and freshly ground black pepper to taste

■ Special Equipment: pastry bag with a plain tip (optional)

This delicious cheese dish can be served either as an appetizer or as a cheese course after the meal. Best of all, it can be cooked in advance and reheated just before serving.

1 Preheat the oven to 450 degrees F. Assemble *mise en place* trays for this recipe (see page 6).

2 Stack the phyllo sheets on a baking sheet, brushing each one with some of the melted butter, making sure to brush all the way to the edges of the phyllo. Trim the stack into a 12-inch square. Discard the trimmings. Bake for 3 to 4 minutes, until golden brown. Allow to cool for at least 20 minutes.

3 In a blender or a food processor fitted with the metal blade, blend the Roquefort and Boursin cheese until smooth. Scrape into a bowl and gently but thoroughly fold in the whipped cream. Fold in the chives and Cognac, and season to taste with salt and pepper.

4 Using a very sharp knife, cut off a 3 x 12-inch strip from the cooled phyllo stack. Set aside.

5 Spoon the cheese mixture into a pastry bag fitted with a plain tip, and pipe evenly over the baked rectangle, making sure the piped lines touch each other. Or, gently spread the cheese over the phyllo with a spatula. Cover with plastic wrap and refrigerate for 1 hour, or until the cheese is firm.

6 Preheat the oven to 200 degrees F.

7 Lift the plastic wrap off the cheese-covered phyllo rectangle. Using a sharp knife, cut it into three 3 x 12-inch strips. Stack the strips, one on top of the other. Place the reserved plain strip on the top. Gently lifting each one with a spatula, transfer the napoléon to a baking sheet and warm in the oven for 1 minute.

8 Remove from the oven and cut crosswise into six 2 x 3-inch rectangles. Serve immediately.

❧ Do not put the napoléon together more than four hours before serving or the pastry will get soggy.

Hot and Sweet Red Pepper Dip with Walnuts and Pomegranate ❧ Paula Wolfert

MAKES ABOUT 3 CUPS
PREPARATION TIME: ABOUT 15 MINUTES
CHILLING TIME: AT LEAST 8 HOURS

This is a very tasty dip that, if covered and refrigerated, will last for at least a week. Serve with crisp bread, crackers, or pita triangles.

6 to 8 red bell peppers (about 2½ pounds), roasted, peeled, and seeds and membranes removed (see page 12)

1½ cups coarsely ground walnuts (about 6 ounces)

½ cup crumbled unsalted crackers

2 tablespoons pomegranate molasses

1 tablespoon fresh lemon juice

½ teaspoon ground cumin, plus a pinch

½ teaspoon granulated sugar

¾ teaspoon salt

3 tablespoons olive oil

2 small hot chiles, such as Fresno or hot Hungarian, roasted, peeled, and seeds and membranes removed, or to taste

2 tablespoons toasted pine nuts (see page 13)

1 Assemble *mise en place* trays for this recipe (see page 6).

2 Spread the bell peppers, smooth side up, on paper towels and drain for about 10 minutes.

3 In a food processor fitted with the metal blade, combine the walnuts, crackers, pomegranate molasses, lemon juice, ½ teaspoon of the cumin, the sugar, and salt and process until smooth. Add the bell peppers and process until puréed and creamy. With the motor running, add 2 tablespoons of the oil in a thin stream. Add the chiles. If the dip seems too thick, thin it with 1 to 2 tablespoons water. Transfer to a nonreactive container, cover, and refrigerate for at least 8 hours.

4 Place the dip in a serving dish and sprinkle with the pine nuts and the pinch of cumin. Drizzle with the remaining 1 tablespoon oil.

Soups

Acorn Butternut Squash Soup with Roasted Chestnuts ∾ Curried Cream of Cauliflower and Apple Soup ∾ Eggplant and Crab Garbure with Cumin and Tomato Confit ∾ Mediterranean Seafood Soup ∾ Apple-Cheese Soup ∾ Creamy Carrot Soup ∾ Spanish Fish Soup ∾ Spicy Broth of Bass and Halibut Flavored with Lovage ∾ Sweet Pepper and Yellow Pepper Soup ∾ Chilled Summer Vegetable Soup with Spanish Vinegar and Quinoa Salad ∾ Lettuce Soup ∾ Iced Sweet Pea Soup ∾ Chilled Curried Tomato Soup with Cilantro Cream

Acorn and Butternut Squash Soup with Roasted Chestnuts ❧ David Bouley

SERVES 6

PREPARATION TIME: ABOUT 30 MINUTES

COOKING TIME: ABOUT 1 HOUR AND 45 MINUTES

---

1 pound fresh chestnuts

3 one-pound acorn squash, halved and seeded

3 one-and-one-half-pound butternut squash, halved and seeded

¼ teaspoon freshly grated nutmeg

¼ teaspoon ground cinnamon

1 teaspoon ground mace

2 tablespoons light brown sugar

¼ cup honey

8 tablespoons unsalted butter, melted

2 quarts water

1 rib celery, chopped

Salt and freshly ground white pepper to taste

½ cup celery leaves (optional)

1 cup vegetable oil (if using celery leaves)

¾ cup heavy cream, softly whipped

2 tablespoons minced fresh lemon thyme

■ Special Equipment: chinois; deep-fry thermometer

This is an aromatic soup combining the rich, sweet taste of our American fall squashes with the intense flavor of the roasted French chestnut, all accented by the innovative use of celery water and crisp celery leaves.

---

1 Preheat the oven to 350 degrees F. Assemble *mise en place* trays for this recipe (see page 6).

2 With a sharp knife cut an "x" on one end of each chestnut and place on a baking sheet. Bake for about 20 minutes, until the chestnuts open and the flesh is tender. Transfer to a plate and allow to cool slightly.

3 When the chestnuts are cool enough to handle, peel with a small sharp knife or your fingers. Put the peeled chestnuts in a small saucepan and cover with water. Bring to a simmer and cook for 5 to 6 minutes, until the flesh is soft. Drain and press the flesh through a chinois or other fine sieve into a medium bowl. Set aside.

4 Meanwhile, place the squash halves, cut side up, in a large shallow baking dish. Dust with the nutmeg, cinnamon, mace, and brown sugar. Drizzle with the honey and melted butter. Cover the dish tightly with aluminum foil. Bake for 40 minutes, or until tender.

5 In a medium-sized saucepan, combine the chopped celery and the water, and bring to a boil over medium-high heat. Reduce the heat and simmer for 45 minutes. Strain, discarding the solids. Set the celery water aside.

6 Remove the squash from the oven and scrape the flesh from the skin. Process the squash in a food processor just until almost smooth; there will be some lumps. Press the flesh through a chinois or other fine sieve into a medium-sized saucepan. Slowly stir in the reserved celery water. Season to taste with salt and white pepper.

7 Place the soup over medium heat and simmer for about 4 minutes, or until just heated through.

8 Meanwhile, if using, rinse the celery leaves and pat dry with paper towels. In a small saucepan, heat the oil to 325 degrees F. on a deep-fry thermometer. Fry the leaves for 15 seconds, or until crisp. Lift from the oil with a slotted metal spoon or tongs and drain on paper towels.

9 Fold the whipped cream into the reserved chestnut purée. Stir in the lemon thyme.

10 Ladle the soup into 6 warm soup bowls. Using 2 tablespoons, shape the chestnut mixture into 6 small ovals, placing one in the center of each serving. Garnish with the fried celery leaves, if using, and serve.

❧ You may use 8 ounces canned unsweetened chestnut purée, but you will not get the same roasted flavor you will get when you roast the chestnuts yourself.

❧ If you are using the fried celery leaves as a garnish, choose pale, tender leaves. Fry them until crisp, but not brown. Store, uncovered, at room temperature, for up to 6 hours. However, if weather is damp, do not fry any earlier than 1 hour before use, or they will wilt.

❧ A chinois is a fine-meshed cone-shaped French sieve. While other fine-meshed sieves can be used when a chinois is called for, the result may not be as fine in texture. The shape enables the cook to press as much flavor from the solid ingredients as possible because the solids adhere to the sides of the sieve, making it easy to press against them with the back of a spoon.

Curried Cream of Cauliflower and Apple Soup ❧ Daniel Boulud

SERVES 6

PREPARATION TIME: ABOUT 25 MINUTES

COOKING TIME: ABOUT 30 MINUTES

4 cups Chicken Stock (see page 15)

1½ tablespoons unsalted butter

1 cup chopped onions

2 teaspoons curry powder

¾ teaspoon saffron threads
(or saffron powder)

1 cup sliced tart apples, such as
Granny Smith

4 cups cauliflower florets

1 cup heavy cream

Salt and freshly ground white
pepper to taste

GARNISH:

1 cup diced tart apples, such as
Granny Smith

1 tablespoon water

1 teaspoon curry powder

¼ teaspoon saffron threads
(or saffron powder)

Salt and freshly ground white
pepper to taste

1 tablespoon chopped fresh chives

Smooth and creamy with a sweet, spicy taste, this soup is the perfect starter to any festive meal. The fact that it can be prepared a day in advance and reheated at the last minute makes it an even better first course for the busy host or hostess. The soup is also tasty served cold.

1 Assemble *mise en place* trays for this recipe (see page 6).

2 In a medium-sized saucepan, warm the stock over low heat.

3 In a large saucepan, melt the butter over medium heat. Add the onions, curry powder, and saffron and cook, stirring frequently, for about 2 minutes, until the onions begin to soften. Add the sliced apples and cook, stirring frequently, for 5 minutes. Stir in the cauliflower and warm chicken stock, increase the heat, and bring to a boil. Reduce the heat and simmer for 20 to 30 minutes, until the cauliflower is very tender.

4 Transfer the soup, in batches if necessary, to a blender or a food processor fitted with the metal blade and process until very smooth. Pour into a medium-sized saucepan and stir in the cream. Season to taste with salt and white pepper and keep warm over very low heat.

5 To make the garnish, combine the diced apples and water in a small saucepan over medium heat and bring to a simmer. Stir in the curry powder and saffron, and season to taste with salt and white pepper. Cover and cook for about 3 minutes. Strain through a fine sieve, reserving the solids. Return the apples to the pan to keep warm.

6 Ladle the soup into warm soup bowls. Sprinkle the diced apple and chopped chives over the top.

Eggplant and Crab Garbure with Cumin and Tomato Confit ❧ **Daniel Boulud**

SERVES 6

PREPARATION TIME: ABOUT 1 HOUR

COOKING TIME: ABOUT 40 MINUTES

FAT PER SERVING: 10 GRAMS

SATURATED FAT: 1.2 GRAMS

CALORIES PER SERVING: 166

CALORIES FROM FAT: 25%

1 tablespoon salt, plus more to taste

3 medium-sized eggplant, peeled and cut into thin 1-inch-long strips (avoiding the seedy center)

1 tablespoon olive oil

1½ cups sliced onions (¼ inch thick)

1½ cups sliced leeks (¼ inch thick)

1½ cups thinly sliced carrots

2 cloves garlic, minced

2 bay leaves

2 sprigs fresh thyme

2 teaspoons ground cumin

½ teaspoon ground coriander

8 cups warm Chicken Stock (see page 15)

Freshly ground black pepper to taste

¾ cup jumbo lump crabmeat, picked over for shells and cartilage

Tomato Confit (see page 241)

6 sprigs fresh chervil, for garnish

Garbure is an earthy vegetable soup from the southwest of France. In this recipe, Daniel replaces the fat and flavor of the traditional bacon and goose confit with crab and a tomato confit.

1 Assemble *mise en place* trays for this recipe (see page 6).

2 In a large saucepan, bring 2 quarts of water to boil over high heat. Add the 1 tablespoon salt and the eggplant and cook for about 3 minutes, or until the eggplant is slightly softened. Drain and set aside.

3 In a medium-sized saucepan, heat the oil over medium heat. Add the onions, leeks, carrots, garlic, herbs, cumin, and coriander and sauté for about 6 minutes, or until the vegetables are just soft. Add the stock, blanched eggplant, and salt and pepper to taste, and simmer for about 25 minutes, or until the vegetables are very tender.

4 Remove the bay leaves and thyme sprigs. Gently stir in the crab and then ladle into shallow soup bowls. Gently float the pieces of tomato confit on top of the soup and put a chervil sprig in the center of each. Serve immediately.

NOTE: Cut the vegetables into equal-sized pieces so that they cook uniformly. The soup can be made up to the addition of the crab up to 3 days ahead. If fresh chervil is not available, use flat-leaf parsley.

Mediterranean Seafood Soup ❧ Jean-Michel Diot

SERVES 6

PREPARATION TIME: ABOUT 1 HOUR AND 30 MINUTES

COOKING TIME: ABOUT 35 MINUTES

8 cloves garlic

3 cups water

1 one-pound lobster

½ cup white wine

3 shallots, diced

12 mussels, well scrubbed and bearded

12 clams, well scrubbed

1 four-ounce zucchini

1 four-ounce yellow squash

4 ounces fresh fava beans, shelled (about ⅓ cup, shelled)

2 cups diced, trimmed fennel bulb (about 1¼ pound bulb)

4 ounces sea scallops, rinsed

1 teaspoon tomato paste

¼ cup plus 1 tablespoon olive oil

¾ pound very ripe tomatoes, cored, peeled, seeded, and diced

2 tablespoons chopped fresh basil

1 tablespoon chopped fresh tarragon

4 tablespoons unsalted butter

Salt and freshly ground black pepper to taste

6 large fresh oysters, shucked

This soup is redolent of the sea and of the intensely pure flavors of the South of France. It would make a great Sunday-night supper along with a crisp white wine, crisp baguettes, and crisp greens! The soup begins with water flavored with garlic, and builds from there. No need to make stock. The scallops most readily available are sea scallops, the larger type which must be halved or quartered before using in this recipe. Substitute sliced green beans for fava beans, if necessary.

1 Assemble *mise en place* trays for this recipe (see page 6).

2 Peel the garlic. Crush 2 of the cloves, and set aside.

3 In a medium-sized saucepan, combine the remaining 6 garlic cloves and the water. Bring to a simmer over medium-high heat.

4 Meanwhile, plunge a knife into the lobster just behind the head to kill it instantly. Cut off the claws.

5 Add the lobster body and claws to the garlic water, return to the boil, cover, and cook for about 8 minutes. Remove the lobster from the water and set aside to cool. Continue boiling the liquid for about 15 minutes, or until reduced to 2 cups. Set aside.

6 In a medium-sized saucepan, combine the white wine, shallots, and reserved crushed garlic. Bring to a simmer. Add the mussels and clams, cover, and cook for 2 minutes, until the shells open. Using a slotted spoon, remove the shellfish, discarding any that do not open. Reserve the shellfish cooking liquid. Open the shells and remove the meat. Discard shells.

7 Remove the meat from the tail and claws of the lobster and cut it into ¼-inch-thick slices.

8 Trim the ends of the zucchini and yellow squash and cut in half lengthwise. Put each half, cut side down, on a work surface and cut into slices about ⅛ inch thick. Set aside.

9 Blanch the fava beans in boiling water to cover for 1 minute. Drain and refresh under cold running water. Peel. Set aside in a small bowl.

10 Blanch the fennel in boiling water to cover for 1 minute. Drain and refresh under cold running water. Add to the bowl with the fava beans.

11 Place the scallops on a flat surface and, using a sharp knife, cut horizontally into halves or quarters to make slices about ¼ inch thick. Refrigerate.

12 Combine the reserved garlic water, the shellfish cooking liquid, and the tomato paste in a blender or a food processor fitted with the metal blade. Blend until smooth. With the motor running, add the olive oil, a little at a time. Transfer to a large saucepan. Add the squash slices and bring to a boil over high heat. Cover and simmer for about 6 minutes, or until the squash is just tender but not mushy.

13 Add the diced tomatoes, fava beans, and fennel to the saucepan. Stir in the basil and tarragon. Stir in the butter, a little at a time. Season to taste with salt and pepper.

14 Reduce the heat and add the mussels, clams, scallops, and oysters. Cook for 1 minute, or until the oysters curl around the edges. Add the lobster meat and cook for 1 minute more, until just heated through. Serve in warm soup bowls.

Apple-Cheese Soup ❧ Dean Fearing

SERVES 6

PREPARATION TIME: ABOUT 20 MINUTES

COOKING TIME: ABOUT 45 MINUTES

1 bouquet garni (1 tablespoon white peppercorns, 3 sprigs fresh thyme plus 2 bay leaves tied together in cheesecloth)

¼ cup peanut oil

3 ounces ham scraps or 1 ham bone

1 rib celery, diced

2 cloves garlic, minced

2 onions, diced

8 tart apples, such as Granny Smith, peeled, cored, and quartered

1 cup white port

6 cups Chicken Stock (see page 15)

4 slices apple-smoked or hickory-smoked bacon, for garnish

1 small red apple, such as Red Delicious, for garnish

1 small, tart green apple, such as Granny Smith, for garnish

Juice of 1 lemon

4 tablespoons unsalted butter, softened

¼ cup all-purpose flour

1½ pounds sharp Cheddar cheese, grated

Salt to taste

Tabasco to taste

■ Special Equipment: Cheesecloth; fine sieve

On a cold day, this soup would make a great lunch, especially if served with homemade bread. Dean suggests that if you want a meatless soup, omit the ham and use vegetable broth in place of the chicken stock.

1 Assemble *mise en place* trays for this recipe (see page 6).

2 To make the soup, in a medium-sized saucepan heat the oil over medium-high heat. Add the ham scraps, if using, the celery, garlic, and onions and sauté for about 4 minutes, or until the onions are translucent but not brown. Reduce the heat to medium and add the quartered apples. Cover and cook, stirring frequently, for about 10 minutes, or until the apples soften. Add the port and simmer for 5 minutes more. Add the chicken stock, bouquet garni, and the ham bone, if using, reduce the heat to low and simmer, partially covered, for about 20 minutes, or until the flavors are well blended. Remove the bouquet garni.

3 Meanwhile, in a small skillet, fry the bacon over medium heat for about 5 minutes, or until browned and crisp. Drain on paper towels. Cut into ⅛-inch dice and set aside.

4 Leaving the skin on, cut the green and red apples into ⅛-inch dice to use for garnish. You will need about 2 tablespoons of each color. Put the diced apples in a small glass or ceramic bowl and sprinkle with 1 tablespoon of the lemon juice. Set aside.

5 In a small bowl, knead the softened butter and flour together until smooth to make a beurre manié. Whisk the mixture into the soup to thicken it. Cook for 5 minutes longer, stirring frequently.

6 Add the grated cheese to the soup, stirring constantly, until it is melted.

7 Strain the soup through a fine sieve into the top of double boiler set over gently boiling water to keep the soup hot. (Do not press too hard on the solids.) Season with the remaining lemon juice and salt and Tabasco to taste. Ladle the soup into warm serving bowls and garnish with the diced apples and chopped bacon. Serve hot.

❧ If you want to make this soup a day or so in advance, prepare it through Step 2. Cool and refrigerate. Add the *beurre manié*, and then the cheese and seasonings, when you reheat the soup for serving. Do not prepare the apple and bacon garnish until a few hours before serving. This soup can be completed up to 2 hours before serving, but keep it warm in the top half of a double boiler set over hot water. Do not simmer over direct heat after the cheese has been added or the soup will separate.

❧ Cheesecloth is a kitchen necessity. It can be used for making bouquets garnis (cloth-enclosed herb mixtures) so that they can then be easily removed from the pot, for straining liquids, and for lining molds. It is inexpensive and can be discarded after use.

❧ Creamed butter and flour kneaded together is called a *beurre manié* and is used as a quick thickening liaison in sauces or soups. Kneading the ingredients together prevents lumping.

Creamy Carrot Soup ❧ Pierre Franey

SERVES 6

PREPARATION TIME: ABOUT 15 MINUTES

COOKING TIME: ABOUT 40 MINUTES

(CHILLING TIME, OPTIONAL: AT LEAST 4 HOURS)

2 tablespoons unsalted butter

1 cup minced onions

5 cups sliced carrots

Salt and freshly ground black pepper to taste

4 cups Chicken Stock (see page 15)

½ cup ricotta cheese

2 tablespoons port wine

2 tablespoons chopped fresh dill

This simple soup has great taste, it can be made in advance, and it can be served hot or cold. What more could a home cook ask?

1 Assemble *mise en place* trays for this recipe (see page 6).

2 In a medium-sized saucepan, melt the butter over medium heat. Add the onions and cook, stirring occasionally, for 4 to 5 minutes, until softened.

3 Stir in the carrots and season to taste with salt and pepper. Add the chicken stock and bring to a boil. Reduce the heat and simmer, partially covered, for 30 minutes. Strain, reserving the liquid.

4 Transfer the carrot mixture to a blender or a food processor fitted with the metal blade. Add the ricotta and 1 cup of the reserved liquid. Process until smooth. Scrape back into the saucepan and add the remaining liquid.

5 Return the soup to the heat and bring to a boil. Remove from the heat and stir in the port and dill. Serve hot. Alternately, allow to cool just to warm room temperature, cover, and refrigerate for at least 4 hours until well chilled. Stir in the port and dill just before serving cold.

Spanish Fish Soup ❧ Joyce Goldstein

SERVES 6
PREPARATION TIME: ABOUT 25 MINUTES
COOKING TIME: ABOUT 40 MINUTES

¼ cup olive oil

4 cups finely diced yellow onions

3 large cloves garlic, minced

1 tablespoon red pepper flakes, or to taste

1 bay leaf

4 cups Fish Stock (see page 17)

1 cup fresh orange juice

¼ cup fresh lime or lemon juice

2 teaspoons grated orange zest

Salt and freshly ground black pepper to taste

60 Manila or other very small clams, well scrubbed

1½ pounds monkfish, cleaned and cut into 2-inch chunks

1 pound sea scallops, trimmed of tough side muscle

Orange-Almond Aïoli (see page 263)

*T*he classic *caldo de perro* from Cadiz is made with only fish, fish stock, and the juice of bitter oranges. Joyce is a bit more expansive in her interpretation. She has added some shellfish, a little heat in the form of hot pepper flakes, and a marvelous orange-and-almond aïoli garnish.

---

1 Assemble *mise en place* trays for this recipe (see page 6).

2 In a large sauté pan, heat the oil over medium heat. Add the onions and sauté for about 10 minutes, or until soft and translucent. Stir in the garlic, red pepper flakes, and bay leaf and sauté for 3 minutes. Add the stock and bring to a simmer. Reduce the heat and simmer for 15 minutes. Stir in the orange and lime juices, zest, and salt and pepper to taste.

3 Carefully drop the clams and fish chunks into the pan. Cover and simmer for about 5 minutes, or until the clams open. Carefully drop in the scallops and simmer for another 2 to 3 minutes, or until just cooked through and opaque.

4 Ladle into warm soup bowls. Place a dollop of the aïoli in the center of each bowl and serve immediately.

❧ Flounder or rockfish can be substituted for the monkfish; add to the soup after the clams have cooked for 3 minutes.

❧ You can garnish the soup with large croutons if desired.

❧ Manilla clams are tiny clams, a little larger than a nickel. Substitute small cherrystones if necessary.

Spicy Broth of Bass and Halibut Flavored with Lovage ~ **Gray Kunz**

SERVES 6

PREPARATION TIME: ABOUT 25 MINUTES

COOKING TIME: ABOUT 35 MINUTES

½ pound fresh black sea bass fillet, skinned, trimmed, and cut into ½-inch cubes

½ pound fresh halibut fillet, skinned, trimmed, and cut into ½-inch cubes

Salt and freshly ground black pepper to taste

3 leaves lovage, chopped, or ¼ cup chopped celery leaves

1 teaspoon vegetable oil, or more if necessary

4 cups Fish Stock (see page 17)

4 tablespoons unsalted butter, cut into pieces

2½ tablespoons minced shallots

½ teaspoon minced garlic

Cayenne pepper to taste

½ cup cored, peeled, seeded, and diced tomatoes

¼ cup diced green bell pepper

⅓ cup thinly sliced leeks

■ Special Equipment: mortar and pestle

*T*his is a perfectly simple fish course that can easily become a main course for a light lunch.

----

1 Assemble *mise en place* trays for this recipe (see page 6).

2 Put the lovage in a mortar and add the vegetable oil. Using a pestle, grind into a paste, adding additional oil if necessary for a pesto-like consistency. Alternatively, mince the chopped lovage leaves and mix them with the oil in a small bowl, pressing down and grinding with the edge of a wooden spoon until the mixture forms a paste-like consistency.

3 In a medium-sized saucepan, bring the stock to a boil over medium-high heat. Reduce the heat to low. Using a whisk, beat the butter into the stock, a piece at a time, until emulsified. Do not add the next piece until the one before is incorporated. Stir in the shallots and garlic. Season to taste with salt and black pepper and cayenne. Bring the mixture to a gentle boil.

4 Season the fish with salt and pepper to taste.

5 Add the tomato, pepper, and leeks to the pan and return to a gentle boil. Add the fish. As soon as the liquid returns to a gentle boil, remove the pan from the heat and stir in the lovage mixture. Taste and adjust the seasoning, if necessary.

6 Ladle the fish and broth into 6 warm, shallow soup bowls. Serve immediately.

~ Lovage, called céleri bâtard, or "false celery," in France because its flavor and aroma are similar to celery, is extremely potent. Use it sparingly. Lovage is easy to grow in a vegetable garden. It is sold at greengrocers and farm markets.

As indicated in the recipe, you can substitute celery leaves for lovage if necessary.

❧ If you like the flavor of lovage, make small amounts of lovage "pesto" as described in Step 2, cover and refrigerate. Use it to flavor stews, soups, salads, or sauces or to season roasted or grilled meats.

❧ If you cannot find black sea bass, substitute any firm-fleshed white fish or use all halibut. Recommended substitutes include grouper, striped sea bass, and snapper.

Sweet Pepper and Yellow Pepper Soup ❧ Sheila Lukins

SERVES 6
PREPARATION TIME: ABOUT 35 MINUTES
COOKING TIME: ABOUT 45 MINUTES
FAT PER SERVING: 5.2 GRAMS
SATURATED FAT: 2.4 GRAMS
CALORIES PER SERVING: 190
CALORIES FROM FAT: 23%

2 red bell peppers, cored, seeded, and cut into ¼-inch-thick strips

10 very ripe plum tomatoes, cored, quartered, and seeded

¼ cup fresh lemon juice

½ teaspoon ground ginger

¼ teaspoon freshly ground black pepper, plus more to taste

Salt to taste

2 tablespoons unsalted butter

1 cup chopped onions

1 cup chopped leeks

The richly colored red and yellow peppers are used to make two separate soups that, when combined, form a dish that is as good to eat as it is pretty to behold. For the presentation, the two soups are simultaneously poured down opposite sides of a shallow bowl. This is remarkably easy to do and makes an impressive dinner party first course.

1 Assemble *mise en place* trays for this recipe (see page 6).

2 In a large heavy saucepan, combine the red peppers, tomatoes, lemon juice, ginger, and ¼ teaspoon pepper and bring to a simmer over low heat. Cover and cook, stirring occasionally, for about 30 minutes, or until the peppers are very soft.

3 Transfer to a food processor fitted with the metal blade and process until smooth. Taste and adjust the seasoning with salt and pepper. (You may have to do this in batches.) Pour into a medium-sized saucepan and set aside.

4 Meanwhile, make the yellow pepper soup: In a large saucepan, melt the butter over low heat. Add the onions

6 yellow bell peppers, 3 roasted, peeled, cored, seeded, and chopped (see page 12) and 3 cored, seeded, and chopped

3 small boiling potatoes (about ¾ pound), peeled and sliced

5 cups Chicken Stock (see page 15)

2 tablespoons chopped fresh chives, for garnish

and leeks and season to taste with salt and pepper. Cook, stirring frequently, for about 15 minutes, or until the vegetables are tender and translucent. Add the yellow peppers, potatoes, and stock. Raise the heat and bring to a boil, then reduce the heat and simmer for about 30 minutes, or until the vegetables are very tender.

5 Transfer to a food processor fitted with the metal blade and process until smooth. (You may have to do this in batches.) Pour into a medium-sized saucepan, taste, and adjust the seasoning.

6 Heat both soups over medium heat, stirring frequently, for about 3 minutes, or until just heated through.

7 Fill a measuring cup with a portion of one soup and fill another with the other soup. Slowly pour one soup down one side of a shallow soup bowl while simultaneously pouring the other soup down the opposite side, so that they meet in the middle of the bowl. Fill 5 more bowls the same way, garnish with the chives, and serve immediately.

NOTE: Either of these soups can be served alone. The yellow pepper soup is superb with a splash of extra-virgin olive oil, a grating of Parmesan cheese, and crisp croutons.

———————————

❧ Replace the homemade chicken stock with canned low-sodium chicken broth if desired.

Chilled Summer Vegetable Soup with Spanish Vinegar and Quinoa Salad ❧ Mark Militello

SERVES 6

PREPARATION TIME: ABOUT 45 MINUTES

COOKING TIME: ABOUT 45 MINUTES

CHILLING TIME: AT LEAST 3 HOURS

FAT PER SERVING: 10 GRAMS

SATURATED FAT: 1.2 GRAMS

CALORIES PER SERVING: 347

CALORIES FROM FAT: 25%

2 tablespoons olive oil, plus more for garnish if desired

½ pound sweet onions, such as Vidalia, diced

¾ pound tomatoes, peeled, cored, and quartered

¾ pound red bell peppers, cored, seeded, and diced

½ pound baking potatoes, peeled and diced

½ pound eggplant, diced

½ pound zucchini, diced

2 cloves garlic, chopped

1 small bunch each fresh thyme, basil, and flat-leaf parsley, tied together in a cheesecloth bag

4 cups Chicken Stock (see page 15)

Salt and freshly ground black pepper to taste

About 2 tablespoons Spanish vinegar, such as L'Estornell

Quinoa Salad (see page 124)

1 small piece Parmigiano-Reggiano cheese, for shaving (optional)

■ Special Equipment: Food mill

This soup is a meal in itself! The rich vegetable flavor is enhanced by a touch of vinegar and extended by the grain salad. This is a masterpiece of low-fat cooking.

1 Assemble *mise en place* trays for this recipe (see page 6).

2 In a large saucepan, heat the oil over medium heat. Add the onions and sauté for about 5 minutes, or until soft but not brown. Add the tomatoes, bell peppers, potatoes, eggplant, zucchini, garlic, herb bundle, and stock. Raise the heat and bring to a boil, then reduce the heat and simmer for about 30 minutes, or until the vegetables are soft. Pass the vegetables through the medium-sized plate of a food mill into a nonreactive container. Season with salt and pepper to taste, cover, cool, and refrigerate for at least 3 hours, or until chilled.

3 When ready to serve, stir vinegar to taste into the soup.

4 For each serving, spoon Quinoa Salad into a ½-cup mold and invert the molds into the center of a large shallow soup bowl. Ladle equal portions of soup around the salads. If desired, drizzle oil onto the soup and shave a bit of Parmesan on top. Serve immediately.

NOTE: Chop each vegetable into equal-sized pieces so that they cook uniformly.

Lettuce Soup ❧ Jacques Pépin

SERVES 6

PREPARATION TIME: ABOUT 25 MINUTES

COOKING TIME: ABOUT 50 MINUTES

---

5 tablespoons unsalted butter

1 cup chopped onions

1 cup chopped leeks, washed and drained

8 cups Turkey or Chicken Stock (see page 15)

4 cups diced, peeled baking potatoes

1 teaspoon salt

2 small heads Boston lettuce, leaves separated, washed, and dried

*N*ot only is this soup easy to make—it is delicately beautiful to look at. A French favorite not often seen in the American kitchen, lettuce soup, which has a potato base, can be served hot or cold.

---

1 Assemble *mise en place* trays for this recipe (see page 6).

2 In a large saucepan, heat 3 tablespoons of the butter over medium heat. Add the onions and leeks and sauté for about 2 minutes. Add the stock, potatoes, and salt and bring to a boil. Reduce the heat to low and simmer, partially covered, for about 40 minutes, until the potatoes are very tender.

3 Transfer the mixture to a blender or a food processor fitted with the metal blade, and blend until smooth. You may have to do this in batches to avoid overflow. Return the soup to the pan and set over low heat.

4 Stack the lettuce leaves a few at a time, roll them up cigar fashion, and slice into chiffonade (thin strips).

5 In a medium-sized saucepan, heat the remaining 2 tablespoons of butter. Add the chiffonade and sauté for about 3 minutes, until wilted. Stir into the soup. Adjust seasoning to taste.

6 Ladle the soup into 6 warm soup bowls and serve immediately.

Iced Sweet Pea Soup ～ Anne Rosenzweig

SERVES 6

PREPARATION TIME: ABOUT 25 MINUTES

COOKING TIME: ABOUT 20 MINUTES

CHILLING TIME: AT LEAST 4 HOURS

2 tablespoons coriander seeds

3 tablespoons unsalted butter

¾ cup minced Vidalia or other sweet onion

3½ cups Chicken Stock (see page 15)

5 cups fresh peas or thawed frozen petite peas

½ cup freshly grated coconut (see Note)

1 cup heavy cream

1 cup tightly packed fresh spinach leaves

Salt and freshly ground white pepper to taste

2 to 3 tablespoons crème fraîche

¼ cup chopped fresh cilantro

Unusual flavors combine to make a wonderfully refreshing cold soup. However, when the weather requires a bit of warmth to start the meal, you can also serve it hot.

1 Assemble *mise en place* trays for this recipe (see page 6).

2 In a small sauté pan, toast the coriander seeds over medium heat for about 5 minutes, or until they begin to smoke and release their oils. Transfer to a plate to cool and then place in a spice grinder and process until fine.

3 In a large saucepan, melt the butter over medium heat. Add the onions, reduce the heat, and cook for 10 minutes, stirring occasionally, until the onions soften, but do not brown. Add the ground coriander and stock, increase the heat to medium, and cook for about 2 minutes, until heated through. Bring to a simmer and stir in the peas and coconut. Cook for about 5 minutes, or until the peas are tender. Stir in the cream and spinach and cook for about 1 minute, or until the spinach begins to wilt.

4 Transfer to a blender or a food processor fitted with the metal blade. Blend or process until smooth. Season to taste with salt and pepper. Pour into a glass or ceramic bowl and refrigerate for 4 hours, or until thoroughly chilled. Taste and adjust the seasoning.

5 Ladle the soup into 6 well-chilled, shallow soup bowls. Garnish each serving with a dollop of crème fraîche and a sprinkling of cilantro. Serve immediately.

～ If you substitute packaged grated coconut for fresh, be sure to buy unsweetened coconut.

～ You can substitute sour cream for the crème fraîche.

Chilled Curried Tomato Soup with Cilantro Cream ~ Marie Simmons

SERVES 6

PREPARATION TIME: ABOUT 30 MINUTES

COOKING TIME: ABOUT 25 MINUTES

CHILLING TIME: AT LEAST 1 HOUR

2 tablespoons olive oil

1½ cups finely chopped onions

3 cloves garlic, minced

1 to 1½ tablespoons curry powder, or to taste

One-and-one-half 35-ounce boxes strained tomatoes (about 6½ cups)

3 cups plain low-fat yogurt, at room temperature, stirred until smooth

Salt and freshly ground black pepper to taste

¼ cup milk, if needed

Cilantro Cream (recipe follows)

This cool soup is made creamy with the addition of the cilantro topping.

1 Assemble *mise en place* trays for this recipe (see page 6).

2 In a large saucepan, combine the oil and onions and cook over low heat, stirring frequently, for about 5 minutes, or until the onions are soft and golden. Add the garlic and curry powder to taste and cook, stirring constantly, for 1 minute. Stir in the tomatoes, cover, and cook for about 15 minutes, or until the flavors are well blended. Uncover and let cool to lukewarm.

3 Transfer to a food processor fitted with the metal blade and process until smooth. (This may have to be done in batches.) Transfer to a nonreactive bowl and whisk in the yogurt and salt and pepper to taste. Cover and refrigerate for at least 1 hour, or until chilled.

4 If necessary, thin the soup by whisking in the milk, a little at a time. Pour into chilled shallow soup bowls. Swirl a dollop of Cilantro Cream into each serving and serve immediately.

CILANTRO CREAM

MAKES ABOUT 1 CUP

½ cup plain low-fat yogurt

2 tablespoons heavy cream (optional)

½ cup packed fresh cilantro leaves

Combine the yogurt, cream, and cilantro in a food processor fitted with the metal blade and process until smooth. Transfer to a container, cover, and refrigerate for at least 1 hour, or until well chilled.

Salads

Cool Lamb Salad with Flageolet, Cumin, and Roasted Peppers ❧ Bean, Zucchini, and Pepper Salad ❧ Gingered Green Bean Salad ❧ Grilled and Chilled Salmon Salad with Artichoke Guacamole ❧ Jícama Salad ❧ Appaloosa, Butterscotch, and Chestnut Bean Salad ❧ Fennel Salad ❧ Quinoa Salad ❧ Parsley Salad with Bulgur, Mint, and Tomatoes ❧ Flaked Parsley Salad with Black Olives

Cool Lamb Salad with Flageolet, Cumin, and Roasted Peppers ❧ **Mario Batali**

SERVES 6

PREPARATION TIME: ABOUT 1 HOUR

MARINATING TIME: AT LEAST 12 HOURS

COOKING TIME: ABOUT 1 HOUR

FAT PER SERVING: 17 GRAMS

SATURATED FAT: 4 GRAMS

CALORIES PER SERVING: 340

CALORIES FROM FAT: 47%

One 1½-pound boneless leg of lamb, butterflied

3 tablespoons olive oil

2 cups plain nonfat yogurt

1 bunch fresh rosemary, leaves only

1 bunch fresh mint

6 cloves garlic

¼ cup black peppercorns

1 large head frisée

1 tablespoon extra-virgin olive oil

1 teaspoon fresh lemon juice

Coarse salt and freshly ground black pepper to taste

Marinated Flageolets (recipe follows)

Roasted Peppers (recipe follows)

Cumin-Scented Yogurt (recipe follows)

A bit of Provence, a bit of the Middle East, and a taste of Italy absolutely define Mario Batali's approach to contemporary cooking in this spectacular main-coarse salad. To cut back on calories and fat, reduce the amount of lamb.

1 Assemble *mise en place* trays for this recipe (see page 6).

2 Put the lamb in a shallow nonreactive dish In a food processor fitted with the metal blade, combine the yogurt, olive oil, yogurt, rosemary, mint, garlic, and peppercorns, and using quick on and off pulses, process just until the herbs and garlic are chopped. Do not purée. Pour over the lamb, cover, and refrigerate for at least 12 hours.

3 Prepare a charcoal or gas grill or preheat the broiler.

4 Grill the lamb for about 12 minutes on each side for medium rare. Place on a warm platter and let rest for about 10 minutes. If broiling, broil the lamb about 4 inches from the heat source.

5 Toss the frisée with the extra-virgin olive oil, lemon juice, and coarse salt and pepper to taste. Place equal portions on each plate and top with the flageolets and roasted peppers. Slice the lamb on the diagonal into ¼-inch-thick slices and arrange over the salads. Spoon the yogurt over the top and around the salad. Serve immediately.

NOTE: Mario suggests using Coach Farm whole goats' milk yogurt in the recipes.

CUMIN-SCENTED YOGURT

MAKES ABOUT 1 CUP

FAT PER 3-TABLESPOON SERVING: 0

SATURATED FAT: 0

CALORIES PER SERVING: 21

CALORIES FROM FAT: 0%

---

1 cup plain nonfat yogurt

1 teaspoon fresh lemon juice

1 tablespoon toasted ground cumin
(see Note)

¼ teaspoon salt

In a blender, process the yogurt, juice, cumin, and salt for about 1 minute, or until smooth. Serve immediately or store, covered and refrigerated, for up to 1 week.

NOTE: Toast the cumin in a small skillet over low heat, stirring once or twice, for approximately 2 minutes, or just until lightly browned and aromatic.

MARINATED FLAGEOLETS

MAKES ABOUT 2 CUPS

FAT PER ⅓-CUP SERVING: 6.9 GRAMS

SATURATED FAT: 1 GRAM

CALORIES PER SERVING: 117

CALORIES FROM FAT: 53%

---

1 cup dried flageolets or small white beans, rinsed and picked clean

¼ cup red wine vinegar

3 tablespoons extra-virgin olive oil

¼ teaspoon fresh oregano or ⅛ teaspoon dried

¼ teaspoon cayenne pepper

¼ large red onion, thinly sliced

Coarse salt and freshly ground black pepper to taste

1 Put the beans in a large saucepan, add 6 cups cold water, and soak for about 8 hours.

2 Drain and rinse the beans, return to the pan, and add 6 cups cold water. Bring to a boil over high heat, reduce the heat, and simmer for about 45 minutes, or until al dente. Drain, transfer the beans to a nonreactive bowl, and set aside to cool.

3 In a small bowl, whisk together the vinegar, oil, oregano, and cayenne. Toss in the onion and season to taste with coarse salt and pepper. Pour over the beans and set aside to marinate for at least 30 minutes. Serve at room temperature, or store, covered and refrigerated, for up to 1 day. Bring to room temperature before serving.

ROASTED PEPPERS

MAKES ABOUT 1 CUP

FAT PER 3-TABLESPOON SERVING: 0.1 GRAM

SATURATED FAT: 0.1 GRAM

CALORIES PER SERVING: 7

CALORIES FROM FAT: 6%

2 large red bell peppers, roasted, peeled, cored, and seeded (see page 12)

1 teaspoon extra-virgin olive oil

Coarse salt and freshly ground black pepper to taste

Using tiny decorative cutters or a sharp paring knife, cut the roasted peppers into triangles, stars, or other fancy shapes. Put in a small bowl and toss with the oil and coarse salt and pepper to taste. Serve at room temperature, or store, covered and refrigerated, for up to 2 days. Bring to room temperature before serving.

Bean, Zucchini, and Pepper Salad ❧ Jean-Michel Bergougnoux

SERVES 6

FAT PER SERVING: 5.2 GRAMS

SATURATED FAT: 0.7 GRAM

CALORIES PER SERVING: 109

CALORIES FROM FAT: 40%

1 pound zucchini, julienned (avoid the seedy centers)

1½ pound yellow waxed beans, trimmed

1 red bell pepper

2 bunches fresh basil, leaves only

Coarse salt to taste

2 tablespoons olive oil

Use this salad with Jean-Michel's braised beef, or as a side dish to balance out any other rich and luscious entrée you create. If wax beans are unavailable, you can replace them with green beans, but the salad will not be as colorful.

1 Assemble *mise en place* trays for this recipe (see page 6).

2 Blanch the zucchini in boiling salted water for 1 minute. Drain and refresh under cold running water. pat dry and set aside.

3 Blanch the beans in boiling lightly salted water for 1 minute. Drain and refresh under cold running water Drain and set aside.

Freshly ground black pepper to taste

■ Special Equipment: Mortar and pestle

4 Using a vegetable peeler, remove the thin outer skin from the bell pepper. Cut the pepper in half and remove the core, membrane, and seeds. Cut into a fine julienne.

5 Put the basil leaves in a large mortar and pestle and add coarse salt to taste. Pulverize, using the pestle, while slowly adding the oil to make a thick paste.

6 In a large bowl, combine the zucchini, beans, and bell pepper. Add the basil paste and toss to coat. Season to taste with additional salt if necessary and pepper.

NOTE: The vegetables and basil paste can be prepared up to 1 day ahead. Store, covered and refrigerated, and combine just before serving. You can make the basil paste in a mini food processor, but it will not have the same texture as that made using a mortar and pestle.

Gingered Green Bean Salad ∿ Jane Brody

SERVES 6

PREPARATION TIME: ABOUT 15 MINUTES

COOKING TIME: ABOUT 5 MINUTES

CHILLING TIME: AT LEAST 30 MINUTES

FAT PER SERVING: 7.4 GRAMS

SATURATED FAT: 0.7 GRAM

CALORIES PER SERVING: 107

CALORIES FROM FAT: 56%

(ANALYSIS WITHOUT ALMONDS)

FAT PER SERVING: 1.7 GRAMS

SATURATED FAT: 0.2 GRAM

CALORIES PER SERVING: 42

CALORIES FROM FAT: 34%

1 pound green beans, trimmed and cut into 2-inch-long pieces

1 tablespoon finely shredded fresh ginger

⅓ cup sliced blanched almonds

*T*his wholesome salad with an Asian twist is made without oil. It has the added virtue of keeping, covered and refrigerated, for up to five days. To cut back on the fat, omit the almonds, or use half the amount.

1 Assemble *mise en place* trays for this recipe (see page 6).

2 In the top half of a vegetable steamer set over boiling water, steam the beans for about 5 minutes, or until just tender. Rinse under cold running water and pat dry.

3 In a medium bowl, combine the beans, ginger, and almonds.

4 In a small bowl, whisk together the mustard and water to make a paste. Stir in the sugar, vinegar, soy sauce, and, if using, the salt. Pour over the bean mixture and toss to coat. Cover and refrigerate for at least 30 minutes before serving.

1 to 2 teaspoons dry mustard, or to taste

About 1½ teaspoons water

1 teaspoon granulated sugar

1½ tablespoons distilled white vinegar or rice vinegar

1 tablespoon reduced-sodium soy sauce

1 teaspoon salt, or to taste (optional)

NOTE: Do not substitute powdered ginger for fresh ginger. Fresh ginger is readily available in supermarkets and green-grocers.

Grilled and Chilled Salmon Salad with Artichoke Guacamole ❧ Todd English

SERVES 6

PREPARATION TIME: ABOUT 1 HOUR

MARINATING TIME (SALMON ONLY): 1 TO 24 HOURS

COOKING TIME: ABOUT 1 HOUR AND 15 MINUTES

---

3 tablespoons chopped fresh thyme

1 clove garlic, finely minced

½ cup olive oil

1 pound skinless, boneless salmon fillet

6 large artichokes, stems and tough outer leaves removed

2 lemons, halved

2 cups milk

1 ripe tomato, cored, seeded, and diced

¼ cup finely diced red onion

1 teaspoon dark Asian sesame oil

Artichoke bottoms replace the avocado and the sesame oil adds an unexpected dimension to this unusual "guacamole," served with a chilled salmon salad. Although this is a rather involved recipe, so much can be done in advance that it is not as difficult as it as first seems.

1 Prepare *mise en place* trays for this recipe (see page 6).

2 In a small shallow nonreactive baking dish, combine the thyme and garlic with 2 tablespoons of the olive oil. Place the salmon in the mixture and turn to coat both sides. Cover and refrigerate for at least 1 hour, or up to 24 hours.

3 In a large nonreactive pot, cover the artichokes with water. Squeeze the juice of 3 of the lemon halves into the pot and then add the 3 lemon halves. Cover and bring to a boil over medium-high heat. Reduce the heat and simmer for 45 minutes, or until the outer leaves come loose with a slight tug. Drain and place upside down on paper towels to cool.

Salt and freshly ground black pepper to taste

3 tablespoons balsamic vinegar

2 tablespoons Dijon mustard

1 tablespoon minced shallots

1 cup Japanese bread crumbs (*panko*) or other crisp bread crumbs

Vegetable oil

1 bunch fresh chervil, snipped into tiny sprigs

4 When cool, remove and discard the outer layer of artichoke leaves. Remove the remaining leaves from the artichokes until you reach the very small tender leaves (take care to avoid the sharp thorns on the tips). Place 36 to 42 of the largest leaves in a shallow container, add the milk, cover, and refrigerate until ready to use.

5 Using a sharp knife, remove and discard the small leaves and the hairy choke of the artichokes to expose the meaty bottoms. Cut the bottoms into ¼-inch dice and put in a small bowl. Gently fold in the tomatoes, onions, and sesame oil. Squeeze in the juice from the remaining lemon half and season to taste with salt and pepper. Stir gently, cover, and set aside.

6 In a small bowl, whisk together the vinegar and mustard. Slowly add the remaining 6 tablespoons olive oil, whisking constantly until emulsified. Stir in the shallots and set aside.

7 Prepare a charcoal or gas grill or preheat the broiler.

8 Grill the salmon for about 8 minutes, turning once, or until just barely cooked in the center. Set aside.

9 Put the bread crumbs in a large plastic bag and set aside.

10 Pour vegetable oil into a large deep heavy frying pan to a depth of about 2 inches and heat over high heat until very hot but not smoking. A few at a time, remove the artichoke leaves from the milk and put in the bag with the bread crumbs, tossing to coat. Shake off the excess crumbs and fry the leaves for about 1 minute, or until golden. Drain on paper towels. Repeat with the remaining leaves.

11 Place a dollop of the artichoke "guacamole" on the wide end of each fried artichoke leaf. Flake about 1 tablespoon of salmon on top and garnish with a tiny sprig of chervil. Serve immediately.

Jícama Salad ～ Dean Fearing

MAKES ABOUT 2½ CUPS

½ small zucchini, cut into fine julienne about ⅛-inch thick

½ small jícama, peeled and cut into fine julienne about ⅛-inch thick

½ small red bell pepper, seeds and membranes removed, cut into fine julienne about ⅛-inch thick

½ small yellow bell pepper, seeds and membranes removed, cut into fine julienne about ⅛-inch thick

½ small carrot, peeled and cut into fine julienne

¼ cup peanut oil

2 tablespoons fresh lime juice

Salt to taste

Cayenne pepper to taste

Dean's salad makes a colorful and crunchy accompaniment to his warm lobster taco, and also works very well with any grilled fish, meat, or poultry.

In a medium-sized bowl, combine all the vegetables, oil, and lime juice. Season to taste with salt and cayenne pepper. Toss to mix well. Serve immediately.

～ Although the jícama salad may be prepared several hours ahead, covered and refrigerated, do not add the salt until almost ready to serve as it will cause the vegetables to lose their crispness.

～ A mandoline makes uniform julienne strips from the vegetables.

Appaloosa, Butterscotch, and Chestnut Bean Salad ❧ Ron Hook

SERVES 6

PREPARATION TIME: ABOUT 30 MINUTES

COOKING TIME: ABOUT 40 MINUTES

SOAKING TIME: 1 HOUR

CHILLING TIME: AT LEAST 2 HOURS

FAT PER SERVING: 0.4 GRAM

SATURATED FAT: 0.1 GRAM

CALORIES PER SERVING: 87

CALORIES FROM FAT: 4%

½ cup each Appaloosa, butterscotch, and chestnut beans, rinsed and picked clean (see Note)

1 bay leaf

½ cup fresh lemon juice

¼ cup balsamic vinegar

2 tablespoons Roasted Garlic pulp (see page 20)

3 large fresh sage leaves

½ teaspoon coarse salt

½ teaspoon freshly ground black pepper

1 medium onion, thinly sliced

3 tablespoons finely grated carrot

1 tablespoon chopped fresh flat-leaf parsley

1 head red-leaf lettuce, separated into leaves, washed, and dried

This hearty salad is deliciously heart-healthy: Low in fat and cholesterol, it's filled with tasty goodness. Serve it as a side dish or a casual main course.

1 Assemble *mise en place* trays for this recipe (see page 6).

2 In a large saucepan, combine the beans with water to cover by 1 to 2 inches and bring to a boil over high heat. Immediately remove the pan from the heat and let stand for 1 hour.

3 Drain the beans, rinse, and cover with fresh cold water. Add the bay leaf and bring to a boil over high heat. Reduce the heat and simmer for about 40 minutes, or until the beans are tender. Drain and discard the bay leaf. Transfer to a heat-proof bowl.

4 In a blender, combine the lemon juice, vinegar, garlic, sage, and coarse salt and pepper. Add ¼ cup of the cooked beans and process until smooth. Pour over the remaining warm beans and toss to coat. Stir in the onion, 2 tablespoons of the carrot, and the parsley. Cover and refrigerate for at least 2 hours.

NOTE: You can use any combination of dried beans to make this salad. However, try to use those that have a good color balance, such as kidney, cranberry, and white beans.

Fennel Salad ～ Matthew Kenney

2 medium-sized bulbs fennel, cut into small dice

1 tablespoon plus 1½ teaspoons minced shallots

¾ teaspoon freshly ground toasted coriander seeds

3 tablespoons fresh lemon juice

1 tablespoon plus 1½ teaspoons sherry wine vinegar

½ to ⅔ cup walnut oil

Salt and freshly ground black pepper to taste

Matthew's fennel salad makes a beautiful bed for his ahi tuna tartare appetizer. This crunchy, anise-flavored dish is also a wonderful accompaniment to any grilled fish dish.

1 Assemble *mise en place* trays for this recipe (see page 6).

2 Put the fennel in a bowl.

3 In another bowl, combine the shallots, coriander, lemon juice, and vinegar. Whisk in the oil and season to taste with salt and pepper. Pour over the fennel and toss to combine. Serve immediately.

NOTE: Fennel quickly discolors, so it should not be cut more than 30 minutes before use. Although lemon juice inhibits discoloration, do not use more than called for in the dressing, as it would make the salad too acidic.

Quinoa Salad ～ Mark Militello

½ cup quinoa, rinsed

1 cup water

½ cup finely diced seeded cucumber

½ cup peas, blanched

½ cup corn kernels, blanched

¼ cup finely diced fennel

¼ cup finely diced celery

¼ cup chopped fresh basil

2 tablespoons chopped fresh mint

¼ cup fresh lemon juice, or more to taste

This quinoa salad rounds out mark's delicious chilled summer vegetable soup. Serve this crunchy grain salad on its own, or as a side accompaniment at a barbecue or pack it up for a summer picnic.

1 Assemble *mise en place* trays for this recipe (see page 6).

2 In a medium-sized saucepan, combine the quinoa and water and bring to a boil over high heat. Reduce the heat and simmer for about 10 minutes, or until all the water has been absorbed and the quinoa is tender. Set aside to cool.

1 tablespoon extra-virgin olive oil

Sea salt and freshly ground black pepper to taste

3 In a nonreactive bowl, combine the cucumber, peas, corn, fennel, celery, herbs, lemon juice, and oil. Add the quinoa, toss, and season to taste with sea salt and pepper. Cover and marinate at room temperature for 1 hour to allow the flavors to develop.

4 Just before serving, adjust the seasoning with extra lemon juice, salt, and/or pepper if necessary.

NOTE: You will have more than enough salad to garnish the soup, which you can serve as a side dish or with greens for another meal. Store, covered and refrigerated, for up to 2 days.

Parsley Salad with Bulgur, Mint, and Tomatoes ❧ Chris Schlesinger

SERVES 6

PREPARATION TIME: ABOUT 20 MINUTES

SOAKING TIME: 30 MINUTES

FAT PER SERVING: 1.6 GRAMS

SATURATED FAT: 0.5 GRAM

CALORIES PER SERVING: 89

CALORIES FROM FAT: 15%

⅓ cup medium-fine bulgur, rinsed

1 cup water

3 tomatoes, peeled, cored, seeded, and finely diced

1 red onion, finely diced

1 cucumber, peeled and finely diced

3 cups finely chopped fresh flat-leaf parsley

¼ cup finely chopped fresh mint

1 teaspoon minced garlic

This is Chris's version of the traditional Middle Eastern salad called tabbouleh. You can make it with any size bulgur grain, but medium-fine gives the best result.

1 Assemble *mise en place* trays for this recipe (see page 6).

2 In a bowl, combine the bulgur and water, cover, and set aside for 30 minutes. Drain in a fine sieve and use your hands to squeeze out any excess water. Transfer to a large bowl.

3 Add the tomatoes, onions, cucumber, parsley, mint, garlic, lemon juice, oil, and Tabasco and salt to taste. Serve immediately, or cover and refrigerate for up to 4 hours. Bring to room temperature before serving. Use the lettuce leaves for scooping up and eating the salad.

NOTE: Do not make this more than 4 hours in advance, or the vegetables will get soggy.

½ cup fresh lemon juice (about 3 lemons)

⅓ cup extra-virgin olive oil

2 to 6 drops Tabasco sauce

Salt to taste

1 head romaine lettuce, separated into leaves, washed, and dried

Flaked Parsley Salad with Black Olives ❧ Paula Wolfert

SERVES 6

PREPARATION TIME: ABOUT 25 MINUTES

¼ pound (about 2 large bunches) very fresh curly parsley, washed and thoroughly dried

24 Kalamata or Niçoise olives, rinsed, drained, pitted, and slivered

3 tablespoons minced shallots

½ teaspoon Worcestershire sauce

3 tablespoons olive oil

1 tablespoon cider vinegar or rice wine vinegar

Salt and freshly ground black pepper to taste

3 tablespoons freshly grated Pecorino-Romano cheese

This unusual recipe uses everyday curly parsley and is delicious with fish. Do not mix this ahead of time.

1 Assemble *mise en place* trays for this recipe (see page 6).

2 Remove the parsley leaves from the stems, discarding the stems, and tear each leaf into tiny bits. You should have about 4 loosely packed cups of parsley flakes.

3 In a large bowl, combine the parsley, olives, shallots, Worcestershire, oil, vinegar, and salt and pepper to taste and toss gently. Transfer to a serving bowl and sprinkle with the cheese. Serve immediately.

NOTE: To insure the parsley is completely dry use a salad spinner.

Entrées

Brasied Beef ✽ Beef Shank Terrine with Leeks ✽ Fillet of Beef with Raisin and Black Olive Sauce ✽ Sofrito of Baby Lamb ✽ Roasted Pork Loin ✽ Braised Lamb Shanks with Dried Mediterranean Fruits ✽ Roast Leg of Lamb with Red Chile Crust ✽ Red Pepper-Crusted Tenderloin of Beef ✽ Roasted Pork Tenderloins with Tapenade ✽ Fillet of Beef with Horseradish Sauce ✽ Roast Rack of Veal ✽ Lamb Tagine with Almonds and Dates ✽ Fillet of Beef in the Modena Manner ✽ Chipotle Lamb Chops ✽ Patria Pork over Boniato Purée with Black Bean Broth ✽ Lamb Stew with Fall Fruit and Vegetables ✽ London Broil with Lime-Marinated Onions ✽ Grilled Beef Tenderloin with Tomatillo Sauce and Blue Corn Crêpes ✽ The Best Leg of Lamb ✽ Stuffed Breast of Veal ✽ Braised Lamb Shanks with White Bean Purée ✽ Ten-Chile Chili ✽ Seared Marinated Breast of Chicken with Tomato and Basil ✽ Cornish Game Hens with Crumb and Sausage Stuffing ✽ Guinea Hen with Quince Purée and Chanterelles ✽ Chicken in Parchment with Thyme ✽ Roast Poussin with Green Olives, Preserved Lemon, and Garlic ✽ Chicken in Green Herb Sauce ✽ Squab with Cabbage and Mashed Potatoes ✽ Grilled Honey-Basil Chicken ✽ Roasted Turkey Breast with Port and Dried Cranberry Sauce ✽ Scallopine of Turkey Breast with Morel and Cognac Sauce ✽ Fricassee of Turkey and Brown Rice ✽ Duck with Turnips and Medjoul Dates ✽ Quail with Coffee and Spice Rub ✽ Jamaican Jerk Chicken ✽ Herb-Marinated Chicken, Shiitake Mushrooms, and Roasted Potatoes Vinaigrette ✽ Guajillo-Maple Glazed Turkey ✽ Swordfish with Pine Nuts and Raisins ✽ Red Snapper in a Salt Crust with Herb Dressing ✽ Broiled Pompano with Pickles and Vegetables ✽ Red Snapper with Tomatoes and Caramelized Garlic ✽ Fillet of Snapper with Tomato, Onion, and Garlic ✽ Striped Bass with Chayote Squash ✽ Grilled Swordfish and Fennel with Charred Tomatoes, Oil-Roasted Garlic, and Balsamic Vinegar ✽ Spice-Crusted Tuna with Asparagus and Seaweed-Wrapped Noodles ✽ Shrimp and Artichoke Casserole ✽ Roasted Salmon with Morrocan Barbecue Sauce ✽ Roast Salmon with Morrocan Spices ✽ Grilled Swordfish ✽ Achiote-Fried Catfish ✽ Big Easy Seafood-Okra Gumbo ✽ Trout Cooked in Vernaccia di Oristano ✽ Striped Bass with Artichokes ✽ Seared "Steak Cut" Haddock with Lentil Ragout ✽ Sole with Tomato Fondue and Saffron Pasta ✽ Salmon with Onion Confit, Winter Vegetables, and Red Wine Sauce ✽ Grilled Salmon with Black Pepper and Ginger ✽ Spice-Rubbed Swordfish ✽ Mussels "Saganaki" ✽ Vegetable Paella ✽ Spring Vegetable Stew with Pesto ✽ Creamy Polenta with Roasted Wild Mushrooms and Fried Sage Leaves ✽ Wild Mushroom Crêpes ✽ Beet Tartare

Braised Beef with Bean, Zucchini, and Pepper Salad ❧ Jean-Michel Bergougnoux

SERVES 6

PREPARATION TIME: ABOUT 1 HOUR

COOKING TIME: ABOUT 2 HOURS AND 35 MINUTES

FAT PER SERVING: 20 GRAMS

SATURATED FAT: 6 GRAMS

CALORIES PER SERVING: 853

CALORIES FROM FAT: 22%

1 tablespoon olive oil

4 pounds beef chuck or top round roast, well trimmed

2 carrots, peeled and finely diced

1 large onion, finely diced

2 ribs celery, finely diced

2 medium-sized tomatoes, cored and quartered

1 head garlic, cut in half crosswise

1 long strip orange zest

1 bunch fresh flat-leaf parsley

4 sprigs fresh thyme

1 bay leaf

1 teaspoon black peppercorns

6 cups dry white wine

Sauce Hachée (see page 280)

Bean, Zucchini, and Pepper Salad (see page 118)

■ Special Equipment: Large heavy-bottomed oven-proof skillet with lid

This wonderful braised beef incorporates all of the flavors and many of the colors of Provence. It is delicious served at room temperature, too.

1 Assemble *mise en place* trays for this recipe (see page 6). Preheat the oven to 350 degrees F.

2 In a large heavy-bottomed oven-proof skillet, heat the oil over medium heat. Add the beef and brown well on all sides, about 5 minutes. Transfer to a plate.

3 Add the carrots, onions, and celery to the skillet and sauté 3 minutes, or until tender.

4 Return the beef to the skillet, add the tomatoes, garlic, orange zest, parsley, thyme, bay leaf, peppercorns, and wine and bring to a boil. Cover, transfer to the oven, and bake for 2½ hours, or until the beef is very tender but still firm to the touch. Do not allow the liquid to boil—it should barely simmer as the meat braises; reduce the oven temperature if necessary.

5 Lift the beef from the skillet and cut it into 6 slices. Place a slice on each plate and spoon 2 tablespoons sauce over it. Mound the salad next to the meat.

Beef Shank Terrine with Leeks and Horseradish Sauce ❧ Daniel Boulud

SERVES 6

PREPARATION TIME: ABOUT 45 MINUTES

COOKING TIME: ABOUT 2 HOURS AND
30 MINUTES

CHILLING TIME: 24 HOURS

---

10 pounds well trimmed beef shank, cut into large pieces, or 1 whole beef shank, well trimmed

2 carrots, peeled and chopped

2 ribs celery, chopped

1 sprig fresh thyme

2 whole cloves

1 bay leaf

1 tablespoon salt, or to taste

5 peppercorns

10 large leeks, washed, trimmed, and green part removed

1½ tablespoons unflavored gelatin

2 tablespoons cold water

2 tablespoons fresh tarragon leaves

Freshly ground black pepper

Horseradish Sauce (see page 276)

½ cup peeled, seeded, and diced tomatoes

1 tablespoon minced fresh chives

■ Special Equipment: 12 x 4 x 4-inch terrine mold or loaf pan

This terrine is great on its own as a light summer lunch, served with a salad, a crisp baguette, a bowl of fresh fruit—and, of course, a light French wine!

---

1 Assemble *mise en place* trays for this recipe (see page 6).

2 Put the beef in a large heavy saucepan and add enough cold water to cover. Bring to a boil, reduce the heat to low, and simmer for 30 minutes, skimming the surface frequently.

3 Add the carrots, celery, thyme, cloves, bay leaf, salt, and peppercorns, and simmer for 1½ hours.

4 Meanwhile, tie a piece of kitchen twine around each leek to hold it together. Distribute the leeks around the beef. Cover and cook for 30 to 45 minutes longer, or until meat is fork-tender. Remove from the heat and let the meat cool slightly in the liquid.

5 Using a slotted spoon, carefully remove the leeks from the pan. Untie them, place in a shallow dish, and set aside.

6 Carefully transfer the beef shank to a shallow dish, and set aside.

7 Strain the stock through a coarse sieve, and discard the solids. Strain again through an extra-fine sieve. Skim the fat from the surface of the stock. (Or refrigerate it for several hours and then lift the hardened fat from the surface.)

8 Measure 2 cups of the stock into a small saucepan and heat over very low heat. Reserve the remaining stock for another purpose.

9 Meanwhile, in a small bowl, combine the gelatin and cold water and let sit for about 5 minutes, or until softened. Stir the gelatin into the hot stock until dissolved. Add the tarragon and season to taste with salt and pepper. Set aside and keep warm.

10 Line a 12 x 4 x 4-inch terrine mold with plastic wrap, allowing about a 3-inch overhang all around.

11 Pull the meat from the bones, breaking it into small pieces. Put a layer of meat on the bottom of the terrine. Arrange whole leeks in 2 parrallel lines down the pan. Continue making alternate layers of meat and leeks, finishing with a layer of meat.

12 Pour the hot stock mixture over the terrine, pressing down with a spatula to make sure it is evenly distributed in the mold. Fold the plastic wrap up over the top to cover. Refrigerate for 24 hours.

13 To unmold, open the plastic wrap and use it to lift the terrine out of the mold. Unwrap the terrine and discard the plastic wrap. Cut the terrine into ¾-inch-thick slices using an electric knife or a very sharp serrated knife.

14 Place 2 slices of the terrine on each serving plate. Spoon a little Horseradish Sauce around the edge, and garnish with the diced tomatoes and chives.

❧ **To produce a really clear jellied stock, line the sieve with a double thickness of cheesecloth before straining the stock the second time.**

Fillet of Beef with Raisin and Black Olive Sauce ❧ Roberto Donna

SERVES 6

PREPARATION TIME: ABOUT 15 MINUTES

COOKING TIME: ABOUT 1 HOUR AND 10 MINUTES

MARINATING TIME (BEEF ONLY): AT LEAST 2 HOURS

MACERATING TIME (RAISINS AND COGNAC): AT LEAST 2 HOURS

---

4 cups Veal Stock (page 16)

1 one-and-a-half-pound beef tenderloin, trimmed and cut crosswise into 6 pieces

⅓ cup olive oil

3 cloves garlic, sliced

3 fresh rosemary sprigs

½ cup raisins

¼ cup Cognac

1 tablespoon prepared black olive purée

Profoundly concentrated flavors heighten the taste of the tender fillet. I think that this dish could also be done with pork or tender lamb loins with the same aromatic result.

---

1 Assemble *mise en place* trays for this recipe (see page 6).

2 Put the beef in a shallow dish. Add the olive oil, garlic, and rosemary, and toss to coat. Cover with plastic wrap and refrigerate at least 2 hours.

3 Meanwhile, in a small bowl combine the raisins and Cognac. Set aside at room temperature to macerate for 2 hours.

4 In a medium-sized saucepan, simmer the veal stock over medium heat for 45 minutes to 1 hour, or until reduced to 1½ cups. Set aside.

5 Remove the beef from the marinade and pat dry with paper towel. Discard the garlic and reserve the oil and rosemary separately.

6 Drain the raisins, reserving the Cognac.

7 Preheat the oven to 175 degrees F.

8 In a large sauté pan, heat the reserved oil over high heat. Add the reserved rosemary and then add the beef and cook, turning once, for 4 to 5 minutes, until it has a nice crispy crust. Remove the rosemary from the pan as soon as it starts to darken. Add the Cognac and continue to cook for 30 seconds to 1 minute, until the Cognac has evaporated. Transfer the beef to a warm serving dish and keep warm in the oven. Spoon off any fat from the pan.

9 Add the veal reduction to the sauté pan, stir in the olive purée, and cook over medium-high heat for 2 minutes, or until reduced to a rich sauce. Stir in the raisins.

Place beef on warmed dinner plates. Pour the sauce over the beef, and serve.

∾ Black olive purée, which is sometimes called olivata, is available at Italian groceries, specialty markets, and many supermarkets.

Sofrito of Baby Lamb with Romesco Sauce ∾ Andrew D'Amico

SERVES 6

PREPARATION TIME: ABOUT 30 MINUTES

COOKING TIME: ABOUT 4½ HOURS

¼ cup olive oil

One 6-pound leg of lamb

2 bulbs garlic, split in half crosswise

2 cups finely diced onions

1 cup finely diced fennel

2 sprigs fresh thyme

2 sprigs fresh rosemary

2 sprigs fresh cilantro

2 bay leaves

Romesco Sauce (see page 279)

Coarse salt to taste

This succulent dish traces its beginnings to the Spanish countryside. This is served with the meat removed from the bone and kept warm in a beautiful chafing dish. If serving the lamb as an entrée, add roasted potatoes and a crisp green vegetable.

---

1 Assemble *mise en place* trays for this recipe (see page 6).

2 Preheat the oven to 350 degrees F.

3 In a roasting pan or casserole with a tight-fitting lid, heat the oil over medium heat. Add the lamb and sear, turning frequently, for about 6 minutes, or until brown on all sides.

4 Add the garlic, onions, and fennel and sauté for about 10 minutes, or until the vegetables are golden brown. Add the thyme, rosemary, cilantro, bay leaves, and 3 cups of water. Cover and roast for 45 minutes.

5 Turn the meat and check the water level. If the vegetables look dry, add 1 more cup of water. Continue to roast, turning and adding water, ½ cup at a time, when necessary, for an additional 1 hour and 15 minutes.

6 Using a pastry brush, thinly coat the lamb on all sides with Romesco Sauce. Sprinkle with salt. Cover and return to the oven for 1 hour longer.

7 Turn the lamb, brush with Romesco Sauce, and season with coarse salt. Return to the oven, uncovered, and roast for approximately 45 minutes longer, or until the meat easily falls from the bone. Transfer to a large chafing dish and serve with the remaining sauce on the side.

Roasted Pork Loin with Acorn Squash Torte and Red Chile Sauce ~ Robert Del Grande

SERVES 6

PREPARATION TIME: ABOUT 1 HOUR

COOKING TIME: ABOUT 3 HOURS

Acorn Squash Torte (see page 244)

1 two-and-one-half- to three-pound boneless, center-cut pork loin, with a layer of fat on top

Salt and freshly ground black pepper to taste

Red Chile Sauce (see page 278)

½ cup sour cream

6 fresh cilantro sprigs

This is a particularly appealing "company's coming" recipe, as there is almost no last-minute work, yet the results are impressive at the table.

1 Preheat the oven to 350 degrees F. Assemble *mise en place* trays for this recipe (see page 6).

2 Begin preparing the Acorn Squash Torte.

3 Lower the oven to 300 degrees F.

5 Season the pork with salt and pepper to taste. Set a large skillet over medium-high heat and when it is hot, sear the pork, beginning with the fat side and then turning so all sides are browned. Transfer the pork to a rack in a roasting pan. Roast for about 1 hour and 15 minutes, until the pork is cooked but still moist and retaining some faint pink color. The internal temperature should be at least 150 degrees F.

5 Meanwhile, to finish making the Acorn Squash Torte.

6 Prepare the Red Chile Sauce.

7 About 25 minutes before the pork is done, remove it from the oven. Lower the oven rack to the bottom rung of the oven and put the pork on it. Position the other oven rack above the pork, leaving ample room for the torte. (If you have 2 ovens, there is no need to move the pork to the lower third of the oven. Bake the torte in the second oven.)

11 When the pork is done, remove it from the oven and let it rest for 15 minutes.

12 While the pork is resting, reheat the red chile sauce in the top half of a double boiler over gently boiling water.

13 Spoon equal portions of the torte into the centers of warm dinner plates. Carve the pork into thin slices and fan at least 3 slices around the torte for each serving. Spoon the red chile sauce over the pork. Garnish each serving with a spoonful of sour cream and a sprig of cilantro.

Braised Lamb Shanks with Dried Mediterranean Fruits ❧ Jean-Michel Diot

SERVES 6

PREPARATION TIME: ABOUT 1 HOURS AND 20 MINUTES

COOKING TIME: ABOUT 3 HOURS AND 15 MINUTES

MARINATING TIME: 12 HOURS

---

1 small leek, trimmed

½ bunch fresh flat-leaf parsley

5 to 6 sprigs fresh sage

1 sprig fresh thyme

1 bay leaf

6 lamb shanks

Perhaps the Arab traders left their mark on the South of France with the flavors of this dish, redolent with cumin, coriander seed, and dried fruits. It is great for entertaining since the dish is even better after it has rested for a day or two.

---

1 Assemble *mise en place* trays for this recipe (see page 6).

2 Make a bouquet garni by tying the leek, parsley, sage, thyme, and bay leaf together with a piece of kitchen twine. In a Dutch oven, combine the lamb shanks, carrots, garlic, shallots, 2 tablespoons of the olive oil, the cumin seed, coriander seed, salt, pepper, and the bou-

3 carrots, peeled and diced

6 cloves garlic, crushed

3 shallots, diced

¼ cup plus 2 tablespoons olive oil

1 tablespoon cumin seed

1 teaspoon coriander seed

1 tablespoon coarse salt, or to taste

1 tablespoon cracked black pepper, or to taste

4 cups dry white wine

2 tablespoons all-purpose flour

3 ripe tomatoes, cored, quartered, and seeded

3 cups water

6 dried figs

6 dried apricots

6 dried dates

2 tablespoons raisins

1 bunch fresh mint, washed and dried

3 tart apples, such as Granny Smith

6 fennel bulbs, trimmed, cored, and cut into ⅛-inch-thick slices

Grated zest and juice of 1 orange

quet garni. Add the wine and stir to mix. Cover and place in the refrigerator to marinate for 12 hours.

3 Preheat the oven to 300 degrees F.

4 Remove the lamb shanks from the marinade. Strain the marinade, reserving the liquid. Reserve the vegetables and bouquet garni separately.

5 In the Dutch oven, heat 2 tablespoons of the olive oil over medium-high heat. Add the lamb shanks and sear, turning frequently, for 10 to 15 minutes, or until well browned. Transfer to paper towels to drain.

6 Add the marinated vegetables to the pot and cook for 5 to 6 minutes, until they have just begun to release their liquid. Transfer to a bowl with a slotted spoon, and set aside.

7 Using a wooden spoon, stir the flour into the juices remaining in the pot. Cook, stirring constantly, for about 3 minutes, or until the flour is golden brown.

8 Return the lamb shanks and vegetables to the pot. Add the tomatoes, the reserved marinade, and the bouquet garni. Increase the heat to high and bring to a boil. Reduce the heat and simmer for about 20 minutes, or until the liquid is reduced by half.

9 Stir in 2 cups of the water. Cover and transfer to the oven. Cook for about 2 hours or until the meat is very tender.

10 Meanwhile, dice the figs, apricots, dates, and raisins. Cut the mint leaves into fine julienne and combine with the diced fruit. Set aside.

11 About 45 minutes before the meat is ready, peel and core the apples and cut into ⅛-inch-thick slices.

12 In a large ovenproof sauté pan, heat the remaining 2 tablespoons of oil over medium heat. Add the fennel and sauté for about about 5 minutes, just until it begins to brown. Stir in the apples and orange zest and juice. Stir in the remaining 1 cup of water, cover, and cook in the oven for 30 minutes.

13 Arrange the fennel mixture in the center of a large platter. Place the lamb shanks on top. Cover with a piece of aluminum foil to keep warm.

14 Place the Dutch oven over high heat, bring the liquid to a boil for about 5 minutes, until reduced and slightly thickened. Skim off any fat that rises to the surface. Strain into a saucepan and stir in the dried fruit mixture. Simmer for 4 to 5 minutes, until fruit softens. Season to taste with salt and pepper.

15 Ladle some of the sauce over the top of the lamb. Serve with the remaining sauce on the side.

Roast Leg of Lamb with Red Chile Crust and Jalapeño Preserves ❧ Bobby Flay

SERVES 8

PREPARATION TIME: ABOUT 45 MINUTES

COOKING TIME: ABOUT 1 HOUR AND 10 MINUTES

1 tablespoon pasilla chile powder (see page 12)

1 tablespoon toasted cumin seeds (see page 13)

2 tablespoons olive oil

Salt and freshly ground black pepper to taste

1 six-pound boned and tied leg of lamb

Jalapeño Preserves (see page 269)

This is a great dish for a buffet because not only is it good served warm, it is just as tasty at room temperature. Like all the other items on this menu, the lamb makes a wonderful dinner on its own, especially when served with the Sweet Potato Gratin (see page 245).

1 Preheat the oven to 450 degrees F. Assemble mise en place trays for this recipe (see page 6).

2 In a large bowl, combine the chile powder, cumin, olive oil, and salt and pepper to taste. Rub the meat on all sides with the mixture to coat. Let the meat sit for at least 30 minutes and for as long as 2 hours at cool room temperature.

3 Place the lamb on a rack in a roasting pan. Roast for 15 minutes. Reduce the oven temperature to 350 degrees

F. and cook for 30 minutes more, or until a meat thermometer inserted into the center registers 145 degrees F. for rare. Transfer the lamb to a cutting board, cover loosely with aluminum foil, and let rest for about 10 minutes.

4 Slice the lamb against the grain into ¼-inch slices and arrange on a serving platter. Garnish with the Jalapeño Preserves.

Red Pepper-Crusted Tenderloin of Beef with Wild Mushroom-Ancho Chile Sauce and Black Bean-Goat Cheese Torta ❧ Bobby Flay

SERVES 8
PREPARATION TIME: ABOUT 40 MINUTES
COOKING TIME: ABOUT 1 HOUR AND 20 MINUTES

---

6 dried New Mexico red chiles

2 tablespoons cracked black peppercorns

1 seven-pound tenderloin of beef, trimmed

1 tablespoon vegetable oil

Salt and freshly ground black pepper to taste

Wild Mushroom-Ancho Chile Sauce (see page 280)

Black Bean-Goat Cheese Torta (see page 246)

This is Bobby's Southwestern version of the classic French steak au poivre. When he demonstrated this recipe in class, he made it in individual portions, but we have substituted a whole tenderloin—easier to serve to a buffet crowd.

---

1 Preheat the oven to 300 degrees F. Assemble *mise en place* trays for this recipe (see page 6).

2 Spread the chiles on a rimmed baking sheet and toast in the oven for 1 minute. Remove the stems and seeds, put the cleaned chiles in a blender or food processor fitted with the metal blade and blend or process just until coarsely chopped. The chiles should be approximately the same consistency as the cracked peppercorns. Return the chiles to the baking sheet, add the cracked peppercorns and toss well.

3 Increase the oven temperature to 400 degrees F.

4 Using kitchen twine, tie the tenderloin about every 2 inches so that it retains its shape while cooking. Rub the tenderloin all over with the oil and season to taste with salt and pepper. Roll the tenderloin in the chile-pepper mixture on the baking sheet.

5 Heat a roasting pan in the oven for 2 minutes, or until very hot. Place the tenderloin in the center of the pan and cook for 12 minutes. Turn the tenderloin over and cook for about 12 minutes more, or until a meat thermometer inserted into the center registers 140 degrees F., for rare. Transfer the tenderloin to a cutting board. Cover loosely with aluminum foil and let rest for 10 minutes.

6 Slice the tenderloin into ⅜-inch-thick slices. Arrange the slices down the center of a serving platter. Top with the Wild Mushroom-Ancho Chile Sauce and garnish the platter with wedges of the Black Bean-Goat Cheese Torta.

∾ Kitchen twine, or any medium-weight untreated cotton thread, is another kitchen necessity. It is used not only for tying up meat and poultry, but also for bouquets garnis, soufflé collars, and many other tasks.

Roasted Pork Tenderloins with Tapenade and Charred Yellow Pepper Sauce ∾ **Bobby Flay**

SERVES 6

PREPARATION TIME: ABOUT 30 MINUTES

COOKING TIME: ABOUT 20 MINUTES

---

3 pork tenderloins, about 1 pound each

½ cup plus 1 tablespoon Black Olive Tapenade (see page 271)

2 tablespoons Spanish paprika

This is guaranteed to be an "in-demand" dinner party recipe. The flavors blend together beautifully, the colors are stupendous, and every part of the dish can be done in advance. Plus, it tastes just as good served at room temperature.

---

1 Assemble *mise en place* trays for this recipe (see page 6).

2 Preheat the oven to 350 degrees F.

Salt and freshly ground black pepper
to taste

¼ cup olive oil

1½ cups Charred Yellow Pepper
Sauce (see page 276)

3 Using a very sharp knife, make a lengthwise cut along
the side of 1 tenderloin, taking care not to cut all the way
through. Gently push the tenderloin open to butterfly it.
Spread 3 tablespoons of the tapenade down the length
of the opening, fold the meat over into its original shape,
and tie closed with kitchen twine. Season liberally with
the paprika and salt and pepper. Repeat with the remaining tenderloins.

4 In a large sauté pan, heat the oil over medium-high
heat. Add the loins and sear for about 5 minutes, or until
lightly browned on all sides. Transfer to a rimmed baking sheet or roasting pan and roast for about 12 minutes,
or until just cooked through (and the internal temperature reaches 160 degrees F). Allow to rest for 5 minutes.

5 Cut the tenderloin crosswise into ½-inch-thick slices
and arrange down the center of a serving platter. Serve
with the charred yellow pepper sauce.

Fillet of Beef with Horseradish Sauce ❧ Pierre Franey

SERVES 6

PREPARATION TIME: ABOUT 25 MINUTES

COOKING TIME: ABOUT 12 MINUTES

1¼ pounds center-cut fillet of beef

4 cups Beef Stock (see page 16)

1 bay leaf

2 sprigs fresh parsley

3 sprigs fresh thyme, chopped, or
½ teaspoon dried thyme

Salt and freshly ground black pepper
to taste

*Although, for this menu, the meat should be cooked just
before serving, all the other components of the recipe
can easily be prepared in advance. However, the beef is also
terrific cold, so the dish could be cooked early in the day,
especially during warm weather, when cold meals are
always welcome.*

1 Assemble *mise en place* trays for this recipe (see
page 6).

2 Carefully tie the meat lengthwise and crosswise with
kitchen twine, leaving a long end of string as a handle to
facilitate removing the meat from the cooking liquid.

1 large leek, white part only, washed and cut into julienne (about 2 cups)

1 large parsnip, peeled and cut into julienne (about 2 cups)

2 carrots, peeled and cut into julienne (about 2 cups)

1 small onion, halved and finely sliced (about ½ cup)

Horseradish Sauce (see page 276)

3 In a large, heavy saucepan or flame-proof casserole with lid, combine the stock, bay leaf, parsley, thyme, and salt and pepper to taste. Add the beef, leaving the length of string outside the pan.

4 Cover the pan, bring the stock to a simmer over medium-high heat, and cook for exactly 5 minutes. Immediately add the leeks, parsnips, carrots, and onion and stir to distribute them. Cover and simmer for exactly 7 minutes. Remove from the heat and let stand, covered, for 5 minutes.

5 Remove the beef from the pan and cut into thin slices (no more than ½-inch thick). Arrange on a warm platter. Spoon the vegetables around the meat and spoon a little of the liquid over all. Serve with the Horseradish Sauce passed on the side.

❧ If you cannot buy a center-cut fillet but instead buy an end of the fillet, trim the tapering ends before cooking.

❧ You can, of course, lift the meat from the pan with tongs rather than using the string as a handle, but do not pierce it with a fork.

❧ Substitute drained white bottled horseradish for grated horseradish in the horseradish sauce, if necessary.

Roast Rack of Veal with Parsnip Purée and Chipotle Beurre Blanc ❧ Vincent Guerithault

SERVES 6

SERVES 6
PREPARATION TIME: ABOUT 30 MINUTES
COOKING TIME: ABOUT 1 HOUR AND 30 MINUTES

RACK OF VEAL:

1 four-pound rack of veal

Salt and freshly ground black pepper to taste

1 tablespoon extra-virgin olive oil

Parsnip Purée (see page 247)

Chipotle Beurre Blanc (see page 282)

■ Special Equipment: steamer; meat thermometer or instant-read thermometer; double boiler

Rack of veal is a truly spectacular cut of meat, perfect for special occasions. The beurre blanc adds a bit of smoky taste and a tinge of amber color to the mellow, juicy meat.

1 Preheat the oven to 350 degrees F. Assemble *mise en place* trays for this recipe (see page 6).

2 Wipe the veal rack with a paper towel and season with salt and pepper to taste.

3 In an ovenproof skillet or roasting pan, heat the oil over medium-high heat until almost smoking. Add the veal and sear the meat on all sides for 4 to 6 minutes, or until well browned.

4 Roast the veal, rib side down, for 1½ hours, or until a meat thermometer or instant-read thermometer registers 150 degrees F. when inserted into the center. Transfer to a cutting board, cover loosely with aluminum foil and allow to rest for 15 minutes before slicing.

5 Meanwhile, make the parsnip purée and the chipotle beurre blanc.

6 Slice the veal into chops. Place a mound of parsnip purée in the center of each warm dinner plate. Arrange one or two chops on top. Spoon the Chipotle Beurre Blanc over the meat. Serve immediately.

❧ Because it usually has to be special-ordered from the butcher, replace the rack of veal with a more economical rolled veal roast weighing about 3½ pounds, if you prefer.

Lamb Tagine with Almonds, Dates, and Toasted Bulgur ❧ Matthew Kenney

SERVES 6

PREPARATION TIME: ABOUT 1 HOUR

COOKING TIME: ABOUT 2 HOURS

¼ cup olive oil

1½ pounds boneless lamb shoulder, cut into ¾-inch cubes

1 large onion, halved and sliced

1½ cups sliced carrots

¾ cup minced shallots

3 cloves garlic, minced

One 1-inch piece fresh ginger, peeled and minced

½ teaspoon saffron threads

1 tablespoon freshly ground toasted cumin seeds

1 tablespoon paprika

1 tablespoon ground cinnamon

1 teaspoon ground cardamom

¼ teaspoon ground allspice

About 3 cups Chicken Stock (see page 15)

¾ cup honey

¼ to ½ cup sliced pitted dates

Salt and freshly ground black pepper to taste

Cayenne pepper to taste

¼ cup plus 2 tablespoons chopped fresh flat-leaf parsley

Toasted Bulgur (see page 249)

1 cup chopped toasted almonds

A tagine is a slowly simmered stew that is traditionally cooked in a wide earthenware dish with a conical lid (also called a tagine). This particular stew brings Morocco right into your kitchen by relying on the exotic dimension of sweet almonds, dates, and honey. It could also be served with couscous in place of bulgur.

---

1 Assemble *mise en place* trays for this recipe (see page 6).

2 In a large Dutch oven, heat the oil over medium heat. Add the lamb and sear for about 5 minutes, or until well browned on all sides. Transfer to paper towels to drain.

3 Add the onions, carrots, shallots, garlic, and ginger to the Dutch oven and stir to combine. Add the saffron, cumin, paprika, cinnamon, cardamom, and allspice and cook, stirring occasionally, for about 10 minutes, or until the vegetables soften.

4 Return the lamb to the Dutch oven, stir, and add just enough stock to barely cover the lamb. Reduce the heat, cover, and simmer gently for about 1 hour, or until the lamb is fork-tender and the liquid has reduced to a sauce-like consistency. Do not allow to boil.

5 Stir in the honey and ¼ cup dates. Taste for sweetness and add up to ¼ cup more dates if desired. Season to taste with salt and pepper and cayenne. Stir in ¼ cup of the parsley.

6 Mound the bulgur in the center of 6 plates. Spoon the tagine over the top and garnish with the almonds and the remaining 2 tablespoons parsley. Serve immediately.

NOTE: You can add chopped celery, potatoes, turnips, or other firm vegetables as well as diced prunes to the tagine.

Fillet of Beef in the Modena Manner ～ Marta Pulini

SERVES 6

PREPARATION TIME: ABOUT 15 MINUTES

COOKING TIME: ABOUT 30 MINUTES

2 pounds beef tenderloin, trimmed of all fat

1 bunch fresh sage

1 bunch fresh thyme

4 sprigs fresh rosemary

2 cloves garlic, peeled

Salt and freshly ground black pepper to taste

2 tablespoons unsalted butter

2 tablespoons olive oil

3 tablespoons fine-quality balsamic vinegar

This is an easy-to-prepare dinner party main course. Use the absolute best Aceto Balsamico Tradizionale Di Modena (balsamic vinegar) to finish, for the authentic taste.

1 Preheat the oven to 400 degrees F. Assemble *mise en place* trays for this recipe (see page 6).

2 Using a very sharp knife, butterfly the tenderloin by cutting it almost in half down its entire length. Open out and flatten slightly.

3 Chop all the herbs and the garlic very fine and mix together. Add salt and pepper to taste and chop again to mix. Sprinkle half the mixture over the cut side of the meat. Reshape the fillet and, using kitchen twine, tie in 6 or 8 places along the length. Rub the outside with the remaining herb mixture.

4 In a large roasting pan, melt the butter with the olive oil over medium-high heat. Add the meat and sear until well browned on all sides. Transfer to the oven and roast for 12 minutes. Turn the meat and cook for 12 minutes more for rare meat; for medium-rare meat, cook for 18 minutes on each side. Remove from the oven and allow to rest for a few minutes.

5 Slice the meat crosswise into ¼-inch slices, discarding the twine, and fan out on a warm serving platter. Drizzle with the balsamic vinegar and serve immediately.

Chipotle Lamb Chops with Creamed Corn Pudding and Three Tomato Salsas ∾ Stephan Pyles

SERVES 6

PREPARATION TIME: ABOUT 1 HOUR

COOKING TIME: ABOUT 1 HOUR

MARINATING TIME (SALSAS ONLY): ABOUT 30 MINUTES

---

3 tablespoons olive oil

½ cup chopped Vidalia or other sweet onion

¼ cup chopped carrot

2 tablespoons chopped celery

2 sprigs fresh thyme or ¾ teaspoon dried thyme

3 sprigs fresh rosemary

½ cup dry red wine

¾ cup veal or beef stock (see page 16)

2 teaspoons chipotle chile purée

2 tablespoons unsalted butter

Salt to taste

12 one-inch-thick rib lamp chops

Creamed Corn Pudding (see page 251)

Tomatillo Salsa (see page 287)

Red Tomato Salsa (see page 287)

Yellow Tomato Salsa (see page 283)

These salsas do very well indeed made the morning before serving and refrigerated. Remember that they must be assembled at least 30 minutes before serving to give the flavors time to meld. If time or energy is a factor, make only one or two salsas, although the effect will not be quite as impressive.

---

1 Prepare a medium-hot fire in charcoal or gas grill or preheat the broiler. If using a grill, toss a handful of soaked aromatic wood chips on the coals about 5 minutes before grilling the lamb chops. Assemble *mise en place* trays for this recipes (see page 6).

2 Meanwhile, in a medium-sized saucepan, heat 2 tablespoons of the oil over medium heat. Add the onion, carrot, and celery and sauté for 4 to 5 minutes, until the vegetables soften a little. Add the thyme and 1 sprig of the rosemary and sauté for 1 minute more. Add the wine and cook for 10 minutes, or until the liquid is reduced to about 2 tablespoons. Lower the heat and add the stock and chile purée. Simmer for 3 minutes. Whisk in the butter, a tablespoon at a time, and season to taste with salt.

3 Strain the sauce through a fine sieve into the top half of a double boiler. Place over simmering water and keep warm until ready to serve.

4 Brush the lamb chops with the remaining 1 tablespoon of oil. Season to taste with salt. Toss the remaining 2 sprigs of rosemary on the charcoal. (If using a broiler, save the rosemary for another use.) Grill the chops for about 6 to 8 minutes for medium rare, turning once.

5 Place a generous amount of Creamed Corn Pudding in the center of warm serving plates. Place 2 lamb chops at the edge of the pudding, crossing the bones over each other. Drizzle the warm sauce over the chops. Garnish

each plate with a heaped tablespoon of each salsa. Pass extra salsa on the side.

___

❧ Whether grilling or broiling, you may want to dip rosemary sprigs in a little olive oil and brush lamb chops several times during cooking.

Patria Pork over Boniato Purée with Black Bean Broth ❧ Douglas Rodriguez

2½ pounds pork tenderloin, trimmed of all fat

¼ cup white vinegar

3 bay leaves

½ cup chopped white onions

¾ cup chopped fresh cilantro

2 tablespoons fresh thyme leaves

2 tablespoons fresh oregano leaves

8 cloves garlic

1 tablespoon cumin seeds

2 tablespoons coarse salt

Freshly ground black pepper to taste

3 cups water

2 tablespoons olive oil

8 cachucha chiles or other hot green chiles, or to taste, seeded and finely diced

½ cup fresh lime juice (about 4 limes)

Black Bean Broth (recipe follows)

Boniato Purée (recipe follows)

The flavors, colors, and texture of this dish perfectly illustrate Doug's cooking, which is zesty, slightly offbeat, and very delicious. Doug uses the more traditional Latin boneless pork butt for this recipe, but we chose pork tenderloin to create a lighter version.

___

1 Assemble *mise en place* trays for this recipe (see page 6).

2 Put the pork in a nonreactive baking pan large enough to hold it comfortably. In a blender, combine the vinegar, bay leaves, onions, ¼ cup of the cilantro, the thyme, oregano, garlic, cumin, coarse salt, and pepper to taste. With the motor running, slowly add the water and blend to a purée. Pour over the pork, cover, and refrigerate for at least 12 hours, turning occasionally.

3 Preheat the oven to 300 degrees F.

4 Put the pan holding the pork and marinade into the oven and roast, covered, for about 2½ hours, or until the pork is very well done and almost falling apart. Cool in the liquid for about 1 hour. Lift the pork from the pan and, using 2 forks, pull apart into shreds.

5 In a large heavy sauté pan, heat the oil over medium-high heat. Add the shredded pork, chiles, and the

remaining ½ cup chopped cilantro and sauté for about 10 minutes, or until the meat is crispy. Add the lime juice, toss, and remove from the heat.

6 Place a scoop of Boniato Purée in the center of each plate, arrange some pork on top, and ladle the Black Bean Broth all around. Serve immediately.

BLACK BEAN BROTH

MAKES ABOUT 2 CUPS
FAT PER 2½-TABLESPOON SERVING: 0.3 GRAM
SATURATED FAT: 0
CALORIES PER SERVING: 62.5
CALORIES FROM FAT: 4%

---

1 pound dried black beans, rinsed and picked clean

2 bay leaves

1 teaspoon ground cumin

1 teaspoon chopped fresh oregano

8 cups cold water

6 red bell peppers, cored, seeded, and quartered

2 white onions, quartered

20 cloves garlic

■ Special Equipment: Juice extractor

1 In a large saucepan, combine the beans, bay leaves, cumin, oregano, and water and bring to a boil over high heat. Reduce the heat and simmer for about 2 hours, or until the beans soften.

2 Process the bell peppers, onions, and garlic in a juice extractor and add the extracted juice to the beans, discarding the pulp. Cook the beans for an additional 30 minutes, or until tender.

3 Strain the cooking liquid through a fine sieve into a saucepan. (Reserve the beans for another use.) Bring the liquid to a boil over high heat, reduce the heat, and simmer for about 20 minutes, or until reduced to 2 cups. Serve hot.

BONIATO PURÉE

MAKES ABOUT 6 CUPS
FAT PER 1-CUP SERVING: 0.6 GRAM
SATURATED FAT: 0.2 GRAM
CALORIES PER SERVING: 176
CALORIES FROM FAT: 3%

---

1 In a large saucepan, combine the boniato, milk, and water and bring to a boil over high heat. Reduce the heat and simmer for about 1 hour, or until the boniato is very tender when pierced with a fork. Drain, reserving the cooking liquid.

1½ pounds boniato, peeled and diced

4 cups skim milk

2 cups water

Salt to taste

2 Using a potato masher, mash the boniato, adding just enough of the reserved liquid to keep it moist. Season to taste with salt and serve hot.

NOTE: The purée can be made up to 2 days ahead, covered, and refrigerated. Reheat in a microwave or in the top half of a double boiler over boiling water.

❧ Boniato, also called Cuban sweet potato, is sold in Latin and Asian markets.

Lamb Stew with Fall Fruits and Vegetables ❧ Alain Sailhac

SERVES 6

PREPARATION TIME: ABOUT 2 HOURS

COOKING TIME: ABOUT 4 HOURS AND 30 MINUTES

SOAKING TIME (BEANS ONLY): AT LEAST 6 HOURS

¼ pound dried black beans, soaked in cold water for 6 hours

1 tablespoon unsalted butter

2 firm tart apples, such as Jonathan or McIntosh, peeled, cored, and sliced

1 tablespoon all-purpose flour

7 cups cold water

Juice of 1 lemon

Salt

1 lemon, halved

4½-pound artichokes

4 red-skinned potatoes (about 1 pound)

Complex flavors combine to make a beautiful and very aromatic fall casserole. The lamb could be served alone, with just its delicious sauce, accompanied by rice or noodles, a crisp salad, and a bottle of young red wine.

1 Assemble *mise en place* trays for this recipe (see page 6).

2 Drain the beans and place in a large saucepan with enough fresh cold water to cover by at least 2 inches. Bring to boil over high heat, reduce the heat, and simmer for 1½ hours, or until soft.

3 Meanwhile, in a medium-sized sauté pan, melt the butter over medium heat. Add the apples and sauté for 6 to 8 minutes, until golden brown. Remove from the heat.

4 Drain the beans, reserving ½ cup of the cooking liquid. In a blender or a food processor fitted with the metal blade, combine the beans, sautéed apples, and reserved bean-cooking liquid. Blend for about 1 minute, until smooth. (Bits of black bean will still be visible.) Transfer to a bowl and set aside.

¼ cup olive oil

4 pounds boneless stewing lamb, trimmed and cut into 2-inch cubes

2 carrots, peeled and diced

2 ribs celery, diced

3 large onions, chopped

1 whole bulb garlic, cloves separated, peeled, and chopped

Freshly ground black pepper to taste

1 cup Lamb Stock (see page 16), or water

8 ounces button mushrooms, wiped clean, trimmed, and quartered

8 ounces pleurotte or oyster mushrooms, wiped clean, trimmed, and halved

1 cup diced, peeled, and seeded tomatoes

1 tablespoon minced fresh flat-leaf parsley

1 teaspoon minced fresh thyme

1 teaspoon minced fresh oregano

5 In a large saucepan, beat together the flour and 1 cup of the water. Stir in 3 more cups of water, the lemon juice, and 1½ teaspoons of salt. Bring to a boil over medium-high heat. Immediately remove from the heat and set aside to cool for about 15 minutes.(This mixture, known as a blanc, will be used to cook the artichokes and insure that they will not discolor.)

6 Cut the stem off 1 of the artichokes. Bend the leaves back and snap them off, leaving the edible leaf bottoms attached to the base. Continue to remove the leaves until you reach the soft crown of leaves in the center. Cut off this core of leaves. Using a small, sharp knife, trim the base evenly to remove all the greenish parts and create a perfect round. To keep the artichoke from discoloring, rub the cut surfaces frequently with the halved lemon as you work. Drop the artichoke into the blanc, and repeat with the remaining artichokes. If the artichokes are not completely covered, add additional water, as necessary.

7 When all the artichokes are trimmed, put the pan over medium-high heat and bring to a boil. Reduce the heat and simmer for 30 minutes, or until the artichoke bottoms are tender when pierced with a knife.

8 Drain the artichokes well and rinse under cold running water. Pat dry with paper towels. Scoop out the chokes (fuzzy interior) with a teaspoon and discard. Pat dry. Cut the artichoke bottoms into quarters and set aside.

9 Cut the potatoes lengthwise. Using a very sharp knife, trim the potatoes into perfectly uniform ovals (to resemble large olives), by turning them in your fingers as you cut away the flesh.

10 Put the potatoes in a medium-sized saucepan, with enough cold water to cover. Add salt to taste and a few drops of lemon juice. Cover and bring to a boil over medium-high heat. Reduce the heat and simmer for 8 to 10 minutes, or until just tender. Drain and set aside.

11 In a very large, deep sauté pan or Dutch oven, heat 1 tablespoon of the olive oil over medium-high heat. Sauté the meat, in 2 or 3 batches, for about 10 minutes, until browned. Do not crowd the pan. Spoon off liquid as it accumulates in the pan. When all the meat is browned, set the lamb aside.

13 Pour off the fat in the pan. Add 1 cup of water and deglaze over medium heat, stirring to scrape up any brown bits sticking to the bottom. Cook for 8 to 10 minutes, stirring, until most of the liquid has evaporated. Return the lamb to the pan.

14 Heat 1 tablespoon of the olive oil in a medium-sized sauté pan over medium-high heat. Add the carrots, celery, and onions and sauté for 10 to 12 minutes, until browned. Add the chopped garlic and sauté for 1 minute longer.

15 Add the stock and 2 more cups of water to the meat, increase the heat, and bring to a boil. Add the sautéed vegetables, reduce the heat to low, cover, and simmer for 1½ hours, or until the lamb is very tender.

16 Skim the fat from the top of the stew. Using a slotted spoon, transfer the meat to a platter and set aside.

17 Strain the cooking liquid and vegetables through a fine sieve into a large saucepan, pushing against the solids to extract all the liquid. Discard the solids. Stir in the bean and apple purée. Add the lamb and keep warm over very low heat.

18 Meanwhile, in a medium-sized saucepan, heat the remaining 2 tablespoons of olive oil over medium heat. Add the mushrooms and sauté for 8 minutes, or until tender. Stir in the artichokes and potatoes to just heat through. Check the seasonings.

19 Spoon the lamb with the sauce into the center of a serving platter. Arrange the vegetable mixture around it. Sprinkle the tomatoes over the vegetables. Sprinkle with the minced parsley, thyme, and oregano, and serve immediately.

London Broil with Lime-Marinated Red Onions and Pineapple Ketchup ❧ Chris Schlesinger

SERVES 6

PREPARATION TIME: ABOUT 15 MINUTES

MARINATING TIME (ONIONS ONLY): AT LEAST 2 HOURS

COOKING TIME: ABOUT 20 MINUTES

FAT PER SERVING: 10.2 GRAMS

SATURATED FAT: 3.5 GRAMS

CALORIES PER SERVING: 288

CALORIES FROM FAT: 33%

3 red onions, very thinly sliced

¼ cup plus 2 tablespoon fresh lime juice (about 3 limes)

Tabasco sauce to taste

2 tablespoons coarse salt

¼ cup coarsely cracked black pepper

1½ pounds London broil (top round), about 1 inch thick

¼ cup plus 2 tablespoons all-purpose flour

Pineapple Ketchup (see page 268)

Onions marinated as they are here would highlight any grilled meat or poultry just as deliciously as they do this stove-top London broil. They could also serve as a fat-free garnish on a sandwich or burger.

1 Assemble *mise en place* trays for this recipe (see page 6).

2 In a nonreactive container, combine the onions, lime juice, and Tabasco. Cover and refrigerate, tossing occasionally, for at least 2 hours or up to 8 hours.

3 Rub the coarse salt and pepper into the meat and sprinkle 3 tablespoons flour over each side. Heat a dry large heavy nonstick skillet over high heat. Add the meat and sear for about 7 minutes per side for rare. Slice on the diagonal into ¼-inch-thick slices. Serve immediately, garnished with the marinated onions and pineapple ketchup.

❧ For meat that is more well done, sear until it is almost the degree of doneness you prefer. Remove the meat from pan and allow to rest for 2 minutes before cutting. The resting time allows the meat to finish cooking.

Grilled Beef Tenderloin with Tomatillo Sauce and Blue Corn Crêpes ❧ Jimmy Schmidt

SERVES 6

PREPARATION TIME: ABOUT 25 MINUTES

COOKING TIME: ABOUT 1 HOUR AND 30 MINUTES

RESTING TIME (CRÊPE BATTER ONLY):
30 MINUTES

---

8 to 10 tomatillos, husked, washed, and diced

1 cup heavy cream

1 tablespoon unsalted butter

2 cups diced red onions

2 cups red wine

2 cups Beef Stock (see page 16)

Salt to taste

12 three-ounce beef tenderloin steaks (filet mignon)

2 tablespoons ground cumin

½ cup diced, roasted red bell peppers (see page 12)

½ cup diced chipotle chiles in adobo sauce (see Glossary)

2 tablespoons snipped chives

2 tablespoons chopped, fresh cilantro

12 Blue Corn Crêpes (recipe follows)

12 sprigs fresh cilantro

Jimmy Schmidt told us that this dish was inspired by his love of fajitas, which he felt were too much like peasant food to serve in a sophisticated Southwestern restaurant. Surely this interpretation of the traditional folk dish will shine at the most elegant dinner party.

---

1 Assemble *mise en place* trays for this recipe (see page 6).

2 In a small saucepan, combine ½ cup of the diced tomatillos and the cream. Bring to a simmer over medium heat and cook for about 10 minutes, or until the mixture is thick enough to coat the back of a spoon. Strain through a fine sieve into a small bowl, pressing on the solids. Discard the solids. Set aside.

3 In a saucepan, melt the butter over medium heat. Add the onions and sauté for about 5 minutes, or until translucent. Add the red wine and cook for about 20 minutes, or until the wine has completely evaporated. Transfer the mixture to a blender or food processor fitted with the metal blade. Blend or process until puréed. Strain through a fine sieve into a small bowl, pressing on the solids. Discard the solids. Set aside.

4 Prepare a charcoal or gas grill or preheat the broiler.

5 Meanwhile, in a large saucepan, bring the stock to a simmer over high heat. Reduce the heat and simmer for about 10 minutes, or until reduced to 1 cup. Add the tomatillo cream and red onion purée. Season to taste with salt. Pour into the top half of a double boiler set over hot water, cover and and keep warm.

6 Rub the beef steaks with the cumin. Grill the beef, turning once, for 4 to 5 minutes for rare. Cook for an additional 2 minutes for medium and an additional 4 to 6 minutes for well done.

7 Stir the remaining diced tomatillos, the roasted peppers, chipotles, chives, and chopped cilantro into the sauce. Place a warm crêpe in the center of each warm dinner plate. Place 2 fillets, overlapping slightly, on the lower half of each crêpe. Spoon a little sauce over the top, then fold the crêpe over the meat. Garnish with the sprigs of cilantro and serve immediately.

Blue Corn Crêpes

MAKES 16 CRÊPES

½ cup all-purpose flour

6 large eggs, beaten

1 cup stone-ground blue cornmeal

⅔ cup milk

1 teaspoon salt

Unsalted butter, for cooking the crêpes

■ Special Equipment: nonstick 6-inch crêpe pan

1 In a medium-sized bowl, beat the flour and eggs together.

2 In another bowl, beat the cornmeal and milk together. When well combined, whisk into the flour and egg mixture, and stir in the salt. Cover and let the batter rest for 30 minutes.

3 In a 6-inch, nonstick crêpe pan or skillet, melt about ¼ teaspoon of butter over medium-high heat. Using a 1-ounce ladle (⅛ cup measuring cup), add just enough crêpe batter to cover the bottom of the pan, tilting it to allow the batter to spread evenly. Cook for about 1 minute, or until lightly browned. Flip the crêpe and cook the other side for 1 minute.

4 Transfer the crêpe to a piece of wax paper. Continue to make the crêpes, adding half-teaspoons of butter to the pan as needed. Layer the cooked crêpes between wax paper and keep warm.

The Best Leg of Lamb with Baba Ghanoosh ❧ Nancy Silverton and Mark Peel

SERVES 6

PREPARATION TIME: ABOUT 1 HOUR

MARINATING TIME: AT LEAST 4 HOURS

COOKING TIME: ABOUT 1 HOUR AND 10 MINUTES

FAT PER SERVING: 30 GRAMS

SATURATED FAT: 9.7 GRAMS

CALORIES PER SERVING: 703

CALORIES FROM FAT: 39%

One 4½-pound leg of lamb, trimmed of excess fat

3 large cloves garlic, thinly sliced

About 1 tablespoon olive oil

Coarse salt and freshly ground black pepper to taste

6 ounces fresh rosemary (about 8 bunches)

Baba Ghanoosh (see page 254)

Nancy and Mark call for an enormous bouquet of rosemary, an herb traditionally served with lamb for good reason. Even if the rosemary didn't impart a wonderful flavor to the meat, the intoxicating aroma coming from the oven would be reason enough to use it in quantity. Have the butcher remove the small bone from the leg of lamb to make slicing it easier. Serve smaller portions of lamb to reduce calories and fat amounts.

---

1 Assemble *mise en place* trays for this recipe (see page 6).

2 Make narrow 1-inch-deep slits all over the lamb and insert the garlic slices in them. Rub the lamb all over with olive oil and coat heavily with coarse salt and pepper. Wrap tightly in plastic wrap and refrigerate for at least 4 hours, or overnight.

3 Preheat the oven to 500 degrees F.

4 Heat an oven-proof skillet or heavy saucepan large enough to hold the lamb comfortably over high heat. Add the lamb and brown on all sides. Remove to a platter and pour off all but 1 tablespoon of fat from the pan. Cover the bottom of the pan with a bed of rosemary (using half to two thirds of the rosemary) and place the lamb on top. Cover the lamb with the rest of the rosemary.

5 Roast for 20 minutes, then reduce the oven temperature to 375 degrees F and roast for about 40 minutes longer, or until the lamb is medium-rare.

6 Take the entire pan outdoors and carefully ignite the rosemary on top of the lamb. Allow it to burn itself out; use a tight-fitting lid to extinguish the flames if necessary. Brush off the woody stems and let the meat rest for 10 to 15 minutes.

7 Cut the lamb into thin slices. Spread the Baba Ghanoosh on a serving platter and lay the lamb slices on top. Pour any accumulated lamb juices over all and serve immediately.

NOTE: If you live in an apartment or the weather is inclement, omit flaming the rosemary. But if possible, give it a try, as the charred rosemary imparts a great flavor to the lamb.

Stuffed Breast of Veal ❧ André Soltner

SERVES 6

PREPARATION TIME: ABOUT 45 MINUTES

COOKING TIME: ABOUT 2 HOURS AND 30 MINUTES

STUFFING:

1 tablespoon unsalted butter

1 small onion, sliced

¾ cup milk

2 cups cubes of crustless, home-style white bread

8 ounces boneless stewing veal, cut into 1-inch cubes (from neck or shoulder)

8 ounces pork butt, cut into 1-inch cubes

2 medium eggs

1 tablespoon chopped fresh parsley

2 tablespoons Cognac

Salt and freshly ground black pepper to taste

From Chef Soltner: "In the small town of Thann, which is the town I come from in Alsace, every year there is a Poitrine de Veau Festival. The festival is held on a weekend in late spring when the weather is warm. The whole town comes and people from the region all around.

"A giant tent is set up. There is music and dancing, which goes on long into the night. The town orders huge amounts of poitrine de veau, and it is sold by the slice. All the money goes to the town—for the fire department, or for something like that. Of course, with all that poitrine de veau, the people drink a large amount of cold beer, and also a great deal of Alsatian white wine. Everyone has a good time. Some people say that this dish was brought to Alsace by the Romans. It could be. But the festival is a local invention."

1 Assemble *mise en place* trays for this recipe (see page 6).

2 To make the stuffing, in a large sauté pan, melt the butter over medium heat. Add the onion and sauté for about 5 minutes, until softened. Remove from the heat and set aside.

3 In a medium-sized saucepan, warm the milk over low

VEAL:

3 pounds boned breast of veal, trimmed of fat

Salt and freshly ground black pepper

1 tablespoon unsalted butter

1 tablespoon peanut oil

1 cup chopped carrots

1 cup diced onions

½ cup diced celery

1 cup dry white wine

½ cup water

■ Special Equipment: Trussing needle and kitchen twine

heat. Remove from the heat, and add the bread cubes, and soak for about 3 minutes.

4 Remove the bread from the milk and squeeze it gently to remove most, but not all, of the milk. Put the cubes in a large bowl and stir in the onions.

5 Process the cubed veal and pork, in batches, in a food processor fitted with a metal blade or a blender until just chopped. Do not overprocess. Add the chopped meat to the bread and onions and stir to combine. Stir in the eggs, parsley, and Cognac and season to taste with salt and pepper.

6 Preheat the oven to 325 degrees F.

7 To prepare the veal, cut a pocket in the side of the breast of veal, being careful not to cut all the way through the meat. Carefully fill the pocket with the stuffing, making sure the pocket is well packed. Using a trussing needle and kitchen twine, sew the pocket closed. Generously season the stuffed breast all over with salt and pepper.

8 In a roasting pan, heat the butter and oil over medium heat. Add the meat and sear for about 12 minutes, or until well browned on all sides. Add the carrots, onions, and celery. Season to taste with salt and pepper.

9 Roast for 1 hour, turning the meat once during roasting, and basting occasionally with the pan juices.

10 Reduce the oven temperature to 300 degrees F. and add the wine and water to the roasting pan. Cover the meat with a sheet of buttered parchment paper or a loose lid of buttered aluminum foil and roast for about 1 hour and 15 minutes longer, basting frequently.

11 Remove the pan from the oven and transfer the meat to a cutting board. Cover loosely with aluminum foil and allow to rest for 15 minutes.

12 Skim the fat from the pan juices. Taste and adjust the seasoning with salt and pepper, if necessary.

13 Remove the string from the meat and discard. Cut the meat into ½-inch-thick slices. Arrange on a serving platter and spoon the pan juices around the meat. Serve immediately.

❧ Sewing up a stuffed breast of veal is a simple task. Trussing needles, which resemble oversized sewing needles, are sold in kitchenware shops. Use them as you would any needle, but your stitches need only be tidy enough to hold the filling in place. They are removed after the veal is cooked.

❧ Breast of veal is not an everyday item in the butcher shop, and you will probably have to special order it a few days before the party. Ask the butcher to remove the bone (it should weigh about 3 pounds after boning) and, if you like, to cut the pocket for you.

❧ A small, sharp knife is the best tool for making the pocket in the veal. Insert the blade and cut a slit along the side of the meat. Do not let the knife cut all the way through the meat. Then insert the blade in the slit again and wiggle it up and down to open the pocket a little.

❧ This stuffing would be good with chicken, turkey, and boned pork too.

❧ If the stuffing is made earlier in the day, keep it refrigerated. Do not stuff the veal until ready to cook, as bacteria can grow.

Braised Lamb Shanks with White Bean Purée ❧ Tom Valenti

SERVES 6

PREPARATION TIME: ABOUT 30 MINUTES

SOAKING TIME (BEANS ONLY): 8 HOURS

COOKING TIME: ABOUT 2 HOURS AND 40 MINUTES

This is Chef Tom Valenti's best-known signature dish and I guarantee it deserves its starring role on his menu. It is a terrific do-ahead winter meal!

---

1 Assemble *mise en place* trays for this recipe (see page 6).

2 Preheat the oven to 325 degrees F.

6 lamb shanks

Salt and freshly ground black pepper to taste

½ cup olive oil

8 ribs celery, sliced

2 large carrots, sliced

1 large onion, diced

5 cloves garlic, minced

2 cups red wine

2 cups Veal Stock (see page 16)

Two 32-ounce cans Italian plum tomatoes, drained and crushed

6 anchovy fillets

20 black or green peppercorns

2 bay leaves

White Bean Purée (see page 254)

3 Season the shanks with salt and pepper to taste. In a large sauté pan, heat the olive oil over medium heat. Add the shanks and sear for about 6 minutes, or until browned on all sides. Transfer to a large flame-proof casserole or roasting pan.

4 In the same pan, sauté the celery, carrots, onions, and garlic over medium heat for 30 seconds, taking care not to burn any particles that have stuck to the bottom of the pan. Add 1 cup of the wine and stir to deglaze the pan. Scrape the mixture over the shanks.

5 Add the veal stock, the remaining 1 cup wine, the tomatoes, anchovies, peppercorns and bay leaves to the casserole. The shanks should be almost covered with liquid; if necessary, add some water. Stir to combine. Bring to a boil over medium-high heat, remove from the heat, and cover tightly.

6 Bake for 2½ hours, or until the meat is almost falling off the bone. Using tongs or a slotted spoon, remove the shanks and set aside, covered with aluminum foil to keep warm. Strain the cooking liquid through a fine sieve into a medium-sized saucepan and simmer for about 5 minutes over medium heat, or until reduced and thickened slightly.

7 Place an equal portion of bean purée on each plate. Place a shank alongside and spoon some sauce over the top. Pass the remaining sauce on the side.

NOTE: You can prepare the shanks ahead of time, up to the point of straining off the liquid. Reheat them in a 350-degree-F oven for about 20 minutes and complete the recipe as instructed.

Ten-Chile Chili ❧ Brendan Walsh

SERVES 12

PREPARATION TIME: ABOUT 45 MINUTES

COOKING TIME: ABOUT 7 HOURS

---

3 pounds Spanish onions, chopped

¾ pound slab bacon, diced

5 pounds lean beef chuck, trimmed and cut into ¼-inch by 1½-inch strips

¾ cup diced celery

½ cup chopped dried mulato chiles

½ cup chopped dried pasilla chiles

½ cup chopped dried ancho chiles

5 dried chiles pequín

1 cup ancho chile powder (see page 12)

⅓ cup ground toasted coriander seeds (see page 13)

⅓ cup ground cumin seeds

1 tablespoon plus 2 teaspoons cayenne pepper

5 bay leaves

4 cups peeled, seeded, and chopped ripe plum tomatoes

2 cups Beef or Chicken Stock (see pages 16 and 15)

½ cup tequila, such as Cuervo Gold

¼ cup seeded, minced serrano chiles

¼ cup seeded, minced jalapeño chiles

3½ ounces canned chipotle chiles in adobo (see Glossary), chopped (half of a seven-ounce can)

*B*rendan's chili calls for 10 chiles, with each one imparting its own special aromatic scent to the final dish. The chef says that this is one instance when more is better! I agree. However, if you cannot find all of the chiles, don't panic. Simply up the quantity of those you can find. The dish will still taste very good. This recipe serves at least 12 hungry people, so it is the perfect chili to make when you are expecting a crowd.

---

1 Assemble *mise en place* trays for this recipe (see page 6).

2 In a large Dutch oven, cook the bacon, stirring frequently, over medium-high heat for 5 minutes, or until the fat is rendered. Using a slotted spoon, remove the bacon and drain on paper towels. Drain off all but 2 to 3 tablespoons of bacon fat.

3 Add a quarter of the beef to the pot and cook, stirring, for 2 to 3 minutes. Remove the meat and drain on paper towels. Repeat with the remaining meat, cooking in batches.

4 When all the meat has been browned, add the onions to the pot. Lower the heat and cook, stirring frequently, for 15 to 20 minutes, or until caramelized. Add the celery and cook for 4 to 5 minutes, or until tender.

5 Return the meat to the pot. Stir in the chopped dried chiles, chiles pequín, chile powder, ground coriander, ground cumin, cayenne, and bay leaves. Add the tomatoes, stock, and tequila and stir to blend. Stir in the minced chiles, chipotle chiles, ham hock, rosemary, sage, and oregano. Raise the heat and bring to a simmer. Reduce the heat to medium-low and cook, partially covered, for 6 hours, stirring occasionally, or until the chili

1 smoked ham hock
1 sprig fresh rosemary
1 sprig fresh sage
1 sprig fresh oregano
Salt to taste

GARNISH:

1 tablespoon olive oil
1 cup seeded, julienned red bell peppers
1 cup seeded, julienned yellow bell peppers
1 cup seeded, julienned poblano chiles
1 cup seeded, julienned Anaheim chiles
1 jalapeño chile, seeded and julienned

- Special Equipment: large Dutch oven

is thick and the flavors are intensely blended. Taste and add salt, if necessary.

6 To prepare the garnish, about 20 minutes before the chili is ready, heat the olive oil in a large saucepan over medium-high heat. Add the julienned bell peppers and chiles and sauté for 4 to 5 minutes, or until just softened. Remove from the heat, cover to keep warm, and set aside.

7 To serve, remove the ham hock, bay leaves, and herb sprigs from the chili. Serve the chili in bowls, topped with a spoonful of julienned peppers. Serve the Cilantro Rice on the side.

Fresh tomatoes can be replaced with chopped, canned Italian plum tomatoes. The ham hock can be replaced with 1 smoked turkey leg.

Seared Marinated Breast of Chicken with Tomato and Basil — Lidia Bastianich

SERVES 6
PREPARATION TIME: ABOUT 40 MINUTES
COOKING TIME: ABOUT 25 MINUTES
MARINATING TIME: AT LEAST 8 HOURS

MARINADE AND CHICKEN:

½ cup olive oil
4 cloves garlic, crushed

Simple but full of flavor, this dish is a home cook's dream. The chicken can marinate overnight and the sauce can be made early in the day. It could be served over pasta for a less formal meal, or at room temperature for an easy summer lunch.

1 Assemble *mise en place* trays for the marinade and chicken (see page 6).

1 tablespoon minced fresh rosemary

1 tablespoon minced fresh sage

Salt and freshly ground black pepper to taste

2 pounds skinless, boneless chicken breasts, split and trimmed

SAUCE:

¼ cup olive oil

8 cloves garlic, crushed

1 pound ripe plum tomatoes, cored, peeled, seeded, and thinly sliced, juices reserved

Red pepper flakes to taste

Salt and freshly ground black pepper to taste

½ cup shredded fresh basil leaves

2 To make the marinade, in a small bowl, combine the olive oil, garlic, rosemary, sage, and salt and pepper to taste.

3 Slice the chicken breasts on the diagonal into thirds. Using a large knife or cleaver, lightly pound each piece to flatten slightly. Place in a shallow glass or ceramic dish. Pour the marinade over the chicken, cover, and refrigerate for at least 8 hours, turning occasionally.

4 Assemble the *mise en place* trays for the sauce (see page 6).

5 To make the sauce, in a medium-sized saucepan, heat 3 tablespoons of the olive oil over moderate heat. Add the garlic and sauté for about 4 minutes, or until lightly browned. Stir in the tomatoes with their juices, the red pepper flakes, and salt and pepper to taste. Simmer for 5 minutes. Stir in half of the basil leaves. Remove from the heat and cover to keep warm.

6 Heat a large sauté pan over medium-high heat until very hot. Drain the chicken, discarding the marinade. Add the chicken to the hot pan, without crowding, and sauté for 5 to 10 minutes, or until golden brown on both sides and just cooked through. (Cook the chicken in batches or in 2 pans if necessary.) Transfer to a large, warm serving platter.

7 Drizzle the remaining 1 tablespoon olive oil over the tomato sauce and pour over the chicken. Sprinkle the remaining basil over the top and serve.

Cornish Game Hens with Crumb and Sausage Stuffing ❧ James Beard

SERVES 6

PREPARATION TIME: ABOUT 15 MINUTES

COOKING TIME: ABOUT 1 HOUR AND 30 MINUTES

---

6 Rock Cornish game hens (about 1 pound each), rinsed and patted dry

½ cup unsalted butter

¼ cup sliced scallions

8 ounces bulk sausage meat

1 tablespoon chopped fresh tarragon

2 teaspoons salt, or to taste

1 teaspoon freshly ground black pepper, or to taste

4 cups fresh bread crumbs (see page 13)

¼ cup chopped fresh parsley

*I*ndividual game hens are a great alternative to the mammoth holiday turkey. They require a shorter cooking time and particularly appeal to those who want both white and dark meat. Serve this entrée with James' Beet and Carrot Purée (see page 240).

---

1 Preheat the oven to 400 degrees F. Assemble *mise en place* trays for this recipe (see page 6).

2 In a large sauté pan, melt the butter over medium-high heat. Add the scallions and sauté for 4 minutes, or until just limp. Stir in the sausage meat, tarragon, salt, and pepper. Cook for 8 to 10 minutes, or until the sausage begins to lose its pinkness. Add the bread crumbs and parsley and stir until well combined. Remove from the heat and let cool completely.

3 Place an equal portion of the stuffing into each of the hens. Truss the cavities closed (see Glossary) by sewing with kitchen twine, or secure them with skewers.

4 Place the stuffed hens on a rack in a large roasting pan, breast side up. Roast for 15 minutes. Turn hens over and baste for another 15 minutes with the accumulated juices.

5 Reduce the oven temperature to 350 degrees F. Turn the birds breast side up, baste again, and roast for about 45 minutes longer, or until just tender; do not overcook.

6 Remove the pan from oven and allow the hens to rest for 5 minutes before serving. Spoon the pan juices over the hens and serve on warm dinner plates.

❧ To test the hens for doneness, wiggle the legs and pierce the joint between the body and thigh with a sharp knife. If legs move freely and the juices run clear, the birds are ready.

❧ Do not stuff the birds until just before cooking. Harmful bacteria may develop in the stuffing as it sits in the uncooked bird.

Guinea Hen with Quince Purée and Chanterelles ~ David Bouley

SERVES 6

PREPARATION TIME: ABOUT 30 MINUTES

COOKING TIME: ABOUT 2 HOURS

---

2 pounds button mushrooms, wiped clean, trimmed, and chopped

2 quarts water

6 large quinces, peeled, quartered, and seeded

6 cups Chicken Stock (see page 15)

⅓ cup chopped celery

⅓ cup chopped carrot

⅓ cup chopped onion

1 sprig fresh thyme

1 bay leaf

⅛ teaspoon dried marjoram

Salt and freshly ground black pepper to taste

3 two-and-one-half-pound guinea hens

1 teaspoon walnut oil

2 pounds chanterelles, wiped clean, trimmed, and sliced

8 shallots, minced

¼ cup fresh tarragon leaves

1 roasted clove garlic (see page 20)

■ Special Equipment: chinois

Quinces are fall fruits, related to apples and pears, but they cannot be eaten raw. When cooked, they provide the perfect accent to many dishes. Look for firm, yellow-skinned fruit and store in a cool, dry place—but not the refrigerator. To capture the true essence of Chef Bouley's dish, buy chanterelles from Nova Scotia, if possible.

---

1 Assemble *mise en place* trays for this recipe (see page 6).

2 In a medium-sized saucepan, combine the button mushrooms and water over medium-high heat. Bring to a boil. Reduce the heat and simmer for about 45 minutes, or until the liquid has reduced to ½ cup. Strain into a bowl, pressing on the mushrooms. Discard the solids and reserve the liquid.

3 Meanwhile, in a medium-sized saucepan combine the quinces, chicken stock, celery, carrot, onion, thyme, bay leaf, and marjoram. Bring to a boil over medium-high heat. Reduce the heat and simmer for 25 to 30 minutes, until the quinces are very soft. Drain the liquid and reserve for another use. Discard the thyme and bay leaf. Pass the remaining solids through a chinois or other fine sieve into a small saucepan. Taste and adjust the seasoning with salt and pepper. Set aside.

4 Preheat the oven to 375 degrees F.

5 Generously season the guinea hens with salt and pepper. Put in a shallow pan and roast for about 45 minutes, or until cooked through and the juices run clear when the flesh is pricked with the tip of a sharp knife. Remove from the oven and let rest for 10 minutes before carving.

6 While the hens are roasting, heat the walnut oil in a large sauté pan over medium heat. Add the chanterelles,

shallots, and tarragon. Sauté for about 10 minutes, or until the vegetables are very soft. Push the roasted garlic pulp from the skin and add to the chanterelles. Add the reserved mushroom liquid and stir to combine. Remove from the heat and keep warm.

7 Place the quince purée over low heat just to warm through.

8 Using a boning knife, remove the breast halves from the hens. Slice each half, diagonally, into thin slices. Remove the legs with the thighs attached.

9 Spoon the warm quince purée into the centers of 6 warm dinner plates. Arrange a sliced breast half around one side of each serving of purée. Lay the legs on the other side. Arrange the chanterelle mixture on top of the breast meat, and drizzle some of the liquid from the chanterelles over all. Serve immediately.

❧ When buying walnut oil, purchase the smallest quantity possible, as it is expensive and it turns rancid very rapidly. A small amount of this flavorful oil adds a distinctive, nutty fragrance to vinaigrettes, baked goods containing walnuts, sautés, or sauces. Store tightly covered in the refrigerator. It usually does not keep for longer than 2 months.

❧ You can substitute small chickens, pheasants, or Rock Cornish game hens for guinea hens.

Chicken in Parchment with Thyme ❧ Antoine Bouterin

SERVES 6

PREPARATION TIME: ABOUT 15 MINUTES

COOKING TIME: ABOUT 25 MINUTES

---

6 skinless, boneless chicken breast halves, trimmed

1 cup chopped leeks, white parts only

½ cup diced celery

1 cup cored, peeled, seeded, and diced tomatoes

Grated zest of 1 lemon

3 cloves garlic, sliced

3 tablespoons chopped scallions

1 tablespoon minced fresh thyme

Salt and freshly ground black pepper to taste

24 to 30 fresh spinach leaves, washed, dried, stems removed

6 tablespoons dry white wine

This recipe calls for the chicken to be cooked in the oven, but you could also place the packets on a covered grill for perfect summertime entertaining.

---

1 Preheat oven to 400 degrees F. Assemble *mise en place* trays for this recipe (see page 6).

2 Cut 6 pieces of heavy-duty aluminum foil into rectangles approximately 18 x 20 inches.

3 Rinse the chicken and pat dry with paper towels. Using a cleaver or heavy knife, slightly flatten each breast half.

4 Combine the leeks and celery. Put about ¼ cup of the vegetables toward the bottom edge of each piece of foil. Lay a chicken breast on top, and put 4 to 5 spinach leaves on top of the chicken.

5 Combine the tomatoes, lemon zest, garlic, scallions, thyme, and salt and pepper to taste. Divide this mixture evenly among the packets, spooning it on top of the chicken. Sprinkle 1 tablespoon of the wine over each one.

6 Fold the top half of each sheet of foil over the chicken so that the edges meet like a book. Fold the bottom edges up to make a 1-inch fold. Fold the 1-inch closure in half, making a ½-inch fold, and fold over once more with a ½-inch fold. Fold the sides in the same way. You should have formed a packet, closed tightly around the ingredients. Place on a large baking sheet and bake for 20 to 25 minutes, or until the foil packages swell up. Serve in the packets, letting your guests slit open the foil at the table, and enjoy the fragrant aroma that steams out.

Roast Poussin with Green Olives, Preserved Lemon, and Garlic ❧ Terrance Brennan

SERVES 6

MARINATING TIME: 48 HOURS

PREPARATION TIME: ABOUT 25 MINUTES

COOKING TIME: ABOUT 20 MINUTES

---

6 poussin, backbones removed

1½ cups olive oil

1 tablespoon chopped garlic

1 tablespoon grated lemon zest

3 pinches of powdered saffron

40 roasted garlic cloves (see page 20), 10 peeled and 30 left unpeeled

1¼ cups Chicken Stock (see page 15)

2 tablespoons Dijon mustard

1½ cups pitted Picholine olives

Preserved Lemons (recipe follows), well drained

¼ cup chopped fresh cilantro

Salt and freshly ground black pepper to taste

▪ Special Equipment: Hand-held immersion blender (optional)

*T*his perfect marriage of flavors is a real crowd pleaser. The saffron provides a rather haunting flavor of exotic places and the preserved lemons add a refreshing zing.

---

1 Assemble *mise en place* trays for this recipe (see page 6).

2 Place the poussin in a glass baking dish large enough to hold them comfortably when laid out flat and add ½ cup of the olive oil, the chopped garlic, lemon zest, and saffron. Toss to coat, cover, and refrigerate for 2 days, turning occasionally.

3 Preheat the oven to 500 degrees F.

4 Drain the excess oil from the poussin and place in a roasting pan, skin side up. Bake for about 20 minutes, or until the poussin are just cooked and the skin is crisp.

5 Meanwhile, in a medium-sized saucepan, bring the stock to a boil over medium heat. Remove the pan from the heat, add the peeled garlic cloves and mustard, and blend well with a hand-held immersion blender or a whisk, until the garlic is puréed. Slowly blend in the remaining 1 cup oil. Stir in the olives, Preserved Lemons, and cilantro. Season with salt and pepper to taste.

6 Place a poussin on each warm plate. Spoon the sauce around the poussin and garnish each with 5 unpeeled roasted garlic cloves. Top with some of the preserved lemon zest. (Do not spoon the sauce over the poussin, or the crisp skin will get soggy.) Serve immediately.

NOTE: The poussin, very small young chickens usually weighing about 1 pound, can be replaced with 3 very small broilers, split in half.

❧ A hand-held immersion blender quickly and smoothly incorporates hot ingredients into a sauce.

QUICK PRESERVED LEMONS

MAKES ABOUT 2 TABLESPOONS
PREPARATION TIME: ABOUT 5 MINUTES
COOKING TIME: ABOUT 10 MINUTES

Zest of 2 large blemish-free lemons, removed with a vegetable peeler or sharp knife and cut into fine julienne

3¼ cups water

2 tablespoons sugar

1 teaspoon salt

This speedy method of preserving lemon zest makes a traditional Middle Eastern flavor accessible to the busy home cook. Once tried, you'll find a million uses for this savory taste.

1 Assemble *mise en place* trays for this recipe (see page 6).

2 Put the lemon zest in a small nonreactive saucepan with 1 cup of cold water. Bring to a simmer over high heat and immediately remove from the heat. Drain and repeat. Drain and set aside.

3 Add the water, sugar, and salt to the saucepan and bring to a boil over high heat. Reduce the heat and simmer for about 2 minutes. Add the zest and simmer for about 5 minutes, until softened. Remove the pan from the heat and cool. Use right away or store in the cooking liquid, covered and refrigerated, for up to 2 weeks.

Chicken in Green Herb Sauce ❧ Giuliano Bugialli

SERVES 6
PREPARATION TIME: ABOUT 35 MINUTES
COOKING TIME: ABOUT 25 MINUTES

1½ ounces (2 to 3 slices) white bread, crusts removed

7 tablespoons fresh rosemary leaves

45 large fresh sage leaves

3 large cloves garlic, peeled

7 tablespoons Chicken Stock (page 15)

*A*n interesting chicken recipe from Tuscany, using the underutilized leg and thigh meat. The intense, fresh herb taste permeates the flavorful meat for a complex yet simple-to-prepare dish.

1 Preheat the oven to 250 degrees F. Assemble *mise en place* trays for this recipe (see page 6).

2 In a food processor fitted with the metal blade, combine the bread, rosemary, sage, garlic, and stock and pulse until finely ground. Set aside.

6 tablespoons olive oil

6 boneless chicken legs, skin on, trimmed of excess fat (from 3½-pound chickens, if possible)

6 boneless chicken thighs, skin on, trimmed of excess fat (from 3½-pound chickens, if possible)

Salt and freshly ground black pepper to taste

1 cup dry white wine

2 scant tablespoons fresh lemon juice

Grated zest of 2 lemons

3 In a large sauté pan, heat the oil over low heat. Add the chicken, increase the heat to medium, and cook for about 15 minutes, turning once, until lightly golden on both sides and the juices run clear when the meat is pierced with the tip of a knife. Remove the pan from the heat. Season the chicken with salt and pepper to taste, and transfer to a large, ovenproof serving platter. Cover with aluminum foil and put in the oven to keep warm.

4 Scrape the bread and herb mixture into the sauté pan, and season with salt and pepper. Set the pan over medium heat and cook the mixture for about 4 minutes, continuously scraping the bottom of the pan with a wooden spoon. Combine the wine and lemon juice and pour into the pan. Cook for about 3 minutes, stirring continuously to deglaze the pan and make a smooth sauce. Strain the sauce through a fine sieve into a bowl, pushing on the solids with the back of a wooden spoon; discard the solids. Taste and adjust the seasonings. Pour the sauce over the chicken and sprinkle the lemon zest over all. Serve immediately.

❧ To grate the lemon peel (or any citrus fruit) with ease, Chef Bugialli suggests covering the side of a grater with a piece of parchment paper. Rubbing the citrus fruit back and forth, turn the fruit as the peel is scraped off. Lift the parchment paper off the grater. Instead of being stuck in the grater, the tiny bits of peel remain on the paper and can be scraped into a bowl. The unwanted, bitter, white pith is left behind.

Squab with Cabbage and Mashed Potatoes ✺ Christian Delouvrier

SERVES 6

PREPARATION TIME: ABOUT 45 MINUTES

COOKING TIME: ABOUT 2 HOURS AND 30 MINUTES

CABBAGE:

1 small head of green cabbage (about 2 pounds) cored, quartered, and separated into leaves

6 strips bacon

3 onions, chopped

2 tablespoons duck fat

Salt and freshly ground black pepper to taste

POTATOES:

6 large baking potatoes

6 tablespoons unsalted butter

1 tablespoon white truffle oil

Salt and freshly ground black pepper to taste

½ ounce white truffle, cut into fine julienne

SAUCE:

6 squab wings (see below)

3 onions, coarsely chopped

3 carrots, coarsely chopped

6 tablespoons dry white wine

4 sprigs fresh thyme

6 cloves garlic

Squab is a lovely dish to serve in the autumn. The tender birds, served with white truffles, strike the perfect note after the elegant foie gras appetizer.

1 Preheat the oven to 400 degrees F. Assemble *mise en place* trays for this recipe (see page 6).

2 To prepare the cabbage, blanch the leaves for 1 minute in enough lightly salted boiling water to cover. Drain.

3 Fry the bacon in an ovenproof skillet over medium-high heat until the fat is rendered. Drain and crumble the bacon. Set aside. Discard all but 2 tablespoons of fat.

4 Add the onions to the pan and cook in the bacon fat for 3 to 5 minutes, until just softened. Add the damp cabbage leaves. Set a piece of waxed or parchment paper directly on top of the cabbage. Cover the pan with a lid or aluminum foil. Braise in the oven for 10 to 12 minutes, until the cabbage is tender. Transfer the cooked cabbage and onions to a clean bowl, and set aside.

5 To prepare the potatoes, puncture each one with a fork and wrap in aluminum foil. Bake for about 1 hour, until fork tender. Trim about ¾ inch off each end of the potatoes. Cut the potatoes in half lengthwise and scoop out the flesh, taking care not to tear the skin. Leave a thin layer of potato flesh on the skins to strengthen them. Set the potato skins aside to cool.

6 Put the potato flesh in a saucepan over medium heat and add the butter and truffle oil. Mash with a fork until the butter is fully incorporated and the potatoes are smooth. Stir in the julienned truffles.

7 Using kitchen scissors, a small sharp knife, or a 2-inch cookie cutter, cut six 2-inch circles from the potato

3 one-pound squabs, wings removed

3 sprigs fresh thyme

3 bay leaves

3 cloves garlic

3 tablespoons unsalted butter

Freshly grated white truffles

skins. Spoon small mounds of potato on the potato skin circles and set aside to keep warm.

8 To make the sauce, heat a heavy roasting pan or skillet over high heat. When hot, add the squab wings and cook, stirring, for 8 to 10 minutes, until juices are released and caramelized on the bottom of the pan. Add the onion, garlic, and carrots and cook for about 10 minutes, over medium heat, until the vegetables soften. Add the wine to deglaze the pan. Add enough water to cover the bones and the thyme. Raise the heat to high and reduce the liquid by one third. Strain through a fine sieve, pressing on the solids to extract liquid. Discard the solids and set the sauce aside to keep warm.

9 To roast the squabs, using a small sharp knife, remove the necks and the giblets. Rinse the squabs and pat dry.

10 Insert 1 sprig of thyme, 1 bay leaf, and 1 clove of garlic into the cavity of each squab. Season each one inside and out with salt and pepper. Truss the legs with kitchen twine. Rub the squabs with butter.

11 Set the squabs, breast side up, on a rack in a heavy roasting pan and roast for 30 minutes. Turn the squabs over and continue roasting for 30 minutes longer. Baste with the pan juices and turn the squabs breast side up again. Roast for about 15 minutes longer, until golden brown and the juices run clear when the flesh is pricked with the tip of sharp knife.

12 Meanwhile, melt the duck fat in a large skillet. Add the reserved braised cabbage and cook over high heat for 3 to 4 minutes, until heated through. Drain and toss with the reserved crumbled bacon.

13 Lift each squab from the pan and remove the legs. Slice the meat from the breast.

14 Spoon equal amounts of cabbage on each plate. Top each with half the breast meat and 1 leg from a squab. Arrange the potato mounds around the cabbage. Spoon sauce over the squab and sprinkle with grated truffles. Serve immediately.

- Squab may have to be special-ordered. If you cannot find it, substitute Rock Cornish Game Hens.

- Truffle oil and white truffles are available in specialty shops.

- While there is no substitute for the rich flavor of duck fat, use olive oil or vegetable oil if you cannot find it at your butcher or specialty store.

- Buy uniformly shaped and sized potatoes with smooth, unblemished skin.

Grilled Honey-Basil Chicken ❧ Ron Hook

SERVES 6

PREPARATION TIME: ABOUT 10 MINUTES

MARINATING TIME: AT LEAST 1 HOUR

COOKING TIME: ABOUT 7 MINUTES

FAT PER SERVING: 4.7 GRAMS

SATURATED FAT: 0.8 GRAM

CALORIES PER SERVING: 243

CALORIES FROM FAT: 18%

1½ pounds boneless, skinless chicken breasts, split and pounded to an even thickness

1½ cups raspberry vinegar

¼ cup reduced-sodium soy sauce

¼ cup plus 2 tablespoons Dijon mustard

¼ cup honey

¼ cup plus 2 tablespoons chopped fresh basil

1 teaspoon dried thyme

1 teaspoon freshly ground black pepper

Here's a tasty addition to summer's grill routine. However, you can also prepare this chicken under the broiler when the weather turns cool.

---

1 Assemble *mise en place* trays for this recipe (see page 6).

2 Place the chicken in a shallow glass dish. In a small mixing bowl, combine the vinegar, soy sauce, mustard, honey, basil, thyme, and pepper. Whisk well and pour over the chicken. Cover and refrigerate for at least 1 hour or up to 4 hours, turning occasionally.

3 Prepare a charcoal or gas grill or preheat the broiler. Spray the grilling grid or broiling pan with nonstick vegetable spray.

4 When the coals are very hot, lift the chicken from the marinade and grill or broil for about 3½ minutes on each side, or until just cooked through. Do not overcook.

5 Meanwhile, transfer the marinade to a small saucepan. Bring to a boil over high heat and boil for about 5 minutes, or until reduced by half.

6 Pour the reduced marinade over the chicken and serve immediately.

Roasted Turkey Breast with Port and Dried Cranberry Sauce ❧ Patricia Jamieson

SERVES 6

PREPARATION TIME: ABOUT 1 HOUR

MARINATING TIME: AT LEAST 1 HOUR OR UP TO 8 HOURS

COOKING TIME: ABOUT 1 HOUR AND 15 MINUTES

FAT PER SERVING: 6.5 GRAMS

SATURATED FAT: 1.3 GRAMS

CALORIES PER SERVING: 225

CALORIES FROM FAT: 26%

---

2 tablespoons Dijon mustard

1 tablespoon plus 1 teaspoon orange juice concentrate, thawed

One 1½-pound boneless turkey breast, skin left on

Freshly ground black pepper to taste

⅔ cup dried cranberries

½ cup water

1 tablespoon vegetable oil

2 onions, chopped

1 cup plus 1 tablespoon port wine

3 tablespoons balsamic vinegar

2 cups Chicken Stock (see page 15)

6 sprigs fresh thyme

½ teaspoon crushed black peppercorns

Two to three ½-inch-wide strips orange zest

2½ teaspoons arrowroot

A low-calorie holiday bird with no leftovers! If you bone the turkey breast yourself, by all means make a dark turkey stock with the bones. Roast them first and then proceed as for Chicken Stock (see page 14).

---

1 Assemble *mise en place* trays for this recipe (see page 6).

2 In a small bowl, combine the mustard and orange juice concentrate. Set aside.

3 Starting at the tip of the turkey breast, peel back the skin, leaving it attached at the wishbone end. Trim any fat and membrane from the turkey. Put the turkey in a shallow glass dish and rub the meat all over with the mustard mixture. Season generously with pepper. Stretch the skin back over the flesh and secure with toothpicks so that it covers the top of the breast well. Cover and refrigerate for at least 1 hour, or up to 8 hours.

4 In a small saucepan, combine the cranberries and water and bring to a boil over medium heat. Reduce the heat and simmer for 3 minutes. Drain, reserving the cooking water. Set the cranberries and cooking liquid aside separately.

5 In a medium-sized saucepan, heat 2 teaspoons of the oil over medium-low heat. Add half the onions and cook, stirring occasionally, for about 10 minutes, or until tender and golden. Add 1 cup of the port and the vinegar, raise the heat to high, and bring to a boil. Boil for about 5 minutes, or until reduced by half. Add the stock, the reserved cranberry water, 2 thyme sprigs, and the crushed peppercorns. Return to a boil and boil for 10 minutes, or until reduced by half. Set aside.

6 Preheat the oven to 325 degrees F. Lightly oil a small roasting pan or an oven-proof skillet that can accommodate a rack.

7 Place the remaining onions and 4 thyme sprigs and the orange zest in the center of the prepared pan and set a rack over them. Lightly spray the rack with vegetable oil spray. Set the turkey breast on the rack and roast for about 45 minutes, or until a meat thermometer inserted in the thickest part registers 160 to 165 degrees F and the juices run clear when the turkey is pierced in the thickest part. Transfer the turkey to a carving board, cover loosely, and let rest for 10 to 20 minutes. (The internal temperature will increase to 170 degrees F upon resting.)

8 Remove the rack from the roasting pan and place the pan over medium heat. Pour in the port reduction and bring to a boil, stirring to scrape up any brown bits. Strain through a fine sieve into a small saucepan, pressing down on the onions.

9 Place the pan over medium heat and bring to a simmer. In a small bowl, dissolve the arrowroot in the remaining 1 tablespoon port, and add to the sauce. Cook, stirring constantly, for about 3 minutes, or until the sauce thickens slightly and is glossy. Stir in the cranberries and adjust the seasoning with pepper.

10 Remove the toothpicks and discard the turkey skin. Holding the knife more or less parallel to the cutting board, slice the turkey. Arrange the slices on a platter or individual plates, spoon a little sauce over the meat, and pass the rest on the side.

NOTE: The port reduction and the plumped cranberries can be prepared up to 8 hours ahead. Store separately, covered and refrigerated. The recipe can be doubled. If you do so, allow extra time for the sauce to reduce.

❧ As with all recipes in the book, if using canned broth in place of homemade stock, use reduced-sodium broth.

❧ The turkey skin serves as a blanket to prevent the turkey from drying out as it roasts, but it is removed before serving to cut the fat.

Scallopine of Turkey Breast with Morel and Cognac Sauce ❧ Jacques Pépin

SERVES 6

PREPARATION TIME: ABOUT 35 MINUTES

COOKING TIME: ABOUT 50 MINUTES

SOAKING TIME (MUSHROOMS ONLY): ABOUT 30 MINUTES

---

3 ounces dried morels

4 cups lukewarm water

6 slices turkey breast, each about 6 ounces and about 1⅜-inch thick

1½ teaspoons salt, or more to taste

1 teaspoon freshly ground black pepper, or more to taste

2 to 3 tablespoons unsalted butter

½ cup chopped shallots

1 tablespoon finely chopped garlic

2 tablespoons Cognac

1½ cups heavy cream

1 teaspoon potato starch or cornstarch (optional)

Few drops of fresh lemon juice

Scallopine of turkey breast is much less expensive than veal but just as elegant with the morels and Cognac—a typically practical French solution!

---

1 Assemble *mise en place* trays for this recipe (see page 6).

2 In a bowl, combine the morels and water. Let the mushrooms soak for about 30 minutes, until reconstituted and softened.

3 Drain the morels, reserving the soaking liquid. Remove any dirty or sandy stems. Cut in half lengthwise, or quarter if very large.

4 Strain the reserved soaking liquid through a fine sieve lined with paper towels into a small saucepan. Bring to a boil over medium-high heat. Reduce the heat to low and simmer for about 30 minutes, until reduced to 1 cup.

5 Preheat the oven to 175 degrees F.

6 Season the turkey slices on both sides with the salt and pepper.

7 In a large skillet, melt 1 tablespoon of the butter over medium-high heat. When hot, add 2 of the turkey slices. Cook for about 2 minutes, turning once. Arrange in a single layer in a large shallow ovenproof dish, and keep warm in the oven. Cook the remaining turkey slices in the same way, adding more butter as needed.

8 When all the turkey is cooked, add the shallots and garlic to the skillet. Reduce the heat to medium and cook for about 30 seconds. Add the Cognac to the skillet. Carefully ignite the Cognac and flambé; it will extinguish almost immediately.

9 Add the reduced mushroom liquid and the cream. Bring to a boil, stirring to scrape up any browned bits.

Stir in the juices that have accumulated around the turkey slices. Strain the sauce into a clean saucepan. Stir in the morels, place over medium heat, and bring to a boil. Reduce the heat and simmer for about 3 minutes. Season to taste with salt and pepper. If the sauce seems thin, dissolve the potato starch or cornstarch in 1 tablespoon of cold water and whisk it into the simmering sauce so that it thickens enough to thinly coat the back of a spoon. Stir in the lemon juice.

10 Arrange the turkey slices on a warm serving platter and spoon the sauce and mushrooms over them. Serve immediately.

❧ You can slice the turkey from a whole turkey breast half, or you can buy packaged turkey cutlets, which are usually cut about ⅜ inch thick.

❧ Whenever you work with raw poultry, be sure to wash the work surfaces and utensils, as well as your hands, with warm, soapy water before proceeding with another task. This prevents the spread of salmonella bacteria.

❧ Even cooked turkey should not be left at room temperature for longer than necessary. Refrigerate any leftovers as soon as the main course is over.

Fricassee of Turkey and Brown Rice ❧ Jacques Pépin

SERVES 6

PREPARATION TIME: ABOUT 30 MINUTES

COOKING TIME: 1 HOUR AND 45 MINUTES TO 2 HOURS

---

2 turkey legs and 2 turkey wings (about 5 pounds)

3 tablespoons unsalted butter

This is a great dish with which you can feed a crowd. It is inexpensive, nutritious, and easy to make ahead of time. And, if there are any leftovers, it's even better when reheated.

---

1 Assemble *mise en place* trays for this recipe (see page 6).

1½ pounds yellow onions, chopped

4 ounces loose-packed sun-dried tomatoes, chopped

3 tablespoons chopped garlic

1 teaspoon ground cumin

½ teaspoon red pepper flakes

3 bay leaves

2 teaspoons salt

1 teaspoon freshly ground black pepper

1½ cups brown rice

5 cups water

1 cup tiny peas, blanched in boiling water for 1 minute

1¼ cup chopped fresh parsley

2 Using a cleaver, cut each turkey leg into 5 pieces and each wing into 2 pieces. Remove any tough tendons.

3 In a large skillet or Dutch oven, melt the butter over medium heat. Add the turkey pieces and sear, turning frequently, for about 15 minutes, or until well browned on all sides.

4 Add the onions and cook for about 10 minutes until the onions soften. Add the sun-dried tomatoes, garlic, cumin, hot pepper flakes, bay leaves, and salt and pepper. Stir in the rice and water, increase the heat, and bring to a boil. Cover, reduce the heat, and simmer for about 1 hour and 10 minutes, or until all the liquid has been absorbed and the turkey meat and rice are very tender.

5 Remove from the heat, and remove the bay leaves. Stir in the peas and parsley, and serve immediately.

❧ Fresh peas are best for this recipe, but you may use high-quality frozen or canned tiny peas.

❧ You can have the butcher chop the turkey into pieces. Ask him to remove the tendons at the same time.

Duck with Turnips and Medjoul Dates ❧ Alfred Portale

SERVES: 6

PREPARATION TIME: ABOUT 45 MINUTES

COOKING TIME: ABOUT 6 HOURS AND 20 MINUTES (6 HOURS FOR THE SAUCE)

---

2 four-and-a-half-pound Muscovy ducks

Ducks and dates are made for each other: both are wonderfully sweet and juicy. Although this recipe takes time to prepare because you must make Duck Stock, the actual preparation is surprisingly easy.

---

1 Preheat oven to 400 degrees F. Assemble *mise en place* trays for the sauce portion of the recipe (see page 6).

SAUCE:

Reserved bones and trimmings from
ducks

1 tablespoon olive oil

1 onion, coarsely chopped

3½ cups dry red wine

1 head garlic, halved crosswise

1 teaspoon black peppercorns

3 sprigs fresh thyme or ½ teaspoon
dried thyme

2 bay leaves

½ teaspoon caraway seeds

DUCK:

6 tablespoons unsalted butter

4 large turnips, peeled and very
thinly sliced

6 medjoul dates, pitted and thinly
sliced lengthwise

4 teaspoons sweet butter

1 ounce olive oil

Salt and freshly ground black pepper

2 Cut off the duck legs and cut apart at the joint. Remove the meat from thighs, leaving it intact; remove the breast halves from the carcass, leaving them intact. Cover and refrigerate the breast and thigh meat. Chop the duck bones and trimmings into pieces.

3 To make the sauce, spread the bones and trimmings in a single layer in a large roasting pan and roast, stirring several times, for about 20 minutes, or until lightly browned.

4 Meanwhile, heat the olive oil in a large sauté pan. Cook the onions over medium-high heat for about 10 minutes, until softened and lightly browned. Remove from the heat.

5 Transfer the bones to a large stockpot and add the onions. Add the wine and enough water to cover the bones. Add the garlic, peppercorns, thyme, bay leaves, and caraway seeds. Bring to a boil over high heat, and then reduce the heat and simmer, partially covered, for 4 to 6 hours, skimming any foam that rises to the surface during cooking. Add more water if necessary.

6 Spoon the fat from the surface of the stock, or blot it with a folded paper towel. Strain the stock through a sieve into a saucepan, pressing against the solids to extract as much liquid as possible. Discard the solids. Strain the stock a second time through a fine-mesh sieve into a saucepan. Bring to a boil over medium heat and cook for 20 to 30 minutes, until reduced to about 1½ cups. The sauce will be slightly syrupy. Set aside.

7 To prepare the duck, assemble the *mise en place* trays for the remaining ingredients (see page 6).

8 Melt 2 tablespoons of the butter in a large sauté pan over medium-high heat. Sauté the turnips for 3 to 4 minutes, until softened and lightly browned around the edges. Add the dates during the last minute of cooking and season to taste with salt and pepper, remove from the heat, and cover to keep warm.

9 Bring the duck sauce to a boil over high heat. Reduce to a simmer and whisk in the remaining 4 tablespoons of butter, a tablespoon at a time, waiting until each one is incorporated before adding the next. Adjust the seasonings and cover to keep warm.

10 In a large sauté pan, heat olive oil over medium heat. Season the duck breasts and thighs with salt and pepper and add to the pan, skin side down. Cook for 4 to 5 minutes, until the skin is crispy. Turn and cook for 4 to 5 minutes longer, until medium-rare. Transfer to a platter or cutting board and let rest for a few minutes.

11 Slice the breasts and thighs on the diagonal into thick slices. Fan the slices in a semi-circle around the center of 6 serving plates. Gather date slivers in a bunch, wrap them with a few turnip slices and stand them lengthwise in the center of each plate. Gently fold turnip slices to form rounded cushions and place around the bundle of dates so that it stands up. Continue adding turnip folds to the base, and intersperse with more date slivers. Spoon the sauce around the outside of the duck, and in a circle around the base of the turnip mixture.

☙ If serving six people and you don't want to plate the duck individually, fan the duck on a platter and create one turnip and date centerpiece, and serve the rest of the portions on the side.

Quail with Coffee and Spice Rub and White Bean Ragout ❧ Anne Rosenzweig

SERVES 6

PREPARATION TIME: ABOUT 45 MINUTES

COOKING TIME: ABOUT 1 HOUR AND 30 MINUTES

MARINATING TIME: 8 HOURS

SPICE RUB:

2 tablespoons sesame seeds

25 coriander seeds

20 black peppercorns

3 cloves

2 juniper berries

¼-inch piece cinnamon stick

½-inch piece bay leaf

3 tablespoons espresso coffee beans

1 teaspoon salt, or more, to taste

12 quail, butterflied

2 tablespoons corn oil

White Bean Ragout (see page 251)

This is an unusual, taste bud-shocking combination, yet absolutely delicious. The mellow bean ragout offers the perfect accompaniment to the quail.

---

1 Preheat the oven to 300 degrees F. Assemble *mise en place* trays for this recipe (see page 6).

2 Put the sesame and coriander seeds, peppercorns, cloves, juniper berries, cinnamon stick, and bay leaf in separate, flattened piles on a non-stick baking sheet with sides. Toast in the oven for 25 to 30 minutes, or until the sesame seeds are golden brown. Remove from the oven and let cool slightly.

3 Measure 1 tablespoon of the sesame seeds and set aside. Place the remaining seeds and spices in a spice grinder. Add the coffee beans and 1 teaspoon salt. Process until finely ground.

4 Rub the spice mixture evenly over the skin side of the quail. Cover and refrigerate for 8 hours or overnight.

5 Preheat the oven to 325 degrees F.

6 Prepare the White Bean Ragout.

7 In a large, heavy skillet, heat the oil over medium-high heat. Add 3 or 4 quail, skin-side down, and cook for about 2 minutes, or until lightly browned. Turn and cook for 4 to 6 minutes longer, or until medium rare. Sprinkle with some of the reserved sesame seeds and remove from the pan. Cover and keep warm in the oven. Cook the remaining quail.

8 Spoon the ragout onto 6 warm plates. Lay 2 quail on either side of the plate and serve immediately.

❧ If quail are unavailable, substitute 1-pound Rock Cornish game hens and serve one per person.

Jamaican Jerk Chicken with Banana-Guava Ketchup ❧ Chris Schlesinger

SERVES 6

PREPARATION TIME: ABOUT 20 MINUTES

CHILLING TIME: AT LEAST 2 HOURS

COOKING TIME: ABOUT 1 HOUR

FAT PER SERVING: 8.6 GRAMS

SATURATED FAT: 2.2 GRAMS

CALORIES PER SERVING: 199

CALORIES FROM FAT: 40%

---

10 Scotch Bonnet or other very hot chiles, stemmed

3 scallions, finely chopped

¼ cup yellow mustard

Juice of 2 limes

2 tablespoons fresh orange juice

2 tablespoons white vinegar, plus more if necessary

2 tablespoons dried rosemary

2 tablespoons dried basil

2 tablespoons dried thyme

2 tablespoons chopped fresh flat-leaf parsley

2 tablespoons mustard seeds

1 teaspoon salt

1 teaspoon freshly ground black pepper

6 chicken leg-thigh quarters (thighs with legs attached), skin removed

Banana-Guava Ketchup (see page 267)

Chicken thighs and legs are used in this recipe because their center bones allow them to withstand long, slow grilling and still remain juicy.

---

1 Assemble *mise en place* trays for this recipe (see page 6).

2 In a blender, combine the chiles, scallions, mustard, lime and orange juices, vinegar, herbs, mustard seeds, salt, and pepper and process to a thick paste. If the paste seems too thick, thin with a little more vinegar. Transfer to a nonreactive container, cover, and refrigerate for at least 2 hours.

3 Prepare a charcoal or gas grill.

4 Generously rub the chicken with the seasoning paste. Grill, uncovered, over a very low fire for about 1 hour, or until the meat easily pulls away from the bone. (If the heat is properly low, the chicken will not burn or dry out.)

5 Separate the legs from the thighs by cutting through the joint. Serve hot or at room temperature with the Banana-Guava Ketchup.

NOTE: You can also roast this chicken in a 275- or 300-degree-F oven for about 1½ hours, or until the meat easily pulls away from the bone.

The jerk paste will keep, refrigerated, almost indefinitely. Double the amount so that you will have it on hand to add zest to other grilled poultry or meat.

❧ You can replace the chiles with ¼ cup Inner Beauty or other Caribbean-style hot sauce, or a mixture of chiles of varying degrees of heat (you will probably need about 15 chiles to approximate the heat of the Scotch Bonnets).

❧ You can leave the skin on for juicier chicken, but the fat grams will increase accordingly.

Herb-Marinated Chicken, Shiitake Mushrooms, and Roasted Potatoes Vinaigrette on Salad Greens ❧ Marie Simmons

SERVES 6

PREPARATION TIME: ABOUT 45 MINUTES

MARINATING TIME: AT LEAST 30 MINUTES

COOKING TIME: ABOUT 35 MINUTES

FAT PER SERVING: 17 GRAMS

SATURATED FAT: 3 GRAMS

CALORIES PER SERVING: 592

CALORIES FROM FAT: 27%

---

3 cloves garlic, minced

1 tablespoon grated orange or lemon zest

1½ tablespoons plus ½ teaspoon fresh thyme leaves

½ teaspoon salt, plus more to taste

¼ teaspoon coarsely ground black pepper, plus more to taste

3 boneless, skinless chicken breasts, split and pounded thin, or 1½ pounds chicken tenders

6 medium baking potatoes, cut into ¼-inch-thick slices

¼ cup plus 1 tablespoon extra-virgin olive oil

3 tablespoons fruit-flavored red wine vinegar, such as raspberry

6 large shiitake mushroom caps

2 small red bell peppers, cored, seeded, and sliced into thin strips

¼ cup chopped fresh flat-leaf parsley

*M*arie calls this a "salad supper," since all the elements are combined on one plate over salad greens. It is a pristine example of contemporary health-conscious fare.

---

1 Assemble *mise en place* trays for this recipe (see page 6).

2 On a flat plate, combine the garlic, zest, the 1½ tablespoons thyme, ½ teaspoon salt, and ¼ teaspoon pepper. Lay the chicken pieces on the plate and gently rub the mix ture into them. Cover and refrigerate for at least 30 minutes.

3 Preheat the oven to 400 degrees F.

4 Put the potatoes in a bowl. Drizzle with 2 tablespoons of the oil, sprinkle with salt and pepper to taste, and toss to coat. Arrange on a nonstick baking sheet and bake for about 20 minutes, or until golden and crisp on the bottom. Carefully turn and bake for 15 minutes longer, or until tender. Cover and set aside to keep warm.

5 Meanwhile, make the vinaigrette. In a small bowl, whisk together 2 tablespoons of the oil, the vinegar, the remaining ½ teaspoon thyme, and salt and pepper to taste. Set aside.

6 While the potatoes are baking, heat a large nonstick skillet over medium heat until hot enough to evaporate a drop of water on contact. Add 2 teapoons of the oil and tilt the pan to coat. Add the chicken and cook for about 1 minute per side, or until nicely browned and cooked through. (If the chicken pieces are thicker than ¼ inch, you may need to cook them for up to 3 minutes per

9 cups mixed salad greens, such as Boston, bibb, red leaf, arugula, watercress, and/or mâche

side.) Transfer the chicken to a warm plate and cover to keep warm.

7 Add the remaining 1 teaspoon oil to the pan. Add the mushrooms and bell peppers and cook for 2 minutes. Sprinkle with salt to taste, stir gently, and cook for about 2 more minutes, or until just barely tender. Transfer to the plate with the chicken and sprinkle with the parsley.

8 Put the salad greens in a large bowl and toss with half of the vinaigrette. Place equal portions on each plate. If using whole chicken breasts, cut into thin diagonal slices, and arrange the slices or tenders on top of the greens. Cut the mushroom caps into ¼-inch strips and arrange them and the bell pepper strips on top of the chicken. Sprinkle the hot potatoes with the remaining vinaigrette and arrange them around the salads. Serve immediately.

❧ Almost any vegetable works in this salad. Marie particularly recommends steamed green beans, broccoli florets, or sugar snap peas. Sautéed cherry tomatoes also make a pretty—and tasty—addition.

Guajillo-Maple Glazed Turkey with Sautéed Greens, Beets, and Yams ✺ David Walzog

SERVES 6

PREPARATION TIME: ABOUT 45 MINUTES

COOKING TIME: ABOUT 5 HOURS AND 30 MINUTES

GLAZE:

2 large turkey legs

3 heads garlic, halved crosswise

2½ cups pure maple syrup

1 cup chopped white onions

5 sprigs fresh thyme

5 sprigs fresh rosemary

4 cups chicken stock (see page 15)

½ cup guajillo chile purée (see page 12)

1 cup water

TURKEY:

1 fourteen-pound fresh turkey

4 heads garlic, halved crosswise

About 10 sprigs fresh thyme

About 10 sprigs fresh rosemary

Salt and freshly ground black pepper to taste

Sautéed Greens, Beets, and Yams (see page 256)

The sweet-and-spicy glaze keeps the turkey moist and adds enormous zest to the mild-flavored bird. The beautiful color of the glazed skin is further accentuated by the rich red and gold of the vegetables.

1 Preheat the oven to 425 degrees F. Assemble *mise en place* trays for this recipe (see page 6).

2 To make the glaze, split the turkey legs open with a sharp knife and pull apart to butterfly them. Place in a roasting pan and cook for about 1 hour, or until very brown, draining off the fat periodically.

3 Add the garlic, maple syrup, onion, and thyme and rosemary sprigs, and continue to roast for 20 minutes. Reduce the oven temperature to 325 F.

4 Transfer the contents of the roasting pan to a large, heavy saucepan. Stir in the stock, chile purée, and water. Bring to a boil over medium-high heat. Reduce the heat and simmer for 30 minutes.

5 Strain the glaze through a fine sieve into a smaller saucepan. Set aside and keep warm.

6 To roast the turkey, rinse it and pat it dry with paper towels. Put the halved garlic heads, thyme, and rosemary into the cavity. Sprinkle, inside and out, with salt and pepper. Press the legs against the breast and tie in place using kitchen twine. Tuck the wings under the back. Set the turkey on a rack in the roasting pan. Cover the turkey with aluminum foil and roast for 1 hour and 30 minutes.

7 Remove the foil and continue to roast the turkey, basting every 15 minutes with the glaze, for about 2 hours longer, or until the juices run clear when the thigh is pierced with a fork. Remove from the oven and let rest for about 15 minutes before carving.

8 Meanwhile, prepare the vegetables.

9 Place the turkey on a warm serving platter and surround with the vegetables. Reheat and pass the remaining glaze on the side.

Swordfish with Pine Nuts and Raisins ～ Colman Andrews

SERVES 6

PREPARATION TIME: ABOUT 20 MINUTES

COOKING TIME: ABOUT 25 MINUTES

2 pounds swordfish, about 1 inch thick, cut into 2 x 3-inch pieces

¼ cup all-purpose flour

2 tablespoons Spanish olive oil

1½ cups dry white wine

¾ cup fresh orange juice

1½ tablespoons fresh lemon juice

24 toasted blanched almonds

2 sprigs fresh flat-leaf parsley, minced

2 sprigs fresh mint, leaves only, minced

2 sprigs fresh marjoram or oregano, leaves only, minced

½ cup golden raisins, plumped in water and drained

½ cup toasted pine nuts (see page 13)

Coarse salt and freshly ground black pepper to taste

Relying on an unusual combination of sweet and sour flavors, Colman has created a unique way to cook fish. The sauce works equally well with chicken breasts.

1 Assemble *mise en place* trays for this recipe (see page 6).

2 Dredge the swordfish pieces in the flour. In a large nonstick skillet, heat the oil over medium heat. Add the fish and cook for about 5 minutes, or until lightly browned on all sides. Drain on paper towels and set aside.

3 Return the skillet to the heat, add the wine and citrus juices, bring to a boil, and boil, stirring frequently, for about 15 minutes, or until the liquid is reduced to ¾ cup.

4 While the liquid is reducing, pulverize the almonds in a mortar and pestle. Add the herbs and about 1 tablespoon of the reducing liquid and work into the almonds to form a thick paste. This is called a picada.

5 Add the raisins, pine nuts, and picada to the skillet and stir to combine. Return the fish to the skillet and cook, stirring gently, for about 3 minutes, or until the fish is hot and opaque throughout and the flavors are well blended. Season to taste with coarse salt and pepper. Serve immediately, with rice or a green salad if desired.

NOTE: Unless you use a mortar and pestle to pulverize the almonds, the sauce will be chunky rather than smooth. If you don't have one, use a food processor fitted with the metal blade and pulse just until the nuts are smooth, taking care not to overprocess them.

Red Snapper in a Salt Crust with Herb Dressing ❧ Francesco Antonucci

SERVES 6
PREPARATION TIME: ABOUT 15 MINUTES
COOKING TIME: ABOUT 60 MINUTES

SNAPPER:

1 bunch fresh rosemary, rinsed and patted dry

1 bunch fresh sage, rinsed and patted dry

1 bunch fresh thyme, rinsed and patted dry

3 cloves garlic

2 three-to-four-pound red snappers or 1 six-to-eight-pound red snapper, scales, skin, and tail intact, rinsed and patted dry

4 pounds coarse sea salt or kosher salt

¼ cup all-purpose flour

2 tablespoons water

*T*he salt crust sounds overpowering but in actuality it holds in moisture while imparting a delicate and pleasing salty flavor. You can use this method to cook any whole fish with scales. Splash a bit of citrus on before serving to heighten the flavor even more. This is wonderful with sautéed greens.

---

1 Preheat the oven to 400 degrees F. Assemble *mise en place* trays for this recipe (see page 6).

2 Divide each bunch of herbs into 4 equal portions. Combine these portions to make 4 bunches of mixed herbs. Using kitchen twine, tie each bunch together. Place 2 bunches of herbs and 1½ cloves of garlic in the cavity of each fish. If using 1 fish, make 2 bunches of herbs and put all 3 cloves of garlic in the cavity.

3 In a large bowl, combine the sea salt, flour, and water. Mix to make a rough dough. Spread evenly in a 3-inch-deep baking pan large enough to hold the fish flat. Lay the fish in the center of the salt mixture and generously cover them with salt mixture gathered up from the sides of the pan, patting the mixture firmly with your fingertips to help it adhere. Bake, uncovered, for 1 hour. (As it bakes the salt will form a compact crust.)

Juice of ½ lemon

Salt and freshly ground white pepper to taste

1 cup extra-virgin olive oil

½ cup water

1 teaspoon minced fresh rosemary

1 teaspoon minced fresh flat-leaf parsley

1 teaspoon dried oregano

½ teaspoon minced garlic

4 Meanwhile, make the dressing. In a small bowl, combine the lemon juice and salt and white pepper to taste. Slowly whisk in the olive oil. When emulsified, whisk in the water, minced fresh herbs, oregano, and garlic.

5 Remove the fish from the oven. Gently crack the salt crust open and carefully remove the crust along with the fish skin. Use kitchen shears to cut through the crust and skin, if necessary. Brush any loose salt off the fish. Using 2 spatulas, lift the fish onto a warm serving platter. Pour the herb dressing over the top, and serve immediately.

❧ For a more elaborate Italian dinner, serve pasta before the fish course and a simple grilled poultry or meat afterwards. Vegetables can be served as a separate course or with the main course.

Broiled Pompano with Pickles and Vegetables ❧ Daniel Boulud

SERVES 6

PREPARATION TIME: ABOUT 40 MINUTES

COOKING TIME: ABOUT 13 MINUTES

FAT PER SERVING: 11 GRAMS

SATURATED FAT: 4.2 GRAMS

CALORIES PER SERVING: 210

CALORIES FROM FAT: 51%

---

2 tablespoons olive oil

2 scallions, minced

½ cup finely minced celery

¼ cup diced zucchini (¼-inch dice)

1 red bell pepper, roasted, peeled, cored, seeded, and cut into ¼-inch dice (see page 12)

This savory dish explodes with exuberant tastes. The pickle-vegetable garnish offers satisfaction with little fat. The percentage of calories from fat seems high because the calories per serving is low.

---

1 Assemble *mise en place* trays for this recipe (see page 6).

2 In a medium-sized saucepan, heat 1½ teaspoons of the oil over medium heat. Add the scallions and celery and sauté for about 5 minutes, or until the vegetables soften. Add the zucchini and sauté for 3 minutes. Stir in the roasted pepper, capers, cornichons, horseradish, lemon segments, lemon juice, and 1½ teaspoons of the oil. Season to taste with coarse salt and pepper, remove from the heat, and cover to keep warm.

1 tablespoon capers, preferably French, drained

1 tablespoon coarsely chopped cornichons

1½ teaspoons grated fresh horseradish

2 lemons, peeled and cut into membrane-free segments

2 tablespoons fresh lemon juice

Coarse salt and freshly ground black pepper to taste

Six 4-ounce skinless pompano fillets

1 teaspoon minced fresh thyme

18 small celery leaves, washed and dried, for garnish

3 Preheat the broiler.

4 Brush a broiling pan and the fillets with the remaining 1 tablespoon oil. Sprinkle the fish with the thyme and coarse salt and pepper to taste and broil for about 2½ minutes on each side, or until just cooked through.

5 Place a fillet on each warm plate, spoon the warm pickle garnish on top, and garnish each with 3 celery leaves.

Red Snapper with Tomatoes and Caramelized Garlic ❧ Antoine Bouterin

SERVES 6

PREPARATION TIME: ABOUT 15 MINUTES

COOKING TIME: ABOUT 1 HOUR

3 pounds red snapper fillets, skinned

6 tablespoons peanut oil

22 cloves garlic, peeled (2 to 3 heads)

2 tablespoons sugar

6 large ripe tomatoes, cored, peeled, seeded, and chopped

1 large onion, thinly sliced

1 cup Chicken Stock (see page 15)

This dish epitomizes the sunny flavors of Provence. Without doubt, it is a dish for garlic-lovers.

1 Assemble *mise en place* trays for this recipe (see page 6).

2 Remove any bones from the fish, rinse it, and pat dry with paper towels. Cut into 2-inch chunks. Cover and refrigerate until ready to cook.

3 In a small sauté pan, heat 2 tablespoons of the oil over medium heat. Add the garlic cloves and sauté for 6 to 7 minutes, until lightly browned. Stir in the sugar. Cook, stirring continuously, for about 3 minutes, until the garlic is caramelized.

½ teaspoon minced fresh thyme

3 large, fresh basil leaves, minced

2 large, fresh sage leaves, minced

1 bay leaf

Pinch of ground cumin

Salt and freshly ground black pepper to taste

6 sprigs fresh parsley

4 Using a slotted spoon, transfer the garlic cloves to a paper towel to drain. Mash 4 of the cloves and set aside. Keep the remaining 18 cloves warm.

5 In a large sauté pan, heat 2 tablespoons of the oil over medium heat. Add the chopped tomatoes and cook, stirring frequently, for 20 to 30 minutes, until all the liquid has evaporated. The tomatoes will be smooth and thick. Remove from the heat.

6 In a medium-sized sauté pan, heat the remaining 2 tablespoons of oil over medium heat. Add the onion and sauté for about 5 minutes, until softened and lightly browned. Stir in the mashed garlic, the tomatoes, stock, thyme, basil, sage, bay leaf, cumin, and salt and pepper to taste. Add the fish and cook, stirring occasionally, for about 10 minutes, until cooked through. Remove the bay leaf.

7 Place equal portions of the fish and vegetable sauce in the center of 6 warm dinner plates. Garnish each plate with 3 garlic cloves and a sprig of parsley.

Fillet of Snapper with Tomato, Onion, and Garlic ~ Charles Bowman

SERVES 6

PREPARATION TIME: ABOUT 20 MINUTES

COOKING TIME: ABOUT 50 MINUTES

⅓ cup plus 2 tablespoons olive oil

1½ cups chopped onions

1 cup thinly sliced carrots

3 cloves garlic, sliced

1¼ cups dry white wine

This traditional fish preparation is found in homes and restaurants throughout Greece. Its popularity is equaled only by its aromatic flavor and ease of preparation.

---

1 Assemble *mise en place* trays for this recipe (see page 6).

2 In a large heavy skillet, heat ⅓ cup of the oil over medium heat. Add the onions, carrots, and garlic and sauté for about 10 minutes, or until very soft but not browned. Stir in the wine and cook, stirring occasionally,

Two 14½-ounce cans whole tomatoes, drained and chopped

1 cup water

¼ cup plus 2 tablespoons chopped fresh flat-leaf parsley

Salt and freshly ground black pepper to taste

Six 6-ounce fillets red snapper, skin on

for about 15 minutes, or until the wine has evaporated. Stir in the tomatoes, water, ¼ cup of the parsley, and salt and pepper to taste, and bring to a boil. Reduce the heat and simmer, uncovered, for about 15 minutes, stirring frequently, until slightly thickened. Set aside to cool slightly.

3 Preheat the oven to 400 degrees F.

4 Rub both sides of the fish with the remaining 2 tablespoons olive oil. Season lightly with salt and pepper and set aside.

5 Spoon about a third of the tomato sauce into a shallow baking dish just large enough to hold the fillets. Arrange the fish, skin side down, on the sauce. Spoon the remaining sauce over the fish and bake for about 12 minutes, or until the fish flakes easily when tested with a fork and the sauce is bubbling.

6 Place the fillets on warm plates, spoon the sauce over, and sprinkle with the remaining 2 tablespoons parsley. Serve immediately, with rice or couscous if desired.

NOTE: You can replace the red snapper with striped bass, black sea bass, or any other firm-fleshed, nonfatty fish fillets.

———

❧ An easy method for chopping canned tomatoes is to cut them up in the can using clean kitchen shears.

Striped Bass with Mango-Black Bean Salsa, Chayote Squash, and Mango Sauce ❧ Ed Brown

SERVES 6

PREPARATION TIME: ABOUT 1H HOURS

COOKING TIME: ABOUT 10 MINUTES

FAT PER SERVING: 9.2 GRAMS

SATURATED FAT: 1.6 GRAMS

CALORIES PER SERVING: 273

CALORIES FROM FAT: 31%

Six 7-ounce striped bass fillets, skin side scored (see Note)

Coarse salt and freshly ground black pepper to taste

2 tablespoons olive oil

3 chayote squash, peeled, seeded, and cut into julienne

Mango Sauce (see page 278)

Mango-Black Bean Salsa (see page 284)

The zesty flavors mask the fact that there is not a lot of fat in this easy-to-put-together tropical recipe. You could replace the striped bass with sea bass or grouper.

1 Assemble *mise en place* trays for this recipe (see page 6).

2 Season the fish with coarse salt and pepper to taste. In a heavy sauté pan large enough to hold the fish comfortably, heat 1 tablespoon of the oil over medium-high heat. Place the fish skin side down in the pan and cook for 2½ minutes. Turn and cook for about 2½ minutes longer, or until the fish is firm and the flesh is opaque. Remove to a warm platter and cover with foil to keep warm.

3 In another sauté pan, heat the remaining 1 tablespoon oil over medium heat. Add the squash, season to taste with coarse salt and pepper, and sauté for about 3 minutes, or until slightly softened.

4 Place equal portions of squash on each plate and lay a fillet on top. Drizzle the sauce around and spoon about 2 tablespoons of the salsa at the side of each fillet. Serve immediately.

NOTES: To score the bass, use a small sharp knife to lightly cut a crisscross pattern into the skin.

You can cook the squash while the fish is cooking, although it will take some kitchen juggling. You may need to use 2 pans to cook the fish—and another tablespoon of oil.

Grilled Swordfish and Fennel with Charred Tomatoes, Oil-Roasted Garlic, and Balsamic Vinegar ~ Ed Brown

SERVES 6

PREPARATION TIME: ABOUT 45 MINUTES

COOKING TIME: ABOUT 40 MINUTES

GRILLING TIME: ABOUT 10 MINUTES

FAT PER SERVING: 10 GRAMS

SATURATED FAT: 2.1 GRAMS

CALORIES PER SERVING: 237

CALORIES FROM FAT: 39%

---

1 large bulb fennel

3 large beefsteak tomatoes, cored and cut into 4 slices each

2 tablespoons extra-virgin olive oil

1½ teaspoons fresh thyme leaves

Coarse salt and freshly ground black pepper to taste

Six 5-ounce swordfish steaks, at least ¾ inch thick

3 tablespoons balsamic vinegar

Oil-Roasted Garlic (recipe follows; optional)

1 tablespoon fresh rosemary leaves

6 sprigs fresh rosemary, for garnish

Ed Brown uses thirty-year-old balsamic vinegar in this dish; if you don't have any on hand, substitute any fine-quality balsamic vinegar for the very expensive "Champagne" variety. Again, this is Ed Brown at his best—great flavor, beautiful presentation, and health-conscious ingredients. His unique way of roasting garlic adds interest to the plate, but because it also adds calories and fat, you may choose to eliminate the garlic garnish.

---

1 Assemble *mise en place* trays for this recipe (see page 6).

2 Trim the fennel and cut lengthwise into 6 slices. Cut a "V" in the bottom of each slice to remove the tough core. Blanch in a saucepan of boiling salted water for 3 minutes, drain, and pat dry. Set aside.

3 Sprinkle the tomatoes with 1 teaspoon of the oil, the thyme, and coarse salt and pepper to taste. Place a non-stick griddle or cast-iron skillet over high heat. When hot, char the tomatoes, a few at a time, for about 30 seconds on each side, until darkened. Set aside.

4 Prepare a charcoal or gas grill or preheat the broiler. Ignite some extra coals and keep them ready in a metal bucket or second grill.

5 Toss the fennel with 2 teaspoons of the oil and coarse salt and pepper to taste. Grill over medium-hot coals for about 2 minutes on each side, or until well colored. Set aside and cover to keep warm. Add the ignited charcoal to the grill to increase the heat.

6 Brush the swordfish with the remaining 1 tablespoon oil and season to taste with coarse salt and pepper. Grill over hot coals for about 3 minutes on each side, or until the center is just firm, for medium-rare. If broiling, broil the fennel about 5 inches from the heat and the swordfish closer to the heat source. Using 2 tablespoons of the vinegar, brush the fish on each side.

7 Place a slice of fennel in the center of each plate. Cut each tomato slice in half and arrange 4 pieces of tomato in a pinwheel design around the fennel on each plate. Randomly place 3 roasted garlic cloves on each plate and sprinkle with the rosemary. Drizzle the remaining vinegar over the plates. Cut each fish steak in half on the bias and place on top of the fennel, slightly overlapping the halves. Garnish with the rosemary sprigs and serve immediately.

NOTE: If fresh herbs are not available, do not replace with dried—instead, use chopped parsley for seasoning and garnish.

OIL-ROASTED GARLIC

18 large cloves garlic
3 cups olive oil

In a small nonreactive saucepan, combine the garlic and oil and simmer over low heat for about 40 minutes, or until the garlic is very soft. Drain, reserving the oil for another use, and serve.

Spice-Crusted Tuna with Asparagus and Seaweed-Wrapped Noodles ~ David Burke

SERVES 6
PREPARATION TIME: ABOUT 1 HOUR AND 15 MINUTES
COOKING TIME: ABOUT 30 MINUTES

¼ cup black peppercorns
¼ cup fennel seeds
¼ cup coriander seeds
¾ tablespoon allspice berries

Again, flavors from all over the world unite to make a contemporary American dish. This is as visually appealing as it is delicious. One of the benefits of this recipe is that the Seaweed-Wrapped Noodle rolls can be made separately and served as an hors d'oeuvre with the yogurt and curry mixture as a dipping sauce.

1 Assemble *mise en place* trays for this recipe (see page 6).

¼ cup curry powder

¾ tablespoon coarse salt

18 thin asparagus spears, approximately the same diameter, trimmed

4 ounces soba noodles

2 tablespoons tahini paste

½ cup soy sauce

1 tablespoon rice wine vinegar

3½ tablespoons chopped fresh cilantro

Cayenne pepper to taste

6 sheets nori

¾ cup plain yogurt

½ cup Dijon mustard

6 four-ounce fresh tuna steaks

¼ cup Curry Oil (see page 265)

2 Combine the peppercorns, fennel seeds, coriander seeds, and allspice berries in a spice or coffee grinder or a mini food processor and process until very fine. Transfer to a shallow bowl and stir in the curry powder and salt. Set aside.

3 Place the asparagus spears on a steamer rack. Steam for 2 to 3 minutes or until crisp-tender. Pat dry and set aside.

4 Cook the soba noodles in boiling, salted water according to the package directions. Drain well (do not rinse).

5 In a medium-sized bowl, combine the noodles, tahini, ¼ cup of the soy sauce, vinegar, 1½ tablespoons of the cilantro, and cayenne to taste.

6 Generously brush the nori sheets with the remaining soy sauce. Place equal portions of the noodle mixture about 1 inch from the bottom edge of each nori sheet. Fold the bottom edge of each sheet over the filling and roll up to make a firm log. Set aside.

7 In a small bowl, combine the yogurt, mustard, and the remaining 3 tablespoons cilantro. Set aside.

8 Dredge the tuna steaks with the spice mixture, pressing it gently into the flesh.

9 In a large sauté pan, heat 3 tablespoons of the Curry Oil over medium-high heat. When the oil is very hot, add the tuna steaks. Sear for 30 seconds per side. Remove from the heat and drain on paper towels.

10 Using a small sharp knife, pierce 3 holes into the side of each steak. Gently push an asparagus spear into each hole, pushing the asparagus as far into the steak as possible. Trim off any excess asparagus so that none extends from the side of the steak.

11 Thinly slice each tuna steak and arrange on 6 serving plates. You will be able to see the asparagus in each slice. Slice each nori noodle roll crosswise on the diagonal. Arrange the nori rolls beside the tuna. Drizzle the plate with the yogurt mixture and the remaining 1 tablespoon Curry Oil.

Mrs. Reardy's Shrimp and Artichoke Casserole ~ Craig Claiborne

SERVES 6

PREPARATION TIME: ABOUT 20 MINUTES

COOKING TIME: ABOUT 45 MINUTES

7 tablespoons unsalted butter

1 pound medium shrimp (unshelled)

4½ tablespoons all-purpose flour

¾ cup milk

¾ cup heavy cream

Salt and freshly ground black pepper to taste

4 ounces fresh mushrooms, sliced (about 1¼ cups)

1 nine-ounce package frozen artichoke hearts, thawed and well drained

2 tablespoons sherry

1 tablespoon Worcestershire sauce

¼ cup freshly grated Parmesan cheese

Paprika

Ah, for the days of cholesterol, fat, and calorie ignorance! I suspect that you could replace the butter with canola oil, the milk and cream with skim milk. But I also suspect the result would be less than rich and delicious. Save this recipe for a day when calories don't count and enjoy yourself!

1 Preheat the oven to 375 degrees F. Assemble *mise en place* trays for this recipe (see page 6). Grease a 2-quart casserole or baking dish with 1 tablespoon of the butter.

2 In a pan of rapidly boiling salted water, cook the shrimp for 3 minutes or until just opaque. Drain and refresh under cold running water. Peel and devein. Set aside.

3 In a medium-sized saucepan, melt 4½ tablespoons of the butter over medium-high heat. Whisk in the flour until blended. Gradually whisk in the milk and cream, and cook, whisking constantly, for 3 to 4 minutes, until the sauce is thick and smooth. Season to taste with salt and pepper. Remove from the heat and set aside.

4 In a small sauté pan, melt the remaining 1½ tablespoons butter over medium heat. Add the mushrooms and sauté for about 5 minutes, or until softened. Remove from the heat.

5 Arrange the artichokes in the bottom of the prepared casserole. Scatter the shrimp over the artichokes. Spoon the mushrooms over the shrimp and artichokes.

6 Add the sherry and Worcestershire sauce to the cream sauce. Pour over the shrimp and artichokes. Sprinkle with the Parmesan cheese and dust with paprika.

7 Bake for 30 minutes, or until golden and bubbling. Serve hot.

~ You can substitute canned artichoke hearts. Be sure to use those packed in water—not marinated artichoke hearts.

Roasted Salmon with Moroccan Barbecue Sauce ❧ Patrick Clark

SERVES 6

PREPARATION TIME: ABOUT 15 MINUTES

COOKING TIME: ABOUT 1 HOUR

FAT PER SERVING: 25.1 GRAMS

SATURATED FAT: 5 GRAMS

CALORIES PER SERVING: 923

CALORIES FROM FAT: 24%

Moroccan Barbecue Sauce (see page 277)

Six 4-ounce skinless salmon fillets

Coarse salt and freshly ground black pepper to taste

2 tablespoons cracked black pepper

2 tablespoons fennel seeds

*P*atrick serves this aromatic salmon on a bed of Couscous and Sautéed Savoy Cabbage (see page 241) for a complete, light-tasting main course.

1 Assemble *mise en place* trays for this recipe (see page 6).

2 Prepare the Moroccan Barbecue Sauce.

3 Preheat the oven to 400 degrees F.

4 Season the salmon to taste with coarse salt and pepper, lay on a heavy-duty baking sheet, and bake for 7 minutes. Remove from the oven and lightly coat each side with the sauce. Sprinkle with the cracked pepper and fennel seeds and roast for an additional 3 minutes, or until the fish is opaque and just beginning to flake. Serve hot, drizzled with additional sauce.

Roast Salmon with Moroccan Spices ❧ Gary Danko

SERVES 6

PREPARATION TIME: ABOUT 1 HOUR

COOKING TIME: ABOUT 45 MINUTES

3 tablespoons chopped fresh cilantro

3 tablespoons chopped fresh flat-leaf parsley

1½ tablespoons cumin seeds

1 tablespoon Hungarian paprika

*T*his dish makes a dramatic and aromatic statement when it is presented at the table. As you cut open the foil wrapper, the sensual Moroccan spices waft out to enrapture your dinner guests. A tempting alternative to plain poached salmon, this can be served hot, cold, or at room temperature.

1 Assemble *mise en place* trays for this recipe (see page 6).

2 Preheat the oven to 350 degrees F.

3 In a small bowl, combine the cilantro, parsley, cumin, paprika, saffron, and coarse salt. Whisk in the oil, lemon

½ teaspoon crumbled saffron threads

1 tablespoon coarse salt

¼ cup extra-virgin olive oil

1½ tablespoons fresh lemon juice

1½ teaspoons harissa or Tabasco, or to taste

One 8-pound salmon, cleaned, head left on and fins and tail removed, rinsed, and patted dry

- Special Equipment: Instant-read thermometer

juice, and harissa. Generously coat the salmon on all sides with the spice mixture.

4 Center a sheet of heavy-duty aluminum foil 18 inches wide and 2 feet long, shiny side up, on a baking sheet large enough to hold the fish. Put the fish and any remaining marinade in the center of the foil. Cover with a matching sheet of foil. Fold up and tightly crimp the edges together to make an airtight packet.

5 Roast for about 45 minutes, or until an instant-read thermometer registers 140 degrees F when inserted through the foil into the thickest part of the fish. Remove and let rest for 5 minutes without opening the foil.

6 Transfer the entire packet to a serving platter and cut the foil open at the table. Lift off large pieces of fish and spoon the cooking juices over them as you serve.

NOTE: If you make this marinade, known as chermoula, in advance, do not add the saffron until the last minute, or the flavor will be lost.

 ❧ Any large firm-fleshed fish, such as red snapper, can be substituted for the salmon.

Grilled Swordfish with Pineapple–Red Chile Salsa ❧ Dean Fearing

SERVES 6

PREPARATION TIME: ABOUT 25 MINUTES

COOKING TIME: ABOUT 5 MINUTES

CHILLING TIME (SALSA ONLY): AT LEAST 2 HOURS

---

6 seven-ounce swordfish steaks, trimmed of skin and dark membrane

This is a wonderfully light fish dish, low in fat and really rich in flavor. It's a spectacular warm-weather recipe and great for summer entertaining. Although not necessary, cooking the swordfish on an outdoor grill allows the flavors of the fish to shine.

---

1 Prepare a charcoal or gas grill or preheat the broiler. Assemble *mise en place* trays for this recipe (see page 6).

3 tablespoons sesame oil

Salt to taste

Pineapple-Red Chile Salsa (see page 285)

2 Brush the swordfish with the sesame oil and season to taste with salt.

3 Put the fish on the preheated grill or under the broiler so that it is 2 to 3 inches from the heat. Cook for 2 minutes, or just long enough to lightly color the side facing the heat. If using a grill, this should be long enough to mark that side with grill marks. Turn the fish over and cook for 2 minutes longer or until the flesh is firm. (To prevent overcooking and keep the fish moist, allow no more than 5 minutes total cooking time for each ½ inch of thickness at the thickest part.)

4 Ladle about ½ cup of the Pineapple–Red Chile Salsa into the centers of 6 warm dinner plates. Place the swordfish steaks on top and serve immediately.

❧ If using an outdoor grill, make sure the grids are very clean. To prevent the fish from sticking, lightly brush the grids with vegetable oil before grilling.

Achiote-Fried Catfish with Salsa Fresca ❧ Marilyn Frobuccino

SERVES 6

PREPARATION TIME: ABOUT 35 MINUTES

COOKING TIME: ABOUT 40 MINUTES

CHILLING TIME (CATFISH ONLY): AT LEAST 2 HOURS

CHILLING TIME (SALSA ONLY): AT LEAST 30 MINUTES

---

4 to 5 six- to seven-ounce catfish fillets (about 2 pounds), cut into 18 long strips

A southern tradition, catfish is frequently used in South-western and Cajun cooking as it readily takes to a variety of strong seasonings. This mild-flavored, low-fat fish is now farm-raised and available across the country.

---

1 Assemble *mise en place* trays for this recipe (see page 6).

2 Rinse the catfish strips under cold running water. Pat dry with paper towels.

2 tablespoons ground annatto seeds

2 tablespoons plus 2 teaspoons chile powder

2 tablespoons plus 1 teaspoon finely minced garlic

½ cup olive oil

4 large eggs

2 cups coarse-ground yellow cornmeal

1½ teaspoons ground cumin

1 tablespoon salt, or to taste

Vegetable oil, for shallow frying

Salsa Fresca (see page 288)

■ Special Equipment: deep-fry thermometer

3 In a glass or ceramic dish, combine the ground annatto, 2 tablespoons of the chile powder, 2 tablespoons of the garlic, and the olive oil. Add the catfish strips and rub the mixture over the fish. Cover and refrigerate for up to 2 hours.

4 Preheat the oven to 200 degrees F.

5 In a shallow bowl, lightly beat the eggs. In another shallow bowl, combine the cornmeal, cumin, salt, and the remaining 2 teaspoons chile powder and 1 teaspoon garlic.

6 One at a time, dip the seasoned catfish strips into the beaten egg, coating well. Then dip into the cornmeal mixture, making sure all sides are well coated. Place the strips on a wire rack.

7 Heat about ½ inch of vegetable oil in a large skillet over medium-high heat to 375 degrees F. on a deep-fry thermometer. Fry the catfish strips, 3 at a time, turning once, for about 6 minutes, or until golden. Drain on paper towels. Put the cooked strips on a wire rack and keep warm in the oven until all strips are cooked.

8 Arrange 3 strips of catfish on each serving plate and spoon the Salsa Fresca on the side. Serve immediately.

Big Easy Seafood-Okra Gumbo ∿ Emeril Lagasse

SERVES 6

PREPARATION TIME: ABOUT 40 MINUTES

COOKING TIME: ABOUT 35 MINUTES

FAT PER SERVING: 7.9 GRAMS

SATURATED FAT: 1.3 GRAMS

CALORIES PER SERVING: 428

CALORIES FROM FAT: 19%

2 tablespoons plus 1 teaspoon olive oil

This is a wonderful party dish—rich, aromatic, and filling. Serve it with crisp toasts and a crisp white wine or maybe a light beer.

1 Assemble *mise en place* trays for this recipe (see page 6).

2 In a large saucepan, heat 2 tablespoons of the oil over medium heat. Add the onions, celery, bell peppers, shallots, and garlic and sauté for about 7 minutes, or until the onions are translucent.

2 medium-sized onions, cut into
½-inch dice

2 ribs celery, cut into ½-inch dice

1 green bell pepper, cored, seeded,
and cut into ½-inch dice

1 red bell pepper, cored, seeded, and
cut into ½-inch dice

1 tablespoon minced shallots

1 teaspoon minced garlic

3 plum tomatoes, peeled, seeded,
and chopped

¼ pound okra, trimmed and sliced
¼ inch thick

8 cups Fish Stock (see page 16)

½ pound boneless firm-fleshed fish,
such as grouper, bass, or snapper,
cut into chunks

½ pound shrimp, peeled and
deveined

¼ pound crabmeat, picked over for
shells and cartilage

1 tablespoon chopped fresh basil

2 teaspoons chopped fresh oregano

1 teaspoon chopped fresh thyme

2 bay leaves

2 tablespoons Emeril's Creole
Seasoning (recipe follows)

2 tablespoons gumbo filé powder

Worcestershire sauce to taste

Tabasco sauce to taste

1 cup shucked oysters, with their
liquid

6 cups hot cooked white rice

3 Stir in the tomatoes and okra and cook for 5 minutes.
Add the stock, bring to a simmer, and simmer for about
20 minutes, or until the okra is tender.

4 Meanwhile, in a large sauté pan, heat the remaining
1 teaspoon oil over medium heat. Add the fish pieces,
shrimp, and crab and sauté for about 3 minutes, or until
the fish is firm but not cooked through. Drain off the
liquid and set the fish and seafood aside.

5 Add the basil, oregano, thyme, bay leaves, Creole
seasoning, filé powder, and Worcestershire sauce and
Tabasco to taste to the simmering stock and stir to combine. Add the reserved fish and seafood, taste, and adjust
the seasonings. Add the oysters with their liquid and
cook for about 1 minute, or until they plump.

6 Place equal portions of rice in each shallow bowl.
Ladle the gumbo over the top and serve immediately.

NOTE: The gumbo stock base can be made early in the
day. Reheat and add the fish and seafood just before
serving.

EMERIL'S CREOLE SEASONING

MAKES ABOUT ¾ CUP

2½ tablespoons paprika

2 tablespoons coarse salt

2 tablespoons garlic powder

1 tablespoon freshly ground black pepper

1 tablespoon onion powder

1 tablespoon cayenne pepper

1 tablespoon dried oregano

1 tablespoon dried thyme

In a glass or ceramic container with an airtight lid, combine all the ingredients. Cover and shake well to combine. Store, covered, for up to 6 months.

Trout Cooked in Vernaccia di Oristano ❧ Carlo Middione

SERVES 6
PREPARATION TIME: ABOUT 30 MINUTES
COOKING TIME: ABOUT 30 MINUTES

⅓ cup extra-virgin olive oil

2 cloves garlic, minced

1 large carrot, peeled and finely chopped

1 large yellow onion, finely chopped

2 ribs celery, finely chopped

1 large, ripe tomato, cored, peeled, seeded, and finely chopped

1 lemon, washed and thinly sliced

Vernaccia di Oristano wine from Sardegna is as different as night from day from the better-known Vernaccia di San Gemignano, a Tuscan wine. It is not yet readily available in American markets, and Carlo Middione suggests approximating the taste of Vernaccia di Oristano by mixing three parts California golden sherry with one part dry white vermouth. For that essential undertaste of bitterness so characteristic of the wine, Carlo adds a well-crushed kernel from the pit of a peach or apricot per quart of the wine mixture. This, he says, adds just enough of the amaro taste, which gives "ballast" to the flavor of the finished dish.

---

1 Assemble *mise en place* trays for this recipe (see page 6).

⅓ cup chopped fresh parsley

½ teaspoon ground oregano

Salt and freshly ground black pepper to taste

6 eight-ounce trout, cleaned

About 2 cups Vernaccia de Oristano, or a mixture of sherry and dry vermouth (see above)

2 In a sauté pan large enough to hold all the trout, heat the olive oil. Add the garlic and sauté oven medium heat for 3 minutes, or until deep gold. Stir in the carrots, onions, celery, tomatoes, lemon, parsley, and oregano. Add salt and pepper to taste. Cook, stirring, for about 10 minutes, or until all the vegetables are lightly browned.

3 Reduce the heat and spread the vegetables evenly over the bottom of the pan. Arrange the trout snugly on top of the vegetables. Add enough wine to come halfway up the trout. Cover loosely with a lid or foil and cook for 5 minutes. Carefully turn the trout with a slotted spatula and cook for about 5 minutes more, or until cooked through. Remove the trout to a warm platter and cover with aluminum foil to keep warm.

4 Strain the vegetables and pan liquid through a fine sieve, pushing down on the solids to extract all the juices. Discard the solids. Pour the cooking liquid into a medium-sized saucepan and simmer over medium heat for about 10 minutes, or until reduced to 1 cup.

5 Place the trout on serving plates and spoon the sauce over the top. Serve immediately.

❧ Since this dish must be cooked at the last minute, organize your *mise en place* trays well to speed preparation.

❧ You may need to use 2 sauté pans, particularly if you decide to leave the heads on the trout for presentation purposes.

❧ California golden sherry is made by such wineries as Christian Brothers and Almaden. Good dry white vermouth is made by Cinzano and Martini and Rossi. Vermouth has a higher alcohol content than a dry white wine and, therefore, is more in keeping with the spirit of the Vernaccia di Oristano.

Striped Bass with Artichokes and Aïoli ❧ Wayne Nish

SERVES 6

PREPARATION TIME: ABOUT 45 MINUTES

COOKING TIME: ABOUT 55 MINUTES

RESTING TIME (AIOLI ONLY): 8 HOURS

6 small artichokes, trimmed, or large artichoke hearts (not marinated)

1 whole head garlic, halved crosswise

1 lemon, quartered

1 tablespoon chopped fresh thyme

Salt and freshly ground black pepper to taste

6 six-ounce striped bass fillets with skin

Kosher salt to taste

¼ cup extra-virgin olive oil

Aïoli (see page 262)

Aïoli is the richly flavored garlic mayonnaise favored throughout Provence as an accompaniment to lightly steamed or grilled poultry, fish, or fresh vegetables. Here, it highlights a simply cooked bass.

1 Preheat the oven to 300 degrees F. Assemble *mise en place* trays for this recipe (see page 6).

2 Cook the artichokes in boiling, salted water for 12 to 15 minutes, or until tender. Drain and let cool slightly.

3 Cut the artichokes in half lengthwise. Place the artichokes, garlic, lemon, thyme, and salt and pepper to taste in a small ovenproof dish. Cover tightly with aluminum foil and bake for 20 minutes. Uncover and set aside to cool.

4 Heat 2 ten-inch, medium-weight skillets over medium-high heat for 4 to 5 minutes.

5 Lightly season both sides of the fish with kosher salt.

6 Pour half the olive oil into each pan. Place 3 of the fish fillets in each pan, skin-side down. Cover the pan with a lid or another skillet laid upside down so that it resembles a dome. Cook the fish for 6 minutes, without turning. Transfer to paper towels to drain.

7 Place a fish fillet in the center of each warm dinner plate. Lay 2 artichoke halves next to each one. Spoon Aïoli over all, or place on one side of the plate, and pass the remaining Aïoli on the side.

❧ The striped bass can be replaced with red snapper or another firm-fleshed saltwater fish.

Seared "Steak-Cut" Haddock with Lentil Ragout and Citrus Shallot Sauce ❧ Charles Palmer

SERVES 6
PREPARATION TIME: ABOUT 20 MINUTES
COOKING TIME: ABOUT 50 MINUTES

Lentil Ragout (see page 250)

HADDOCK:

2 tablespoons grapeseed oil

Salt and freshly ground black pepper to taste

6 six-ounce, thick-cut, fresh haddock steaks (1¼ to 1½ inches thick)

3 tablespoons minced shallots

3 tablespoons unsalted butter

1 tablespoon olive oil

1¼ cups Chicken Stock (see page 15)

Zest and juice of 2 lemons

1 tablespoon minced fresh parsley

1 teaspoon minced fresh thyme

In this recipe, Charlie treats the fish as though it were a piece of steak. The interesting combination of textures and flavors creates a contemporary taste for this mild, low-fat fish.

---

1 Assemble *mise en place* trays for this recipe (see page 6).

2 Prepare the Lentil Ragout.

3 To prepare the haddock, heat the grapeseed oil in a large, nonstick skillet over medium-high heat. Season the haddock steaks with salt and pepper to taste and place in the hot pan. Cook for 5 to 7 minutes, or until golden brown and lightly crusted on the bottom. Turn the fish and sear the other side. Transfer to a plate and cover with aluminum foil to keep warm.

4 Reduce the heat to medium and add the shallots and butter to the pan. Cook for 2 minutes, or until the butter starts to brown and foam. Add the olive oil and stock and cook, stirring occasionally, for 10 minutes, or until the liquid is reduced by half. Whisk in the lemon juice and zest and minced herbs. Adjust the seasoning with salt and pepper.

5 Spoon equal portions of lentil ragout onto 6 warm dinner plates. Place the haddock steaks on the plates and spoon the pan sauce over and around the fish.

Sole with Tomato Fondue and Saffron Pasta ❧ Georges Perrier

SERVES 6

PREPARATION TIME: ABOUT 30 MINUTES

COOKING TIME: ABOUT 40 MINUTES

FAT PER SERVING: 6 GRAMS

SATURATED FAT: 1 GRAM

CALORIES PER SERVING: 420

CALORIES FROM FAT: 15%

---

1 tablespoon toasted saffron threads

1 cup water

1 pound imported dried fettuccine

Salt to taste

Six 4-ounce Dover sole fillets

Salt and freshly ground black pepper to taste

¼ cup all-purpose flour

2 tablespoons plus 1 teaspoon olive oil

Tomato Fondue (see page 281)

2 tablespoons chopped fresh chives

Georges normally makes fresh saffron egg pasta for this dish but, in the interest of saving calories, we have substituted more ordinary dried pasta. If you can find saffron-flavored dried pasta, by all means use it.

---

1 Assemble *mise en place* trays for this recipe (see page 6).

2 In a small saucepan, combine the saffron and water and bring to a boil over high heat. Reduce the heat and simmer for about 30 minutes, or until the liquid is reduced to 3 tablespoons. Strain, discarding the saffron, and set the liquid aside.

3 Bring a large pot of salted water to a boil over high heat. Add the pasta and cook for about 9 minutes, or until al dente.

4 Meanwhile, season the sole with salt and pepper and then lightly dredge with the flour, shaking off the excess. In a nonstick sauté pan large enough to hold the fish comfortably, heat 2 tablespoons of the oil. Cook the sole for about 30 seconds on each side, until opaque. Remove from the heat and cover to keep warm.

5 Drain the pasta and toss with the reserved saffron water, the remaining 1 teaspoon oil, and salt to taste. Place equal portions of the hot pasta in the center of 6 plates. Lay a fillet on top and ladle 3 tablespoons Tomato Fondue over each. Sprinkle with the chives and serve immediately.

NOTE: If you decide to make your own fresh pasta, add the saffron water to the dough rather than using it as a seasoning.

❧ Replace the Dover sole with petrale sole, lemon sole, rex sole, or any other member of the flounder family.

❧ Toast the saffron in a nonstick skillet over medium heat for about 30 seconds, just until fragrant.

Salmon with Onion Confit, Winter Vegetables, and Red Wine Sauce ❧ Debra Ponzek

SERVES 6

PREPARATION TIME: ABOUT 1 HOUR AND 15 MINUTES

COOKING TIME: ABOUT 1 HOUR AND 45 MINUTES

RED WINE SAUCE:

2 tablespoons unsalted butter

⅓ cup chopped onions

⅓ cup chopped leeks

⅓ cup chopped celery

2 fresh thyme sprigs

½ pound salmon (or other fish) bones, well rinsed

1½ cups red wine

1 cup Veal Stock (see page 16)

Salt and freshly ground black pepper to taste

WINTER VEGETABLES:

2 beets, scrubbed

5 small new potatoes, scrubbed

Salt and freshly ground black pepper to taste

½ large butternut squash, peeled, seeded, and cut into ¼-inch dice

1 large turnip, peeled and cut into ¼-inch dice

1 tablespoon unsalted butter

2 tablespoons chopped fresh parsley

2 tablespoons chopped fresh thyme

This is a wonderfully aromatic dish, full of intense flavors that balance the delicate salmon. You could use almost any sweet, delicate fish, such as sea trout, white fish, or trout, as well as any combination of crisp vegetables you like.

---

1 Assemble *mise en place* trays for this recipe (see page 6).

2 To make the sauce, melt 2 tablespoons of the butter in a medium-sized saucepan over medium-high heat. Add the onion, leeks, celery, and thyme sprigs and stir to coat with the butter. Lay the fish bones on top of the vegetables, cover and reduce the heat to low. Cook for 5 to 10 minutes, or until any flesh remaining on the bones is opaque.

3 Stir in the wine and cook, uncovered, for about 15 minutes, or until the liquid is reduced by three-quarters. Add the stock and cook for about 30 minutes, or until the sauce is thick enough to coat the back of a spoon. Strain through a fine sieve into a small saucepan. Season to taste with salt and pepper. Set aside.

4 To prepare the winter vegetables, put the beets in a small saucepan and add enough water to cover. Bring to a boil over high heat. Reduce the heat and simmer for 20 minutes, or until tender when pierced with a fork. Drain and cool.

5 Meanwhile, put the potatoes in a medium-sized saucepan and add enough water to cover. Add a little salt to the water. Bring to a boil over high heat. Reduce the heat and simmer for about 12 minutes, or until tender when pierced with a fork. Drain and cool.

6 Peel the cooked beets and potatoes and cut into ¼-inch dice. Toss with the squash and turnip, season with salt and pepper, and set aside.

Onion confit:

3 tablespoons duck fat or olive oil

3 pounds red onions, thinly sliced

5 tablespoons granulated sugar

3 tablespoons sherry vinegar

Salt and freshly ground black pepper to taste

Salmon:

2 teaspoons olive oil

6 six-ounce salmon fillets

Salt and freshly ground black pepper to taste

7 To make the onion confit, melt the duck fat or oil in a large sauté pan over medium heat. Add the sliced red onions and sprinkle with the sugar. Cook, stirring occasionally, for 30 minutes, or until the onions are uniformly glazed and deep brown. Sprinkle with the vinegar and cook for 2 minutes more. Season to taste with salt and pepper. Remove from the heat and set aside.

8 Preheat the oven to 400 degrees F.

9 To prepare the salmon, in a large ovenproof sauté pan, heat the olive oil over medium-high heat. Season the salmon with salt and pepper and sear on both sides for 1 minute, or until just crisp. Transfer the pan to the oven and roast for 4 minutes, or until medium rare.

10 In a nonstick sauté pan, melt the butter over medium-high heat. Add the diced winter vegetables and season to taste with salt and pepper. Cook for 5 minutes, or until just crisp-tender and golden. Stir in the chopped herbs. Remove from the heat and cover with aluminum foil to keep warm.

11 Meanwhile, heat the red wine sauce over low heat.

12 Place the onion confit on one side of 6 warm serving plates. Lay the salmon partially on the confit and spoon the vegetables on the other side of the salmon. Spoon the warm sauce around the vegetables and serve immediately.

Grilled Salmon with Black Pepper and Ginger ❧ Wolfgang Puck

SERVES 6

PREPARATION TIME: ABOUT 20 MINUTES

COOKING TIME: 45 TO 55 MINUTES

1½ cups white wine

¾ cup sherry

6 scallions, trimmed and chopped

5½ tablespoons chopped fresh ginger

½ cup heavy cream

8 tablespoons unsalted butter

Salt and freshly ground white pepper to taste

3 cups plus 3 tablespoons peanut oil

1 bunch spinach, trimmed, washed, and thoroughly dried

4½ tablespoons cracked black pepper

6 six-ounce fresh, skinless salmon fillets

Exotic tastes simply presented make this a special entrée. It is easy to do on a grill, but equally good cooked under a hot broiler.

---

1 Prepare a charcoal or gas grill or preheat the broiler. Assemble *mise en place* trays for this recipe (see page 6).

2 In a medium-sized saucepan, combine the wine, sherry, scallions, and 1 tablespoon of the ginger. Bring to a simmer over medium heat and simmer for 10 to 12 minutes, or until reduced by half.

3 Slowly whisk in the cream and cook gently for 15 to 20 minutes, or until the sauce is thick enough to coat the back of a spoon.

4 Whisk the butter into the sauce, waiting until each tablespoon is incorporated before adding the next. Remove from the heat and season to taste with salt and white pepper. Strain through a fine sieve into a small saucepan. Set aside.

5 In a deep, heavy saucepan, heat 3 cups of the oil over medium-high heat. When very hot, cook the spinach leaves, a few at a time, for 20 seconds, or until crisp. Using a slotted spoon, remove the leaves from the oil and drain on paper towels.

6 Combine the remaining 4½ tablespoons ginger and the cracked pepper. Season the salmon with salt to taste, and then generously coat with the ginger-pepper mixture. Drizzle the remaining 3 tablespoons of oil over both sides of the salmon. Grill or broil the salmon for 4 to 5 minutes on each side, or until firm but still rare in the center.

7 Meanwhile, in the top half of a double boiler, reheat the sauce over low heat.

8 Spoon the sauce into the center of 6 warm plates. Lay a salmon fillet on the sauce. Arrange the spinach leaves to the side, and serve immediately.

❧ Be sure the spinach leaves are completely dry before frying. If they are even a little wet, the oil will spatter. In any event, use caution when dropping them into the hot oil and do not crowd the pan. Although these can be fried ahead of time, they are best when fried immediately before serving.

Spice-Rubbed Swordfish with Mango-Lime Salsa ❧ Chris Schlesinger

SERVES 6
PREPARATION TIME: ABOUT 30 MINUTES
GRILLING TIME (fish only): ABOUT 15 MINUTES
FAT PER SERVING: 7.7 GRAMS
SATURATED FAT: 1.6 GRAMS
CALORIES PER SERVING: 220
CALORIES FROM FAT: 32%

---

3 tablespoons cumin seeds

3 tablespoons chile powder

2 tablespoons coarse salt

2 tablespoons cracked black pepper

1½ tablespoons curry powder

1½ tablespoons ground cinnamon

Six 4-ounce swordfish steaks, about ¾ inch thick

Mango-Lime Salsa (see page 286)

Refreshing and easy to prepare, this slightly smoky swordfish is a wonderful addition to your repertoire of low-fat summer grilling.

---

1 Assemble *mise en place* trays for this recipe (see page 6).

2 In a heavy sauté pan, combine the cumin, chile powder, coarse salt, pepper, curry powder, and cinnamon and toast over medium heat, stirring frequently, for about 4 minutes, or until slightly smoky. Set aside to cool.

3 Prepare a charcoal or gas grill or preheat a broiler.

4 Rub the fish on both sides with the cooled spice mixture. Grill over medium-hot coals for about 7 minutes on each side, or until opaque throughout. If broiling, broil the fish 5 to 6 inches from the heat source. Serve with the Mango-Lime Salsa on the side.

NOTE: The spice rub can be made up to 1 month ahead, tightly covered, and kept in a cool, dark spot.

Mussels "Saganaki" ❧ Paula Wolfert

SERVES 6

PREPARATION TIME: ABOUT 30 MINUTES

SOAKING TIME: 45 MINUTES;

COOKING TIME: ABOUT 10 MINUTES

---

3 pounds mussels

1 tablespoon coarse salt, plus more to taste

½ cup water

1 to 2 tablespoons fresh lemon juice, or more to taste

¼ teaspoon freshly ground black pepper, plus more to taste

1 tablespoon olive oil

2 teaspoons minced seeded long hot green chile, or more to taste

⅓ cup plus 2 tablespoons chopped fresh flat-leaf parsley

½ cup peeled, seeded, and chopped fresh tomatoes or drained, seeded, and chopped canned tomatoes

½ teaspoon mashed garlic

5 large fresh spearmint or other mint leaves, torn into shreds

¼ teaspoon crumbled dried oregano, preferably Greek

1 teaspoon dry mustard

Pinch of red pepper flakes

3 ounces imported feta cheese, preferably Bulgarian

A saganaki is a shallow pan with two handles, but any a deep sauté pan will work just about as well for this combination of shellfish and feta cheese. The flavors may surprise your taste buds, but I'm sure you will find it quite delicious.

---

1 Assemble *mise en place* trays for this recipe (see page 6).

2 Scrub the mussels and pull off the beards. Rinse in several changes of water and put in a bowl of cool water. Add the sea salt and let stand for at least 30 minutes to purge the mussels of sand. Drain.

3 Place the mussels in a saganaki or large deep sauté pan. Add the water, cover, and cook over high heat for about 2 minutes, or just until the mussels open; do not overcook. Using tongs or a slotted spoon, transfer the mussels to a bowl to cool. Strain the cooking liquid through several layers of damp cheesecloth into a bowl and set aside.

4 Remove the mussels from their shells and cut off any remaining beards. Strain any liquid collected in the bowl and add to the reserved mussel broth. Sprinkle the mussels with lemon juice and pepper to taste.

5 In a medium-sized nonreactive skillet, heat the olive oil over medium-low heat. Add 2 teaspoons minced chile and ⅓ cup of the parsley and cook for 1 minute, stirring. Add the reserved mussel cooking liquid, the tomatoes, garlic, mint, oregano, mustard, red pepper flakes, and the remaining ¼ teaspoon pepper. Raise the heat to high and bring to a boil. Reduce the heat and simmer for 5 minutes, stirring often, or until the sauce has reduced to about 1¼ cups. If desired, add more minced green chile to taste. Return to the boil for just a second. Transfer to a bowl and allow to cool for about 10

minutes, until tepid. Add the mussels to the sauce, cover, and refrigerate.

6 Twenty minutes before serving, soak the feta in cold water for 15 minutes. Drain and cut into ½-inch cubes.

7 In a large skillet, heat the mussels and sauce over medium-low heat just until heated through. Do not allow the sauce to boil. Add the feta cheese and cook, stirring, for 2 minutes. Taste and adjust the seasoning. Serve immediately, sprinkled with the remaining 2 tablespoons chopped parsley.

___

➤ If you buy cultivated, farm-raised mussels, there is no need to soak them. Ask the fish merchant where the mussels come from; soaking diminishes their flavor.

Vegetable Paella ➤ Dominick Cerrone

SERVES 6

PREPARATION TIME: ABOUT 1½ HOURS

COOKING TIME: ABOUT 30 MINUTES

___

1 large tomato, peeled, cored, seeded, and chopped

2 tablespoons minced onion

7 cups Vegetable Stock (see page 18)

1½ tablespoons saffron threads

1½ tablespoons Hungarian paprika

1 bay leaf

⅓ cup extra-virgin olive oil

3 cups Arborio rice

½ cup fresh peas

⅓ cup diced roasted red bell pepper

This is a dazzling vegetarian dish that can be adapted to any time of the year using fresh seasonal vegetables. When presented at the table, it resembles an edible kaleidoscope.

___

1 Assemble *mise en place* trays for this recipe (see page 6).

2 In a small bowl, toss the tomatoes and onions to combine.

3 In a medium-sized saucepan, combine the stock, saffron, paprika, bay leaf, and tomato mixture and bring to a boil over medium-high heat. Immediately reduce the heat to a simmer.

4 Heat the paella pan over medium-high heat. Add the oil and when very hot, stir in the rice. Cook, stirring constantly, for about 3 minutes, or until golden brown. Add 6 cups of the simmering stock, reduce the heat until barely simmering, and cook, without stirring, for about

½ to ¾ cup each of at least 6 of the following: blanched sliced carrots, fennel, celery, asparagus, and/or artichoke hearts; blanched corn kernels, sliced broccoli, and/or sliced cauliflower florets; blanched trimmed string beans, sugar snap peas, snow peas, and/or sliced mushrooms; shredded spinach and/or endive

¼ cup chopped fresh herbs [1 tablespoon each parsley and chives combined with any other herb(s) you desire]

Olive oil spray (optional)

■ Special Equipment: Paella pan or other wide shallow two-handled pan (about 14 inches in diameter)

20 minutes, or until the rice is barely al dente (see Note); place the vegetables decoratively over the rice as it cooks. Begin with the peas and roasted peppers and add the other vegetables according to the degree of doneness you desire. When the rice is al dente, turn off the heat and rest for about 10 minutes.

5 Sprinkle the paella with the herbs and, if desired, spray a bit of olive oil spray over the dish to make it glisten. Serve immediately, bringing the pan to the table.

NOTE: The extra cup of stock should be added if all the liquid has been absorbed before the rice is done. When setting up the decorative vegetable pattern, use one vegetable, such as asparagus, to outline sections.

_____

❧ If the paella pan is larger than the stove burner, set it off center and rotate it frequently for even cooking.

Spring Vegetable Stew with Pesto ❧ Bradley Ogden

SERVES 6
PREPARATION TIME: ABOUT 1 HOUR
COOKING TIME: ABOUT 20 MINUTES

_____

1 cup fresh fava beans (1 pound unshelled)

½ cup fresh peas (8 ounces unshelled)

1 small head broccoli, divided into small florets (about 2 cups)

5 cups Vegetable Stock (see page 18)

1 pound thick asparagus spears, peeled and cut into 2-inch pieces (about 2 cups)

You would have to be Peter Rabbit to make a fresher tasting stew. It's light enough to make a delightful first course, but served with homemade bread, it makes a lovely spring lunch.

_____

1 Assemble _mise en place_ trays for this recipe (see page 6).

2 In a large saucepan of lightly salted, boiling water, cook the fava beans for 2 minutes, or until just tender. Using a strainer or slotted spoon, remove the beans from the boiling water. Refresh under cold running water and drain well. Remove the skins from the beans and discard. Set the beans aside.

1 medium fennel bulb, trimmed, cored, and cut into 1-inch dice (about 1½ cups)

2 tomatoes, cored, peeled, seeded, and diced

1 yellow squash, trimmed, peeled, and cut into ¼-inch-thick slices (about 2 cups)

¾ pound small curly spinach leaves, trimmed, rinsed, and dried

Kosher salt and freshly ground black pepper to taste

⅓ cup fresh chervil leaves

2 tablespoons fresh tarragon leaves

Pesto (see page 270)

3 Add the peas and broccoli florets to the boiling water and cook for 30 seconds. Drain, rinse under cold running water, and drain well. Set aside.

4 In a large pot, bring the stock to a boil over high heat. Add the asparagus and fennel and cook for 30 seconds.

5 Add the fava beans, peas, broccoli, and the remaining vegetables and cook for 3 minutes, or until the spinach has wilted; do not overcook. Season to taste with salt and pepper. Stir in the chervil and tarragon.

6 Ladle the stew into 6 warm, shallow soup bowls. Generously spoon the Pesto over the top, and serve immediately.

❧ Use any fresh spring vegetables in this stew—for example, black-eyed peas could replace the peas. Young bitter greens, such as mustard and kale, could be added or could replace the spinach. Fresh corn kernels could also be used later in the season, when corn is at its most succulent.

Creamy Polenta with Roasted Wild Mushrooms and Fried Sage Leaves ❧ Bradley Ogden

SERVES 6

PREPARATION TIME: ABOUT 20 MINUTES

COOKING TIME: ABOUT 1 HOUR

1½ cups water

1½ cups Chicken Stock (see page 15)

9 cloves garlic, 8 cloves sliced, 1 clove minced

¾ cup polenta

The earthy mushrooms add extra body and fullness to the polenta. Without the mushrooms, the rich polenta is a terrific side dish, excellent served with a plate of grilled vegetables.

1 Preheat the oven to 350 degrees F. Assemble *mise en place* trays for this recipe (see page 6).

2 In a medium-sized, heavy-bottomed, ovenproof saucepan, bring the water, stock, and minced garlic to a full boil over high heat. Slowly whisk in the polenta. Reduce

6 cups any combination of flavorful mushrooms, such as shiitakes, morels, chanterelles, Italian browns, or cèpes, trimmed

4½ tablespoons olive oil

4½ tablespoons balsamic vinegar

3 sprigs fresh thyme

3 sprigs fresh rosemary

Kosher salt and freshly cracked black pepper to taste

3 tablespoons unsalted butter

⅔ cup crème fraîche, at room temperature

¼ cup freshly grated, aged Monterey Jack cheese

¼ cup freshly grated Parmesan cheese

Fried Sage Leaves (recipe follows)

the heat and cook for 5 minutes, stirring constantly with a wooden spoon. Cover, transfer to the oven, and bake for 45 minutes, stirring 2 or 3 times to prevent sticking.

3 Meanwhile, combine the mushrooms, sliced garlic, olive oil, vinegar, thyme, rosemary, and salt and pepper to taste in a shallow roasting pan. About 20 minutes before the polenta is ready, place the pan on a rack in the lower half of the oven and roast for 20 minutes, or until lightly browned and tender.

4 Remove the polenta and mushrooms from the oven. Beat the butter, crème fraîche, and cheeses into the polenta. Taste and adjust the seasoning with salt and pepper.

5 Spoon the polenta onto 6 warm plates. Spoon the mushrooms over the polenta. Garnish with the Fried Sage Leaves and serve immediately.

◆ Crème fraîche is available in the refrigerated foods section of specialty stores and some supermarkets.

◆ Polenta is both Italian cornmeal and the dish made from it. It is served as a main course or side dish, depending on the ingredients added to it and the rest of the menu. In the first stages of cooking, it is important to stir polenta continuously. In Italy, many cooks use a stick to stir polenta, but a long-handled wooden spoon works fine.

FRIED SAGE LEAVES

MAKES ABOUT ⅔ CUP

1 cup peanut oil
⅔ cup fresh sage leaves
Salt to taste

1 In a small sauté pan, heat the oil over high heat until very hot. Add a few sage leaves and fry for about 45 seconds, until the leaves are crisp and the edges begin to curl. Using a slotted spoon or long-handled strainer, remove the crisp leaves and drain on paper towels. Continue frying until all leaves are cooked.

2 Lightly sprinkle each batch of leaves with salt as they are fried. Store at room temperature until ready to use.

❧ Wipe the sage leaves clean with a paper towel. If you must wash them, be sure they are completely dry before frying.

Wild Mushroom Crêpes ❧ Jean-Georges Vongerichten

SERVES 6
PREPARATION TIME: ABOUT 30 MINUTES
COOKING TIME: ABOUT 45 MINUTES
CHILLING TIME (CREPE BATTER ONLY):
AT LEAST 20 MINUTES

6 tablespoons unsalted butter
1 shallot, chopped
1 clove garlic, chopped
4 ounces fresh porcini mushrooms, wiped clean, trimmed, and roughly chopped
4 ounces fresh shiitake mushrooms, wiped clean, trimmed, and roughly chopped

This is a basic crêpe recipe made special with mushrooms and a soy vinaigrette. Any type of wild mushrooms may be used.

1 Assemble *mise en place* trays for this recipe (see page 6).

2 In a medium-sized sauté pan, melt 2 tablespoons of the butter over medium-high heat. Add the shallot and garlic and sauté for about 3 minutes, until translucent.

3 Stir in the mushrooms and season to taste with salt and pepper. Reduce the heat and sauté for about 5 minutes, or until all the liquid from the mushrooms has evaporated.

4 Transfer the mushrooms to a blender or a food processor fitted with the metal blade. Process, using on/off

4 ounces fresh button mushrooms, wiped clean, trimmed, and roughly chopped

Salt and freshly ground black pepper to taste

1 tablespoon minced fresh chervil

1 tablespoon minced fresh chives

1 cup all-purpose flour

3 large eggs

1 cup milk

¼ cup soy sauce

¼ cup fresh lemon juice

1 cup olive oil

turns, until finely chopped. Scrape the mushrooms into a bowl and stir in the chervil and chives. Set aside.

5 In a small saucepan, melt the remaining 4 tablespoons of butter over medium heat. Heat for about 3 minutes, or until golden brown. Take care the butter does not burn. Remove from the heat.

6 In a bowl, whisk together the flour, eggs, milk, and salt to taste until smooth. Whisk in browned butter. Cover and refrigerate for 20 minutes.

7 Preheat the oven to 400 degrees F.

8 To make the crêpes, heat a 6- or 7-inch nonstick crêpe pan over medium heat. Pour in just enough batter (about 2 tablespoons) to cover the bottom of the pan. Cook for 1 minute, or until light brown on the bottom and set. Carefully turn the crêpe and cook the other side for about 1 minute, or just until golden. Lift the crêpe from the pan and lay on a sheet of wax paper. Continue making the crêpes until you have made 8, stacking one on top of the other as you go. Use any leftover batter to make extra crêpes and freeze them for another use.

9 Lay the crêpes out on a work surface. Spread an equal portion of mushrooms evenly over the top of 7 of the crêpes.

10 Neatly stack the mushroom-topped crêpes, one on top of the other on a small non-stick baking sheet. Place the plain crêpe on top. Bake for about 10 minutes, until the top crêpe is lightly browned.

11 Meanwhile, in a bowl, whisk together the soy sauce and lemon juice. Whisk in the olive oil.

12 Remove the crêpe stack from the oven and cut into 6 wedges.

13 Ladle 2 to 3 tablespoons of the soy vinaigrette into the centers of 6 warm plates. Place a wedge of crêpe on each plate and serve immediately.

🖎 You may have a little more soy vinaigrette than you need for this recipe. Store, covered and refrigerated, for up to a week. Use as dressing for meat, poultry or salads.

🖎 When serving the vinaigrette as a garnish, as in this recipe, do not overmix: You want the soy to "bead" out of the oil (form little droplets).

🖎 If you want to make the crêpes ahead of time and store them in the refrigerator, stack them between sheets of waxed paper. (This will make them easier to separate.) There is no need to bring them to room temperature before spreading the mushroom mixture on them.

🖎 If you make extra crêpes, stack them between sheets of waxed paper, wrap the stack in a double thickness of plastic, and freeze for up to 1 month.

Beet Tartare 🖎 Jean-Georges Vongerichten

SERVES 6

PREPARATION TIME: ABOUT 25 MINUTES

COOKING TIME: ABOUT 1 HOUR

CHILLING TIME: 30 MINUTES

----

1 pound beets, trimmed, washed, and quartered

1 shallot, chopped

2 teaspoons chopped cornichons

2 teaspoons chopped capers

2 teaspoons chopped fresh parsley

1 teaspoon mayonnaise

Salt and freshly ground black pepper to taste

Tabasco to taste

1 teaspoon sherry wine vinegar

3 tablespoons extra-virgin olive oil

Chef Vongerichten got this idea from steak tartare. In his bistro restaurant, JoJo, he sometimes serves the beet tartare topped with a sautéed sea scallop. He has also used golden beets, which taste very good, but the "beef" tartare symbolism doesn't work without the deep red beets!

----

1 Preheat the oven to 300 degrees F. Assemble *mise en place* trays for this recipe (see page 6).

2 Spread the beets in a shallow baking dish. Add enough water to come ½ inch up the sides of the pan. Cover tightly with aluminum foil and roast for 1 hour. Remove the foil and cool the beets in their cooking juices.

3 Peel the beets, reserving the cooking juices. Put the beets in a blender or a food processor fitted with the metal blade, and process until just chopped.

4 Transfer the beets to a bowl. Stir in the shallot, cornichons, capers, parsley, and mayonnaise. Season to taste with salt, pepper, and Tabasco. Cover and refrigerate for at least 30 minutes.

5 Using a soup spoon, scoop out a heaping mound of beets. Use a second spoon to form the mound into a quenelle (a rounded oval). Set a quenelle in the center of each of 6 serving plates. Let the quenelles come to room temperature.

6 In a bowl, whisk together the reserved beet-cooking juices, the vinegar, and olive oil. Season to taste with salt and pepper. Drizzle in a circle around the edge of the beet quenelles and serve.

✌ Do not chop the ingredients too fine or you will lose the juices.

✌ Do not serve ice-cold. The flavor is better at room temperature.

✌ You can form the quenelles without refrigerating the beet mixture, but it is easier if the mixture is cold. You can also form the quenelles with your hands. Dampen your hands first with cold water to keep the beets from sticking.

Pasta

Potato Gnocchi with Fresh Sage Sauce ❧ Fusilli with Twenty-Minute Tomato Sauce, Hot Chiles, and Arugula ❧ Pasta Packages with Veal Sauce ❧ Shells with Shrimp, Broccoli, Bread Crumbs, and Chile Pepper ❧ Risotto with Porcini ❧ Spaghetti with Saffroned Onions, Greens, Fennel, Sun-Dried Tomatoes, and Currants ❧ Ziti with Lentils and Kale ❧ Shells "Al Forno" with Mushrooms and Radicchio ❧ Shrimp Ravioli with Tomatoes and Olives ❧ Penne with Asparagus ❧ Open Ravioli of Wild Mushrooms and Caramelized Onion ❧ Orecchiette with Zucchini and Yellow Squash ❧ Fusilli with Tomatoes and Bread Crumbs ❧ Smoked Salmon, Salmon Roe, and Pasta Salad ❧ Bow Tie Pasta with Mussels and Zucchini

Potato Gnocchi with Fresh Sage Sauce ❧ Lidia Bastianich

SERVES 6

PREPARATION TIME: ABOUT 45 MINUTES

COOKING TIME: ABOUT 45 MINUTES

6 large Idaho or russet potatoes, peeled and cut into quarters

2 large eggs, beaten

1 tablespoon salt

Freshly ground white pepper to taste

About 4 cups sifted, unbleached all-purpose flour

Fresh Sage Sauce (recipe follows)

1 cup freshly grated Parmigiano-Reggiano cheese

■ Special Equipment: Potato ricer, food mill, or old-fashioned potato masher

*G*nocchi are Italian dumplings made from flour, farina, or, as in this case, potatoes. Sometimes they are made with the addition of either eggs and cheese, or both. When Lidia makes them, they are silky and light as a feather. With her recipe, yours should be also.

1 Assemble *mise en place* trays for this recipe (see page 6).

2 Place the potatoes in a large saucepan with enough cold water to cover by several inches. Bring to a boil over high heat, lower the heat, and simmer for 15 minutes, or until tender. Drain well. Push the potatoes through a ricer or a food mill into a medium-sized bowl, or mash with an old-fashioned potato masher and allow to cool thoroughly, about 30 minutes.

3 Mound the potatoes on a cool work surface, such as a marble slab. Make a well in the center, and add the beaten eggs, 1 teaspoon of the salt, and white pepper to taste. Using both hands, work the mixture together, slowly adding 3 cups flour. Scrape the dough up from the surface with a pastry scraper or knife and keep blending until you have a smooth dough that is still sticky on the inside. The whole process should take no longer than 10 minutes (the more you work this dough, the more flour it absorbs). Sprinkle the dough with a little flour.

4 Cut the dough into 8 equal pieces. Sprinkle your hands with flour and using both hands, roll each piece on a lightly floured surface into a ½-inch-thick rope, continuously sprinkling flour on the work surface and your hands as you work the dough. Cut each rope into ½-inch pieces and set the pieces on an ungreased baking sheet. Indent each gnocchi with your thumb or score

with the tines of fork. (The texture on the gnocchi will help the sauce adhere.)

5 Meanwhile, bring a 6-quart saucepan of water to a boil over high heat. Just as it comes to a boil, add the remaining 2 teaspoons salt.

6 Drop the gnocchi into the boiling water a few at a time, stirring the water continuously with a wooden spoon. Boil for 2 to 3 minutes, until the gnocchi rise to the top. Using a slotted spoon, transfer the gnocchi to a warm serving platter. Let the water return to a boil before adding each new batch of gnocchi.

7 Pour the Fresh Sage Sauce over the gnocchi, stir in the grated cheese and pepper to taste, and serve immediately.

Fresh Sage Sauce

MAKES ABOUT 4 CUPS

1 cup unsalted butter

8 to 10 large fresh sage leaves, quartered

2 cups heavy cream

1 cup Chicken Stock (page 15)

Salt and freshly ground white pepper to taste

In a medium-sized saucepan, melt the butter over medium heat. Add the sage and sauté for 2 minutes. Stir in the cream and stock, bring to a simmer, and simmer for 5 minutes. Season to taste with salt and pepper. Serve warm.

Fusilli with Twenty-Minute Tomato Sauce, Hot Chiles, and Arugula ✢ Mario Batali

SERVES 6

PREPARATION TIME: 10 MINUTES

COOKING TIME: ABOUT 20 MINUTES

FAT PER SERVING: 12.2 GRAMS

SATURATED FAT: 4.2 GRAMS

CALORIES PER SERVING: 475

CALORIES FROM FAT: 23%

½ cup chopped carrots

2 tablespoons olive oil

1 medium onion, finely diced

3 cloves garlic, minced

2 tablespoons balsamic vinegar

2 tablespoons fresh thyme leaves

1 tablespoon red pepper flakes

One-and-one-third 35-ounce boxes strained tomatoes (about 6 cups; see Note)

Salt to taste

1 pound imported dried fusilli pasta

1 bunch arugula, trimmed, washed, dried, and cut into ¼-inch chiffonade

One 2-ounce piece Pecorino-Romano cheese, for grating (optional)

Quick, healthy, and delicious—with a touch of heat! What more could the home cook ask? (Except, perhaps to have Mario himself cook it for you!)

1 Assemble *mise en place* trays for this recipe (see page 6).

2 In a food processor fitted with the metal blade, combine the carrots and oil and process until the carrots are minced. Transfer to a large saucepan, stir in the onions and garlic, and cook over medium heat, stirring frequently, for about 7 minutes, or until the onions begin to brown.

3 Add the vinegar, thyme, and pepper flakes and cook, stirring, for 1 minute. Add the tomatoes, raise the heat to high, and cook, stirring frequently, for about 8 minutes, or until the sauce thickens slightly. Season to taste with salt. Remove from the heat and cover to keep warm.

4 Meanwhile, bring a large pot of salted water to a boil over high heat. Add the pasta and cook for about 9 minutes, or until al dente. Drain, add to the sauce, and toss to combine. Return to the heat for 1 minute, just to heat through.

5 Remove from the heat and toss in the arugula. Pour into a warm serving dish and serve immediately. Grate the cheese over individual servings if desired.

NOTE: Pomi brand produces excellent boxed strained tomatoes.

Pasta Packages with Veal Sauce ～ Giuliano Bugialli

SERVES 6

PREPARATION TIME: ABOUT 1 HOUR AND 30 MINUTES

COOKING TIME: ABOUT 2 HOURS

SOAKING TIME (SPINACH ONLY): ABOUT 30 MINUTES

DRAINING TIME (RICOTTA ONLY): ABOUT 1 HOUR

VEAL SAUCE:

1 tablespoon minced garlic

1 tablespoon fresh rosemary leaves

2 tablespoons olive oil

1 four-ounce piece fatty prosciutto or pancetta, diced

1 pound veal stew meat, cut into large pieces

⅛ teaspoon freshly grated nutmeg, or to taste

Pinch of ground cinnamon

1 cup dry red wine

Salt and freshly ground black pepper to taste

3 tablespoons tomato paste

2 cups Chicken Stock or Veal stock (see page 15 and 16)

BALSAMELLA SAUCE:

8 tablespoons unsalted butter

1 clove garlic, peeled

¼ cup unbleached all-purpose flour

4 cups milk

This deliciously rich pasta dish comes from Parma. It is not for the diet-conscious, as it has many eggs, lots of cheese, and some other fat as well. However, the taste is definitely worth an occasional splurge.

---

1 Assemble *mise en place* trays for this recipe (see page 6).

2 To make the veal sauce, mash the garlic and rosemary together.

3 In a medium-sized heat-proof casserole, heat the olive oil over medium heat. Add the garlic mixture and the prosciutto and sauté for about 3 minutes, stirring constantly. Add the veal and sauté for about 5 minutes, or until lightly golden. Season with nutmeg and cinnamon and mix well. Add the wine, bring to a simmer, and simmer for about 10 minutes. Remove the casserole from the heat and strain the contents through a fine sieve. Pour the liquid back into the casserole and season to taste with salt and pepper.

4 Transfer the solids in the sieve to a meat grinder and finely grind into a bowl. Add the ground meat to liquid in the casserole and return to medium heat.

5 Whisk together the tomato paste and 1 cup of the stock. Add this to the casserole. Bring to a simmer, cover, and simmer for at least 1 hour, adding additional broth as needed, until the sauce is reduced and quite thick. Taste and adjust the seasoning with salt and pepper. You should have about 3 cups of sauce. Set the sauce aside.

6 To make the balsamella sauce, melt the butter in a medium-sized saucepan over medium heat. Add the garlic and sauté for 1 minute. Remove and discard the garlic. Stir the flour into the butter to make a roux, and cook for 1 to 2 minutes. Whisk in the milk. Cook, whisk-

SPINACH FILLING:

Coarse sea salt or kosher salt

2 pounds fresh spinach, tough stems removed, soaked for 30 minutes in cold water

¼ pound ricotta cheese, very well drained (see Note)

½ pound mascarpone cheese

½ cup freshly grated Parmigiano-Reggiano cheese, plus extra for serving if desired

1 extra-large egg

3 extra-large egg yolks

Freshly grated nutmeg to taste

Salt and freshly ground black pepper to taste

PASTA:

About 2¼ cups unbleached all-purpose flour

4 extra-large egg yolks

Pinch of salt

¼ cup cold water

2 tablespoons olive oil

2 tablespoons unsalted butter, at room temperature

■ Special Equipment: Meat grinder; pasta machine.

ing continuously, for 5 to 8 minutes, or until thickened. Scrape into a bowl and place a piece of buttered waxed paper directly on the surface to prevent skin from forming. Set aside.

7 To make the spinach filling, bring a large pot of cold water to a boil over medium heat, and when the water reaches a boil, add salt to taste. Drain the spinach and add to the pot. Boil for 5 minutes, drain, and refresh under cold running water. Squeeze the spinach almost dry and finely chop. You will have about 2½ cups of loosely packed chopped spinach.

8 Combine the spinach, ricotta, mascarpone, Parmigiano, egg, and egg yolks in a bowl and mix well. Stir in the nutmeg, salt and pepper to taste. Cover and refrigerate until needed.

9 To make the pasta, mound the flour on a clean, flat work surface (preferably wood). Make a well in the center and add the egg yolks and salt.

10 Using a fork, mix the eggs and salt together and then begin to incorporate the flour by pulling it into the eggs from the inner rim of the well. Using your hands, begin incorporating more flour by pushing it under the dough that is forming to keep it from sticking to the surface. Push some of the flour aside, incorporating it only as you need it, and continue working the dough until well blended and no longer sticky. Lift the dough to the side of the work surface. Wash your hands and poke a dry finger into the dough. If it comes out clean, the dough needs no additional flour. If it comes out sticky, incorporate more flour.

11 Using a pastry scraper, clean the work surface of all flour and any caked dough bits. Place the dough on the clean surface and knead it by pushing down with the palm of one hand. Fold the dough over and continue kneading, pushing and folding, for 3 minutes and no longer than 8 minutes, until very smooth. Divide the dough into 2 or 3 pieces to make it easier to work with.

12 Using a hand-cranked pasta machine, stretch each piece of dough into sheets a little less than $\frac{1}{16}$-inch thick (usually the last setting). Cut the pasta sheet into 6-inch squares.

13 In a shallow dish, combine the water and olive oil. Set aside.

14 Preheat the oven to 375 degrees F. Generously butter a 13½-inch-by-8¾-inch baking dish with the butter.

15 Bring a large saucepan of water to a boil and when it reaches a boil, add salt to taste. Cook the pasta squares in batches for 8 to 10 seconds, or until just barely firm. Using a slotted spoon, transfer the pasta to the water and oil mixture to stop further cooking. Remove the pasta squares and arrange in a single layer on clean, moistened cotton kitchen towels to rest. You should have 24 to 26 pasta squares.

16 Place 2 heaping tablespoons of the spinach filling in the center of each pasta square. Fold each one up as if you were wrapping a package: fold two sides into the center over the top of the mixture so that there is a seam; then tuck each end under. Carefully transfer to the buttered baking dish and arrange them, seam side up, in a single layer. Pour the balsamella sauce over the top. Bake for 20 minutes, or until heated through.

17 Meanwhile, reheat the veal sauce over medium-low heat for 8 to 10 minutes, stirring occasionally, until heated through.

18 Remove the baking dish from the oven and spoon the veal sauce over the pasta packages. Serve immediately, with additional grated Parmigiano, if desired.

NOTE: To drain ricotta, place it in a fine sieve set over a bowl. Allow to drain for 1 hour before using.

❧ You can replace the homemade pasta with commercially made pasta sheets, although most commercially made pasta sheets are not thin as homemade ones.

Shells with Shrimp, Broccoli, Bread Crumbs, and Chile Pepper ❧ Biba Caggiano

SERVES 6

PREPARATION TIME: ABOUT 20 MINUTES

COOKING TIME: ABOUT 20 MINUTES

---

2 pounds broccoli, stalks removed and florets separated

⅓ cup extra-virgin olive oil

¾ pound medium shrimp, shelled, deveined, rinsed, and well drained

2 tablespoons fresh white bread crumbs (see page 13)

4 anchovy fillets, separated from one another

3 cloves garlic, minced

Generous pinch of red pepper flakes, or more to taste

Salt to taste

1 pound dried pasta shells, orecchiette, or penne

This simple seafood pasta dish requires only three-quarters of a pound of shrimp to feed six nicely—an economy that pays off handsomely in the cholesterol department, too.

---

1 Assemble *mise en place* trays for this recipe (see page 6).

2 In a steamer basket, steam the broccoli over boiling water for 4 minutes, or until tender. Refresh under cold running water and set aside.

3 In a large skillet, heat the oil over medium heat until nearly smoking. Add the shrimp and cook, stirring continuously, for 1 to 2 minutes, or until opaque. Using a slotted spoon, transfer the shrimp to a plate.

4 Immediately stir the bread crumbs into the skillet, and stir for 10 seconds, or until the crumbs are lightly golden. (The pan is very hot and the bread crumbs will brown in no time at all.) Stir in the anchovies and garlic. Cook for 15 to 20 seconds, stirring, until the garlic is browned and cooked. Return the shrimp to the skillet and add the broccoli florets and red pepper flakes. Season to taste with salt and cook, stirring continuously, for 1 minute. Remove from the heat.

5 Bring a large pot of water to a boil. When it boils, add salt and cook the pasta for about 10 minutes, or until al dente. Drain well, reserving some of the cooking water.

6 Add the pasta to the skillet and set over medium heat. Cook for 1 to 2 minutes, stirring continuously, until the pasta, shrimp, and vegetables are well combined. If the pasta looks dry, add 2 to 3 tablespoons of the reserved cooking water. Taste and adjust the seasoning with salt and red pepper flakes. Serve immediately.

❧ If you have organized your *mise en place* well, this recipe will come together in minutes.

Risotto with Porcini ❧ Roberto Donna

SERVES 6

PREPARATION TIME: ABOUT 25 MINUTES

COOKING TIME: ABOUT 60 MINUTES

1 cup Veal Stock (page 16)

6 porcini mushroom caps, wiped clean, plus 7 ounces fresh porcini mushrooms, trimmed and wiped clean

1 bulb garlic

¼ cup olive oil

6 cups Chicken Stock (page 15)

6 tablespoons unsalted butter

½ large onion, minced

½ teaspoon minced fresh sage

½ teaspoon minced fresh rosemary

1 pound Arborio rice (see Note)

¾ cup dry white Italian wine, such as Pinot Grigio

Salt and freshly ground black pepper to taste

Risotto can be a home cook's nightmare, only because it must be made at the last minute and stirred constantly while the rice absorbs the liquid. But, with its rich, creamy taste, it's a fantastic dream to eat. And like any dream, it is worth a little effort.

1 Preheat the oven to 375 degrees F. Assemble *mise en place* trays for this recipe (see page 6).

2 In a small saucepan, bring the veal stock to a boil over medium heat. Reduce the heat and simmer for about 20 minutes, or until reduced to 2 tablespoons. Remove from the heat, cover, and set aside.

3 Put the porcini caps in a small baking pan. Cut the garlic bulb in half crosswise and add to the pan. Drizzle 3 tablespoons of the olive oil over the mushrooms and garlic. Set aside.

4 Cut the remaining mushrooms into ¼-inch pieces and set aside.

5 In a medium-sized saucepan, bring the chicken stock to a simmer over medium heat. Reduce the heat to low and keep hot.

6 In a medium-sized saucepan, melt 4 tablespoons of the butter with remaining 1 tablespoon olive oil over low heat. Add the onion and cook, stirring, for about 10 minutes, or until translucent. Raise the heat to medium-high and stir in the sage, rosemary, and diced porcini. Sauté for 2 minutes. Stir in the rice, reduce the heat to medium, and toast, stirring occasionally, for 3 minutes, or until the rice is glistening. Add the wine and cook, stirring continuously, for about 1 minute, or until all the liquid has been absorbed by the rice.

7 As soon as the wine has been absorbed, begin adding the hot chicken stock to the rice ½ cup at a time, cooking and stirring until each addition is absorbed. This should take no more than 15 to 20 minutes, as you want the rice to be creamy but still al dente.

8 Meanwhile, roast the porcini caps for 10 minutes, or until just tender. Turn off the oven and open the door or remove and cover to keep warm.

9 Remove the risotto from the heat. Add the remaining 2 tablespoons butter and salt and pepper to taste, and stir until the rice is very creamy. Spoon into a warm serving bowl. If necessary, reheat the reduced veal stock. Place the porcini caps on top, and drizzle with the warm veal stock. Serve immediately.

NOTE: Arborio rice is Italian, medium-grain rice that is especially good for risotto. Buy it in specialty shops, the gourmet section of the supermarket, or an Italian grocery.

❧ Even though risotto must be made at the last minute, this dish will all come together easily if you are well organized.

❧ You can buy frozen veal stock in gourmet or specialty shops.

Spaghetti with Saffroned Onions, Greens, Fennel, Sun-Dried Tomatoes, and Currants ❧ Joyce Goldstein

SERVES 6

PREPARATION TIME: ABOUT 30 MINUTES

COOKING TIME: ABOUT 15 MINUTES

---

1 cup currants

¼ teaspoon crushed saffron threads

2 tablespoons dry white wine

Coarse salt to taste

1 pound spaghetti

¾ cup olive oil

4 onions, sliced ¼ inch thick

2 cups ⅛-inch-thick fennel slices

¾ to 1 cup finely julienned dry-packed sun-dried tomatoes (see Note)

2 tablespoons minced anchovy fillets

1 tablespoon minced garlic

1½ pounds Swiss chard or escarole, trimmed, washed, dried, and cut into a fine chiffonade

This unusual pasta dish finds its roots in Sicily, with the Arabic influences of saffroned onions and currants combined with indigenous fennel and sun-dried tomatoes. It is complex in flavor and rich in taste, yet inexpensive and easy to prepare.

---

1 Assemble *mise en place* trays for this recipe (see page 6).

2 In a small bowl, combine the currants and hot water to cover. Set aside to plump for at least 10 minutes. In a small cup, combine the saffron and wine. Set aside to soak.

3 Bring a large pot of salted water to a boil over high heat. Add the spaghetti and stir to prevent clumping. Cook for about 12 minutes, or until al dente.

4 Meanwhile, in a large sauté pan, heat the oil over medium heat. Add the onions and sauté for about 4 minutes, or until soft. Add the saffron mixture and cook for 1 minute. Stir in the fennel, sun-dried tomatoes, anchovies, and garlic and sauté for 3 minutes.

5 Drain the currants and add to the onion mixture. Stir in the Swiss chard and cook, stirring, for about 2 minutes, or until wilted.

6 Drain the pasta and transfer to a large shallow bowl. Add the sauce, toss to combine, and serve immediately on warm plates.

NOTE: Sun-dried tomatoes vary widely in quality and saltiness. If they are sweet, use the larger amount called for in the recipe; if salty, use the lesser.

Joyce says "no cheese, please" on this pasta. However, she says, you could add some chunks of grilled tuna for an even more flavorful and filling dish.

Ziti with Lentils and Kale ❧ Patricia Jamieson

SERVES 6

PREPARATION TIME: ABOUT 30 MINUTES

COOKING TIME: ABOUT 45 MINUTES

FAT PER SERVING: 6.7 GRAMS

SATURATED FAT: 0.6 GRAM

CALORIES PER SERVING: 490

CALORIES FROM FAT: 12%

½ cup green lentils, preferably Le Puy

1½ teaspoons olive oil

1 medium-sized onion, chopped

1 medium-sized carrot, chopped

4 cloves garlic, minced

2 ounces prosciutto, trimmed of fat and chopped (about ¼ cup)

2 cups Chicken Broth (see page 15)

1 teaspoon chopped fresh rosemary or pinch of dried

1 teaspoon fresh thyme leaves or ½ teaspoon dried

One 28-ounce can plum tomatoes, drained and chopped

4 cups coarsely chopped kale (about ½ bunch)

Salt and freshly ground black pepper to taste

1 pound imported dried ziti

¼ cup freshly grated Parmigiano-Reggiano cheese (optional)

*L*entils make this sauce so robust that it becomes an interesting alternative to long-simmered more traditional sauces. Large pasta shapes, such as ziti, fusilli, or rotini, are ideal because the lentils nestle in their holes and crevices.

---

1 Assemble *mise en place* trays for this recipe (see page 6).

2 In a medium-sized saucepan, cover the lentils with cold water, bring to a boil over high heat, and boil for 5 minutes to soften. Remove from the heat, drain, rinse under cold running water, and set aside.

3 In a nonstick sauté pan, heat the oil over medium heat. Add the onions, carrots, garlic, and prosciutto and sauté for about 5 minutes, or until the vegetables soften. Stir in the lentils, add the broth and herbs, and bring to a boil. Reduce the heat, cover, and simmer for about 15 minutes. Add the tomatoes and kale and simmer for an additional 20 minutes, or until the lentils and kale are tender. Season to taste with salt and pepper.

4 Meanwhile, bring a large pot of salted water to a boil over high heat. Add the pasta and cook for about 10 minutes, or until al dente. Drain and transfer to a large warm shallow bowl.

5 Add the sauce to the pasta and toss to combine. Taste and adjust the seasonings with salt and pepper. Serve immediately, passing the cheese on the side if desired.

Shells "Al Forno" with Mushrooms and Radicchio ❧ Johanne Killeen and George Germon

SERVES 6

PREPARATION TIME: ABOUT 30 MINUTES

COOKING TIME: ABOUT 45 MINUTES

---

6 tablespoons unsalted butter

6 ounces shiitake mushrooms, wiped clean, stemmed and cut into ¼-inch slices

Salt to taste

1 pound medium-sized dried conchiglie (pasta shells)

2½ cups heavy cream

½ cup freshly grated Parmigiano-Reggiano cheese

½ cup shredded Bel Paese cheese

½ cup crumbled Gorgonzola cheese

2 heads (about 1 pound) radicchio, halved, cored, and shredded

6 fresh sage leaves, shredded

*H*ere is a richly delicious "make ahead" casserole filled with the flavors of earthy mushrooms, sharp radicchio, and pungent cheeses. Johanne and George recommend a good imported dried pasta, such as De Cecco or Del Verde, or any pasta that is 100-percent semolina.

---

1 Preheat the oven to 450 degrees F. Assemble *mise en place* trays for this recipe (see page 6). Generously butter a 9-inch square baking dish.

2 In a medium-sized sauté pan, melt 4 tablespoons butter over medium heat. Add the mushrooms and sauté for 5 minutes, or until tender. Add salt to taste. Remove from the heat and set aside.

3 Bring a large pot of water to a boil over high heat. When the water boils, add a little salt. Cook the pasta for about 10 minutes, until al dente. Drain well.

4 In a large bowl, combine the cream, Parmigiano-Reggiano, Bel Paese, Gorgonzola, mushrooms, and radicchio. Add the drained pasta and toss to combine. Add the sage leaves and season to taste with salt.

5 Transfer the pasta to the prepared dish. Dot with the remaining 2 tablespoons butter. Bake for 30 minutes, or until bubbly and golden brown on top. Serve immediately.

❧ The mushroom stems not needed for this recipe can be used to enrich soups, stocks, and sauces.

❧ Conchiglie is a shell-shaped pasta available in many sizes, from very small (generally for soup) to large (for stuffing).

Shrimp Ravioli with Tomatoes and Olives ～ Michael Lomonaco

SERVES 6

PREPARATION TIME: ABOUT 1 HOUR AND 15 MINUTES

COOKING TIME: ABOUT 25 MINUTES

SAUCE:

¼ cup plus 2 tablespoons olive oil

2 ounces canned anchovies, drained

½ to 1 teaspoon red pepper flakes, to taste

3 pounds very ripe plum tomatoes, cored, peeled, seeded, and chopped

2 tablespoons chopped shallots

2 tablespoons plus 1½ teaspoons chopped garlic

4 ounces Niçoise olives, pitted and chopped

¼ cup small capers, well drained

3 tablespoons chopped fresh flat-leaf parsley

1½ tablespoons chopped fresh basil

Freshly ground black pepper to taste

RAVIOLI:

1 pound large shrimp, peeled and deveined

1 tablespoon plus 1½ teaspoons olive oil

3 tablespoons chopped shallots

1½ teaspoons chopped garlic

3 tablespoons chopped fresh flat-leaf parsley

This type of Italian tomato sauce is known as puttanesca, a word that, in polite company, trans-lates to "street-walker." It's a naughty name for a zesty and quite addictive sauce. Try it simply spooned over linguine or spaghetti.

---

1 Assemble *mise en place* trays for this recipe (see page 6).

2 To make the sauce, heat the oil in a large sauté pan over medium heat. Add the anchovies and red pepper flakes and cook for about 4 minutes or until the anchovies "melt."

3 Add the tomatoes and cook, stirring occasionally, for 5 to 10 minutes, until very soft. Stir in the shallots, garlic, olives, capers, parsley, and basil. Season to taste with pepper. Remove the pan from the heat and set aside.

4 To make the ravioli filling, use a sharp knife to cut the shrimp into nuggets the size of peas.

5 In a medium-sized sauté pan, heat the oil over medium heat. Add the shrimp and sauté for 2 minutes, or until just cooked. Stir in the shallots, garlic, parsley, cilantro, and thyme. Season to taste with salt and pepper. Remove from the heat and allow to cool (about 20 minutes).

6 When the shrimp mixture is cool, stir in the egg white.

7 Separate the wonton wrappers. Using a small pastry brush dipped in cold water, moisten the edges of 1 wonton wrapper. Place 1 teaspoon of the cooled shrimp mixture in the center. Fold over diagonally into a triangle and pinch the edges together to seal. Put the ravioli on a parchment-lined baking sheet and continue making ravioli until all the wrappers are used.

8 Meanwhile, in a large pot, bring 2 quarts of water to a boil over high heat. When boiling, lightly salt the water.

3 tablespoons chopped fresh cilantro

1½ tablespoons chopped fresh thyme

Salt and freshly ground black pepper to taste

1 egg white, lightly beaten

1 package wonton wrappers (about 50 wrappers)

9 Drop the ravioli into the boiling water one by one. Stir gently to prevent sticking and return the water to a slow boil. Cook for 1 to 2 minutes, until the ravioli bob to the surface of the pot. Lift the ravioli out of the water with a slotted spoon and carefully put into a colander to drain.

10 While the ravioli are cooking, warm the sauce over low heat.

11 Place the ravioli on a warm serving platter, and spoon the warm sauce over the top. Serve immediately.

❧ The ravioli could also be made with traditional pasta dough, but the wonton wrappers make an especially easy preparation.

Penne with Asparagus ❧ Carlo Middione

SERVES 6

PREPARATION TIME: ABOUT 25 MINUTES

COOKING TIME: ABOUT 30 MINUTES

Spring bursts forth with sweet asparagus peeking through this rich pasta dish. If you prefer, substitute another green vegetable.

1 pound thin asparagus stalks, trimmed and cut into 2-inch pieces

¼ cup extra-virgin olive oil

2 cloves garlic, minced

1½ pounds ripe Italian plum tomatoes, cored, peeled, seeded, and finely chopped

14 ounces dried penne

1 cup freshly grated Pecorino Romano cheese, plus extra for serving, if desired

1 Assemble *mise en place* trays for this recipe (see page 6).

2 Bring a large saucepan of water to a boil. When it boils, add salt and cook the asparagus for 4 minutes. Turn off the heat and, using a slotted spoon or tongs, transfer the asparagus to a bowl and cover to keep warm. Reserve the water for cooking the pasta.

3 In a large saucepan, heat the olive oil over medium heat. Add the garlic and cook for 2 to 3 minutes, until golden. Stir in the tomatoes and cook for about 10 minutes.

2 large eggs, lightly beaten

Salt and freshly ground black pepper to taste

4 Meanwhile, return the asparagus water to a boil. Add the pasta and cook for 7 minutes, or until just barely al dente. Drain, leaving a little water clinging to the pasta.

5 Put the pasta in a large, heated casserole or a ceramic serving bowl set over a pan of simmering water. Stir in the asparagus and cheese. Add the beaten eggs and stir gently for 3 to 4 minutes, until the pasta is well coated and glossy. Stir in the tomato sauce and season to taste with salt and pepper. Serve immediately on warm dinner plates, with extra grated cheese passed at the table if desired.

✎ To heat the casserole, set it in a warm (250 degree F.) oven while you prepare the rest of the dish.

✎ The heat of the penne actually cooks the eggs. Adding the cheese before the eggs creates an insulation that keeps the eggs from getting too hot too quickly and curdling.

Open Ravioli of Wild Mushrooms and Caramelized Onion ✎ Charles Palmer

SERVES 6

PREPARATION TIME: ABOUT 2 HOURS

COOKING TIME: ABOUT 1 HOUR

This beautiful first course is not as difficult as first glance might indicate. Much can be done in advance to rate those "oohs" and "ahs" at the table.

PASTA:

1 cup semolina flour

1 cup bread flour

2 large eggs

3 tablespoons olive oil

1 teaspoon salt, or more to taste

2 tablespoons chopped fresh parsley

1 Assemble *mise en place* trays for this recipe (see page 6).

2 To make the pasta, in the bowl of a heavy-duty mixer, combine the flours, eggs, olive oil, and 1 teaspoon salt. Beat at low speed until mixed. Add the parsley, increase the speed to medium, and continue to beat until the dough forms a smooth ball. If the dough seems dry, add cold water, 1 teaspoon at a time.

Approximately 3 tablespoons ice water

FILLING:

1 tablespoon olive oil

1 large Spanish onion, halved and thinly sliced

1 cup sliced chanterelle mushrooms

1 cup coarsely chopped oyster mushrooms

Salt to taste

¾ cup Chicken Stock (see page 15)

1 tablespoon unsalted butter

1 tablespoon plus 1 teaspoon chopped fresh parsley

2 teaspoons chopped fresh chives

Freshly ground black pepper to taste

Tomato Compote (recipe follows)

Chive Oil (see page 264)

12 small chive stalks

■ Special Equipment: pasta machine (optional)

3 Using a pasta machine, roll the dough into thin sheets with the machine on the next-to-last setting. Alternately, roll out into a thin sheet on a lightly floured surface.

4 Cut the pasta dough into twelve 4-by-4-inch squares. Stack the squares, placing a sheet of plastic wrap or parchment paper between each square, and wrap the stack in parchment or waxed paper. Set aside. Reserve the remaining dough for another use.

5 To make the filling, in a large non-stick sauté pan, heat the olive oil over medium heat. Add the onions, reduce the heat to low and cook, covered, for 10 minutes. Raise the heat to medium-low and cook, uncovered, for 10 to 15 minutes longer, or until the onions are well caramelized. Using a slotted spoon, remove the onions from the pan and set aside.

6 Add the mushrooms to the pan and sprinkle lightly with salt. Raise the heat to medium and cook for 1 minute, or until well coated with the pan juices. Stir in the Chicken Stock and butter. Cook, stirring occasionally, for about 8 minutes, or until the mushrooms are tender and the liquid has reduced to a rich sauce.

7 Stir in the reserved caramelized onions, 1 teaspoon parsley, and the chopped chives. Season to taste with salt and pepper. Remove from the heat and cover to keep warm.

8 Meanwhile, in a large saucepan, bring 2 quarts of water to a boil over high heat. Salt lightly.

9 Add the pasta squares to the boiling water and cook for 1 minute, or until al dente. Drain well.

10 Spoon the mushroom mixture into the bottom of each of 6 shallow soup bowls. Place one pasta square in each bowl over the mushroom mixture. Spoon the Tomato Compote on top of the ravioli and drizzle the Chive Oil on top. Garnish with chive stalks and the remaining 1 tablespoon parsley, and serve immediately.

If not using pasta dough immediately, wrap it tightly in plastic and let it rest at room temperature. Do not refrigerate, and do not allow it to sit for more than three hours or dough will toughen and be unusable. You may, however, cut the pasta in squares, wrap them as instructed in the recipe, and let them sit at room temperature for up to 8 hours.

To save time, purchase commercially prepared pasta sheets and cut into desired size. If these are not available, you could use dried lasagna noodles. Cook as directed on the package and cut into four-inch squares.

TOMATO COMPOTE

MAKES ABOUT 1 CUP

1½ cups cored, peeled, seeded, and chopped ripe tomatoes

1 tablespoon chopped sun-dried tomatoes packed in oil, drained

1 tablespoon olive oil

¼ teaspoon red pepper flakes, or to taste

Salt and freshly ground black pepper to taste

2 tablespoons chopped fresh basil

2 tablespoons chopped fresh chives

1 In a small saucepan, combine the fresh and sun-dried tomatoes. Stir in the olive oil, red pepper flakes, and salt and pepper to taste, and bring to a simmer over medium heat. Reduce the heat and cook gently for 15 to 20 minutes, until thickened.

2 Remove from the heat and stir in the basil and chives. Serve warm.

Orecchiette with Zucchini and Yellow Squash ❧ Marie Simmons

SERVES 6

PREPARATION TIME: ABOUT 15 MINUTES

COOKING TIME: ABOUT 10 MINUTES

FAT PER SERVING: 4.3 GRAMS

SATURATED FAT: 0.5 GRAM

CALORIES PER SERVING: 331

CALORIES FROM FAT: 12%

---

1 pound imported dried orecchiette pasta

1 tablespoon olive oil

2 scallions, chopped

1 clove garlic, minced

3 medium-sized zucchini, thinly sliced

2 yellow squash, thinly sliced

1 tablespoon freshly grated Parmigiano-Reggiano or Pecorino Romano cheese, plus, if desired, additional for serving

Salt and freshly ground black pepper to taste

Since both zucchini and yellow squash are very moist, they require very little cooking. If you undercook the vegetables slightly, the hot pasta and the addition of a little of the boiling pasta water will complete the cooking yet allow the vegetables to retain their bright color and crispness. A light dusting of robustly flavored Parmigiano-Reggiano or Pecorino Romano cheese provides a blast of flavor with a minimum of fat and calories. This serves as a very light and graceful primi piatti, or first-course pasta dish, as well as a simple main course.

---

1 Assemble *mise en place* trays for this recipe (see page 6).

2 Bring a large pot of salted water to a boil over high heat. Add the pasta and cook for about 10 minutes, or until al dente. Scoop out ½ cup of the cooking water and set it aside, then drain the pasta.

3 Meanwhile, in a medium-sized sauté pan, heat the oil over medium heat. Add the scallions and garlic and sauté for 2 minutes. Add the zucchini and yellow squash and sauté for about 3 minutes, or until the vegetables just begin to soften. Add the pasta, the reserved pasta cooking water, and the cheese and toss to coat. Season to taste with salt and pepper. Spoon into warm pasta bowls and, if desired, offer additional cheese on the side.

Fusilli with Tomatoes and Bread Crumbs ❧ Alice Waters

SERVES 6

PREPARATION TIME: ABOUT 25 MINUTES

COOKING TIME: ABOUT 1 HOUR AND 25 MINUTES
(1 HOUR FOR THE BREAD CRUMBS)

1 large loaf country-style bread, crust removed

½ cup extra-virgin olive oil

4 cloves garlic, chopped

12 large, ripe, red tomatoes, cored, peeled, seeded, and chopped

1 large bunch fresh parsley, chopped

½ cup fresh basil leaves, chopped

6 sprigs fresh thyme leaves, chopped

Salt and freshly ground black pepper to taste

Balsamic or red wine vinegar to taste (optional)

1½ pounds dried fusilli pasta

You must have very ripe, sweet tomatoes and good rustic bread for the true taste to come through in this simple but delicious dish.

1 Preheat the oven to 275 degrees F. Assemble *mise en place* trays for this recipe (see page 6).

2 Cut the bread into pieces. In a food processor fitted with the metal blade, process the bread, in batches, to coarse crumbs. You will have about 6 cups of crumbs. Spread in a shallow baking tray and toast in the oven for 1 hour, or until dry and crisp but not brown.

3 In a large sauté pan, heat the olive oil over medium heat. Add the bread crumbs and garlic and cook, stirring constantly, for 10 minutes, or until the crumbs are golden. Pour into a bowl and set aside.

4 In a glass or ceramic bowl, combine the tomatoes and chopped herbs. Season to taste with salt and pepper. Add a splash of vinegar to intensify the flavor of the tomatoes, if you desire.

5 In a large pot, bring 4 quarts of salted water to a boil over high heat. Cook the pasta until al dente. Drain well.

6 Transfer the pasta to a warm, shallow serving bowl. Pour the tomatoes over the top and toss to combine. Add the bread crumbs and toss to combine. Serve immediately.

❧ This is a dish that waits for no one. Serve it as soon as it is assembled, or the bread crumbs will turn soggy.

Smoked Salmon, Salmon Roe, and Pasta Salad ❧ Alice Waters

SERVES 6

PREPARATION TIME: ABOUT 30 MINUTES

COOKING TIME: ABOUT 25 MINUTES

CHILLING TIME: ABOUT 4 HOURS

Juice of 2 limes (about ⅓ cup)

2 teaspoons Dijon mustard

Grated zest of 1 lemon

12 quail eggs (see note)

Salt and freshly ground black pepper to taste

½ cup extra-virgin olive oil, or to taste

⅔ pound thin green beans or haricot verts, trimmed

1 bunch fresh cilantro, washed and dried

1 bunch watercress, washed and dried

1 pound dried tubular pasta such as ditali or penne, or small shells

½ cup chopped pitted Niçoise olives

1½ cups tiny fresh peas

5 scallions, trimmed and sliced

8 ounces thinly sliced smoked salmon, cut into narrow strips

6 ounces salmon caviar

This salad will never seem as delicious to us as it was the first time Alice made it. But, if you use only the best ingredients, you'll come very close!

---

1 Assemble *mise en place* trays for this recipe (see page 6).

2 In a glass or ceramic bowl, whisk together the lime juice, mustard, and lemon zest. Set aside.

3 Put the quail eggs in a medium-sized saucepan and add enough cold water to cover. Bring to a boil over high heat. Immediately remove from the heat, drain, and rinse under cold running water.

4 Peel the quail eggs and slice in half lengthwise. Arrange on a plate and season to taste with salt, pepper, and 2 tablespoons of the olive oil. Cover and refrigerate.

5 In a medium-sized saucepan of boiling salted water, blanch the beans for 2 minutes, or until bright green and crisp-tender. Drain and refresh under cold running water. Pat dry and set aside.

6 Remove the leaves from half of the cilantro and watercress and chop the leaves. Set these aside. Trim the remaining cilantro and watercress sprigs, wrap in damp paper towels, and refrigerate.

7 In a large pot, bring 4 quarts of salted water to a boil over high heat. Cook the pasta until al dente. Drain well.

8 Transfer the pasta to a large serving bowl, add the remaining 6 tablespoons of olive oil and toss well. Stir in the lime dressing, chopped cilantro and watercress, beans, olives, peas, and scallions until well mixed. Stir in the salmon and caviar. Wipe the edge of the bowl. Cover and refrigerate for 4 hours, or until well chilled.

9 When ready to serve, garnish the salad with the reserved cilantro and watercress sprigs, and nestle the quail eggs among them. Serve immediately.

NOTE: Quail eggs are sold in specialty stores. Hens' eggs are too large to substitute. If you cannot find quail eggs, omit them from the recipe.

Bow Tie Pasta with Mussels and Zucchini ～ Paul Bartolotta

SERVES 6

PREPARATION TIME: ABOUT 30 MINUTES

COOKING TIME: ABOUT 20 MINUTES

FAT PER SERVING: 11.5 GRAMS

SATURATED FAT: 1.9 GRAMS

CALORIES PER SERVING: 424

CALORIES FROM FAT: 25%

1½ tablespoons extra-virgin olive oil

1 tablespoon minced garlic

54 mussels, well scrubbed and debearded

2¼ cups dry white wine

6 bay leaves

Pinch of red pepper flakes

3 medium-sized zucchini, cut on the diagonal into ⅛-inch-thick slices

6 tomatoes, peeled, cored, seeded, and diced

1½ tablespoons chopped fresh flat-leaf parsley

1 pound imported dried bow tie pasta

Salt and freshly ground black pepper to taste

This ambrosial combination of flavors truly is a one-dish meal filled with nutritious goodness.

---

1 Assemble *mise en place* trays for this recipe (see page 6).

2 In a large saucepan, heat 1 tablespoon of the oil over medium heat. Add the garlic and sauté for 1 minute. Add the mussels, wine, bay leaves, and pepper flakes, cover, and steam for about 5 minutes, or until the mussels open. Using a slotted spoon, transfer the mussels to a bowl. Discard any that have not opened. Bring the broth to a boil over high heat and cook for 3 to 4 minutes to burn off the acidity of the wine. Remove from the heat.

3 In a large sauté pan, heat the remaining 1½ teaspoons oil over medium heat. Add the zucchini and sauté for about 5 minutes, or until slightly softened. Stir in the tomatoes, mussels, and broth, remove from the heat, and set aside.

4 Meanwhile, bring a large pot of salted water to a boil over high heat. Add the pasta and cook for about 10 minutes, or until al dente. Drain.

5 Add the pasta to the sauce and heat, stirring constantly, over medium heat for about 3 minutes, or until the natural starch of the pasta thickens the sauce. Add the parsley, season to taste with salt and pepper, and serve immediately.

Side Dishes

Beet and Carrot Purée ❧ Tomato Confit ❧ Couscous and Sautéed Savoy Cabbage ❧ Fattoush ❧ Grain Pilaf ❧ Acorn Squash Torte ❧ Sweet Potato Gratin with Chiles ❧ Black Bean-Goat Cheese Torta ❧ Parsnip Purée ❧ Wild Rice-Orzo Pilaf ❧ Roasted Sweet Potatoes ❧ Toasted Bulgur ❧ Lentil Ragout ❧ Creamed Corn Pudding ❧ White Bean Ragout ❧ Potato Shoes ❧ Roasted Onions with Mustard Vinaigrette ❧ Baba Ganoosh ❧ White Bean Purée ❧ Cilantro Rice ❧ Black Pepper-Scallion Cornbread ❧ Couscous with Greens ❧ Sweet and Sour Pumpkin or Butternut Squash

Beet and Carrot Purée ❧ James Beard

SERVES 6

PREPARATION TIME: ABOUT 20 MINUTES

COOKING TIME: ABOUT 1 HOUR AND 15 MINUTES

1 pound young beets, trimmed and scrubbed

1 tablespoon vegetable oil

1 pound carrots, peeled, trimmed, and thinly sliced

4 tablespoons unsalted butter, at room temperature

⅛ teaspoon freshly grated nutmeg

Salt and freshly ground black pepper to taste

The beautiful color of this vegetable purée simply sings "fall." It can be prepared well ahead of time, which makes it a perfect holiday side dish.

1 Preheat the oven to 300 degrees F. Assemble *mise en place* trays for this recipe (see page 6).

2 Rub the beets with the oil and wrap in aluminum foil. Place on a baking sheet and bake for 1 hour, or until the beets are tender when pierced with a fork. Let cool slightly.

3 Meanwhile, place the carrots in a medium-sized saucepan and add enough water to cover. Bring to a boil over high heat. Lower the heat and simmer, covered, for about 15 minutes, or until tender. Drain well and set aside.

4 Peel the beets and discard the skins. Cut the beets into quarters.

5 Put the beets, carrots, butter, and nutmeg in a food processor fitted with the metal blade, and process until smooth. Season to taste with salt and pepper.

6 Transfer the purée to a medium-sized saucepan. Cook over medium heat, stirring constantly, for about 3 minutes, or until just heated through. Serve hot.

❧ Reserve the trimmed beet greens to use as a salad vegetable, or steam for a delicious and nutritious green vegetable.

Tomato Confit ❧ Daniel Boulud

MAKES ABOUT 1½ CUPS

---

4 plum tomatoes, peeled, cored, quartered, and seeded

1 large clove garlic, quartered

1 teaspoon ground cumin

½ teaspoon ground coriander

2 teaspoons olive oil

Salt and freshly ground black pepper to taste

*D*aniel uses this confit as a topping in his eggplant and crab garbure soup. These tomatoes can be used as a side dish to any meat, poultry, or vegetable entrée.

---

1 Preheat the oven to 350 degrees F. Assemble *mise en place* trays for this recipe (see page 6).

2 Lay the tomatoes in a small baking pan and sprinkle them with the garlic, spices, oil, and salt and pepper to taste. Bake for about 10 minutes, or until the tomatoes soften. Remove and discard the garlic. Use immediately, or set aside until ready to serve. If necessary, reheat over very low heat just until warm.

NOTE: The confit can be made up to 1 week ahead, covered, and refrigerated. Bring to room temperature and heat just until warm before serving.

Couscous and Sautéed Savoy Cabbage ❧ Patrick Clark

SERVES 6

PREPARATION TIME: ABOUT 20 MINUTES

COOKING TIME: ABOUT 5 MINUTES

FAT PER SERVING: 5.5 GRAMS

SATURATED FAT: 2.2 GRAMS

CALORIES PER SERVING: 195

CALORIES FROM FAT: 25%

---

3 cups water or Chicken Broth (see page 15)

½ cup finely diced carrots

½ cup finely diced zucchini

*T*his easy-to-make combination is the perfect accompaniment for grilled fish or meat. To lower the saturated fat, sauté the cabbage in vegetable oil instead of butter.

---

1 Assemble *mise en place* trays for this recipe (see page 6).

2 In a large saucepan, bring the water to a boil over high heat and add the carrots, zucchini, and onions. Stir in the couscous, cover, remove from the heat, and set aside for about 10 minutes, or until all the liquid is absorbed. Add the oil, if using, and salt and pepper to taste and fluff with a fork. Cover to keep warm.

½ cup finely diced onions

1 cup quick-cooking couscous

1 tablespoon olive oil (optional)

Salt and freshly ground black pepper
to taste

1½ tablespoons unsalted butter or
vegetable oil

1 head savoy cabbage, shredded,
blanched, and patted dry

3 In a large sauté pan, heat the butter over medium-low heat. Add the cabbage and sauté for about 3 minutes, or until just warmed through. Season to taste with salt and pepper.

4 Spoon the couscous onto one half of a large warm serving platter, mound the cabbage next to it, and serve immediately.

Fattoush ～ Andrew D'Amico

SERVES 6

PREPARATION TIME: ABOUT 30 MINUTES

TOASTING TIME: ABOUT 10 MINUTES

---

6 day-old 6-inch pita breads, cut
into ½-inch squares

2 cloves garlic, minced

1 serrano chile, seeded and minced

1 teaspoon salt, plus more to taste

½ cup fresh lemon juice

½ teaspoon ground sumac

¼ cup extra-virgin olive oil

¼ cup virgin olive oil

Freshly ground black pepper to taste

3 large ripe but firm tomatoes,
peeled, cored, seeded, and cut into
¼-inch dice

2 scallions, cut into ¼-inch dice

1 small red onion, cut into ¼-inch
dice

1 small red bell pepper, cored,
seeded, and cut into ¼-inch dice

*T*his hearty bread salad has its roots in Syria. Related to the Tuscan panzanella, an equally filling side dish, fattoush is an excellent accompaniment to grilled or roasted meats.

---

1 Assemble *mise en place* trays for this recipe (see page 6).

2 Preheat the oven to 350 degrees F.

3 Place the pita on a nonstick baking sheet and bake for 10 minutes, or until golden brown. Set aside.

4 In a mini food processor fitted with the metal blade (or in a mortar and pestle), process (or grind) the garlic, chile, and salt until a paste forms. Transfer to a small bowl and stir in the lemon juice and sumac. Whisk in the oils and season to taste with salt, if necessary, and pepper.

5 In a salad bowl, combine the tomatoes, scallions, onions, bell peppers, cucumbers, lettuce, parsley, mint, and cilantro. Add the dressing and toss to combine. Toss in the toasted pita and serve immediately.

1 large cucumber, peeled, seeded, and cut into ¼-inch dice

1 large head Romaine lettuce, inner leaves only, coarsely chopped

½ cup chopped fresh flat-leaf parsley

½ cup chopped fresh mint

½ cup chopped fresh cilantro

■ Special Equipment: Mini food processor

Grain Pilaf ❧ Gary Danko

SERVES 6

PREPARATION TIME: ABOUT 15 MINUTES

COOKING TIME: FROM 4 TO 60 MINUTES, DEPENDING ON GRAIN CHOSEN

MILLET:

2 tablespoons olive oil or unsalted butter

¼ cup minced onion

1 cup millet

2½ cups water

Coarse salt to taste

BULGUR OR QUINOA:

2 tablespoons olive oil or unsalted butter

¼ cup minced onion

1 cup bulgur or well-washed quinoa

2 cups water

Coarse salt to taste

Gary loves to experiment with grains. He frequently cooks a number of different ones and combines them to create a new taste—as well as an interesting side dish. For this pilaf, combine all four or only two of the suggested grains to serve with the salmon. To serve six people, you will need to start with about two cups of uncooked grain, so mix and match the grains accordingly. If you cook all four grains, you will have twice as much pilaf as you need, but it is delicious cold or reheated the next day.

1 Assemble *mise en place* trays for this recipe (see page 6).

2 To prepare the millet, in a medium-sized saucepan, heat the oil over medium heat. Add the onions and sauté for about 3 minutes, or until just softened. Stir in the millet and sauté for 1 minute. Add the water and coarse salt to taste and bring to a boil. Reduce the heat, cover, and just barely simmer for 15 to 20 minutes, or until tender. Remove from the heat and keep warm.

3 To prepare the bulgur or quinoa, in a medium-sized saucepan, heat the oil over medium heat. Add the onions and sauté for 3 minutes, or until just softened. Stir in the grain and sauté for 1 minute. Add the water and coarse

WEHANI RICE:

2 tablespoons olive oil or unsalted butter

¼ cup minced onion

1 cup Wehani rice

3 cups water

Coarse salt to taste

COUSCOUS:

2 tablespoons olive oil or unsalted butter

¼ cup minced onion

1 cup couscous

1 cup boiling water

Coarse salt to taste

salt to taste and bring to a boil. Reduce the heat, cover, and just barely simmer for 15 minutes, or until tender. Remove from the heat and allow to rest for 5 minutes.

4 To prepare the rice, in a medium-sized saucepan, heat the oil over medium heat. Add the onions and sauté for about 3 minutes, or until just softened. Stir in the rice and sauté for 1 minute. Add the water and coarse salt to taste and bring to a boil. Reduce the heat, cover, and just barely simmer for 50 minutes, or until tender. Remove from the heat and keep warm.

5 To prepare the couscous, in a medium-sized saucepan, heat the oil over medium heat. Add the onions and sauté for about 3 minutes, or until just softened. Stir in the couscous and sauté for 15 seconds. Immediately add the boiling water and remove the pan from the heat. Cover and allow to rest for 5 minutes.

6 Fluff the grains with a fork before serving and combine.

❧ Most grains can be kept warm, tightly covered, in a very low oven for up to 1 hour. You can also reheat them, tightly covered, in a 300-degree-F oven for about 20 minutes.

Acorn Squash Torte ❧ Robert Del Grande

SERVES 6

2 large acorn squash

1 tablespoon plus 1 teaspoon unsalted butter

2 tablespoons plus 2 teaspoons light brown sugar

3 poblano chiles, roasted (see page 12), peeled, seeded, and chopped

This is a perfect side dish for Robert's roasted pork loin and red chile sauce. It is also a wonderful creamy, spicy accompaniment for any dinner where you are looking for a twist on comfort food.

1 Preheat the oven to 350 degrees F. Assemble *mise en place* trays for this recipe (see page 6).

2 Wash and dry the acorn squash. Cut in half lengthwise and scrape out the seeds. Put 1 teaspoon of butter

3 ounces mild goat cheese

¼ cup minced fresh cilantro

1⅓ cups heavy cream

4 large eggs, separated

and 2 teaspoons of sugar in each cavity. Set in a baking dish and bake for 1 to 1¼ hours, or until the flesh is soft. Allow to cool.

3 Lower the oven to 300 degrees F.

4 Scrape out the squash flesh into a bowl, discard the skin, and mash lightly with a potato masher or fork. You should have about 3½ cups of squash.

5 Grease a 10-inch square baking dish with butter.

6 Combine the chiles, goat cheese, and minced cilantro with the squash flesh. Season with salt and pepper to taste. Stir in the cream until well incorporated.

7 In a clean bowl, using an electric mixer set on high speed, beat the egg whites to soft peaks. In a separate bowl, beat the egg yolks and then gently fold the yolks into the egg whites. Fold the whipped egg mixture into the squash mixture and pour into the prepared baking dish. Place the baking dish in a larger roasting pan and add water to the larger pan to a depth of about 1 inch.

8 Bake the torte for 40 to 50 minutes or until set and a cake tester inserted into the center comes out clean.

Sweet Potato Gratin with Chiles ❧ Bobby Flay

SERVES 8

PREPARATION TIME: ABOUT 15 MINUTES

COOKING TIME: ABOUT 1 HOUR

---

3 tablespoons unsalted butter, at room temperature

2 chipotle chiles in adobo sauce (see Glossary)

5 cups heavy cream

Zanne Zakroff, executive food editor of Gourmet *magazine, enjoyed this dish at a class so much that she has since made it part of her Thanksgiving menu. She especially loved the play of the mild sweet potatoes against the smoky flavor imparted by the chipotle chiles. I think it is much more exciting to serve than the traditional holiday potato casserole, and it's always a smash at a cocktail buffet—holiday time or not. If you'd like to go a little lighter, cut one cup of the cream; however, the volume of the sweet potatoes absorbs the richness of the full amount.*

9 sweet potatoes, peeled and thinly sliced (about 8 cups)

Salt and freshly ground white pepper to taste

1 Preheat the oven to 350 degrees F. Assemble *mise en place* trays for this recipe (see page 6).

2 Generously butter a shallow 4-quart casserole. Set aside.

3 In a blender or food processor fitted with the metal blade, combine the chiles and cream and blend until smooth.

4 Place a layer of sliced sweet potatoes in the casserole. Pour some chile cream over the top and season with salt and pepper. Continue layering until all the potatoes are used, ending with cream.

5 Bake for 1 hour or until the potatoes are tender and the top is lightly browned and bubbling. Serve hot or at room temperature.

Black Bean-Goat Cheese Torta ❧ Bobby Flay

SERVES 8

1 cup cooked black beans (see page 19) or canned black beans, well drained

1 small onion, chopped

1 clove garlic, minced

¾ cup Chicken Stock (see page 15) or water

1 tablespoon ground cumin

Salt and freshly ground black pepper to taste

20 three-inch fresh flour tortillas (see page 21) or store-bought flour tortillas

2 cups finely crumbled goat cheese

These are very impressive and delicious sides. They go well with beef, chicken, or pork.

1 Preheat the oven to 500 degrees F. Assemble *mise en place* trays for this recipe (see page 6).

2 In a medium-sized saucepan, combine the beans, onion, garlic, and stock. Bring to a simmer over medium heat and cook for about 10 minutes. Drain the beans and reserve the liquid.

3 In a blender or food processor fitted with the metal blade, combine the bean mixture and cumin. Season to taste with salt and pepper. Blend or process until smooth, adding enough of the reserved liquid to make a thick purée. Transfer the purée to a bowl.

4 Spread about 2 teaspoons of bean purée on one side of each of 16 tortillas. Sprinkle equal portions of the cheeses on top. Stack the tortillas so that each stack has

1½ cups finely grated white Cheddar cheese

2 tablespoons olive oil

2 tablespoons ancho chile powder (see page 12)

4 tortillas and there are 4 stacks total. Top each stack with a plain tortilla and press down lightly. Brush the tops with olive oil and sprinkle with ancho chile powder.

5 Carefully transfer the tortas to an ungreased baking sheet and bake for 5 minutes, or until heated through, the cheese melts on the inside and the tops are crisp. Cut in half. Serve warm or at room temperature.

❧ To make 3-inch tortillas from regular store-bought tortillas, cut out a 3-inch circle of waxed paper. Stack 3 or 4 tortillas. Lay the paper pattern on top and cut around it with sharp kitchen scissors.

Parsnip Purée ❧ Vincent Guerithault

SERVES 6

2 pounds parsnips, peeled and cut into 1-inch pieces

1½ cups heavy cream

2 tablespoons unsalted butter, softened

Salt and freshly ground black pepper

Parsnips are a sweet and delicious vegetable. This purée makes a creamy accompaniment to Vincent's Roast Rack of Veal. Serve it also with roast chicken to round out a satisfying winter dinner.

---

1 Assemble *mise en place* trays for this recipe (see page 6).

2 Steam the parsnips in a covered steamer basket set over boiling water for 20 minutes, or until tender when pierced with a fork. Transfer the parsnips to a blender or food processor fitted with the metal blade.

3 In a small saucepan, heat the cream over medium heat until small bubbles begin to appear around the edges. Do not boil. Add to the parsnips. Add the butter and salt and pepper to taste, and blend or process for 15 to 20 seconds until smooth. Transfer the purée to the top half of a double boiler over simmering water. Cover and keep warm until serving.

Wild Rice-Orzo Pilaf ❧ Patricia Jamieson

SERVES 6

PREPARATION TIME: ABOUT 20 MINUTES

COOKING TIME: ABOUT 50 MINUTES

FAT PER SERVING: 6.7 GRAMS

SATURATED FAT: 0.5 GRAM

CALORIES PER SERVING: 244

CALORIES FROM FAT: 24%

---

2 teaspoons vegetable oil

1 large onion, chopped

1 rib celery, finely chopped

1¼ cups wild rice, rinsed

2¾ cups Chicken Stock (see page 15), heated to boiling

1 sprig fresh thyme or ½ teaspoon dried

½ cup orzo

2 tablespoons finely chopped scallions

2 tablespoons finely chopped fresh flat-leaf parsley

1 teaspoon grated orange zest

Salt and freshly ground black pepper to taste

¼ cup chopped toasted pecans or almonds, for garnish (optional)

A romatic wild rice gives a rich and flavorful dimension to this pilaf. It is a particularly festive side dish for entertaining or the holidays, with the added bonus that it can be prepared ahead of time.

---

1 Assemble *mise en place* trays for this recipe (see page 6).

2 In a large heavy saucepan, heat the oil over medium heat. Add the onions and celery and sauté for about 5 minutes, or until the vegetables soften. Stir in the wild rice. Add the stock and thyme and bring to a simmer. Reduce the heat to medium-low, cover, and cook gently for about 50 minutes, or until the rice is tender and all the liquid is absorbed.

3 Meanwhile, cook the orzo in a medium-sized saucepan of boiling barely salted water for about 7 minutes, or until just tender. Drain in a sieve and rinse under warm running water.

4 Stir the orzo, scallions, parsley, and zest into the rice. Season to taste with salt and pepper. Put in a serving bowl, garnish with the nuts if desired, and serve immediately.

NOTE: The pilaf can be made up to 2 days ahead, covered, and refrigerated. To reheat, place in a casserole sprayed with nonstick vegetable spray. Cover and bake in a preheated 325-degree-F oven for about 20 minutes, until heated through.

Roasted Sweet Potatoes ❧ Patricia Jamieson

SERVES 6

PREPARATION TIME: ABOUT 10 MINUTES

ROASTING TIME: ABOUT 15 MINUTES

FAT PER SERVING: 2.3 GRAMS

SATURATED FAT: 0.3 GRAM

CALORIES PER SERVING: 108

CALORIES FROM FAT: 19%

---

2 medium-sized sweet potatoes, peeled and cut into ¼-inch-thick slices

1 tablespoon olive oil

Salt and freshly ground black pepper to taste

These are a healthy alternative to the traditional holiday sweet potato casserole. They are so good you will find them to be almost addictive at any time of the year.

---

1 Assemble *mise en place* trays for this recipe (see page 6). Preheat the oven to 450 degrees F.

2 Lightly spray a heavy-duty baking sheet with nonstick vegetable spray. On the pan, toss together the potatoes, oil, and salt and pepper to taste. Spread the potatoes out into a single layer and roast, turning once, for about 15 to 20 minutes, or until tender and golden. Serve immediately.

Toasted Bulgur ❧ Matthew Kenney

SERVES 6

1½ cups coarse-ground bulgur

3 tablespoons olive oil

1 large onion, chopped

¼ teaspoon hot green chile, such as jalapeño or serrano, seeded and chopped, or to taste

2 teaspoons tomato paste

1¾ cups plus 2 tablespoons boiling water

1 tablespoon plus 1½ teaspoons fresh lemon juice

¼ cup chopped fresh flat-leaf parsley

1 Assemble *mise en place* trays for this recipe (see page 6).

2 Preheat the oven to 300 degrees F.

3 Spread the bulgur on a baking sheet and toast in the oven, stirring frequently, for about 7 minutes, or until light brown. Take care not to let bulgur get too dark, or it will taste burned. Set aside.

4 In a large skillet, heat the oil over medium heat. Add the onions and chile and sauté for about 4 minutes, or until the onions are soft and translucent. Stir in the bulgur and tomato paste, add the water, and bring to a boil. Stir gently, reduce the heat, cover, and cook for about 20 minutes, or until all the water has been absorbed and the bulgur is tender. Stir in the lemon juice, parsley, and salt and pepper to taste. Remove from the heat, cover, and let rest for 5 minutes before serving.

Salt and freshly ground black pepper
to taste

NOTE: If you prepare the bulgur early in the day, do so only up to the point of adding the lemon juice and parsley. To reheat, moisten with about ¼ cup Chicken Stock (see page 14) and warm over low heat. Add the lemon juice, parsley, and salt and pepper to taste just before serving. This may also be served at room temperature.

Lentil Ragout ❧ Charles Palmer

SERVES 6

6 sprigs fresh parsley

4 sprigs fresh thyme

1 clove garlic

6 black peppercorns

2 tablespoons olive oil

¾ cup diced onions

½ cup diced carrots

1 cup green French lentils (Le Puy lentils), picked through, rinsed, and drained

2 cups Chicken Stock (see page 15)

½ cup peeled, sliced, cooked, small new potatoes

Salt and freshly ground black pepper to taste

This ragout is a hearty and flavorful side dish for Charlie's seared "steak cut" haddock, but will work with true steak, chicken, or any other seared or grilled fish.

1 Assemble *mise en place* trays for this recipe (see page 6).

2 Wrap the parsley and thyme sprigs, garlic, and peppercorns in a cheesecloth bag and tie securely to make an herb sachet.

3 In a medium-sized saucepan, heat the olive oil over medium-high heat. Add the onions and carrots and cook for 2 minutes. Add the lentils and cook for 2 minutes. Add the stock and herb sachet and bring to a simmer. Simmer for 20 to 30 minutes, until all the liquid has been absorbed and the lentils are tender. Remove from the heat and discard the sachet. Stir in the potatoes, season to taste with salt and pepper, and cover to keep warm until serving.

Creamed Corn Pudding ❧ Stephan Pyles

SERVES 6

5 ears fresh corn, husks and silks removed

½ cup heavy cream

3 medium eggs

2 medium egg yolks

¼ cup diced red bell pepper

1 serrano chile, seeded and minced

1 tablespoon minced fresh cilantro

2 teaspoons pure maple syrup

⅛ teaspoon ground cinnamon

Salt and freshly ground black pepper to taste

1 Assemble *mise en place* trays for this recipe (see page 6).

2 Preheat the oven to 375 degrees F. Generously grease a 9-inch square baking dish with butter.

3 Using a sharp knife, cut the kernels from the corn into a bowl. Scrape the cob to release all the milk. You should have about 3 cups of corn.

4 In another bowl, combine the cream, eggs, egg yolks, bell pepper, chile, cilantro, maple syrup, and cinnamon and beat well. Stir in the corn kernels and their milk and season to taste with salt and pepper. Pour into the prepared baking dish.

5 Bake for 25 to 35 minutes, or until a knife inserted into the center comes out clean. Serve warm.

White Bean Ragout ❧ Anne Rosenzweig

SERVES 6

3 ounces slab bacon, cut in ¼-inch dice

1 cup finely chopped carrots

1 cup finely chopped onions

1 cup Chicken Stock (see page 15)

¼ cup red wine

5½ cups cooked Great Northern beans (see page 19) or rinsed and drained canned white beans

This ragout is perfect mellow accompaniment to the quail Anne makes with a coffee and spice rub. Make the ragout as an interesting side dish for any chicken or meat entrée.

1 Assemble *mise en place* trays for this recipe (see page 6).

2 In a large saucepan, sauté the bacon over medium heat for about 5 minutes, or until all the fat has been rendered.

1 tablespoon minced fresh thyme

4 cups chopped fresh kale

½ cup chopped fresh parsley

4 tablespoons unsalted butter

Freshly ground black pepper to taste

3 Add the carrots and onions and sauté for 3 minutes. Add the stock and wine and bring to a simmer. Cook, stirring occasionally, for 15 to 20 minutes, or until most of the liquid has evaporated.

4 Stir in the beans and thyme. Cook for about 4 minutes. Stir in the kale, parsley, and butter. Season to taste with salt and pepper. Remove from the heat and keep warm until serving.

Potato Shoes ❧ Nancy Silverton and Mark Peel

SERVES 6

PREPARATION TIME: ABOUT 10 MINUTES

COOKING TIME: ABOUT 30 MINUTES

FAT PER SERVING: 9.2 GRAMS

SATURATED FAT: 0.9 GRAM

CALORIES PER SERVING: 264

CALORIES FROM FAT: 31%

5 small baking potatoes (4 to 6 ounces each)

¼ cup vegetable oil

Coarse salt and freshly ground black pepper to taste

*N*ancy and Mark call these "shoes" because they truly resemble the soles of shoes for very tiny feet! If you like potatoes, you will love these.

1 Assemble *mise en place* trays for this recipe (see page 6). Preheat the oven to 450 degrees F.

2 Cut the potatoes lengthwise into ½-inch-thick slices. (Do not peel.)

3 In an oven-proof skillet large enough to hold the potatoes in a single layer, heat the oil over medium heat and cook the potatoes for about 5 minutes, or until the bottoms are well browned. (You may need to use 2 skillets.)

4 Sprinkle the potatoes with coarse salt and pepper to taste and bake, without turning, for about 20 minutes, or until tender. Serve immediately, bottom side up.

❧ A cast-iron skillet is best for this recipe, although any oven-proof skillet works well.

❧ You can also cut and brown the potatoes in this fashion and then place under any roast (a leg of lamb is particularly good) to roast, without turning, in the fat and juices of the meat. However, this increases the fat and calorie content of the potatoes.

Roasted Onions with Mustard Vinaigrette ❧ Nancy Silverton and Mark Peel

SERVES 6

PREPARATION TIME: ABOUT 15 MINUTES

ROASTING TIME: ABOUT 1 HOUR AND 30 MINUTES

STANDING TIME: ABOUT 15 MINUTES

FAT PER SERVING: 9 GRAMS

SATURATED FAT: 1.2 GRAMS

CALORIES PER SERVING: 128

CALORIES FROM FAT: 63%

---

3 very large red onions, dry papery outer skin removed and halved through the stem end

2 tablespoons olive oil

1 teaspoon coarse salt

3 tablespoons fresh lemon juice

1½ teaspoons chopped fresh thyme or ⅜ teaspoon dried

1½ teaspoons Dijon mustard

¼ teaspoon coarsely ground black pepper

2 tablespoons extra-virgin olive oil

Nancy and Mark taught us their favorite method for preparing "always-on-hand" onions. It's so easy, and absolutely perfect for dressing up simply grilled meats, poultry, or fish. To save on fat, serve the onions without the vinaigrette. Note that the percentage of calories from fat is high, but the calories and grams of saturated fat are low, making this better for you than you may at first think!

1 Assemble *mise en place* trays for this recipe (see page 6). Preheat the oven to 375 degrees F.

2 In a shallow baking pan just large enough to hold them comfortably, arrange the onions cut side down in a single layer. Drizzle with the 2 tablespoons olive oil and sprinkle with the coarse salt. Roast, basting occasionally with any accumulated juices, for 1½ hours, until the onions are very soft in the center, lightly browned and somewhat caramelized, and just beginning to come apart.

3 In a small bowl, whisk together the lemon juice, thyme, mustard, and pepper. Gradually whisk in the extra-virgin olive oil. (The mixture will not emulsify.) Pour over the warm onions and set aside for about 15 minutes before serving.

❧ To roast small white onions, slice a small piece off the stem end of each so that they can stand upright in the pan. Cut an X about ½ inch deep into the top of each onion. Proceed with the recipe, baking the onions for about 35 to 40 minutes, until very soft. The baking time will depend on their size.

Baba Ghanoosh ～ Nancy Silverton and Mark Peel

MAKES ABOUT 2½ CUPS
FAT PER ½-CUP SERVING: 4.5 GRAMS
SATURATED FAT: 0.6 GRAM
CALORIES PER SERVING: 51
CALORIES FROM FAT: 77%

1 large or 2 small eggplant

2 cloves garlic, minced

3 tablespoons olive oil

1½ teaspoons fresh lemon juice

½ teaspoon coarse salt

½ teaspoon coarsely ground black pepper

Use this baba ghanoosh to accompany Nancy and Mark's leg of lamb, or use it as a dip for pita toasts for a tasty hors d'ouerves.

1 Assemble *mise en place* trays for this recipe (see page 6).

2 Set a large cast-iron skillet over medium-high heat, add the eggplant, and cook for about 1 hour, carefully turning every 15 minutes or so, until the skin gets black and charred. Set aside until cool enough to handle.

3 Trim the stem end(s) from the eggplant and cut in half lengthwise. Carefully scrape out the pulp, discarding the charred skin. (The pulp may be darkened, which will impart a roasted flavor.)

4 Transfer the pulp to a bowl and mash it with a fork, breaking up any large pieces. Add the garlic, oil, lemon juice, coarse salt, and pepper. Cover and let stand for about 4 hours at room temperature, or refrigerate for up to 12 hours. Bring to room temperature before serving.

NOTE: You can use 2 skillets to cook the eggplant if necessary.

White Bean Purée ～ Tom Valenti

SERVES 6

1 pound dried Great Northern beans

4 cloves garlic, 3 crushed and 1 minced

Tom's white bean purée complements his incredible braised lamb shanks perfectly. Try this purée instead of mashed potatoes for an interesting change of pace.

1 Assemble *mise en place* trays for this recipe (see page 6).

4 sprigs fresh thyme

2 bay leaves

3 cups Chicken Stock (see page 15), or more if needed

½ cup white wine

Salt and freshly ground black pepper to taste

½ cup olive oil

1 to 2 tablespoons unsalted butter, at room temperature (optional)

2 Rinse the beans in cold water, discarding any damaged or broken ones. Place in a large bowl, add cold water to cover, and soak for 8 hours, changing the water 3 or 4 times. Drain.

3 In a large saucepan, combine the beans, crushed garlic, thyme, bay leaves, stock, and wine and bring to a simmer over medium heat. Cook for about 1½ hours, or until the beans are tender, adding additional stock or water if the beans get too dry. Season to taste with salt and pepper.

4 In a food processor fitted with the metal blade, purée the beans. With the motor running, slowly add the olive oil and minced garlic and process until smooth. (This may have to be done in batches.) If the purée seems too thick, fold in the butter. Serve hot.

NOTE: You can prepare the beans ahead of time. Reheat over low heat, adding extra stock or water if necessary.

Cilantro Rice ～ Brendan Walsh

SERVES 12
PREPARATION TIME: ABOUT 20 MINUTES
COOKING TIME: ABOUT 30 MINUTES

8 cups cold water

4 cups long-grain white rice

1 tablespoon plus 1 teaspoon coarse salt

3 cups chopped fresh cilantro

2 cups diced red bell peppers

2 cups diced yellow bell peppers

1 cup olive oil

⅔ cup white wine vinegar

Brendan's method for cooking rice should yield perfectly cooked rice every time. His addition of pungent cilantro adds a whole new dimension to plain boiled white rice while giving it a flavor readily associated with Southwestern cooking. This rice can be served warm or at room temperature as a well-seasoned salad.

1 Assemble *mise en place* trays for this recipe (see page 6).

2 In a large saucepan, bring the water to a boil over high heat. Add the rice and salt and bring back to a boil. Immediately lower the heat, cover the pan, and cook for

Freshly ground black pepper to taste

20 minutes. Remove from the heat and let rest, covered, for 10 minutes.

3 Transfer the rice to a large bowl. Stir in the cilantro, bell peppers, olive oil, vinegar, and pepper to taste. Serve immediately or cover and let stand at room temperature.

~ This recipe can be easily tripled for a large crowd.

~ Fresh basil or parsley may be substituted for cilantro.

Sautéed Greens, Beets, and Yams ~ David Walzog

SERVES 6

---

5 large yams, washed

6 large beets, washed

3 bunches beet greens, trimmed, washed, and dried

4 tablespoons unsalted butter

■ Special Equipment: small melon-baller

Use this hearty vegetable dish as an accompaniment to David's guajillo-maple glazed turkey, or to add some "comfort food" to any fall or winter dinner.

---

1 Prepare the mise en place trays for this recipe (see page 6).

2 In separate saucepans, cook the yams and beets in boiling, salted water to cover by several inches for about 20 minutes, or until tender when pierced with a fork. Drain well and allow to cool.

3 Carefully peel the vegetables. Using a small melon-baller, scoop out balls from each vegetable, using as much of the flesh as you can. Set the balls aside in separate bowls.

4 Just before serving, in a large saucepan, melt 2 tablespoons of the butter over medium heat. Add the beet greens, cover and cook for about 2 minutes, or until wilted. Remove from the pan and keep warm.

5 Add the remaining 2 tablespoons of butter and 1 tablespoon of water to the saucepan. When the butter melts, add the reserved vegetable balls. Cook for 1 minute, or until the vegetables are heated through.

♺ If you don't have a melon-baller, cut the beets and yams into 1-inch cubes.

Black Pepper-Scallion Cornbread ♺ David Walzog

SERVES 6

PREPARATION TIME: ABOUT 15 MINUTES

BAKING TIME: ABOUT 25 MINUTES

5 tablespoons unsalted butter

1⅓ cups yellow stone-ground cornmeal

¾ cup all-purpose flour

2½ tablespoons granulated sugar

1 tablespoon salt

1 tablespoon plus 1 teaspoon baking powder

½ teaspoon baking soda

1 cup milk

1 large egg

½ cup chopped scallions (white parts only)

1 tablespoon cracked black pepper

■ Special Equipment: 9-inch round cake pan

1 Preheat the oven to 425 degrees F. Assemble *mise en place* trays for this recipe (see page 6).

2 In a small saucepan, melt 4 tablespoons of the butter. Remove from the heat.

3 Put the remaining 1 tablespoon of butter in a 9-inch round cake pan and heat in the oven while preparing the cornbread batter.

4 In a medium-sized bowl, sift together the cornmeal, flour, sugar, salt, baking powder, and baking soda.

5 In another bowl, whisk the milk, egg, and melted butter together. Add to the cornmeal mixture and stir just to combine. Stir in the scallions and pepper.

6 Take the hot cake pan from the oven and tilt it to distribute the melted butter. Immediately pour the batter into the pan.

7 Bake for about 25 minutes, or until a cake tester inserted into the center comes out clean.

♺ Heating the butter and the pan helps brown the bread. The batter will sizzle when poured into the hot pan. If possible, use a dark-colored cake pan.

Couscous with Greens ✦ Paula Wolfert

½ pound (about 4 bunches) fresh flat-leaf parsley, thick stems discarded, and chopped

¼ pound (about 2 bunches) fresh dill, chopped

¼ pound fennel fronds (fennel tops), chopped

¼ pound (about 2 bunches) scallions, chopped

¼ pound leeks, chopped

½ cup chopped carrot greens or celery leaves (optional)

½ cup olive oil

1 cup chopped onions

3 tablespoons tomato paste

2 tablespoons crushed garlic, plus 6 whole garlic cloves, peeled

2 teaspoons sweet paprika

2 teaspoons ground coriander or tabil

1 teaspoon ground caraway seeds

2 teaspoons salt, or more to taste

1½ to 2 teaspoons red pepper flakes, preferably Aleppo, Turkish, or Near East

2 cups hot water

1 pound (about 2½ cups) medium-grain couscous

1 red bell pepper, cored, seeded, and cut into 6 pieces

1 hot green chile, seeded and minced

■ Special Equipment: Couscous cooker *(couscousière)*, or a large steamer or a large colander that fits inside a large saucepan

This is a delicious, nutritious entrée for vegetarians and those looking for healthy alternatives in their diets.

1 Assemble *mise en place* trays for this recipe (see page 6).

2 In the perforated top of a *couscousière* (or a steamer basket or large colander), combine the parsley, dill, fennel, scallions, leeks, and carrot greens or celery leaves, and set over boiling water. Cover and steam for 30 minutes. Remove from the heat, uncover, and let stand until cool. Squeeze out the excess moisture.

3 In a large sauté pan, heat the oil over medium heat. Add the onions and sauté for 3 minutes, or until tender. Stir in the tomato paste and cook, stirring constantly, for about 2 minutes, or until the paste glistens. Stir in the crushed garlic, paprika, coriander, caraway, salt, and red pepper flakes. Reduce the heat and sauté for about 3 minutes, or until the garlic softens. Add 1 cup of the water, cover, and cook for 15 minutes.

4 Remove from the heat, add the couscous, and stir. Add the steamed vegetables and herbs and stir. Fold in the bell pepper, chile, and garlic cloves.

5 Fill the bottom of the couscousière with water and bring to a boil over high heat. Fasten on the perforated top and put the couscous mixture in the top. (Or put it into the steamer basket or large colander and set over boiling water.) Cover and steam for 30 minutes.

6 Transfer the couscous to a warm serving dish and break up any lumps with a fork. Remove and reserve the garlic cloves and bell pepper. Stir the remaining cup of hot water into the couscous, taste, and adjust the seasoning. Cover with aluminum foil and let stand for 10 minutes. Remove the foil and garnish the couscous with the reserved bell pepper and garlic.

Sweet and Sour Pumpkin or Butternut Squash ❧ Paula Wolfert

SERVES 6

PREPARATION TIME: ABOUT 15 MINUTES

COOKING TIME: ABOUT 15 MINUTES

RESTING TIME (LIQUID): 3 TO 4 HOURS

One 2½-pound pumpkin or butternut squash

About 2 tablespoons coarse salt

¼ cup olive oil

1⅓ cups (about ½ pound) thinly sliced onions

1 teaspoon granulated sugar

¼ cup plus 3 tablespoons white wine vinegar

⅓ cup water

¾ teaspoon salt

½ teaspoon freshly ground black pepper

¼ cup torn fresh mint leaves

This is an interesting way of preparing squash. It serves as either a condiment or a side dish.

1 Assemble *mise en place* trays for this recipe (see page 6).

2 Peel the pumpkin or squash, removing a little flesh with the peel. If using pumpkin, cut the flesh into ¼-inch-thick slices approximately 2½ inches by 3¼ inches. If using butternut squash, start at the neck end and cut into ¼-inch-thick rounds. When you reach the bulb end, cut lengthwise in half, remove the seeds and pulp, and slice the flesh into 1-inch squares about ¼ inch thick. Sprinkle the pumpkin or squash lightly with coarse salt. Using paper towels, blot off the excess moisture, but do not dry completely.

3 In a large nonreactive skillet, heat the oil over medium-high heat. Add the pumpkin or squash, without crowding, and cook for about 5 minutes, turning once or twice, or until golden brown on both sides. Remove with tongs and drain on paper towels, then cover and set aside.

4 Reduce the heat to medium and add the onions and sugar to the skillet. Cook for about 5 minutes, or until the onions are soft and golden brown and just beginning to caramelize. Raise the heat, add the vinegar and water, and bring to a simmer. Cook for about 4 minutes, or until the liquid has reduced by half. Remove from the heat and set aside to mellow for 3 to 4 hours.

5 Layer the pumpkin or squash on a large serving dish, sprinkling the layers with the salt and pepper. Pour the onion mixture over the slices. Garnish with half the torn mint leaves, cover, and refrigerate for about 1 hour, or until chilled.

6 Serve chilled, garnished with the remaining mint leaves.

NOTE: For the sweetest flesh, purchase pumpkin or squash with dull skin that feels heavy for its size. It is essential to use a mild wine vinegar for this recipe. Try the Sasso brand or French Corcellet white wine vinegar for best results. Avoid vinegar with more than 6 percent acidity.

Sauces, Dressings, and Salsas

Aïoli ❧ Orange-Almond Aïoli ❧ Basil Oil ❧ Chive Oil ❧ Curry Oil ❧ Barbecue Spice ❧ Apricot-Peach Chutney ❧ Banana-Guava Ketchup ❧ Pineapple Ketchup ❧ Jícama-Melon Relish ❧ Jalapeño Preserves ❧ Pesto ❧ Mexican Oregano Pesto ❧ Black Olive Tapenade ❧ Green Olive Tapenade ❧ Blue Cheese Dressing ❧ Buttermilk Dressing ❧ Goat Cheese Fondue ❧ Avocado Vinaigrette ❧ Cider Vinaigrette ❧ Ginger Vinaigrette ❧ Red Onion Vinaigrette ❧ Charred Yellow Pepper Sauce ❧ Horseradish Sauce ❧ Moroccan Barbecue Sauce ❧ Mango Sauce ❧ Red Chile Sauce ❧ Romesco Sauce ❧ Sauce Hachée ❧ Wild Mushroom-Ancho Chile Sauce ❧ Tomato Fondue ❧ Chipotle Beurre Blanc ❧ Yellow Tomato Salsa ❧ Mango-Black Bean Salsa ❧ Pineapple-Red Chile Salsa ❧ Mango-Lime Salsa ❧ Red Tomato Salsa ❧ Tomatillo Salsa ❧ Salsa Fresca ❧ Salsa Cruda ❧ Black Bean-Mango Salsa

$\mathcal{A}$ioli ❧ Wayne Nish

MAKES ABOUT 2⅔ CUPS

18 cloves garlic, 6 cloves minced and 12 left whole

¾ cup extra-virgin olive oil

1½ cups peanut oil

6 large egg yolks

¼ cup heavy cream

3 tablespoons fresh lemon juice

2 teaspoons kosher salt

$\mathcal{A}$ioli is a garlic-flavored mayonaise used to top pieces of fish and poultry, and may even be stirred into certain soups. Wayne uses this recipe to accompany his striped bass with artichokes.

1 Assemble *mise en place* trays for this recipe (see page 6).

2 In a small sauté pan, combine the whole garlic cloves and 2 tablespoons olive oil. Cover and cook over very low heat, stirring occasionally, for about 15 minutes, or until the garlic is very soft.

3 In a blender, combine the softened garlic and minced fresh garlic with 4 tablespoons peanut oil and blend until smooth. Set aside.

4 In a medium-sized glass or ceramic bowl, beat the egg yolks with a hand-held electric mixer set at high speed until well blended. While continuing to beat, gradually add ½ cup of the remaining peanut oil in a slow, steady stream until completely emulsified. Stir in the cream and lemon juice and transfer the mixture to a heavy saucepan. Cook over low heat just until bubbles form around the edges. Remove from heat and let the mixture stand for 2 to 3 minutes (this will kill any bacteria in the raw eggs). Return the mixture to the bowl and gradually whisk in the remaining ¾ cup peanut oil until incorporated.

5 Whisk in the garlic purée and salt. Using the mixer set at medium speed, beat in the remaining 10 tablespoons olive oil a little at a time until incorporated.

6 Cover and refrigerate for at least 8 hours before using. Whisk well before serving.

Orange-Almond Aïoli ～ Joyce Goldstein

MAKES ABOUT 1½ CUPS

1 cup mayonnaise

¼ cup fresh orange juice

1 teaspoon fresh lemon juice

½ cup toasted sliced almonds, crushed (see page 13)

2 teaspoons puréed garlic

2 teaspoons grated orange zest

¼ teaspoon salt

Pinch of freshly ground black pepper

Use this aïoli to top Joyce's spanish fish soup or spread it thinly on top of small toast points or toasted baguette slices for a tasty Mediterranean hors d'oeuvre.

1 Assemble *mise en place* trays for this recipe (see page 6).

2 In a nonreactive bowl, whisk together the mayonnaise and orange and lemon juices. Whisk in the almonds, garlic, orange zest, and salt and pepper. Cover and refrigerate until ready to use.

NOTE: To prepare the crushed almonds, grind in a mortar and pestle or crush them with a rolling pin. To prepare the puréed garlic, process a few cloves in a mini food processor or grind in a mortar and pestle.

Basil Oil ～ David Burke

MAKES ABOUT 3 CUPS

2 bunches fresh basil, leaves only

2½ cups extra-virgin olive oil

David Burke drizzles this basil oil on top of his red potato and goat cheese tart recipe, but this is a wonderful oil to have in your kitchen to spice up any dressings or sauces.

1 Dip the basil into a pot of rapidly boiling salted water for 30 seconds. Immediately place into a bowl of lightly salted ice water. Drain and squeeze to remove all the water.

2 In a blender, combine the basil and ½ cup of the olive oil. With the blender running, slowly add the remaining 2 cups of oil. Pour the mixture into a non-reactive container. Cover and let rest for 24 hours.

3 Strain the oil through a double layer of cheesecloth or fine strainer into a glass or ceramic bowl. Use right away or cover and refrigerate for up to 1 month. Let come to room temperature before using.

Chive Oil ❧ Charles Palmer

2 ounces fresh chives

1½ teaspoons cold water

½ cup grapeseed oil

Kosher salt and freshly ground black pepper to taste

This is a fragrant flavored oil used to top Charlie's open ravioli of wild mushrooms and caramelized onions. It can also be stirred into soups, tossed with pasta or rice, or mixed in to salad dressings.

1 Blanch the chives in a small pan of boiling water for 30 seconds. Drain immediately and refresh under cold running water. Pat dry and roughly chop.

2 Place the chives in a blender, add the cold water and blend until just puréed. Do not overprocess or the bright green color will fade. Scrape the purée into a small glass or ceramic bowl. Whisk in the oil and season to taste with salt and pepper. Use right away or cover tightly and store in a cool, dark place.

Curry Oil ❧ David Burke

MAKES ABOUT 2 CUPS

2 cups olive oil
1 shallot, minced
1½ tablespoons curry powder
1 teaspoon fennel seeds
1 teaspoon pink peppercorns
Kosher salt and freshly ground
pepper to taste

David uses this curry oil drizzled around his spice-crusted tuna entrée. This is a great basic recipe for a flavored oil. Serve it with grilled fish, lamb, chicken, or on falafel. Stir into rice in place of butter. Sauté fish or chicken cutlets or stir-fry vegetables. Drizzle a few drops of oil on cream soups before serving.

1 In a medium-sized heavy saucepan, heat ¼ cup of the oil over very low heat. Add the shallot, curry powder, fennel seeds, peppercorns, and salt and pepper to taste. Sauté, stirring constantly, for 2 minutes to allow the curry flavor to develop.

2 Add the remaining oil and simmer gently for about 10 minutes. Remove the pan from the heat and set aside until the solids have settled to the bottom of the pan.

3 Carefully pour the oil into a squeeze bottle or glass jar, leaving the sediment in the pan. Store the oil, tightly covered, in the refrigerator for up to 1 month. Let it come to room temperature before using.

Barbecue Spice ❧ Robert Del Grande

MAKES ABOUT 2½ TEASPOONS

1 tablespoon chile powder
2 teaspoons hot paprika
1 teaspoon all-purpose flour
1 teaspoon granulated sugar
¼ teaspoon ground cinnamon
¼ teaspoon coarse salt
Pinch of ground cloves
Pinch of freshly ground black pepper

Combine all ingredients in a small screw-top jar and shake to mix. Store tightly covered until ready to use.

❧ Use the best chile powder you can buy. If possible, buy pure ground chile powder.

❧ This recipe multiplies easily. Make lots of extra barbecue spice and store, tightly covered, for up to 3 months. Use it to add zest when roasting poultry or meat.

Apricot-Peach Chutney ❧ David Walzog

MAKES ABOUT 6 CUPS
PREPARATION TIME: ABOUT 15 MINUTES
COOKING TIME: ABOUT 35 MINUTES
CHILLING TIME: AT LEAST 3 HOURS

9 ounces dried apricot halves, sliced (about 1½ cups)

4½ ounces dried black currants (about 1 cup)

2 ounces dried cranberries (about ½ cup)

1½ cups apricot purée (organic apricot purée, sold as baby food in natural food stores)

1 cup rice wine vinegar

¾ cup Triple Sec

2 cups water

1 serrano chile, stemmed, seeded, and chopped

2 tablespoons ancho chile powder (see page 12)

1 tablespoon salt

1½ teaspoons freshly ground black pepper

1 cup diced fresh peaches

⅔ cup chopped, toasted pecans

2 teaspoons chopped fresh thyme

What a treat! Homemade chutney replacing the usual cranberry sauce as a relish for the holiday bird. This is typical of David's fresh approach to Thanksgiving dinner. The hint of spice further complements his guajillo chile-glazed turkey.

1 Assemble *mise en place* trays for this recipe (see page 6).

2 In a large, nonreactive saucepan, combine the apricots, black currants, cranberries, apricot purée, vinegar, Triple Sec, and water. Bring to a boil over high heat. Stir in the chile, chile powder, salt, and pepper. Reduce the heat to medium-low, cover and cook for 30 minutes, or until the dried fruits are very soft.

3 Strain the fruit through a fine sieve, reserving the liquid. Put the fruit in a medium-sized glass or ceramic bowl.

4 Return the liquid to the pan and cook over medium-high heat, stirring occasionally, for 5 minutes, or until a very thick syrup forms. (You should have about 1½ cups.)

5 Pour the syrup over the fruit. Stir in the peaches, pecans, and thyme. Cover and refrigerate for at least 3 hours. Bring to room temperature before serving.

❧ To toast the pecans, lay them in a single layer on a baking sheet and toast in a preheated 400 degree F. oven. Toast for 5 to 10 minutes, or until golden. Immediately transfer to a plate to cool.

❧ To make apricot purée, cook ½ pound (1½ cups) of dried apricots in 2 cups of gently simmering water until soft. Transfer the apricots and liquid to a blender or food processor fitted with the metal blade. Blend or process until puréed.

❧ Substitute unsweetened frozen peaches for fresh. Thaw before adding to the chutney.

Banana-Guava Ketchup ~ Chris Schlesinger

MAKES ABOUT 2 CUPS

FAT PER 5-TABLESPOON SERVING: 3 GRAMS

SATURATED FAT: 0.4 GRAM

CALORIES PER SERVING: 186

CALORIES FROM FAT: 14%

1 tablespoon vegetable oil

1 medium yellow onion (about 4 ounces), diced

5 very ripe bananas (about 2 pounds), peeled and cut into 1-inch pieces

½ cup guava paste (see Note)

1½ cups fresh orange juice

2½ tablespoons raisins

2 tablespoons light brown sugar

1 tablespoon curry powder

2 tablespoons white vinegar

¼ cup fresh lime juice (about 2 limes)

Salt and cracked black pepper to taste

Banana-Guava Ketchup will keep, covered, and refrigerated, for up to 6 weeks.

1 Assemble *mise en place* trays for this recipe (see page 6).

2 In a heavy-bottomed saucepan, heat the oil over medium heat. Add the onions and sauté for about 5 minutes, or until very soft. Reduce the heat slightly, add the bananas, and cook, stirring constantly to avoid sticking, for about 5 minutes, or until the bananas are slightly caramelized.

3 Combine the guava paste with 1 cup of the orange juice and stir into the banana mixture. Add the raisins, brown sugar, curry powder, 1 tablespoon of the vinegar, and the remaining ½ cup orange juice and stir to combine. Raise the heat and bring to a boil. Reduce the heat and simmer gently for about 15 minutes, or until the mixture is the consistency of applesauce.

4 Remove from the heat and stir in the lime juice and the remaining 1 tablespoon vinegar. Season with salt and cracked pepper to taste. Serve hot or at room temperature.

NOTE: The guava paste combined with 1 cup orange juice can be replaced by one 12-ounce can guava nectar or 1 cup guava jelly combined with ½ cup orange juice.

Pineapple Ketchup ~ **Chris Schlesinger**

MAKES ABOUT 2½ CUPS
FAT PER SERVING: 5 GRAMS
SATURATED FAT: 0.9 GRAM
CALORIES PER SERVING: 135
CALORIES FROM FAT: 32%

1 tablespoon vegetable oil

1 yellow onion, very thinly sliced

½ large ripe pineapple, peeled, cored, and cut into ½-inch cubes (about 1½ cups)

¼ cup fresh orange juice

¼ cup tamarind water (see Note)

¼ cup packed light brown sugar

Pinch of ground cloves

Salt and coarsely cracked black pepper to taste

Chris' tangy "ketchup" is a wonderful twist on a traditional ketchup. Use this a condiment for his London Broil or for any grilled meats, poultry or fish.

1 Assemble *mise en place* trays for this recipe (see page 6).

2 In a heavy-bottomed sauté pan, heat the oil over high heat until very hot but not smoking. Add the onions, reduce the heat, and sauté for about 7 minutes, or until translucent.

3 Add the pineapple and cook, stirring constantly, for about 3 minutes, or until the pineapple begins to soften.

4 Add the orange juice, tamarind water, sugar, cloves, and salt and cracked pepper to taste. Cook, stirring constantly, for about 5 minutes, or until heated through. Remove from the heat and serve hot or at room temperature. This ketchup keeps, covered and refrigerated, for up to 2 weeks.

NOTE: To make tamarind water, combine 1 tablespoon tamarind syrup with ½ cup hot water. Or dissolve a golf ball-sized piece of tamarind paste in ½ cup very hot water and allow to sit for 10 minutes; strain through a fine sieve to remove all the pulp. Chris also told us that equal parts of molasses, fresh lime juice, and Worcestershire sauce will be a valiant approximation for the natural flavor of tamarind. If necessary, you can substitute ¼ cup white vinegar for the tamarind water.

Jicama-Melon Relish ❧ Stephan Pyles

MAKES ABOUT 2 CUPS

¼ cup jícama, peeled, seeded, and cut into ¼-inch dice

¼ cup cantaloupe melon, peeled, seeded, and cut into ¼-inch dice

¼ cup honeydew melon, peeled, seeded, and cut into ¼-inch dice

2 tablespoons cucumber, peeled, seeded, and cut into ⅛-inch dice

1½ tablespoons red bell pepper, seeded and cut into ¼-inch dice

1 large very ripe mango, peeled, seed removed, and coarsely chopped

1 fresh serrano chile, stemmed, seeded, and finely chopped

Juice of 1 lime

2 teaspoons finely chopped fresh cilantro

Salt and freshly ground black pepper to taste

1 Assemble *mise en place* trays for this recipe (see page 6).

2 In a medium-sized glass or ceramic bowl combine the jícama, melons, cucumber, and red pepper.

3 In a blender or food processor fitted with the metal blade, combine the mango, chile, and lime juice. Blend or process until smooth. Add to the chopped vegetables along with the cilantro, and season to taste with salt and pepper. Toss to mix. Cover and refrigerate until ready to serve.

❧ Cut the vegetables and melon into the size dice specified. With the exception of the cucumber, which is cut into ⅛-inch dice, the dice should be ¼-inch. For these amounts, buy one whole vegetable, piece of fruit, or melon. You will have leftovers, but buying the produce whole rather than pre-cut insures freshness.

Jalapeño Preserves ❧ Bobby Flay

MAKES ABOUT 5 CUPS

---

3 red bell peppers, seeds and membranes removed, diced

6 jalapeño chiles, seeded and diced

4 cups granulated sugar

*B*obby says these preserves are his version of the classic mint jelly that is traditionally served with lamb. They make a wonderful accompaniment to roasted meats.

---

1 Assemble *mise en place* trays for this recipe (see page 6).

2 In a heavy-bottomed, non-reactive saucepan, combine the bell peppers, jalapeños, sugar, and vinegar. Bring to a

¼ cup red wine vinegar

¾ cup (6 ounces) liquid pectin

boil over medium-high heat, stirring frequently to prevent sticking. Reduce the heat to low and simmer for 20 minutes, stirring every 5 minutes. Take care not to let the mixture boil over.

3 Remove from the heat and stir in the pectin. Return the pan to the heat and bring back to a boil. Immediately remove from the heat and pour into a heatproof glass or ceramic bowl. Allow to cool. Cover and refrigerate for 8 hours or overnight before serving.

❧ You can replace the jalapeños with any other hot chile.

❧ For a thicker consistency, increase the number of bell peppers and chiles by 1 or 2 peppers and chiles each.

❧ These preserves make a great hostess gift, packed in a pretty jar, labeled and tied with a ribbon. The preserves keep for up to 1 month in the refrigerator.

Pesto ❧ Bradley Ogden

MAKES ABOUT 1 CUP

2 tablespoons ground almonds

½ cup loosely packed fresh basil leaves

2 tablespoons chopped fresh flat-leaf parsley

½ teaspoon minced garlic

¼ cup olive oil

2 teaspoons balsamic vinegar

1 teaspoon fresh lemon juice

2 tablespoons freshly grated Parmesan cheese

Kosher salt and freshly cracked black pepper to taste

Pesto is a wonderful condiment, and many variations exist. Here, Bradley uses almonds to add a distinctive flavor. He spoons the pesto over his Spring Vegetable Stew. You can add it to soups or stews, toss it with pasta, or serve it with grilled fish or chicken.

1 Assemble *mise en place* trays for this recipe (see page 6).

2 Combine the almonds, basil, parsley, garlic, and olive oil in a blender or food processor fitted with the metal blade and process until smooth.

3 Transfer the purée to a glass or ceramic bowl. Stir in the vinegar, lemon juice, Parmesan cheese, and salt and pepper to taste. Cover and let rest at room temperature for several hours until ready to serve.

Mexican Oregano Pesto ❧ Stephan Pyles

MAKES ABOUT 1 CUP

---

1 cup tightly packed fresh Mexican oregano leaves

2 teaspoons toasted pine nuts (see page 13)

1 clove garlic

¼ cup olive oil

Store this pesto in the refrigerator in a tightly sealed glass jar for up to 2 weeks. Use it to flavor mayonnaise-based salad dressings, vinaigrettes, and pasta dishes. If you can't find Mexican Oregano use any fresh oregano available.

In a blender or food processor fitted with the metal blade, combine the oregano, nuts, and garlic. Blend or process, using quick on/off pulses, until minced. With the motor running, slowly add the oil, processing until smooth. Transfer the pesto to a glass or ceramic bowl. Cover and refrigerate. Bring to room temperature before using.

Black Olive Tapenade ❧ Bobby Flay

MAKES ABOUT 1½ CUPS

---

1 cup pitted black olives

2 anchovy fillets

1 tablespoon minced garlic

1 tablespoon pine nuts

2 tablespoons fresh lemon juice

2 tablespoons olive oil

Salt and freshly ground black pepper to taste

In a blender or a food processor fitted with the metal blade, combine the olives, anchovies, garlic, pine nuts, lemon juice, and oil. Process until well blended but still textured (not as smooth as a purée). Season to taste with salt and pepper. Transfer to a nonreactive container, cover, and refrigerate until ready to use.

❧ Use your favorite brine- or oil-cured black olives for the tapenade.

Green Olive Tapenade ❧ Matthew Kenney

MAKES ABOUT 1½ CUP

3 ounces Picholine olives, pitted (see page 13)

1½ teaspoons drained small capers

1½ anchovy fillets, patted dry

1½ teaspoons fresh lemon juice

¼ cup plus 2 tablespoons olive oil

About 2 tablespoons water

Salt and freshly ground black pepper to taste (optional)

1 In a blender, purée the olives, capers, and anchovies. Add the lemon juice and blend well. With the machine running, add the oil. Add enough water to make a thin sauce-like mixture. Season to taste with salt and pepper, if necessary.

2 Strain through a fine strainer into a bowl, pressing against the solids with the back of a spoon. Cover and refrigerate until ready to use.

Blue Cheese Dressing ❧ Craig Claiborne

MAKES ABOUT 2 CUPS

1 cup mayonnaise

½ cup sour cream

¼ cup crumbled blue cheese

2 tablespoons minced onion

1 teaspoon minced parsley

1 tablespoon fresh lemon juice

1 tablespoon white vinegar

Salt and freshly ground black pepper to taste

Cayenne pepper to taste

This dressing is the traditional accompaniment to Craig Claiborne's bu alo chicken wings, or any chicken wings you may be serving.

Combine the mayonnaise, sour cream, blue cheese, onion, parsley, lemon juice, and vinegar in a bowl. Add salt, pepper, and cayenne to taste. Cover and refrigerate for at least 1 hour.

Buttermilk Dressing ~ **Robert Del Grande**

MAKES ABOUT 1½ CUPS

¼ cup buttermilk

¼ cup heavy cream

2 tablespoons mayonnaise
(see Note)

1 teaspoon pure maple syrup

1 teaspoon fresh lime juice

¼ teaspoon salt

Pinch of freshly ground white pepper

Robert's dressing is used on his appetizer of creamed biscuits and barbecued crabmeat, but is a wonderfully creamy and tasty dressing for a potato salad or to dress hearty greens.

In a bowl, whisk all the ingredients together until smooth. Transfer to a squirt bottle or a small lidded container. Refrigerate until ready to use, but do not let the dressing sit for longer than 1 hour.

NOTE: For a thicker dressing, increase the mayonnaise by 1 tablespoon.

~ Put the Buttermilk Dressing in a squirt bottle, such as those used for ketchup and mustard. Similar squirt bottles can be found in beauty supply stores. This will make it easier to control the drizzle on the crab.

Goat Cheese Fondue ~ **David Burke**

MAKES ABOUT 1 CUP

1 teaspoon unsalted butter

2 shallots, minced

3 ounces semisoft goat cheese

½ cup light cream

½ teaspoon ground cumin

Salt and freshly ground black pepper to taste

This fondue is used in as a topping for David's red potato and goat cheese tart appetizer. Serve the fondue with bread and cheese for a cocktail party.

1 Assemble *mise en place* trays for this recipe (see page 6).

2 In a small sauté pan, melt the butter over medium heat. Add the shallots and sauté for about 2 minutes until just softened.

3 Stir in the cheese and cream. Increase the heat to medium-high and cook, stirring constantly for about 1 minute, or until the cheese has melted. Stir in the cumin and salt and pepper to taste. Remove from the heat and keep warm.

Avocado Vinaigrette ❧ Bobby Flay

MAKES ABOUT 1½ CUPS

½ avocado, seeded

½ jalapeño chile, seeded

2 tablespoons finely chopped red onion

¼ cup fresh lime juice

1 teaspoon granulated sugar

¾ cup olive oil

Salt and freshly ground black pepper to taste

Use this vinaigrette on Bobby's tuna tostada, or as a topping for any grilled fish or vegetables.

1 Assemble *mise en place* trays for this recipe (see page 6).

2 Scoop the flesh from the avocado. In a blender or food processor fitted with the metal blade, combine the avocado, jalapeño, onion, lime juice, and sugar. Blend or process until smooth.

3 With the motor running, slowly add the oil and process until the vinaigrette is quite thick. Season to taste with salt and pepper. Transfer to a squirt bottle or glass ceramic bowl. Cover and refrigerate until ready to use.

❧ **To facilitate "painting" a design on the platter, transfer the vinaigrette to a squirt bottle such as those used for ketchup and mustard. Similar squirt bottles can be found in beauty supply stores.**

Cider Vinaigrette ❧ Christian Delouvrier

MAKES ABOUT ¾ CUP

2 tablespoons cider vinegar

¼ cup plus 2 tablespoons light olive oil

Salt and freshly ground black pepper to taste

½ teaspoon minced fresh chervil

½ teaspoon minced fresh parsley

½ teaspoon minced fresh chives

½ teaspoon minced fresh tarragon

This vinaigrette is ripe with fresh herbs and will liven up any green salad.

1 Assemble *mise en place* trays for this recipe (see page 6).

2 Whisk together the vinegar and oil. Season to taste with salt and pepper. Stir in the minced fresh herbs.

Ginger Vinaigrette ❧ Alfred Portale

MAKES ABOUT 1¼ CUPS

5 ounces fresh ginger, peeled

¾ cup grapeseed oil, or more to taste

¼ cup plus 2 tablespoons fresh lime juice, or more to taste

7 drops Tabasco

1 clove garlic, minced

1 shallot, minced

This vinaigrette is used to marinate the tuna, and dress the salad in Alfred's tuna tartare appetizer. Use this to to add a delicious taste and tang to any green salad.

1 Assemble *mise en place* trays for this recipe (see page 6).

2 Grate the ginger. Wrap the grated ginger in a square of cheesecloth, hold it over a small bowl, and twist the cheesecloth tightly to extract the ginger juice. Stir in the grapeseed oil, lime juice, Tabasco, minced garlic, and shallot. Taste and adjust the flavors with additional oil or citrus juices, if necessary. Set aside.

Red Onion Vinaigrette ❧ Gary Danko

2 tablespoons tarragon vinegar

1 tablespoon Dijon mustard

Coarse salt and freshly ground black pepper to taste

¼ cup plus 2 tablespoons extra-virgin olive oil

¼ cup minced red onion

2 tablespoons drained capers

1 clove garlic, minced

2 teaspoons minced fresh tarragon

Drizzle this vinaigrette over Gary's asparagus and peppers in his asparagus and red onion vinaigrette appetizer, or use the dressing tossed with fresh spinach or even grilled vegetables to make a delicious salad.

1 Assemble *mise en place* trays for this recipe (see page 6).

2 In a small bowl, combine the vinegar, mustard, and coarse salt and pepper to taste. Slowly whisk in the oil until emulsified. Whisk in the onions, capers, garlic, and tarragon. Taste and adjust the seasonings. Set aside.

Charred Yellow Pepper Sauce ~ Bobby Flay

MAKES ABOUT 2½ CUPS

2 roasted yellow bell peppers,
peeled, cored, and seeded

2 shallots, chopped

⅓ cup sherry wine vinegar

1 teaspoon Spanish paprika

1 cup olive oil

Salt and freshly ground black pepper
to taste

Use this sauce to top off Robby's toasted pork tenderloin with black olive tapenade, or to spice up any roasted fish, meat, or vegetable dish.

In a food processor fitted with the metal blade, combine the peppers, shallots, vinegar, and paprika. Process until smooth. With the machine running, slowly add the oil. When well emulsified, season to taste with salt and pepper. Transfer to a nonreactive container and refrigerate until ready to use.

Horseradish Sauce ~ Pierre Franey

MAKES ABOUT ½ CUP

½ cup sour cream

2 tablespoons freshly grated horseradish, or to taste

1 teaspoon white wine vinegar

⅛ teaspoon Tabasco

Salt and freshly ground black pepper
to taste

A classic sauce that accompanies any number of meat dishes.

1 Assemble *mise en place* trays for this recipe (see page 6).

2 In a bowl, combine the sour cream, 2 tablespoons of horseradish, the vinegar, and Tabasco. Stir to blend. Season to taste with salt and pepper, and add more horseradish, if desired.

Moroccan Barbecue Sauce ❧ Patrick Clark

MAKES ABOUT 1 CUP

2½ cups honey

1 cup ketchup

1 cup rice wine vinegar

½ cup soy sauce

Juice of 2 limes

1 tablespoon chile paste with garlic

½ cup chopped fresh cilantro

2 tablespoons chopped fresh ginger

5 star anise

2 small cinnamon sticks

1 tablespoon coriander seeds

1 tablespoon black peppercorns

1 teaspoon ground cardamom

1 teaspoon ground cloves

1 teaspoon ground mace

Patrick coats salmon fillets with this pungent sauce. Use it when you are grilling any fish, chicken, or as a dipping sauce for grilled vegetables.

1 Assemble *mise en place* trays for this recipe (see page 6).

2 In a medium-sized nonreactive saucepan, combine the honey, ketchup, vinegar, soy sauce, lime juice, chile paste, cilantro, ginger, star anise, cinnamon sticks, coriander seeds, peppercorns, cardamom, cloves, and mace and bring to a boil over medium heat. Reduce the heat and simmer, stirring frequently, for about 45 minutes, or until reduced by one third. Strain through a fine strainer into a bowl and discard the solids. Cool to room temperature.

NOTE: Chile paste with garlic is available in Asian markets and specialty food stores. The sauce can be made up to 2 weeks ahead, covered, and refrigerated. Bring to room temperature before serving.

Mango Sauce ❧ Ed Brown

MAKES ABOUT 2 CUPS
FAT PER ⅓-CUP SERVING: 5.3 GRAMS
SATURATED FAT: 0.3 GRAM
CALORIES PER SERVING: 71
CALORIES FROM FAT: 63%

2 mangoes, peeled and cubed, or 8 ounces canned mango purée

½ cup water

2 tablespoons canola oil

¼ cup Champagne vinegar

Pinch of cayenne pepper

Salt to taste

1 Assemble *mise en place* trays for this recipe (see page 6).

2 In a blender, combine all the ingredients and process for about 3 minutes, or until smooth. Use immediately, or pour into a nonreactive container, cover, and refrigerate for up to 2 days.

Red Chile Sauce ❧ Robert Del Grande

MAKES ABOUT 3 CUPS

6 large Ancho chiles, toasted (see page 12) and coarsely chopped

1 orange, peeled, seeded, and chopped into small pieces

3 cups Chicken Stock (see page 15)

½ cup chopped yellow onion

2 cloves garlic, peeled

Pinch of ground cloves

Pinch of ground cumin

Pinch of of ground cinnamon

2 tablespoons unsalted butter

Coarse salt and freshly ground pepper to taste

*R*ed chile sauce goes particularly well with Robert's roasted pork loin. Try this sauce to spice up other roasted meats such as chicken.

1 Assemble *mise en place* trays for this recipe (see page 6).

2 Put the chiles in a bowl with warm water to cover, and soak for 30 minutes until soft and pliable. Drain.

3 Put the chiles, orange, chicken stock, onion, garlic, and spices in a blender or food processor fitted with the metal blade. Blend or process for 30 seconds, or until smooth.

4 In a medium-sized saucepan, heat the butter over medium heat until it browns slightly. Add the chile purée and bring to a boil, stirring constantly. Lower the heat and simmer for 30 minutes. Taste and adjust the seasoning with salt and pepper. Serve warm.

Romesco Sauce ❧ Andrew D'Amico

MAKES ABOUT 1½ CUPS

3 plum tomatoes, halved

2 fresh hot green chiles, such as jalapeño or serrano, halved and seeded

1 red bell pepper, cored, quartered, and seeded

1 small bulb garlic, separated into cloves

½ cup sliced unblanched almonds

1 dried New Mexican red chile

1 cup water

3 tablespoons red wine vinegar

2 tablespoons chopped fresh flat-leaf parsley

1 tablespoon sweet paprika

½ cup olive oil

Salt and freshly ground black pepper to taste

This sauce accompanies Andrew's sofrito of baby lamb. The roasted flavors of the vegetables add a complex element to the sauce. This sauce can be used as a base for a soup or as a glaze for grilled meats.

1 Assemble *mise en place* trays for this recipe (see page 6).

2 Preheat the oven to 350 degrees F.

3 Place the tomatoes, fresh chiles, bell pepper, garlic, and almonds on a nonstick baking sheet, keeping each ingredient separate, and bake for about 20 minutes, removing the items as they are cooked: The almonds will brown quickly, while the vegetables will probably require the full time for their skins to blister and their flesh to soften. Cool, then peel the peppers and garlic. Finely chop the almonds in a spice grinder or finely grind them with a mortar and pestle.

4 In a small saucepan, combine the dried chile and water and bring to a boil over high heat. Reduce the heat and simmer for about 10 minutes, or until the liquid is reduced to ¼ cup. Remove the pan from the heat and cool slightly. Seed and stem the chile and set aside. Reserve the cooking water.

5 In a food processor fitted with the metal blade, combine the green chiles, bell pepper, garlic, dried chile and cooking water, vinegar, parsley, and paprika and process until smooth. With the processor running, slowly add the oil. When well blended, season to taste with salt and pepper. Transfer to a nonreactive bowl and fold in the almonds. Use immediately or cover and refrigerate until ready to use.

❧ You can cook veal shanks, beef shanks, or rack of lamb or rack of veal in this manner. The sauce also serves as a glaze for roast rack of lamb.

Sauce Hachée ❧ Jean-Michel Bergougnoux

MAKES ABOUT 1 CUP

¼ cup dry white wine

1½ teaspoons balsamic vinegar

½ teaspoon Dijon mustard

½ cup olive oil

1 anchovy fillet, drained well and chopped

3 tablespoons peeled, seeded, and diced tomatoes

1 teaspoon chopped Niçoise olives

½ teaspoon chopped capers

½ teaspoon chopped cornichons

1 tablespoon chopped fresh flat-leaf parsley

1½ teaspoons chopped fresh basil

Salt and freshly ground black pepper to taste

This sauce combines Mediterranean ingredients to make a flavorful relish for Jean-Michel's braised beef, but it is also a wonderful accompaniment for any grilled fish or chicken.

1 Assemble *mise en place* trays for this recipe (see page 6).

2 In a small bowl, whisk together the wine, vinegar, and mustard. Whisk in the oil until emulsified. Fold in the anchovy, tomatoes, olives, capers, cornichons, herbs, and salt and pepper to taste. Serve immediately.

NOTE: The sauce can be made up to 1 day ahead, but do not add the herbs until just before serving.

Wild Mushroom-Ancho Chile Sauce ❧ Bobby Flay

MAKES ABOUT 4 CUPS

2 tablespoons unsalted butter

½ cup diced red onion

2 tablespoons minced garlic

2 cups red wine

This chunky and rich sauce goes perfectly with Bobby's roasted pepper-crusted tenderloin of beef.

1 Assemble *mise en place* trays for this recipe (see page 6).

2 In a medium-sized saucepan, melt the butter over medium heat. Add the onion and garlic, reduce the heat,

1 cup sliced shiitake mushrooms (about 6 mushrooms)

1 cup sliced cremini mushrooms (about 6 mushrooms)

1 cup sliced portobello mushrooms, cut the same size as shiitake and cremini mushrooms

3½ cups Chicken Stock (see page 15)

¾ cup dried ancho chile purée (see page 12)

2 tablespoons honey, or to taste

Salt and freshly ground black pepper to taste

and sauté for about 5 minutes, or until just soft. Add the red wine, increase the heat to medium, and simmer for about 15 minutes, or until the liquid is reduced to ¼ cup.

3 Add the mushrooms to the pan and cook for about 5 minutes, or until just softened.

4 Add the chicken stock and bring to a boil. Reduce the heat and simmer for 15 minutes.

5 Whisk in the chile purée and simmer for 5 minutes more. Season to taste with the honey and salt and pepper. Serve warm.

Tomato Fondue ～ Georges Perrier

MAKES ABOUT 2 CUPS

8 ripe tomatoes, peeled, cored, seeded, and chopped

½ cup extra-virgin olive oil

¼ cup balsamic vinegar

3 tablespoons chopped fresh flat-leaf parsley

3 tablespoons chopped fresh chives

Coarse salt and freshly ground black pepper to taste

Tomato fondue is used as a condiment in Georges' dish of sole and saffron pasta. It can be used to top any seared or grilled meat or poultry, or can be tossed with pasta.

1 Assemble *mise en place* trays for this recipe (see page 6).

2 In a medium nonreactive saucepan, combine the tomatoes, oil, and vinegar and bring to a boil over medium-low heat. Cook, stirring frequently, for about 40 minutes, or until thickened and reduced slightly. Remove from the heat and stir in the parsley and chives. Season to taste with coarse salt and pepper. Keep warm until ready to serve.

NOTE: This can be made up to 1 week ahead, covered, and refrigerated. Reheat gently to serve. Reserve leftovers for another use.

Chipotle Beurre Blanc ❧ Vincent Guerithault

MAKES ABOUT 3 CUPS

―――――――

2 chipotle chiles in adobo, well drained (see Glossary)

1 cup dry white wine

1 cup white wine vinegar

1 tablespoon minced shallots

1 cup (2 sticks) unsalted butter, softened

Vincent uses this sauce on his roast rack of veal. It is a delicate and tasty sauce for meat, chicken, or fish.

1 Assemble *mise en place* trays for this recipe (see page 6).

2 Put the chipotles in a blender or food processor fitted with the metal blade and blend or process until smooth.

2 In a small, heavy, nonreactive saucepan, bring the wine, wine vinegar, and shallots to a boil over medium heat. Reduce the heat to low and simmer, uncovered, for 20 to 30 minutes, or until the liquid has evaporated. Whisking vigorously, add the butter, 2 tablespoons at time, making each addition just before the previous one has been totally incorporated. When all the butter has been incorporated, whisk in the chipotle purée. Remove from the heat, cover and keep warm.

―――――――

❧ If you have difficulty puréeing the small amount of chipotle chiles in the blender or food processor, chop them very fine with a sharp knife.

Salsas

*S*alsas are an exciting way to use fruits, beans, and vegetables such as chiles, to create innovative and bold condiments for fish, chicken, quesadillas, and anything else you feel needs topping. Assembling mise en place trays before making your salsa is extremely important because most of the work of making salsas is in preparing the ingredients.

Yellow Tomato Salsa ❧ Stephan Pyles

MAKES ABOUT 2 CUPS

1 pound yellow tomatoes or yellow cherry tomatoes, chopped

1 large shallot, finely minced

1 large clove garlic, finely minced

2 tablespoons finely minced fresh cilantro

1 tablespoon Champagne vinegar or white wine vinegar

2 serrano chiles, seeded and minced

2 teaspoons fresh lime juice

1 tablespoon pure maple syrup (optional)

Salt to taste

In a bowl, combine the tomatoes and their juices, the shallot, garlic, cilantro, vinegar, chiles, lime juice, and maple syrup, if the tomatoes are not sweet enough. Season to taste with salt. Mix well. Cover and refrigerate for at least 2 hours or until very cold.

❧ For speed, chop the tomatoes in a food processor using on/off pulses to ensure they remain chunky.

❧ The salsa can be made early in the day and refrigerated until ready to use.

Mango-Black Bean Salsa ❧ Ed Brown

MAKES ABOUT 3 CUPS
FAT PER ½-CUP SERVING: 1 GRAM
SATURATED FAT: 0.1 GRAM
CALORIES PER SERVING: 84
CALORIES FROM FAT: 10%

⅔ cup finely diced mango
(1 to 2 mangoes)

⅓ cup cooked black beans (see page 19)

½ red bell pepper, cored, seeded, and cut into ¼-inch dice

2 scallions, green parts only, chopped

1 orange, peeled and cut into membrane-free segments

½ lime, peeled and cut into membrane-free segments

1 tablespoon chopped fresh cilantro

1½ cups fresh orange juice

1 teaspoon rice wine vinegar

1 teaspoon extra-virgin olive oil

¼ teaspoon red pepper flakes

Salt to taste

Up to 1 hour before serving, combine all the ingredients in a nonreactive bowl. Let stand at room temperature until ready to serve.

NOTE: The recipes makes more salsa than you will need. Cover and refrigerate it for up to 3 days.

Pineapple-Red Chile Salsa ~ **Dean Fearing**

½ very ripe pineapple, peeled, cored, and coarsely chopped

½ mango or papaya, peeled, seeded, and coarsely chopped

½ red bell pepper, seeds and membranes removed, chopped

½ yellow bell pepper, seeds and membranes removed, chopped

1 small jícama, peeled and chopped

2 teaspoons peeled and grated fresh ginger (from a 3-inch piece)

1 clove garlic, minced

1 serrano chile, seeded and minced

2 dried cayenne chiles, seeded and minced or ⅛ teaspoon ground cayenne pepper

2 teaspoons minced fresh cilantro

2 teaspoons minced fresh basil

2 teaspoons minced fresh mint

1 tablespoon white wine vinegar

1 tablespoon sweet rice vinegar

1 teaspoon soy sauce

1 teaspoon sesame oil

Salt to taste

Juice of 1 lime, or to taste

In a bowl, combine the pineapple, mango, bell peppers, jícama, ginger, garlic, chiles, herbs, vinegars, soy sauce, and sesame oil. Season to taste with salt and the lime juice. Mix well. Cover and refrigerate for at least 2 hours before serving. Bring to room temperature before serving.

~ The salsa must be made at least 2 hours in advance to allow the flavors to blend. It can be made early in the day and refrigerated until about 1 hour before serving. Allow to come to room temperature before serving so that the flavors are subtle against the swordfish. It does not hold up well for longer than 8 to 12 hours.

~ For speed, chop the fruit and vegetables—separately— in a food processor using on/off pulses to ensure they remain chunky.

Mango-Lime Salsa ❧ Chris Schlesinger

MAKES ABOUT 3 CUPS
FAT PER ½-CUP SERVING: 0.4 GRAM
SATURATED FAT: 0.1 GRAM
CALORIES PER SERVING: 82
CALORIES FROM FAT: 4%

2 large ripe but firm mangoes, peeled, pitted, and cut into ¼-inch dice

1 red onion, cut into ¼-inch dice

1 red bell pepper, cored, seeded, and cut into ¼-inch dice

1 green bell pepper, cored, seeded, and cut into ¼-inch dice

½ cup chopped fresh cilantro

¼ cup fresh lime juice (about 2 limes)

¼ cup unsweetened pineapple juice

2 tablespoons Caribbean-style hot sauce, such as Inner Beauty Real Hot Sauce

Salt and freshly ground black pepper to taste

In a nonreactive bowl, combine all the ingredients and stir gently. Serve immediately, or store, covered and refrigerated, for up to 3 days.

NOTE: Chris says the hot sauce should be as hot as you can tolerate. Inner Beauty Real Hot Sauce is fiery.

Red Tomato Salsa ❧ Stephan Pyles

MAKES ABOUT 1½ CUPS

4 small, ripe tomatoes, cored, seeded, and cut into ¼-inch dice

2 cloves garlic, roasted (see page 20), peeled and mashed

⅓ cup finely diced red onion

2 tablespoons finely diced red bell pepper

1 teaspoon fresh lime juice

Salt to taste

Put the tomatoes in a medium-sized glass or ceramic bowl. Stir in the garlic, onion, pepper, and lime juice. Season to taste with salt. Let stand for at least 30 minutes before serving.

Tomatillo Salsa ❧ Bobby Flay

MAKES ABOUT 1⅔ CUPS

8 medium tomatillos, husked, washed, and coarsely chopped

2 tablespoons finely diced red onion

1 tablespoon minced jalapeño chile

¼ cup fresh lime juice

¼ cup chopped fresh cilantro

2 tablespoons olive oil

2 teaspoons honey

Salt and freshly ground black pepper to taste

In a glass or ceramic bowl, combine the tomatillos, onion, chile, lime juice, cilantro, olive oil, and honey. Season to taste with salt and pepper. Cover and refrigerate for at least 1 hour. Allow to come to room temperature before serving.

Salsa Fresca ❧ Marilyn Frobuccino

---

1 large, very ripe pineapple, peeled, halved, and cored

¼ cup plus 3 tablespoons extra virgin olive oil

¼ cup fresh lime juice

1 tablespoon jalapeño-flavored vinegar (see page 24)

1 pickled jalapeño chile, seeded and minced

Salt to taste

1 Roughly chop half of the pineapple using a large, sharp knife or a food processor and set aside. Cut the remaining pineapple crosswise into ¼-inch slices. Generously coat the pineapple slices with 3 tablespoons of the oil.

2 Heat a cast-iron skillet over medium-high heat until very hot and smoking. Place the pineapple slices in the skillet and, turning once, sauté for about 2 minutes, or until pineapple darkens. Transfer to paper towels and allow to cool.

3 Meanwhile, put the chopped pineapple in a blender or food processor fitted with the metal blade, and blend or process until thick and smooth. Add the remaining ¼ cup of olive oil and, using 3 to 4 on/off pulses, process until the mixture begins to emulsify. With the machine running, slowly add the lime juice and jalapeño vinegar in a steady stream. Process just to incorporate. Transfer the mixture to a glass or ceramic bowl.

4 Cut the cooked pineapple into ¼-inch pieces. Stir into the puréed pineapple, along with the jalapeños. Season to taste with salt, if necessary. Cover and refrigerate for at least 30 minutes before serving.

Salsa Cruda ～ Marilyn Frobuccino

8 large, very ripe plum tomatoes, cored, seeded, and cut into ¼-inch dice

4 large tomatillos, washed, husked, and cut into ¼-inch dice

1 pickled serrano chile, minced

¼ cup minced red onion

2 tablespoons minced fresh cilantro

Juice of 1 large fresh lime

Salt to taste

In a medium-sized glass or ceramic bowl, combine the tomatoes, tomatillos, chile, onion, cilantro, and lime juice. Add salt to taste. Cover and allow to marinate at room temperature for 1 hour before serving.

～ The smaller and more evenly the ingredients are cut, the more flavorful the salsa.

～ Pickled serrano chiles are sold in cans in Hispanic markets. If you can't find them, use a pickled jalapeño.

～ The salsa can be made up to 8 hours ahead of time, covered and refrigerated but do not add the salt until just before serving.

Black Bean-Mango Salsa ❧ Bobby Flay

MAKES ABOUT 2¼ CUPS

————————

1 cup cooked black beans (see page 19) or canned black beans, well drained

1 mango, peeled, seeded, and coarsely chopped (about ½ cup)

1 small red onion, diced

½ jalapeño chile, seeded and finely diced

¼ cup lightly packed, chopped fresh cilantro

¼ cup fresh lime juice

2 tablespoons olive oil

Salt and freshly ground white pepper to taste

In a medium-sized glass or ceramic bowl, combine the black beans, mango, onion, chile, cilantro, lime juice, and oil. Season to taste with salt and white pepper.

Desserts

Banana Fritters ❧ Mascarpone with Fruit ❧ Hazelnut Cookies ❧ Quince Tart ❧ Deep Chocolate Marquise ❧ Warm Apricot Tarts with Pistachios ❧ Banana-Pineapple Shake ❧ Sweet Green Tomato Pie ❧ Baklava ❧ Lemon Curd Napoleon ❧ Carrot-Raisin Cake ❧ The Marquesa's Chocolate Cream in a Crust ❧ Orange and Strawberry Tart with Candied Bell Pepper Caramel ❧ Tirami-sù ❧ Coffee Granita with Lemon-Scented Ice Milk ❧ Apple Soufflé on a Platter with Apricot Sauce ❧ Hazelnut Cheesecake ❧ Blueberry Clafoutis ❧ Gratin of Strawberries and Rhubarb with Warm Nutmeg Cream and Pistachio Ice Cream ❧ Banana Cocoa Cake ❧ Lemon Tart ❧ Chocolate Tart with Orange Salad ❧ Chocolate Amaretto Pudding ❧ Chocolate Risotto Pudding ❧ Brown Butter Berry Tart ❧ Blue Corn Biscotti ❧ Maple Sugar-Crusted Apple Pie ❧ Bolo Apple Cake ❧ Thin Apple Tart ❧ Chilled Minted Melon Soup ❧ Gateau Rolla ❧ Chocolate Walnut Tarte ❧ Pumpkin Crème Brûlée ❧ Blackberry-Rhubarb Phyllo Tart ❧ Caramelized Pear and Cranberry Upside-Down Cake ❧ Cranberry-Walnut Tart ❧ Chilled Soup of Santa Rosa Plums Flavored with Vanilla ❧ Chocolate Strudel and Poached Pears with Cinnamon Sauce ❧ Walnut Tart ❧ Vanilla Custard with Maple-Roasted Peanuts ❧ Apricot and Ginger Crisp ❧ Banana-Pecan Strudel with Raisin Brandy Cream ❧ Baked Apples ❧ Pear Clafoutis ❧ Warm Chocolate Cake ❧ Pecan Pie ❧ Sour Cherry Tart ❧ Cranberry-Mango Cobbler with Cinnamon-Pecan Cream ❧ Chocolate Bread Pudding ❧ Crème Brûlée Le Cirque ❧ Walnut Biscotti ❧ Grilled Peached with Blue Cheese and Sweet Balsamic Vinegar Glaze ❧ Passion Fruit Ice Cream with Raspberry Purée and White Chocolate Sauce ❧ Baked Peaches with Warm Blueberry-Thyme Sauce ❧ Apricots Baked with Kirsch and Vanilla ❧ Roasted Caramelized Pears ❧ Plum and Ginger Kuchen ❧ Dried Fig and Apricot Tart ❧ Chocolate Mousse ❧ Pistachio-Fig Tart ❧ Passion Fruit Club with Strawberries ❧ Sweet Potato Pie ❧ Lemon Anise Churros ❧ Apricot and Cherry Tart ❧ Walnut Roll

Banana Fritters ✒ Colman Andrews

MAKES ABOUT 24

PREPARATION TIME: ABOUT 1 HOUR (INCLUDING RESTING TIME)

FRYING TIME: ABOUT 3 MINUTES PER BATCH; ABOUT 12 MINUTES TOTAL

---

1 pound very ripe bananas, peeled and mashed

6 large eggs

½ cup milk

2 to 3 tablespoons dark rum, or to taste

Grated zest of 1 lemon

½ teaspoon ground cinnamon

Pinch of salt

1 teaspoon active dry yeast

3 to 4 cups all-purpose flour

4 cups corn oil

4 large pieces orange peel

About ½ cup confectioners' sugar

These simple doughnut-like treats are easy to make and always draw raves. They are also a marvelous way to use overripe bananas. What's more, you can make them several hours before serving.

---

1 Assemble *mise en place* trays for this recipe (see page 6).

2 In a bowl, combine the bananas and eggs. Add the milk, rum, lemon zest, cinnamon, and salt and whisk until well blended. Add the yeast, whisking, then add just enough flour to make a smooth batter that is the consistency of softly whipped cream. Cover and set aside to rest for 30 minutes.

3 In a large heavy nonstick frying pan, heat the oil over medium-high heat until hot (see Note). Add the orange peel and cook for about 2 minutes, or until the peel begins to brown. Remove and discard the peel, and heat the oil until it registers 360 degrees F on a candy thermometer. Use a soup spoon to form the batter into small ovals, drop the ovals into the oil, a few at a time, and fry for about 3 minutes, or until golden and crisp. Using a slotted spoon, remove the fritters and drain on paper towels. Continue until all the batter has been used.

4 Using a fine sieve or sugar shaker, lightly dust the warm fritters with confectioners' sugar. Serve warm or at room temperature.

NOTE: The oil must be deep enough for the fritters to float freely, or they will brown too quickly and still be raw in the center.

Mascarpone with Fruit ❧ Francesco Antonucci

SERVES 6

PREPARATION TIME: ABOUT 10 MINUTES

¾ pound mascarpone cheese

6 ripe large fruits, such as peaches, pears, or apples

12 ripe, small fruits, such as figs, apricots, or small bunches of grapes, or an assortment of dried fruits

Mascarpone is a double-to-triple-cream cow's milk cheese from Italy's Lombardy region, and frequently sweetened and served with fresh or dried fruit as a dessert. It ranges in texture from very soft, almost runny, to the consistency of room-temperature cream cheese or butter. Its delicate flavor blends well with a wide variety of both savory and sweet seasonings. A small portion of rich, buttery mascarpone requires only a piece of sweet fruit as enrichment to make a most satisfying dessert.

Place the mascarpone cheese on a platter. Serve it with a bowl of the fruit. Let the guests peel and cut the fruit themselves.

❧ Serve whatever fruit is in season, either by the piece or in a large, overflowing centerpiece, allowing your guests to choose whatever they wish.

❧ For the best mascarpone, buy the cheese from a cheese shop or an Italian market.

❧ Instead of fresh fruit, you can serve dried fruit. Or bring white wine or water seasoned with pungent spices to a boil and pour this over the dried fruit. Let it soak for at least 8 hours. The soaking gives the fruit time to absorb the flavors of the wine or spiced water and to plump up.

Hazelnut Cookies ❧ **Lidia Bastianich**

MAKES 20 TO 30 COOKIES

PREPARATION TIME: ABOUT 20 MINUTES

COOKING TIME: ABOUT 30 MINUTES

1 cup finely chopped toasted and skinned hazelnuts (see page 13)

1 cup confectioners' sugar, sifted

⅛ teaspoon ground cinnamon

4 large egg whites

Here is a simple cookie to dip into Vin Santo or a frothy cappuccino. These are good keepers, so make a couple of batches to have on hand.

1 Assemble *mise en place* trays for this recipe (see page 6). Preheat the oven to 400 degrees F. Line 2 baking sheets with parchment paper.

2 In a heavy saucepan, combine the nuts, confectioners' sugar, and cinnamon.

3 In a large bowl, using an electric mixer set on medium-high speed, beat the egg whites until stiff. Gently stir the whites into the nut mixture. Cook over medium heat, stirring constantly, for 8 to 10 minutes, or until golden brown and the mixture pulls away from the sides of the pan. Remove from the heat.

4 Using 2 teaspoons, scoop out rough 1½- to 2-inch mounds of the mixture and place them about 1½ inches apart on the prepared baking sheets. Bake for 10 minutes, or until lightly browned. Lifting the paper by both ends, transfer the cookies, still on the paper, to a wire rack to cool and set. Repeat with the other sheet of parchment paper.

5 Lift the cookies from the paper with a spatula. Store, tightly covered, until ready to serve.

Quince Tart ~ James Beard

SERVES 6

PREPARATION TIME: ABOUT 45 MINUTES

COOKING AND BAKING TIME: ABOUT 2 HOURS
AND 10 MINUTES

CHILLING TIME (PASTRY ONLY): AT LEAST 1 HOUR

COOLING TIME (TART): ABOUT 3 HOURS

FILLING:

6 large quinces

1 cinnamon stick

2 whole cloves

3 cups water

3 cups granulated sugar

Juice of 1 lemon

PASTRY:

2½ cups all-purpose flour

1 cup unsalted butter, cut into small
pieces and softened

2 tablespoons granulated sugar

3 large egg yolks

½ teaspoon ground cinnamon

Grated zest of 1 lemon

GARNISH:

2 tablespoons chopped, toasted
almonds

1 cup heavy cream, gently whipped
to soft peaks

■ Special Equipment: 12-inch fluted
tart pan with removable bottom; pie
weights; pastry cutter (optional).

This tart is an old-fashioned American autumn dessert. Although quinces are usually available only from October through December, they can be wrapped in plastic and refrigerated for up to two months.

1 Assemble *mise en place* trays for this recipe (see page 6).

2 To make the filling, peel and core the quinces, reserving the seeds. Cut the quinces into julienne strips and set aside.

3 Wrap the cinnamon stick, cloves, and quince seeds in a cheesecloth bag and tie securely.

4 In a large, heavy-bottomed saucepan, combine the water, sugar, and lemon juice. Bring to a boil over high heat. Stir in the julienned quinces and the spice bag and return the liquid to a boil. Reduce the heat and simmer, stirring occasionally, for about 1½ hours, or until the quinces are very soft and the mixture has thickened. Remove the pan from the heat and discard the spice bag. Set aside to cool.

5 Meanwhile, to make the pastry, put the flour in a medium-sized bowl and make a well in the center. Add the butter, 2 tablespoons of the sugar, the egg yolks, ground cinnamon, and lemon zest. Using your fingertips, knead to form dough. Gather into a ball and divide into two pieces, one about a third larger than the other. Flatten each into a disk, wrap in plastic, and refrigerate for at least 1 hour, or until firm.

6 Preheat the oven to 375 degrees F.

7 Roll out two thirds of the pastry between 2 pieces of wax paper, or on a lightly floured board, to a circle about 14 inches in diameter. Carefully fit into a 12-inch fluted tart pan with a removable bottom. Trim the edges. Prick

the bottom of the tart with a fork, line it with foil, and weight with pie weights, rice, or beans.

8 Bake the tart shell for 10 minutes. Remove the foil and weights and fill with the cooled quince mixture.

9 Roll out the remaining third of pastry to a 12-inch circle. Using a pastry cutter or a knife, cut into strips ¼ inch to ½ inch wide. Using the longest strips for the center of the tart and, working from the center out, lay half of the strips about ¾ inch apart across the tart. Lay the remaining strips perpendicular to the first strips to form a lattice. Trim off the excess dough and push the ends of the strips into the edge of the crust to seal.

10 Bake the tart for 20 to 30 minutes, or until the pastry is golden brown and the filling is bubbling. Remove from the oven and sprinkle with the almonds. Cool on a wire rack for at least 3 hours, or overnight. Do not refrigerate.

11 Serve at room temperature, with whipped cream.

❧ The pectin in the quince seeds acts as a thickening agent for the tart filling.

❧ The tart is also good served with crème fraîche, sour cream, or vanilla ice cream instead of whipped cream.

Deep Chocolate Marquise ~ David Bouley

SERVES 6

PREPARATION TIME: ABOUT 40 MINUTES

BAKING TIME: ABOUT 15 MINUTES

CHILLING TIME: AT LEAST 4 HOURS

LADYFINGERS:

8 large eggs, separated

1½ cups plus 2 tablespoons granulated sugar

⅞ cup all-purpose flour

⅞ cup cornstarch

2 teaspoons pure coffee extract

2 teaspoons pure vanilla extract

MARQUISE:

6 large egg yolks

1¼ cups plus 2 tablespoons confectioners' sugar

8 ounces bittersweet chocolate, coarsely chopped

1 cup unsalted butter

2 tablespoons orange-flavored liqueur, such as Cointreau or Grand Marnier

Grated zest of 2 oranges (about 2 tablespoons)

½ cup Dutch-processed cocoa powder

1¼ cups heavy cream, softly whipped

Whipped cream, for garnish

6 fresh mint sprigs, for garnish

*T*his rich, dark, luxurious chocolate dessert is a true indulgence. Use the best bittersweet chocolate you can find for the most intense flavor.

---

1 Assemble *mise en place* trays for this recipe (see page 6). Preheat the oven to 325 degrees F. Lightly butter and flour 2 baking sheets. Lightly butter an 8-inch spring-form pan.

2 To make the ladyfingers, using an electric mixer set on medium-high speed, beat the egg yolks with 1 cup plus 2 tablespoons of sugar for 3 to 4 minutes until pale yellow and thick.

3 In another bowl, using an electric mixer set on medium-high speed, beat the egg whites and the remaining ½ cup of sugar until stiff and shiny.

4 Whisk together the flour and cornstarch. Fold the dry ingredients into the egg yolk mixture, alternating with the meringue. When well combined, divide the mixture in half. Stir coffee extract into one half of the batter and vanilla extract into the other half.

5 Spoon the coffee-flavored batter into a pastry bag fitted with a plain tip. Pipe batter onto the baking sheets, making 4-inch strips about ½ inch apart. When all the coffee batter is gone, fill the pastry bag with the vanilla batter and make more ladyfingers.

6 Bake for about 15 minutes until light golden. Cool the ladyfingers completely on wire racks.

7 To make the marquise, put the egg yolks and confectioners' sugar in a medium-sized bowl set over a larger bowl filled with very warm water. Using a hand-held electric mixer set on medium speed, beat until well mixed. Increase the speed to medium-high and beat for 4 to

5 minutes until the mixture is pale yellow and thick. Remove from the water and set aside.

8 In the top half of a double boiler, melt the chocolate over barely simmering water. Transfer to a large bowl and set aside.

9 In a small saucepan, melt the butter over medium-low heat. Stir in the liqueur and orange zest.

10 Whisk the butter mixture into the chocolate, alternating with the cocoa. When well blended, fold in the beaten egg yolk mixture. Fold in the whipped cream.

11 Line the sides of the springform pan with alternating flavors of ladyfingers, positioning them so that they stand up straight around the pan. Spoon the chocolate marquise mixture into the pan and smooth the top with a spatula. Cover with plastic wrap and refrigerate for at least 4 hours.

12 To serve, carefully remove the sides of the springform pan. Slice the cake and serve each piece with whipped cream and a sprig of mint.

❧ You can substitute high-quality ladyfingers sold in French bakeries for homemade ladyfingers. They also are sold packaged in specialty stores. Be sure to buy slender, French-style ladyfingers rather than plump, American style.

Warm Apricot Tarts with Pistachios ～ Daniel Boulud

SERVES 6

PREPARATION TIME: ABOUT 20 MINUTES

COOKING TIME: ABOUT 55 MINUTES

1½ pounds frozen puff pastry, thawed

¾ cup plus 1 tablespoon granulated sugar

¼ cup water

¼ cup heavy cream

9 canned whole apricots or 18 apricot halves packed in water, drained, halved, and pitted (if whole)

1 pint high-quality vanilla ice cream

1 tablespoon chopped, toasted pistachios

6 fresh mint sprigs, for garnish

■ Special Equipment: 6 three-inch round tart molds; 3-inch plain cutter

These tarts taste great made with canned apricots, but you could, in the height of summer, use fresh ones. Or, substitute fresh peaches or nectarines. If you want to make these tarts ahead of time, unmold them while they are still warm—otherwise, the caramel sets and they are impossible to remove from the molds.

---

1 Preheat the oven to 375 degrees F. Lightly butter 6 three-inch round tart molds and set the molds on a baking sheet. Assemble *mise en place* trays for this recipe (see page 6).

2 On a lightly floured surface, roll out the pastry almost paper-thin. Transfer to a baking sheet and prick all over with a fork. Bake for 20 minutes, or until golden. Remove from the oven, and reduce the oven temperature to 350 degrees F.

3 In a heavy saucepan, combine the sugar and water and bring to a boil over medium heat, stirring occasionally until the sugar is dissolved. Lower the heat to a simmer and let the syrup cook for 30 to 40 minutes, without stirring, until it is a deep golden brown. Swirl the syrup occasionally by tilting the pan, but take care, as sugar syrup is very hot.

4 Remove the pan from the heat and carefully stir in the heavy cream. The hot syrup may spatter. Stir until smooth and then pour into the tart molds.

5 Place 3 apricot halves, rounded side up, in an overlapping pattern in each mold. Bake for 5 minutes.

6 Meanwhile, using a 3-inch plain cutter, cut 6 circles from the puff pastry.

7 Remove the molds from the oven and lay a pastry circle on top of each one. Immediately invert the tarts onto warm dessert plates.

8 Place a small scoop of vanilla ice cream in the center of each tart. Sprinkle each one with pistachios, garnish with a mint leaf, and serve.

❧ High-quality vanilla ice cream tastes richer and creamier because it is. According to federal guidelines, ice cream manufacturers can incorporate a certain amount of air into their product: the better the quality, the less air—and the higher the cost. Less air means more cream, flavorings, and, in most cases, care.

Banana-Pineapple Shake ❧ Daniel Boulud

SERVES 6

PREPARATION TIME: ABOUT 15 MINUTES

FREEZING TIME: ABOUT 1 HOUR

FAT PER SERVING: 1.2 GRAMS

SATURATED FAT: 0.1 GRAM

CALORIES PER SERVING: 103

CALORIES FROM FAT: 10%

---

1 small pineapple, peeled, cored, and cut into chunks

2 ripe bananas, cut into chunks

1 cup ice-cold 1% milk

2 tablespoons fresh lime juice

1 teaspoon sugar substitute, such as Equal

Grated zest of 1 lime

6 sprigs fresh mint or small pineapple leaves, for garnish

This exceptionally light dessert is served in Champagne glasses with sprigs of mint. It's equally delicious as a refreshing mid-afternoon snack, for two. Daniel uses sugar substitute in this recipe rather than granulated sugar because its sweetening power is so much greater—a little goes a long way!

---

1 Assemble *mise en place* trays for this recipe (see page 6).

2 In a nonreactive freezer-proof container, combine the pineapple and bananas and freeze for 1 hour, or until firm.

3 In a blender, combine the frozen fruit, milk, lime juice, sugar substitute, and lime zest and process until thick and smooth. Serve immediately in frosted Champagne or tall glasses, garnished with the mint sprigs.

NOTE: To frost glasses, place in the freezer for about an hour.

Sweet Green Tomato Pie ❧ Antoine Bouterin

SERVES 6

PREPARATION TIME: ABOUT 20 MINUTES

BAKING TIME: ABOUT 20 MINUTES

2 lemons

5 tablespoons water

½ cup granulated sugar

½ pound puff pastry, thawed

1 large egg

1 tablespoon arrowroot

4½ tablespoons unsalted butter

3 pounds green tomatoes, cored, peeled, seeded, and sliced into ¼-inch slices

3 large egg whites

1 tablespoon confectioners' sugar

■ Special Equipment: 9-inch tart pan with removable bottom; pastry weights, beans, or rice

This unusual French dessert calls for unripe tomatoes. In rural America, green tomato pie is often served as dessert. In both countries, the recipes were created to utilize bumper crops that gardeners feared would not reach ripeness before the autumn frost. This pie has a wonderful fresh taste, as citrus again heightens the flavor of the tomatoes.

1 Preheat the oven to 400 degrees F. Assemble *mise en place* trays for this recipe (see page 6).

2 Using a sharp knife, carefully remove the yellow-colored peel from 1 of the lemons, avoiding the bitter white pith. Cut the peel into a fine julienne. Grate the zest from the remaining lemon and set aside.

3 In a small saucepan, combine the julienned peel, the water, and 3 tablespoons of the sugar. Bring to a boil over high heat, and cook for 4 to 5 minutes, until all the water has evaporated. Drain the lemon peel on paper towels and set aside.

4 On a lightly floured surface, roll out the pastry to a circle about ⅛ inch thick and approximately 12 inches round. Transfer the pastry to a 9-inch tart pan with a removable bottom. Gently fit the pastry into the pan, and trim off any excess. Prick the bottom of the pastry all over with a fork. Line the pastry shell with aluminum foil and spread pastry weights, dried beans, or rice over the foil. Bake for about 15 minutes, until the pastry is lightly browned. Lift out the foil and weights, and set on a wire rack to cool. Do not turn off the oven.

5 In a small bowl, beat the egg with the arrowroot.

6 In a large sauté pan, melt the butter over medium heat. Cook the tomato slices for about 5 minutes, or until softened, stirring gently every so often and taking care not to tear the slices. Sprinkle 3 tablespoons of the sugar over them and stir gently. Spoon some liquid from the pan into the egg mixture and stir to temper it. Add the egg mixture to the pan, and stir gently. Remove from the heat, and stir in the julienned lemon peel. Pour this mixture into the partially baked pastry shell, and let the filling cool slightly.

7 In a large bowl, using an electric mixer, beat the egg whites until soft peaks form. Add the remaining 2 tablespoons of sugar and beat until stiff peaks form. Fold the lemon zest into the meringue. Using a spatula, spread the meringue evenly over the tomato filling, swirling and lifting the meringue to make an attractive design.

8 Bake for about 5 minutes, until the meringue is golden. Sprinkle with the confectioners' sugar and serve immediately.

_____

❧ When making a tart with a filling as moist as this one, do not expect the pastry to stay firm and crisp. It will soften a little beneath the filling.

Baklava ❧ Charles Bowman

MAKES ABOUT 15 PIECES
PREPARATION TIME: ABOUT 1 HOUR
BAKING TIME: ABOUT 1 HOUR
COOKING TIME: ABOUT 15 MINUTES
RESTING TIME: AT LEAST 4 HOURS, OR UP TO 24 HOURS

_____

2 cups toasted walnuts

2 cups blanched almonds

16 pieces zweibach (or 1 cup dry bread crumbs)

1 tablespoon ground cinnamon

*K*nown *throughout the world as the Greek dessert, flaky baklava is incredibly sweet—and incredibly delicious.*

_____

1 Assemble *mise en place* trays for this recipe (see page 6).

2 Place half of the walnuts and almonds in a food processor fitted with the metal blade. Chop fine, using quick pulses and being careful not to pulverize. Transfer to a large bowl. Repeat with the remaining nuts and add to the bowl.

3 Place half of the zweibach in the food processor and process to make fine crumbs. Add to the nuts. Repeat

2 tablespoons unsalted butter, softened

One 1-pound package phyllo dough, thawed according to the package directions

1½ cups Clarified Butter (see page 20), melted

About 18 whole cloves

3 cups sugar

2¼ cups water

¾ cup honey

One 3-inch cinnamon stick

2 tablespoons brandy

■ Special Equipment: Pizza cutter (optional)

with the remaining zweibach. Add the cinnamon to the nut-crumb mixture and toss to blend.

4 Preheat the oven to 350 degrees F. Butter a 13 x 9-inch glass baking dish with the softened butter.

5 Lay the phyllo sheets on a dry work surface. With a pizza cutter or a long sharp knife, cut the phyllo cross-wise in half to make 2 stacks of 12 x 8½-inch sheets. Lay 4 sheets in the pan. (Since the phyllo is not quite long enough to cover the bottom of the pan completely, as you assemble the baklava, alternate the sheets so that every other layer, more or less, reaches the opposite ends of the pan.) Using a pastry brush, coat the sheets of phyllo with clarified butter. Repeat to make 8 layers of phyllo, leaving the final sheet dry.

6 Sprinkle about 1¼ cups of the nut mixture over the dry sheet of phyllo. Add 4 more sheets of phyllo, brushing each one with butter but leaving the final sheet dry. Sprinkle with another 1¼ cups of the nut mixture. Repeat this procedure two more times, ending with a layer of nuts. Add the remaining sheets of phyllo, brushing each one including the top one with butter.

7 With a long sharp knife, cut the baklava lengthwise into thirds. Then cut these strips on the diagonal into diamond shapes, ending just short of the lengthwise cuts and the sides of the pan. With a short spatula, work around the sides of the pan, tucking the layers of dough in so that the edges are smooth. Stick a clove into the center of each diamond. Bake for about 1 hour, or until golden brown on top. Set on a wire rack to cool completely.

8 In a large saucepan, combine the sugar, water, honey, cinnamon stick, and 3 cloves and bring to a boil over medium heat, stirring with a wooden spoon until the sugar dissolves. Reduce the heat slightly and boil gently for about 10 minutes, until slightly syrupy. Remove from the heat and stir in the brandy. Set aside to cool to lukewarm.

9 Pour the syrup over the cooled baklava. Cover loosely and set aside at room temperature for several hours, or overnight. Finish cutting the baklava just before serving.

Lemon Curd Napoleon ❧ Terrance Brennan

SERVES 6

PREPARATION TIME: ABOUT 45 MINUTES

COOKING TIME: 4 MINUTES

BAKING TIME: ABOUT 5 MINUTES

---

8 large egg yolks

½ cup fresh lemon juice

Grated zest of 2 lemons

¾ cup sugar

8 tablespoons (1 stick) unsalted butter, cubed, at room temperature

6 sheets phyllo dough, thawed according to the package directions

½ cup Clarified Butter (see page 20), melted

½ cup confectioners' sugar

1 pint raspberries, washed and dried

This very sophisticated dessert combines two traditional ingredients in a most unusual way. And, as impressive as it is, it's quite easy to put together.

---

1 Assemble *mise en place* trays for this recipe (see page 6).

2 In a medium-sized heat-proof bowl, combine the egg yolks, lemon juice, and zest. Whisk in the sugar and set the bowl over (not in) a pot of simmering water. Do not let the bottom of the bowl touch the water. Cook, whisking constantly, for about 4 minutes, or until thickened.

3 Remove the bowl from the heat and beat in the room-temperature butter, a piece at a time, until completely incorporated.

4 Put the bowl in an ice water bath and stir the curd frequently until cool. Cover and refrigerate until ready to use.

5 Preheat the oven to 400 degrees F. Line 2 baking sheets with parchment paper.

6 Place 1 phyllo sheet on a dry work surface. Using a pastry brush, liberally coat with clarified butter. Top with 2 more sheets, brushing each with butter. Make a second stack with the 3 remaining sheets of phyllo, buttering each one. Using a sharp round 3-inch cookie cutter, cut out 12 circles from each stack. Sprinkle with confectioners' sugar and arrange on the baking sheets. Cover each baking sheet with a sheet of parchment paper and put another baking sheet on top to hold the phyllo discs flat.

Bake for about 5 minutes, or until golden. Remove the baking sheets and parchment from the top of the phyllo disks and cool on the baking sheets.

7   Place a small dollop of lemon curd in the center of each plate. Place a phyllo disc on top and dab each with a tablespoon of curd. Arrange 4 raspberries on the curd and top each dessert with another phyllo disc. Repeat to make 4 layers, ending with a phyllo disc. Sprinkle with confectioners' sugar and serve immediately.

NOTE: The raspberries can be replaced with any other berry except strawberries, which are too large for an attractive presentation.

_____

❧ When washing raspberries, mist them with a sprayer and turn them upside down on paper towels to dry. If they are handled too much, they tend to disintegrate.

❧ The curd can be made with any citrus fruit.

Carrot-Raisin Cake ❧ Jane Brody

MAKES ONE 9-INCH LOAF; SERVES 6
PREPARATION TIME: ABOUT 30 MINUTES
BAKING TIME:<\FA>BOUT 1 HOUR
FAT PER SERVING: 9.6 GRAMS
SATURATED FAT: 1 GRAM
CALORIES PER SERVING: 415
CALORIES FROM FAT: 21%

_____

1½ teaspoons baking soda

¼ cup warm water

1½ cups finely shredded carrots

1 cup raisins

½ cup plain nonfat yogurt

Jane Brody's "almost-good-for-you" carrot cake has such a wonderful, moist texture and satisfying flavor, no one will guess that it is so low in saturated fat.

_____

1   Assemble *mise en place* trays for this recipe (see page 6). Preheat the oven the 325 degrees F. Lightly spray a 9 x 5-inch loaf pan with nonstick vegetable spray.

2   In a small bowl, combine the baking soda and warm water and set aside.

3   In a large bowl, combine the carrots, raisins, yogurt, sugar, applesauce, oil, egg whites, cinnamon, nutmeg, cloves, and the salt, if desired. Stir in the flours and then stir in the baking soda mixture just until combined.

½ cup granulated sugar, or to taste

½ cup unsweetened applesauce

¼ cup vegetable oil, preferably canola

2 large egg whites

2 teaspoons ground cinnamon

½ teaspoon grated nutmeg

½ teaspoon ground cloves

½ teaspoon salt (optional)

1 cup whole wheat flour

1 cup all-purpose flour

4 Pour the batter into prepared pan and bake for about 1 hour, or until a toothpick or cake tester inserted into the center comes out clean. Cool in the pan on a wire rack for about 10 minutes before turning the cake out onto the rack to cool completely.

The Marquesa's Chocolate Cream in a Crust ❧ Giuliano Bugialli

SERVES 6

PREPARATION TIME: ABOUT 1 HOUR

COOKING TIME: ABOUT 30 MINUTES

CHILLING TIME (CHOCOLATE CREAM AND FILLED MOLDS): ABOUT 1 HOUR TOTAL

COOKIE MOLDS:

2 extra-large egg whites

1 cup confectioners' sugar

¼ cup plus 2 tablespoons sifted, unbleached all-purpose flour

¼ cup milk

1 teaspoon pure orange extract

CHOCOLATE CREAM:

2 ounces bittersweet chocolate, coarsely chopped

A spectacularly delicious chocolate dessert from Liguria— and all the components can be made in advance.

1 Preheat the oven to 400 degrees F. Assemble *mise en place* trays for this recipe (see page 6). Butter 4 baking sheets. Set 6 four-ounce custard cups on a work surface.

2 To make the cookie molds, using a fork, lightly beat the egg whites in a small bowl until foamy. Sift the confectioners' sugar over the whites, mixing with a wooden spoon until the sugar is completely absorbed. Add the flour a tablespoon at a time, mixing with the wooden spoon until incorporated. Combine the milk and orange extract, and stir into the batter until well blended.

3 For each cookie mold, spoon 1 tablespoon of batter onto a prepared baking sheet to form a thin circle about 5 inches in diameter. Place only 3 or 4 circles on each sheet, allowing at least 1 inch between them so that they

8 tablespoons unsalted butter, cut into pieces, at room temperature

1 tablespoon unflavored gelatin

¼ cup cold water

¾ cup hot milk

1 tablespoon brandy

5 extra-large eggs, separated

¼ cup plus 1 tablespoon granulated sugar

2 tablespoons confectioners' sugar

½ cup bittersweet chocolate shavings (page 14)

do not run into each other during baking. Bake 1 sheet of cookies at a time for 4 to 5 minutes, or until the edges of the circles are lightly golden.

4 Using a thin-edged metal spatula, lift the cookies from the baking sheets, one at a time, and immediately fit each one into a custard cup, gently pressing it into the bottom for a neat fit. (If the cookies become too firm to mold, put the baking sheet back in the oven for about 1 minute.) Allow the cookies to cool in the cups for at least 5 minutes, or until firm, and then carefully remove them from the cups and set on a wire rack to cool completely. When cool, set on an ungreased baking sheet or tray. You will need 12 cups, and there is enough batter for a couple of practice cups.

5 To make the chocolate cream, put the chocolate in a medium-sized bowl or the top of a double boiler and melt it over very warm, but not simmering, water. Add the butter and, using a wooden spoon, beat vigorously for about 2 minutes, until well incorporated.

6 Meanwhile, in a small bowl, sprinkle the gelatin over the water. Let it soften for about 5 minutes. Add the hot milk and stir until the gelatin is completely dissolved.

7 Pour the gelatin mixture into the chocolate mixture, stirring continuously with a wooden spoon. Remove the chocolate mixture from the pan of water. Stir in the brandy and then the egg yolks, one at a time. Let cool for about 20 minutes.

8 In a large bowl, using an electric mixer set on medium-high speed, whip the egg whites until foamy. Add the granulated and confectioners' sugar and continue to beat until stiff, about 3 to 4 minutes. Gently fold the meringue into the cooled chocolate mixture. Cover and refrigerate for 30 minutes.

9 Spoon 2 heaping tablespoons of the chocolate mixture into each cooled cookie mold and refrigerate for at least

30 minutes. When ready to serve, sprinkle chocolate shavings over each filled cup.

❧ The cookie shells do not hold up well if made on a humid day.

Orange and Strawberry Tart with Candied Bell Pepper Caramel ❧ David Burke

SERVES 6

PREPARATION TIME: ABOUT 1 HOUR

BAKING AND COOKING TIME: ABOUT 50 MINUTES

CHILLING TIME (PASTRY ONLY): 40 MINUTES

PASTRY:

One 10-inch sheet frozen puff pastry

1 teaspoon ground cinnamon

2 tablespoons granulated sugar

2 tablespoons dark brown sugar

FILLING:

2 pints medium strawberries, rinsed, dried, and hulled

4 oranges

Candied Bell Pepper Caramel (recipe follows)

1 cup heavy cream, gently whipped to soft peaks

Mint sprigs

David Burke loves to shock the palate by using foods in interesting ways—for example, bell peppers in a dessert sauce.

---

1 Assemble *mise en place* trays for this recipe (see page 6).

2 Let the puff pastry thaw at room temperature for about 20 minutes. Roll out the puff pastry between two sheets of wax paper to about ⅛ inch thick. Lay on a baking sheet, cover with wax paper, and refrigerate for 30 minutes.

3 Meanwhile, in a small bowl, combine the granulated sugar, brown sugar, and cinnamon. Set aside.

4 To make the filling, remove the zest from the oranges and put in a bowl. Be sure to peel only the colorful zest—not the bitter white pith.

5 Holding each one over the bowl with the zest, peel the oranges and cut between the membranes to separate into sections. Let the sections and any juice fall into the bowl. Discard the membrane and seeds. Set aside.

6 Preheat the oven to 350 degrees F.

7 Remove the pastry from the refrigerator. Place on a board and invert a 10-inch plate over the pastry. With a

pastry cutter or sharp knife, cut around the plate to make a 10-inch circle. Carefully transfer the pastry to a non-stick baking sheet, lifting it gently or using spatulas to guide it. Using the point of a sharp knife, prick holes in a circular pattern over the entire surface of the pastry. Refrigerate for 10 minutes.

8 Sprinkle half the sugar mixture over the pastry circle. Bake for about 10 minutes or until the pastry is golden brown. Remove the pastry but do not turn off the oven.

9 Using a spatula, carefully slide the baked crust onto a flat plate. Lay the baking sheet over the plate and invert the pastry onto it, so that the bottom is facing up. Sprinkle the pastry with the remaining sugar mixture. Bake for 5 to 7 minutes longer, or until golden brown.

10 Allow the pastry to cool for 5 minutes and then carefully slide it onto a cake platter.

11 Warm the Candied Bell Pepper Caramel in a small nonreactive saucepan over low heat.

12 Spread the whipped cream over the pastry. Arrange the strawberries, points up, in 2 rows around the edge of the pastry. Mound the orange sections, zest, and juices in a heap in the center of the pastry so that the casual look of the oranges contrasts with the neat rows of strawberries. Pour the warm Candied Bell Pepper Caramel over the fruit. Garnish with mint sprigs and serve immediately.

❧ **If you have extra strawberries, slice them and mix in with the orange sections before mounding them on the cream.**

CANDIED BELL PEPPER CARAMEL

MAKES ABOUT 3½ CUPS

¾ cup minced yellow bell pepper

¾ cup minced red bell pepper

1 cup granulated sugar

1 cup apple cider

1 to 2 tablespoons Grand Marnier

3 tablespoons unsalted butter, at room temperature

1 In a medium-sized, heavy, nonreactive saucepan, combine the peppers, sugar, and cider. Cook, stirring occasionally, for about 30 minutes, or until the sauce turns golden brown, thickens, and caramelizes.

2 Remove from the heat and whisk in the Grand Marnier and butter. Cover and refrigerate. Reheat gently before using.

Tirami-sù ～ Biba Caggiano

SERVES 6
PREPARATION TIME: ABOUT 20 MINUTES
COOKING TIME: ABOUT 15 MINUTES
CHILLING TIME: AT LEAST 4 HOURS

ZABAGLIONE:

8 large egg yolks

½ cup granulated sugar

⅓ cup brandy

FILLING AND CAKE:

1½ pounds mascarpone cheese

4 large egg whites

2 tablespoons granulated sugar

2 cups Italian espresso, at room temperature

¼ cup brandy

*T*irami-sù, literally translated as "pick me up," needs no introduction. In the last ten years, this dessert has become more popular in America than in Italy. It is served in one version or another in all types of restaurants. Apparently, the dessert originated in Tuscany in the early 1900s, but many regions claim it as their own.

A true tirami-sù is always made with mascarpone, a delicious, sweet, soft Italian cheese, not unlike a very thick, slightly acidic whipped cream—never with any other cheese or with whipped cream.

Biba's generously portioned recipe is based on a tirami-sù from the fancy Osteria Trattoria Laguna in Cavallino, near Venice, Italy, which she found had a particular extra-light texture that made it simply irresistible. She uses a creamy zabaglione as the custard to avoid using uncooked eggs.

1 Assemble *mise en place* trays for this recipe (see page 6).

2 To make the zabaglione, put the egg yolks and sugar in a large bowl or the top of a double boiler set over

40 high-quality ladyfingers, prefer-ably imported from Italy

½ cup unsweetened cocoa powder

½ cup semisweet chocolate curls, optional (see page 14)

slowly simmering water. Beat with a whisk or hand-held electric mixer set at medium speed until thick and pale yellow. Beat in the brandy and cook for about 10 minutes, whisking constantly, until the zabaglione doubles in volume, is soft and fluffy, and feels hot to the touch. Immediately set the zabaglione over a bowl of ice water and let cool.

3 To make the filling, combine the mascarpone and the cooled zabaglione in the bowl of an electric mixer and beat at low speed to blend.

4 In a large bowl, using clean beaters, beat the egg whites on medium-high speed until foamy. Add the sugar and beat until stiff peaks form. Fold the egg whites into the mascarpone mixture.

5 In a medium-sized bowl, combine the espresso and brandy. One at a time, quickly dip half the ladyfingers into the coffee mixture. Lay them very close together in a 13-by-9-inch baking dish. Spread half the mascarpone mixture evenly over the ladyfingers.

6 Using a fine-mesh strainer, sprinkle half the cocoa powder evenly over the mascarpone. Dip the remaining ladyfingers in the espresso mixture and place side by side on the mascarpone, making another layer. Spread the remaining mascarpone mixture evenly over the lady-fingers, and sprinkle with the remaining cocoa powder. Cover the dish with plastic wrap and refrigerate for at least 4 hours, or overnight.

7 Just before serving, sprinkle semisweet chocolate curls over the tirami-sù, if desired.

❧ American ladyfingers are more spongy than their Italian counterpart, and since real Italian tirami-sù requires a slightly harder cookie, Biba suggests using ladyfingers imported from Italy.

Coffee Granita with Lemon-Scented Ice Milk ~ Dominick Cerrone

SERVES 6

INFUSING TIME (MILK MIXTURE ONLY):
12 HOURS

PREPARATION TIME: ABOUT 30 MINUTES

FREEZING TIME: 2 HOURS

⅔ cup plus 6 tablespoons granulated sugar

3 cups milk

1 cup heavy cream

Zest of 1 large lemon, removed with a vegetable peeler or sharp knife and cut into strips

One 3-inch cinnamon stick

3 cups very hot espresso (or other strong coffee)

4 large egg whites, at room temperature

Cocoa for dusting (optional)

6 sprigs fresh mint

■ Special Equipment: Hand-held immersion blender

Here is a summer dessert that is perfection! Because it is icy-cold, it must be made well in advance. The granita is wonderfully invigorating, rather like eating a refreshing frozen cappuccino.

1 Assemble *mise en place* trays for this recipe (see page 6).

2 In a medium-sized saucepan, combine the ⅔ cup sugar with the milk, cream, lemon zest, and cinnamon stick and bring to a boil over medium heat, stirring to dissolve the sugar. Immediately remove the pan from the heat and pour into a nonreactive container. Cover and refrigerate for at least 12 hours.

3 Dissolve 3 tablespoons of the remaining sugar in the coffee and pour onto a rimmed baking sheet. Place in the freezer and freeze, frequently breaking up the frozen edges with a fork to prevent the mixture from freezing in a solid block. When completely frozen, transfer to a small freezer container and keep frozen.

4 Put a 9 x 13-inch pan in the freezer. Place 6 goblets or coupes in the refrigerator.

5 In a large bowl, using an electric mixer set at medium-high speed, beat the egg whites with the remaining 3 tablespoons sugar until they hold stiff peaks. Refrigerate this meringue.

6 Using a hand-held immersion blender, whip the chilled milk mixture until it holds firm peaks. Fold into the chilled meringue, scrape into the chilled pan, cover, and freeze for 2 hours.

7 When ready to serve, scrape the coffee granita *(Negro)* into the chilled goblets. Place a scoop of ice milk *(Blanco)* on top. Serve immediately, dusted with cocoa if desired, garnishing each with a mint sprig and a cookie.

NOTE: You could also flavor the ice milk with either lemon grass or lemon verbena.

Apple Soufflé on a Platter with Apricot Sauce ❧ Julia Child

SERVES 6

PREPARATION TIME: ABOUT 30 MINUTES

COOKING TIME: ABOUT 30 MINUTES

12 slices home-style white bread

3 tablespoons Clarified Butter (see page 20)

7 tablespoons unsalted butter

3 sweet, firm apples, such as Golden Delicious or McIntosh, peeled, cored, and cut into ⅜-inch dice

11 tablespoons granulated sugar

¼ teaspoon fresh lemon juice

¼ teaspoon ground cinnamon

¼ cup Calvados or bourbon

¼ cup chopped walnuts (optional)

Apricot Sauce (recipe follows)

1 cup milk

¼ cup cornstarch, sifted

1 tablespoon pure vanilla extract

4 large eggs

5 large egg whites

3 tablespoons confectioners' sugar

■ Special Equipment: 8 x 11-inch ovenproof platter; 3-inch round cutter

*F*or this recipe, you need an attractive, ovenproof platter on which you will bake the soufflé and then carry it to the table. This means you need not dig out your soufflé dish! Many of the components can be prepared well in advance, but the soufflé must be baked at the last minute.

1 Assemble *mise en place* trays for this recipe (see page 6).

2 To make the croûtons for the soufflé, use a 3-inch round cutter to cut a round out of each slice of bread.

3 In a medium-sized, nonstick sauté pan, heat the clarified butter over medium heat. Add the bread rounds and sauté, turning once, for 3 to 4 minutes, until golden on both sides. Drain the croûtons on paper towels.

4 In a medium-sized, nonstick saucepan, heat 3 tablespoons of the butter over medium heat. Add the apples and sauté for about 5 minutes, or until almost soft. Stir in 4 tablespoons of the sugar, the lemon juice, and cinnamon. Sauté for about 5 minutes longer, until the apples begin to caramelize. Add the Calvados, increase the heat, and boil rapidly for about 3 minutes, swirling the apples around in the pan, until all the liquid has evaporated. Remove from the heat and stir in the walnuts, if desired. Set aside.

5 Place a rack in the upper third of the oven, and preheat the oven to 425 degrees F. Using 1 tablespoon of butter, butter an 8 x 11-inch ovenproof platter.

6 Spread a little of the Apricot Sauce over each croûton. Arrange them on the buttered platter. Spoon the apples on the croûtons, and top each with a dollop of sauce.

7 In a medium-sized saucepan, whisk the milk into the cornstarch until smooth. Set over medium heat, and whisk in 5 tablespoons of the remaining sugar and the remaining 3 tablespoons of butter. Cook, stirring continuously, for about 4 minutes, or until the mixture comes to a boil. If lumps form, boil for 1 minute longer, beating vigorously until smooth. Remove from the heat and stir in the vanilla. The mixture will be thick and gluey. Beat in the egg yolks, one at a time.

8 In a large bowl, using an electric mixer, beat the egg whites with the remaining 2 tablespoons of sugar until stiff, shiny peaks form. Stir about a quarter of the egg whites into egg yolk mixture to loosen it. Then, carefully and rapidly, fold in the remaining egg whites.

9 Mound the soufflé mixture over the fruit-topped croûtons. Bake for about 12 minutes, or until the soufflé has risen and started to brown. Quickly sprinkle the top of the soufflé with the confectioners' sugar and bake for 2 to 3 minutes longer, until the sugar browns. Serve immediately, with the remaining warmed Apricot Sauce on the side.

~ If you beat the egg whites nicely and fold them in so as not to deflate them, a soufflé baked on a platter should rise a good 3 inches as it bakes. You can make the soufflé base 30 minutes or so in advance, leaving it in the saucepan and covering it with an upside-down bowl. The egg whites will suffer only a slight loss of puffing power.

Apricot Sauce

Makes about 3 cups

8 ounces dried apricots, rinsed and drained

½ cup water

½ cup dry vermouth

1 In a medium-sized saucepan, combine the dried apricots, water, and vermouth. Let soak for at least 1 hour, or overnight if the fruit is especially dry. (You may need to add another ¼ cup of water for longer soaking.)

2 Add the cinnamon stick and lemon to the pan of apricots, and bring to a simmer over medium heat. Cook for 20 minutes.

1 cinnamon stick or ¼ teaspoon ground cinnamon

½ lemon, quartered and seeded

½ cup granulated sugar, or more to taste

16 ounces canned apricot halves packed in water

⅛ teaspoon salt

1 to 2 teaspoons unsalted butter, softened (optional)

3 Stir in the sugar and the canned apricots, with their juices. Reduce the heat to low and cook, stirring frequently to prevent the sauce from scorching and sticking, for 20 to 30 minutes, or until thick and almost caramelized. Taste frequently, and add additional sugar, a tablespoonful at a time, if the sauce is too tart.

4 Transfer the apricot mixture to a blender or a food processor fitted with the metal blade. Blend until smooth. Blend in the butter, if using. Serve hot or cold.

⬦ This sauce can be made up to 1 week in advance, covered, and refrigerated. It can also be frozen for up to 3 months.

Hazelnut Cheesecake ⬦ Craig Claiborne

SERVES 6

PREPARATION TIME: ABOUT 15 MINUTES

BAKING TIME: ABOUT 2 HOURS

COOLING TIME: 1 HOUR IN THE OVEN; 2 HOURS OUTSIDE THE OVEN

2 tablespoons unsalted butter, softened

Approximately ⅓ cup graham cracker crumbs

1½ cups toasted, blanched hazelnuts or toasted, blanched almonds (see page 13)

2 pounds cream cheese, at room temperature

½ cup heavy cream

4 large eggs

1¾ cups granulated sugar

1 teaspoon pure vanilla extract

There is nothing as overwhelmingly wonderful as a cheesecake—smooth, rich, and oh-so-delicious. A real indulgence.

1 Preheat the oven to 300 degrees F. Assemble *mise en place* trays for this recipe (see page 6). Generously grease a 9-by-3-inch-deep springform pan. Sprinkle the graham cracker crumbs over the pan, tilting it so that they cover the bottom and sides. Shake out the excess crumbs. Using 2 large sheets of aluminum foil, double-wrap the outside of the springform pan.

2 Place the nuts in a blender or food processor fitted with the metal blade. If you want the cheesecake to have a crunchy texture, process the nuts for about 20 seconds, until they are coarse-fine. If you want a smooth texture, process for about 1 minute, until they are almost paste-like.

3 Using an electric mixer set at low speed, beat the cream cheese, cream, eggs, sugar, and vanilla in a large bowl. As the ingredients blend, increase the speed to medium-high and continue beating until smooth. Add the nuts and beat until thoroughly incorporated.

4 Scrape the batter into the prepared pan and shake the pan gently to level the mixture. Set the pan inside a slightly wider pan and pour boiling water into the larger pan to a depth of about ½ inch, or until the water comes about halfway up the sides of the springform pan.

5 Bake for 2 hours. Turn off the oven and let the cake cool in the oven for 1 hour.

6 Remove the pans from the oven and lift the cake out of the water bath. Place on a wire rack and allow to sit for at least 2 hours.

7 Carefully remove the sides of the springform pan and set the cheesecake on a serving dish. Serve lukewarm or at room temperature, or refrigerate until about an hour before serving. Let the cake come to room temperature before serving.

_____

❧ You can make this cheesecake in a 9-by-3-inch-deep cake pan. When the cheesecake is completely cool, invert it onto a serving plate by placing the plate over the top of the cake and turning both upside down.

Blueberry Clafoutis ❧ Andrew D'Amico

SERVES 6 TO 8

PREPARATION TIME: ABOUT 20 MINUTES

BAKING TIME: ABOUT 40 MINUTES

½ cup plus 2 tablespoons confectioners' sugar

2 large egg yolks

1 large egg

8 tablespoons (1 stick) unsalted butter, cut into pieces, softened

1 cup all-purpose flour

1 cup hot boiled milk

2 tablespoons kirschwasser, rum, or Chambord

2½ cups ripe blueberries, picked over, rinsed, and dried

■ Special Equipment: 9-inch round flan dish or cake pan

This easy-to-prepare, pudding-like dessert is always well received, especially if the fruit is ripe and sweet. Although French, clafoutis is not from the Mediterranean area but from the Limousin region, where it is traditionally made with dark, juicy cherries.

1 Assemble *mise en place* trays for this recipe (see page 6).

2 Preheat the oven to 400 degrees F. Generously butter a 9-inch flan dish or cake pan.

3 In a large bowl, using an electric mixer set on medium speed, beat ½ cup of the sugar and the egg yolks for 2 to 3 minutes, or until thick. Beat in the whole egg and then gradually beat in the butter, a piece at a time. Beat in the flour. Beat in the milk and kirschwasser and mix until smooth.

4 Pour into the prepared pan and distribute the berries evenly over the top. Bake on the lower rack of the oven for about 40 minutes, or until the top is golden and the center is set. Cool on a wire rack for 10 minutes. Sprinkle with the remaining 2 tablespoons sugar and serve warm.

NOTE: Any ripe berry can be used in place of or in combination with the blueberries. If the berries are not naturally sweet, toss with ¼ cup of sugar and let stand for 30 minutes before adding to the batter. The clafoutis will be puffed when it comes out of the oven, similar to a soufflé, and although it deflates quickly, it will still taste delicious.

Gratin of Strawberries and Rhubarb with Warm Nutmeg Cream and Pistachio Ice Cream ❧ Gary Danko

SERVES 6

PREPARATION TIME: ABOUT 40 MINUTES

BAKING TIME: ABOUT 40 MINUTES

COOKING TIME: ABOUT 30 MINUTES

FREEZING TIME (ICE CREAM ONLY): ABOUT 24 HOURS

---

4 cups sliced strawberries

4 cups sliced rhubarb

1 cup granulated sugar

2 teaspoons ground cinnamon

1½ teaspoons grated nutmeg

Pinch of ground cloves

⅛ teaspoon salt, plus a pinch

¾ cup all-purpose flour

4 tablespoons unsalted butter, cubed and chilled

⅛ teaspoon grated lemon zest

Warm Nutmeg Cream (recipe follows)

Pistachio Ice Cream (recipe follows)

6 whole strawberries

This gratin is a great addition to the traditional American combination of sweet spring strawberries and tart rhubarb. The pistachio ice cream adds a touch of Mediterranean flavor.

---

1 Assemble *mise en place* trays for this recipe (see page 6).

2 Preheat the oven to 350 degrees F. Generously butter a shallow 2-quart baking dish.

3 In a large bowl, combine the strawberries, rhubarb, sugar, 1½ teaspoons of the cinnamon, the nutmeg, cloves, and pinch of salt and toss well. Transfer to the baking dish.

4 In a food processor fitted with the metal blade, combine the flour, butter, lemon zest and the remaining ½ teaspoon cinnamon and ⅛ teaspoon salt. Process, using quick on and off pulses, until the texture is sandy.

5 Sprinkle the cinnamon topping over the fruit and bake for about 40 minutes, or until bubbling and golden brown. Cool for about 10 minutes before serving.

6 Spoon the gratin onto 6 warm dessert plates. Spoon some Warm Nutmeg Cream on top and place a scoop of Pistachio Ice Cream at the side of each serving. Garnish each plate with a whole strawberry and serve immediately.

Warm Nutmeg Cream

MAKES ABOUT 2 CUPS

2 cups heavy cream

½ cup granulated sugar

8 tablespoons (1 stick) unsalted butter

¼ teaspoon grated nutmeg

Pinch of salt

In a small nonstick saucepan, combine the cream, sugar, butter, nutmeg, and salt and bring to a boil over medium heat. Reduce the heat and simmer, stirring occasionally, for about 10 minutes, or until the mixture thickens enough to coat the back of a spoon. Serve warm.

Pistachio Ice Cream

MAKES ABOUT 2 QUARTS

¼ cup plus 2 tablespoons chopped pistachios

1 cup plus 1 tablespoon granulated sugar

¼ teaspoon grated lemon zest

Pinch of ground green cardamom

¼ teaspoon salt, plus a pinch

1 large egg white

3 cups heavy cream

1½ cups milk

½ vanilla bean, split

10 large egg yolks

■ Special Equipment: Ice cream freezer

1 In a food processor fitted with the metal blade, combine the pistachios, 3 tablespoons of the sugar, the lemon zest, cardamom, and pinch of salt. Process until the pistachios are coarsely ground. Add the egg white and process to a fine paste. Transfer to a bowl and set aside.

2 In a medium-sized saucepan, combine 1½ cups of the heavy cream with the milk, vanilla bean, and the remaining ¼ teaspoon salt and bring to a boil over high heat. Immediately remove from the heat and set aside.

3 In a heavy medium-sized saucepan, whisk together the egg yolks, pistachio paste, and the remaining ¾ cup plus 2 tablespoons sugar. Whisking constantly, blend in a bit of the hot cream to temper the eggs. Set over medium heat and whisk in the remaining hot cream. Cook, stirring constantly, for about 15 minutes, or until the mixture thickens enough to coat the back of the spoon. Whisk in the remaining 1½ cups cream and remove from the heat. Remove the vanilla bean. Let the mixture cool to room temperature and then refrigerate until chilled. Or chill the mixture in an ice water bath.

4 Pour into an ice cream freezer and freeze according to the manufacturer's directions. When frozen, transfer to a 2-quart container with a tight-fitting lid. Cover and freeze for at least 24 hours before serving.

NOTE: You can make the pistachio paste as coarse or fine as you like. If you want an absolutely smooth texture to the ice cream, strain the cream mixture through a fine sieve before pouring into the ice cream freezer.

Banana Cocoa Cake ～ Robert Del Grande

SERVES 6

PREPARATION TIME: ABOUT 15 MINUTES

COOKING TIME: ABOUT 30 MINUTES

1½ cups all-purpose flour

½ cup unsweetened cocoa powder

1 teaspoon baking powder

1 teaspoon baking soda

½ teaspoon salt

1 cup granulated sugar

1½ cups mashed very ripe bananas (about 4 medium bananas)

1 cup milk

8 tablespoons (1 stick) unsalted butter, melted

2 large eggs

1 teaspoon pure vanilla extract

1 cup chopped walnuts or pecans

Confectioners' sugar (optional)

Whipped cream (optional)

Ice cream (optional)

■ Special Equipment: 9-inch square cake pan

"Here's one for the quick and easy. Sift the dry, mix the liquid, stir it all together and bake. But only if you pass the test that strikes fear in the hearts of doubting cooks: Is a banana dry or liquid, particularly when mashed? . . ."
—ROBERT DEL GRANDE
(Answer according to Del Grande: liquid)

---

1 Preheat the oven to 325 degrees F. Lightly spray a 9-inch square cake pan with non-stick vegetable oil spray. Assemble *mise en place* trays for this recipe (see page 6).

2 Sift the flour, cocoa, baking powder, baking soda, and salt into a large bowl. Stir in the sugar.

3 In another bowl, combine the bananas, milk, melted butter, eggs, and vanilla, mixing well. Stir into the flour mixture until just combined. Stir in the nuts. Do not overmix.

4 Pour the batter into the prepared pan and smooth the top. Bake for 30 minutes, or until a cake tester inserted into the center comes out clean. Remove from the oven and allow to cool on a wire rack.

5 To serve, warm the cake in a preheated 275 degree F. oven for 10 minutes, if desired.

6 Cut the cake into squares, dust the tops with confectioners' sugar, if desired, and serve with whipped cream or ice cream.

Lemon Tart ∾ **Christian Delouvrier**

SERVES 6
PREPARATION TIME: ABOUT 20 MINUTES
COOKING TIME: ABOUT 25 MINUTES
COOLING TIME: 1 TO 1½ HOURS

½ pound frozen puff pastry, thawed

1 cup fresh lemon juice (about 6 lemons)

6 large eggs

5 large egg yolks

1¼ cups granulated sugar

15 tablespoons unsalted butter, cut into pieces

■ Special Equipment: 9-inch tart pan with removable bottom; pastry weights, dried beans, or rice

This is a perfectly sublime ending to a rich, complex dinner. Once assembled, the tart requires only a minute under the broiler and then an hour to set, making it a breeze to prepare.

1 Preheat the oven to 400 degrees F. Assemble *mise en place* trays for this recipe (see page 6).

2 On a lightly floured surface, roll out the pastry about ⅛ inch thick into a circle approximately 12 inches round. Transfer the pastry to a 9-inch tart pan with a removable bottom. Gently fit the pastry into the pan, and trim off any excess. Prick the bottom of the pastry all over with a fork. Line the pastry with aluminum foil and spread pastry weights, dried beans, or rice over the foil. Bake for 15 minutes, or until lightly browned. Remove from the oven. Lift off the foil and weights and set on a wire rack to cool.

3 Preheat the broiler.

4 In the top half of a double boiler, combine the lemon juice, eggs, egg yolks, and sugar. Set over simmering water. Using a hand-held electric mixer, beat for 8 to 10 minutes, or until the mixture is very thick and clings to the beater.

5 Remove from the heat. Using a whisk, whisk in the butter, a little at a time. Pour the custard into the partially baked pastry shell.

6 Place under the broiler for 1 minute, or until the top is glazed. Let sit at room temperature for 1 to 1½ hours, until the filling is cooled and set, before serving.

———————

∾ To extract as much juice as possible, roll the lemons on the countertop several times, exerting a small amount of pressure. If you wrap the halved lemon in cheesecloth before squeezing it, no pits or pulp will get in the juice (this only works for hand-squeezed lemons).

Chocolate Tart with Orange Salad ∾ Jean-Michel Diot

SERVES 6

———————

1¾ cups unsalted butter, at room temperature

2 cups granulated sugar

5 large eggs

¼ teaspoon salt

1½ cups all-purpose flour

12 ounces bittersweet chocolate

¼ cup cornstarch

2 large egg yolks

1 tablespoon confectioners' sugar

Orange Salad (recipe follows)

■ Special Equipment: 10-inch tart pan with removable bottom. Pastry weights, dried beans, or rice.

A chocolate dessert as seductive as this one tastes even better when served with an orange salad for a slightly acidic accent and refreshing note.

———————

1 Assemble *mise en place* trays for this recipe (see page 6).

2 In a large bowl, using an electric mixer set on medium-high speed, beat 12 tablespoons of the butter, ½ cup of the granulated sugar, 1 of the eggs, and the salt for 3 to 4 minutes, until light colored and thick. Reduce the speed to medium-low and slowly add the flour, about ½ cup at a time, being careful not to overmix the dough. Form the dough into a flattened ball, wrap in plastic, and refrigerate for at least 2 hours.

3 Preheat the oven to 350 degrees F.

4 Lay a large piece of waxed paper on a lightly floured surface and dust the paper with flour. Put the chilled dough on the paper and sprinkle lightly with flour. Lay a second sheet of waxed paper over the dough, and roll it out to a 13-inch circle. Carefully transfer the paper-wrapped pastry to the refrigerator and chill for about 15 minutes.

5 Peel off the top piece of waxed paper and carefully transfer the chilled dough, paper side up, to a 10-inch tart pan with a removable bottom. Gently lift off the remaining piece of waxed paper, fit the pastry into the pan, and trim off any excess. Prick the bottom of the pastry all over with a fork. Line the pastry shell with aluminum foil, and spread pastry weights, dried beans, or rice over the foil. Bake for 10 to 15 minutes, until lightly browned. Lift out the weights and foil and and set on a wire rack to cool. Do not turn off the oven.

6 In the top half of a double boiler, melt the chocolate over barely simmering water. Beat in the remaining 1 cup of butter, a little at a time, until well incorporatedfer to a wire rack to cool for at least 1 hour before serving.

9 Just before serving, dust the tart with confectioners' sugar. Cut into wedges and serve with the Orange Salad on the side.

Orange Salad

Makes about 4 cups

8 oranges

2 tablespoons bitter orange marmalade

3 tablespoons granulated sugar

1 With a small, sharp knife remove the colored peel from 4 of the oranges, being careful to avoid any bitter white pith. Cut the peel into fine julienne.

2 Blanch the julienne in boiling water for 15 seconds. Drain and refresh under cold running water. Pat dry and set aside.

3 Working over a bowl, cut all the peel and pith from all 8 oranges, letting any juices drip into the bowl. Slice between the membranes to free each segment, dropping the segments into the bowl. Squeeze the juice from the membranes and discard them.

4 Add the marmalade, reserved zest, and the sugar to the orange segments. Stir to combine. Cover and refrigerate until ready to serve.

Chocolate Amaretto Pudding ～ Roberto Donna

SERVES 6
PREPARATION TIME: ABOUT 20 MINUTES
COOKING TIME: ABOUT 1 HOUR AND 30 MINUTES
SETTING TIME: AT LEAST 3 HOURS

10 amaretti cookies, crumbled

1½ cups granulated sugar

¼ cup unsweetened cocoa powder

6 large eggs

1 quart milk

1 cup Marsala wine

1 tablespoon plus 1 teaspoon Cognac

1 tablespoon water

This rich, chocolate "bread pudding" uses delicate amaretti cookies for the bread, providing just a hint of one of Italy's favorite flavors.

1 Preheat the oven to 350 degrees F. Assemble *mise en place* trays for this recipe (see page 6).

2 In a heatproof bowl, combine the amaretti with 1 cup plus 2 tablespoons of the sugar, the cocoa, and eggs and stir to blend.

3 In a medium-sized saucepan, bring the milk to a boil over medium heat. Immediately stir into the amaretti mixture. Stir in the Marsala and Cognac, remove from the heat, and set aside.

4 In a small saucepan, combine the water with the remaining ¼ cup plus 2 tablespoons sugar and cook over medium heat, stirring continuously, for 10 minutes, or until dark gold and caramelized. Remove from the heat and carefully pour into the bottom of a 2-quart soufflé dish or mold. Using caution, pour the milk mixture into the mold (it may splatter).

5 Place the soufflé dish into a large baking pan and add enough hot water to come about halfway up the sides of the dish. Bake for 45 minutes to 1 hour, until the center of the pudding is set. Cool completely on a wire rack. When cool, cover and refrigerate for at least 3 hours or overnight.

6 When ready to serve, place a serving plate on top of the soufflé dish and invert to unmold the pudding. Serve immediately, spooning any caramel remaining in the dish over the pudding.

～ **Before boiling milk, wet the bottom of the saucepan with water to prevent the milk from sticking to the bottom of the pot.**

Chocolate Risotto Pudding ❧ Todd English

SERVES 6

PREPARATION TIME: ABOUT 15 MINUTES

COOKING TIME: ABOUT 30 MINUTES

---

6 cups water

1 cup milk

2 large egg yolks

½ cup nonalkalized cocoa powder

¼ cup granulated sugar

1 tablespoon unsalted butter

1½ cups Arborio rice

1 vanilla bean, split lengthwise

Grated zest and juice of 1 small orange

5 ounces semisweet chocolate, coarsely chopped

½ cup raisins, plumped in ½ cup orange liqueur, such as Grand Marnier (optional)

½ cup chopped toasted walnuts (see page 13)

3 small fresh mint sprigs

Both chocolate and rice pudding are desserts fraught with nostalgia. Todd took these childhood memories and created an entirely new dessert with a very grown-up taste.

---

1 Assemble *mise en place* trays for this recipe (see page 6).

2 In a medium-sized saucepan, bring the water to a boil over high heat. Reduce the heat so the water continues to boil gently.

3 In a medium-sized bowl, whisk together the milk, egg yolks, cocoa, and sugar until very smooth. Set aside.

4 In a heavy-bottomed straight-sided medium-sized saucepan, melt the butter over medium heat. Add the rice and stir to coat. Ladle in just enough boiling water to cover the rice, add the vanilla bean, and cook, stirring, until all the liquid has been absorbed by the rice. Continue stirring and adding water, about 1 cup at a time, until all the water is absorbed or the rice is al dente—whichever happens first. This should take no more than 20 to 25 minutes.

5 Stir the milk mixture into the rice. Add the orange zest and juice and cook, stirring constantly, for about 6 minutes, or until the mixture is the consistency of custard (although it will not be as smooth because of the rice). Add the chocolate and cook, stirring constantly, for about 2 minutes, or until it has melted. Remove from the heat. Remove the vanilla bean, stir in the raisins, if using, and any liquid. Pour into a warm serving bowl, sprinkle with the nuts, and garnish with the mint sprigs. Serve immediately.

NOTE: Although this pudding is best served warm, it can also be served at room temperature or chilled.

Brown Butter Berry Tart ❧ Dean Fearing

TART PASTRY:

1½ cups all-purpose flour

2 tablespoons plus 2 teaspoons granulated sugar

8 tablespoons (1 stick) unsalted butter, chilled and cut into ½-inch pieces

1 large egg yolk

2 to 3 tablespoons heavy cream, chilled

FILLING:

1 pint fresh raspberries, blueberries or blackberries, or a combination of all three

6 tablespoons unsalted butter

1 vanilla bean

3 extra-large eggs

¾ cup granulated sugar

⅓ cup all-purpose flour

■ Special Equipment: 10-inch tart pan with a removable bottom or flan ring

This luscious dessert is flavored with browned butter scented with vanilla, giving a nutty taste to the berries. After a relatively light dinner, a home-baked fruit tart is always welcome.

---

1 Assemble *mise en place* trays for this recipe (see page 6).

2 To make the pastry, in a medium-sized bowl, combine the flour and sugar. With your fingers or a pastry blender quickly blend in the butter, a few pieces at a time, until the mixture resembles coarse meal.

3 In a small bowl, blend the egg yolk with 2 tablespoons of cream. Make a well in the center of the flour and pour in the egg mixture. Quickly blend with your fingers to form a soft dough. Add more cream if the dough is dry and crumbly. Do not overmix or the pastry will be tough. Roll the pastry into a ball and flatten slightly. Wrap in plastic wrap and refrigerate for at least 1 hour.

4 To assemble the tart, roll out the pastry on a lightly floured surface or between 2 sheets of plastic wrap to ⅛-inch thick and 14 inches in diameter. Line a 10-inch tart pan or flan ring with the pastry so that it overhangs the edges by about 1 inch. Trim the edges and crimp lightly.

5 Preheat the oven to 375 degrees F.

6 To make the filling, wash and dry the berries. Sprinkle half of the berries in the bottom of the pastry-lined pan. Refrigerate the remaining berries.

7 In a small saucepan, melt the butter over low heat. Add the vanilla bean and heat gently for about 10 minutes or until the butter turns golden brown, being careful not to burn it. Immediately remove from heat. Let the butter cool until tepid.

8 In a medium-sized bowl, using an electric mixer set on high speed, whisk the eggs and sugar until pale and creamy and the batter forms a ribbon when the beaters are lifted.

9 Remove the vanilla bean from the browned butter. (Rinse, dry and set aside for future use.) Slowly pour the butter into the batter, beating on low speed, until all the butter is incorporated. Gently fold the flour into the batter, taking care not to overmix.

10 Pour the batter over the berries in the tart shell. Bake for 35 to 40 minutes, or until set. Remove the tart from the oven and set on a rack to cool.

11 Arrange remaining berries on top of the tart. Serve at room temperature.

Blue Corn Biscotti ~ Bobby Flay

MAKES 26 TO 28 BISCOTTI
PREPARATION TIME: ABOUT 20 MINUTES
BAKING TIME: ABOUT 35 MINUTES
RESTING TIME: AT LEAST 2 HOURS

2½ cups all-purpose flour

1¼ cups granulated sugar

½ cup stone-ground blue cornmeal

3 tablespoons stone-ground yellow cornmeal

1½ teaspoons baking powder

½ teaspoon salt

8 tablespoons (1 stick) unsalted butter, at room temperature

2 large eggs

Even the pastry chef at the Mesa Grill, Wayne Harley Brachman, gives a Southwestern flair to traditional recipes. Here, the blue corn of the Hopi Indians is used to make fabulous, practically addictive cookies inspired by the famous "twice-baked" Italian biscotti. It's this treatment that gives biscotti their distinctive crispy crunch.

---

1 Preheat the oven to 375 degrees F. Line a baking sheet with parchment paper. Assemble *mise en place* trays for this recipe (see page 6).

2 In the bowl of an electric mixer, whisk together the flour, sugar, blue and yellow cornmeal, baking powder, and salt.

3 With the mixer set at its lowest speed, add the butter to the dry ingredients, a little at a time, beating until the mixture resembles coarse meal. Beat in the eggs, one at a

2 tablespoons Anisette or Sambuca liqueur

½ cup coarsely chopped pecans

½ cup coarsely chopped unsalted pistachios

time. Stir the liqueur into the dough until incorporated. Stir in the nuts until the dough is thoroughly blended and holds together in a ball.

4 Transfer the dough to the baking sheet and gently press to form a log measuring approximately 3 inches wide, 1½ inches high, and 10 inches long. Bake for about 25 minutes, or until lightly browned. Remove from the oven and allow to rest for at least 2 hours or for as long as 8 hours.

5 Before second baking, reheat the oven to 350 degrees F.

6 Using a serrated knife, carefully cut the log crosswise into ⅓-inch-thick slices. Lay the slices on the same parchment paper-lined baking sheet and bake for 8 to 10 minutes or until lightly browned around the edges but still slightly soft in the middle. For more even baking, turn the biscotti over after 4 minutes. Remove from the oven and cool on the baking sheet.

Maple Sugar-Crusted Apple Pie ❧ Bobby Flay

SERVES 10 TO 12

PREPARATION TIME: ABOUT 1 HOUR AND 30 MINUTES (INCLUDES CHILLING)

BAKING TIME: ABOUT 20 MINUTES

PIE PASTRY:

¾ cup (1½ sticks) plus 3 teaspoons unsalted butter

2 tablespoons plus 2 teaspoons solid vegetable shortening

2 to 3 teaspoons ice water

3 drops fresh lemon juice

2½ cups all-purpose flour

There is nothing particularly Southwestern about this pie. It's just delicious and one of Bobby Flay's favorite desserts.

1 Assemble *mise en place* trays for this recipe (see page 6).

2 To make the pastry, cut the butter and shortening into pea-sized pieces. Place in the freezer for 30 minutes or until frozen.

3 Combine the ice water and lemon juice. Set aside.

4 In the bowl of an electric mixer, whisk together the flour, maple sugar, and salt. With the mixer at its lowest speed, gradually add the frozen butter. Mix for about 3 minutes, or until the butter begins to break up. Add the frozen shortening and mix for 2 minutes more. Drizzle

2 tablespoons plus 2 teaspoons maple sugar

½ teaspoon salt

FILLING:

8 or 9 tart apples, such as Granny Smith, peeled, cored, and sliced

¼ cup granulated sugar

2 teaspoons ground cinnamon

1 teaspoon freshly grated nutmeg

¼ cup cornstarch

2 tablespoons arrowroot

¼ cup maple syrup

1 large egg

2 tablespoons cold water

■ Special Equipment: 10-inch tart pan

in just enough of the ice water to cause the dough to come together. Gather the dough into a ball and let it rest for 10 minutes.

5 Divide the dough in half and flatten slightly into discs. Wrap in plastic wrap and refrigerate for 30 minutes.

6 Preheat the oven to 400 degrees F.

7 To make the filling, in a large bowl, combine the apples, granulated sugar, cinnamon, nutmeg, cornstarch, and arrowroot. Gently mix in the maple syrup. Set aside.

8 Roll out half of the pastry on a lightly floured surface or between 2 sheets of plastic wrap to a circle about ⅛ inch thick and 14 inches in diameter. Line a 10-inch tart pan with the pastry so that it overhangs the edges by about 1 inch.

9 Spread the apple mixture in the pastry shell, mounding slightly in the center. Roll out the remaining pastry into a circle large enough to cover the apple filling. Lay it over the filling and roll up the edges of the pastry to make a seal. Crimp them together, trimming off any excess dough.

10 In a small bowl, beat the egg with the cold water. Brush this egg wash over the pastry. Sprinkle with half of the maple sugar. Cut a few steam vents in the top. Bake in the center of the oven for 30 minutes.

11 Reduce the oven temperature to 350 degrees F. Sprinkle the remaining maple sugar on top of the pie and bake for about 20 minutes more, or until the pastry is golden and the filling is bubbling. Serve warm.

Bolo Apple Cake ❧ Bobby Flay

MAKES ONE 9-INCH ROUND CAKE
PREPARATION TIME: ABOUT 20 MINUTES
BAKING TIME: ABOUT 45 MINUTES

3 large Granny Smith or other tart apples, peeled, cored, and cut into wedges

¾ cup lightly packed dark brown sugar

2 teaspoons cornstarch

½ cup plus 1 tablespoon dry sherry

2 teaspoons pure vanilla extract

¾ cup cake flour

½ teaspoon baking powder

¼ teaspoon baking soda

Pinch of salt

4 tablespoons unsalted butter, at room temperature

⅓ cup granulated sugar

1 large egg

¼ cup plus 2 tablespoons buttermilk, at room temperature

The flavor of sherry creates an intriguing note and gives a touch of the Spanish palate to this dessert.

1 Assemble *mise en place* trays for this recipe (see page 6).

2 Preheat the oven to 400 degrees F.

3 Put the apples in a 2-quart baking dish. In a medium bowl, whisk together the brown sugar, cornstarch, ½ cup of the sherry, and 1 teaspoon of the vanilla. Pour over the apples and toss to coat. Bake, stirring occasionally, for about 25 minutes, or until the apples are slightly softened and beginning to brown. Remove from the oven, but do not turn off the oven.

4 Sift the flour, baking powder, baking soda, and salt together 3 times. Set aside.

5 In a large bowl, using an electric mixer set on medium-high speed, beat the butter and granulated sugar together for about 5 minutes, or until light and fluffy. Add the egg and beat just until blended. Using a spatula, fold in a third of the flour mixture. Fold in half of the buttermilk and the remaining 1 tablespoon sherry and 1 teaspoon vanilla. Fold in another third of the flour mixture and then the remaining buttermilk. Fold in the remaining flour mixture.

6 Scrape the batter over the warm apples and smooth the top to cover the fruit. Bake for about 20 minutes, or until the cake is golden on top and the center springs back when lightly pressed. Serve warm.

❧ The apples can be replaced by pears.

Thin Apple Tart ❧ Pierre Franey

SERVES 6

PREPARATION TIME: ABOUT 20 MINUTES

COOKING TIME: ABOUT 20 MINUTES

1½ cups all-purpose flour, chilled

6 tablespoons unsalted butter, chilled and cut into pieces

3 tablespoons plus 2 teaspoons granulated sugar

¼ cup cold water

3 large, tart apples, such as Granny Smith, peeled, cored, and thinly sliced

1 tablespoon unsalted butter, melted

■ Special Equipment: dark-colored, 12-inch pie pan or pizza pan

*T*his is one of my favorite French desserts. It is so simple and the apple flavor just shines!

1 Preheat the oven to 450 degrees F. Assemble *mise en place* trays for this recipe (see page 6).

2 Put the flour, butter, and 2 teaspoons of the sugar in a food processor fitted with the metal blade. With the motor running, slowly add the water through the feed tube and process for about 1 minute, until the dough forms a ball.

3 Transfer the dough to a lightly floured surface and roll out into a circle about 13 inches in diameter. Press into a 12-inch shallow black steel or aluminum pie pan or pizza pan about ½ inch deep. Trim any dough that rises up the side of the pan to make a flat round.

4 Sprinkle the dough with 1 tablespoon of the sugar. Arrange the apple slices neatly in an overlapping circular pattern on the dough, starting from the center and forming concentric rings. The center will rise to a slight peak, but it will flatten during baking. If there is space in the middle, fill it with some chopped apple. Sprinkle the apples with the remaining 2 tablespoons of sugar.

5 Bake for about 20 minutes, until the apples are lightly browned and soft and the sugar has begun to brown.

6 Remove the tart from the oven, and turn the oven setting to broil.

7 When the broiler is hot, place the tart under it for 1 minute to caramelize the sugar on top. The rims of the apple slices should be well browned, but watch carefully so that the pastry does not get too brown. Remove from the broiler and brush the top with the melted butter. Cut into wedges and serve hot.

> ❧ Cut the apples as thin as possible. They should be as uniformly shaped as possible for even cooking. You can cut them into either circles or half-moon shapes.

Chilled Minted Melon Soup ❧ Marilyn Frobuccino

SERVES 6

PREPARATION TIME: ABOUT 20 MINUTES

CHILLING TIME: AT LEAST 2 HOURS

---

1 five- to six-pound very ripe Crenshaw melon, peeled, seeded, and cubed

1 five- to six-pound very ripe honeydew melon, peeled, seeded, and cubed

3 tablespoons fresh lime juice

2 tablespoons serrano-flavored vinegar (see page 24)

1 tablespoon minced seeded pickled jalapeño (optional)

3 tablespoons chopped fresh cilantro

3 tablespoons chopped fresh mint

¼ teaspoon ground cinnamon

¼ teaspoon freshly grated nutmeg

6 sprigs fresh mint

This dessert soup is immensely refreshing. Made with very ripe melons, it is light, sweet, and the perfect ending to a zesty meal. This soup also serves as a great first course, particularly with the addition of the jalapeño. If you make this in a blender, you will have to do so in batches.

1 Assemble *mise en place* trays for this recipe (see page 6).

2 Put the melon cubes in a food processor fitted with the metal blade, or a blender. Add the lime juice, vinegar, jalapeño, if using, the cilantro, chopped mint, cinnamon, and nutmeg. Process or blend for 30 to 45 seconds, or until smooth, adding about 2 tablespoons of cold water if necessary to thin to a soupy consistency.

3 Transfer to a glass or ceramic bowl. Cover and refrigerate for at least 2 hours to allow the flavors to develop.

4 Serve in chilled soup bowls, garnished with the fresh mint sprigs.

Gateau Rolla ~ Joyce Goldstein

MAKES ONE 9-INCH CAKE; SERVES 6
PREPARATION TIME: ABOUT 1 HOUR
BAKING TIME: ABOUT 1 HOUR
CHILLING TIME: ABOUT 13 HOURS

MERINGUE LAYERS:

About 2 tablespoons flavorless vegetable oil

5 large egg whites, at room temperature

Pinch of salt

1 cup granulated sugar

1 teaspoon pure vanilla extract

¾ cup finely grated almonds

FILLING:

6 ounces sweet chocolate, coarsely chopped (see Note)

2 tablespoons nonalkalized cocoa powder

3 large egg whites

¾ cup granulated sugar

1½ cups (3 sticks) unsalted butter, at room temperature

This rich dessert is a real crowd pleaser! And it is an even greater boon to the home cook as it is best made at least one day in advance.

1 Assemble *mise en place* trays for this recipe (see page 6).

2 Preheat the oven to 250 degrees F. Trace a circle 9 inches in diameter onto each of four 10-inch squares of parchment paper. Lightly oil 4 baking sheets with vegetable oil and place a piece of parchment paper onto each sheet, tracing side down. Lightly oil the paper. (See Note.)

3 To make the meringue layers, in a large bowl, using an electric mixer set on high speed, beat the egg whites with the salt until they hold stiff peaks. Gradually beat in ¾ cup of the sugar and continue to beat until stiff and glossy. Lower the speed and beat in the remaining ¼ cup sugar and the vanilla. Fold in the almonds just until blended.

4 Spread or pipe the meringue into rounds about ¼ inch thick on the parchment, staying within the outlines of the circles. Bake for about 1 hour, or until just dry. Carefully lift the meringues and paper off the baking sheets and cool on the paper on wire racks.

5 While the meringues are baking, make the filling: Melt the chocolate with the cocoa in the top half of a double boiler set over barely simmering water, stirring frequently until smooth. Set aside to cool.

6 Put the egg whites in a heatproof bowl and set it over a pan of hot water. Using an electric mixer set on high speed, beat until foamy. Gradually beat in the sugar until soft peaks form. Beat in the butter, a bit at a time, then beat in the chocolate mixture until smooth. Transfer to a clean bowl, cover, and refrigerate for about 1 hour, or until firm enough to spread.

7 Carefully peel the cooled meringue off the parchment paper. (If a meringue cracks or breaks, you can patch it with the filling.)

8 Spread equal portions of the chocolate filling over 3 of the meringue circles, spreading it about ¼ inch thick. Stack them on a cake plate. Place the remaining meringue on top and carefully frost the top and sides with the remaining chocolate filling.

9 Refrigerate the cake for about 1 hour, or until the frosting has set. Cover and allow to chill for at least 12 hours, or up to 2 days. Bring to room temperature before serving.

NOTE: This recipe calls for sweet chocolate, which is dark sweet chocolate, sweeter than bittersweet or semi-sweet chocolate. The most widely available brand in the United States is Baker's German Sweet Chocolate.

Only one 10-inch parchment paper square will fit on a baking sheet. You may have to bake these in two batches if your oven is not large enough to hold 4 baking sheets.

Chocolate Walnut Tarte ∾ Vincent Guerithault

SERVES 6

PREPARATION TIME: ABOUT 30 MINUTES

BAKING TIME: ABOUT 25 MINUTES

CHILLING TIME (PASTRY ONLY): ABOUT 2 HOURS AND 30 MINUTES

TART PASTRY:

1 cup all-purpose flour

1 teaspoon granulated sugar

When Vincent Guerithault made this dessert in class, we could hardly keep the audience in its seats. Chef Vincent suggests serving this tart with a scoop each of banana and chocolate ice cream drizzled with chocolate sauce. Talk about a sweet death!

---

1 Assemble *mise en place* trays for this recipe (see page 6).

2 To make the pastry, in a medium-sized bowl, combine the flour and sugar. With your fingertips or a pastry blender, quickly blend in the butter, a few pieces at a

8 tablespoons (1 stick) unsalted butter, chilled and cut into pieces

2 to 3 tablespoons ice water

FILLING:

1½ cups semisweet chocolate chips

1½ ounces semisweet chocolate, chopped

1 cup walnut halves

1 tablespoon plus 1 teaspoon dark rum

2 teaspoons pure vanilla extract

2 tablespoons unsalted butter

½ cup dark brown sugar

1 large egg, lightly beaten

4 firm bananas

■ Special Equipment: 10-inch tart pan with removable bottom; pie weights or dried beans, peas, or rice

time, until the mixture resembles coarse meal. Add the water, a tablespoon at time, and quickly blend with your hands to form a soft dough. Do not overmix, or the pastry will be tough. You may need additional water, but take care not to allow the dough to get sticky. Roll the pastry into a ball and flatten slightly. Wrap in plastic wrap and refrigerate for at least 2 hours.

3 To make the tart, roll out the pastry on a lightly floured surface or between 2 sheets of plastic wrap to a circle about 14 inches in diameter and ⅛ inch thick. Line a 10-inch tart pan with the pastry so that it overhangs the edges by about 1 inch. Trim the edges and crimp lightly. Prick the bottom of the pastry with a fork. Refrigerate for at least 30 minutes.

4 Preheat the oven to 450 degrees F.

5 Line the pastry with lightly buttered parchment paper or aluminum foil, buttered side down. Fill with pie weights, dried beans, or rice. Bake about 15 minutes or until the edges of the pastry are golden and the bottom is set. Remove the weights and parchment and return the tart shell to the oven for 3 to 4 minutes until lightly browned. Cool completely on a wire rack before filling. (Leave the oven on.)

6 To make the filling, in a medium-sized bowl, combine the chocolate chips, chopped chocolate, walnuts, rum, and vanilla extract. Set aside.

7 In a small saucepan, melt the butter and sugar over medium heat, stirring frequently. Bring the mixture just to a boil. Remove from the heat and pour over chocolate mixture, stirring continously until smooth and cooled slightly.

8 Mix in the egg, stirring until incorporated.

9 Peel and slice the bananas and arrange them evenly in the baked tart shell. Spoon the chocolate mixture over the bananas, forming a slight mound in the center. Bake for about 4 minutes, or until the top is slightly crumbly. Do not overbake. Allow to cool completely on a wire rack before serving.

❧ Be sure to let the chocolate mixture cool slightly before stirring in the egg to prevent the egg from "cooking."

Pumpkin Crème Brûlée ❧ Ron Hook

SERVES 6

PREPARATION TIME: ABOUT 10 MINUTES

BAKING TIME: ABOUT 45 MINUTES

FAT PER SERVING: 2 GRAMS

SATURATED FAT: 1.2 GRAMS

CALORIES PER SERVING: 129

CALORIES FROM FAT: 14%

---

10 large egg whites, at room temperature

1 cup canned pumpkin purée

¼ cup granulated sugar

1 cup evaporated skim milk

2 tablespoons heavy cream

2 teaspoons cornstarch

1 teaspoon pumpkin pie seasoning

⅛ teaspoon salt

This is a very light crème brûlée, so we have allowed almost a cup per person. You can, of course, prepare smaller portions to save on calories and fat.

---

1 Assemble *mise en place* trays for this recipe (see page 6). Preheat the oven to 300 degrees F.

2 In a large bowl, combine the egg whites, pumpkin, and sugar and whisk until well blended. Whisk in the milk, cream, cornstarch, pumpkin pie seasoning, and salt.

3 Pour into six 8-ounce glass or ceramic custard cups or ramekins. Place the dishes in a shallow baking dish large enough to hold them comfortably and add enough hot water to come halfway up the sides of the filled dishes.

4 Bake for about 45 minutes, or until the centers are set. Remove the custard cups from the water bath and cool on a wire rack. Serve warm, at room temperature, or chilled.

NOTE: These can be made early in the day, held in the refrigerator, and served chilled or at room temperature. Be sure to use plain pumpkin purée, not sweetened, spiced pumpkin pie filling.

Blackberry-Rhubarb Phyllo Tart ❧ Patricia Jamieson

MAKES ONE 9-INCH TART; SERVES 6

PREPARATION TIME: ABOUT 40 MINUTES

COOKING TIME: ABOUT 2 MINUTES

BAKING TIME: ABOUT 50 MINUTES

FAT PER SERVING: 10 GRAMS

SATURATED FAT: 2.9 GRAMS

CALORIES PER SERVING: 308

CALORIES FROM FAT: 28%

---

1 pound rhubarb, trimmed and cut into 1-inch pieces (about 3 cups)

2 cups fresh blackberries

¾ cup plus 2 tablespoons granulated sugar

1 tablespoon quick-cooking tapioca

2 teaspoons grated lemon zest

2 tablespoons unsalted butter

2 tablespoons vegetable oil, preferably canola

1 large egg white, at room temperature

Six 14 x 18-inch sheets phyllo dough, thawed according to package instructions

1 tablespoon plus 2 teaspoons fine dry bread crumbs

About 2 tablespoons confectioners' sugar, for dusting

This is delicious made with summer's freshest fruit, but it works almost as well with frozen fruit. You don't need to thaw the fruit, but in that case, bake the tart for an additional twenty minutes or so. This is delicious served with low-fat ice cream.

---

1 Assemble *mise en place* trays for this recipe (see page 6). Set the oven rack on the lowest level and preheat the oven to 400 degrees F. Place a heavy-duty baking sheet on the rack to heat. Spray a 9-inch pie plate with nonstick vegetable spray.

2 In a large bowl, combine the rhubarb, berries, sugar, tapioca, and lemon zest and toss to blend. Set aside.

3 In a small saucepan, melt the butter over very low heat. Skim off any foam that rises to the surface and cook for about 2 minutes, or until the butter begins to turn a light, nutty brown. Take care not to burn. Pour into a small bowl and set aside to cool.

4 When the butter is cool, use a fork to whisk in the oil and egg white until well blended.

5 Lay 1 sheet of the thawed phyllo in the prepared pie plate so that the edges hang over the sides. (As you work, keep the sheets of phyllo not being immediately used covered with a damp kitchen towel.) With a pastry brush, brush the phyllo with the egg white mixture. Sprinkle with 1 teaspoon of the bread crumbs. Lay another sheet of phyllo at an angle over the first. Brush with the egg white mixture and sprinkle with 1 teaspoon bread crumbs. Repeat with 3 more sheets of phyllo, brushing with the egg mixture and sprinkling with the crumbs.

6 Spoon the fruit mixture into the phyllo-lined pie plate. Lift a section of the overhanging phyllo, give it a twist, and drape it over the fruit filling to form a ruffle. Repeat with the remaining overhanging phyllo, lifting it at 4 points in all. Brush the ruffled phyllo with the egg white mixture. Lay the remaining sheet of phyllo on a sheet of wax paper and cut it in half lengthwise and then crosswise. Lift each quarter from underneath, bunch it together at the center to form a ruffle, and place it over the exposed fruit in the center of the tart to give the entire tart a ruffled top. (Do not worry if some fruit is still visible; small openings serve as steam vents.) Brush the center ruffles with the egg white mixture.

7 Set the pie plate on the baking sheet in the oven and bake for 10 minutes. Reduce the heat to 350 degrees F and bake for 40 to 50 minutes longer, or until the pastry is golden and the fruit mixture is bubbling. Cool to room temperature on a wire rack.

8 Just before serving, dust the top with confectioners' sugar.

NOTE: The tart is best served the day it is made. If the phyllo ruffles soften, reheat the tart in a 350-degree-F oven to crisp them.

Caramelized Pear and Cranberry Upside-Down Cake ❧ Matthew Kenney

MAKES ONE 9-INCH CAKE; SERVES 6
PREPARATION TIME: ABOUT 20 MINUTES
COOKING TIME: ABOUT 5 MINUTES
BAKING TIME: ABOUT 30 MINUTES

11 tablespoons plus 1 teaspoon unsalted butter

¾ cup lightly packed light brown sugar

Although this dessert is not Mediterranean in flavor, it is one of Matthew Kenney's trademarks and he wanted to share it with the class—and our readers.

1 Assemble *mise en place* trays for this recipe (see page 6).

2 Preheat the oven to 350 degrees F and put a baking sheet on the center rack. Lightly grease a 9-inch round cake pan.

⅓ cup dried cranberries

2 firm but ripe pears, peeled, cored, halved, and sliced ⅛ inch thick

1⅔ cups all-purpose flour

2 teaspoons baking powder

¼ teaspoon salt

⅔ cup granulated sugar

2 large eggs

1 teaspoon pure vanilla extract

2 cups milk

Vanilla ice cream or frozen yogurt (optional)

■ Special Equipment: 9-inch round cake pan

3 In a medium-sized saucepan, melt 6 tablespoons of the butter over medium heat. Stir in the brown sugar and cook, stirring constantly, for about 5 minutes, or until the sugar dissolves. Immediately pour into the prepared cake pan. Sprinkle the cranberries over the sugar syrup and arrange the pear slices on top in a slightly overlapping circular pattern. Set aside.

4 In a small bowl, whisk together the flour, baking powder, and salt.

5 In a large bowl, using an electric mixer set on medium-high speed, cream the remaining ⅓ cup butter and the granulated sugar for 2 to 3 minutes, or until light and fluffy. Add the eggs 1 at a time, and beat until well combined. Add the vanilla. Add the dry ingredients, alternating them with the milk and beating until well blended. Pour the batter over the pears and spread with a spatula to cover the fruit.

6 Set the cake on the preheated baking sheet and bake for about 30 minutes, or until the edges are golden and a cake tester inserted in the center comes out clean. Cool on a wire rack for 5 minutes.

7 Position a serving plate over the cake pan and gently invert. Tap gently to release, and lift the pan off the cake. Serve warm, with scoops of ice cream or yogurt if desired.

NOTE: The dessert pictured was prepared as individual 6-inch cakes. If you chose to bake individual cakes, divide the pears and batter among the smaller cake pans and decrease the baking time to about 20 minutes, or until the edges are golden and a cake tester inserted in the center comes out clean.

Baking the cake on the hot baking sheet helps to caramelize the sugar. If making the cake in advance, invert it onto an oven-proof plate. Just before serving, reheat it in a 300-degree-F oven for about 10 minutes.

Cranberry-Walnut Tart ❧ Johanne Killeen and George Germon

SERVES 6

PREPARATION TIME: ABOUT 20 MINUTES

COOKING TIME: ABOUT 20 MINUTES

CHILLING TIME (PASTRY ONLY): ABOUT 30 MINUTES

TART PASTRY:

2 cups unbleached, all-purpose flour

¼ cup superfine sugar

½ teaspoon coarse salt

1 cup unsalted butter, cut into ½-inch cubes and chilled

¼ cup ice water

FILLING:

2 cups fresh cranberries, rinsed and dried

½ cup chopped walnuts

2 tablespoons superfine sugar

2 tablespoons light brown sugar

2 tablespoons confectioners' sugar

1 cup whipped cream (optional)

This easy-to-make dessert is perfect for the Thanksgiving and Christmas table. The dough is fail-safe and can be used for any tart or pie.

---

1 Preheat the oven to 450 degrees F. Assemble *mise en place* trays for this recipe (see page 6).

2 To make the tart pastry, combine the flour, sugar, and salt in a food processor fitted with the metal blade. Pulse on and off a few times to combine.

3 Add the chilled butter, tossing quickly with your fingers to coat with flour (this prevents the butter cubes from adhering together and helps them to combine more evenly with the flour). Pulse on and off about 15 times, until the mixture resembles small peas.

4 With the motor running, add the ice water all at once through the feed tube and process for about 10 seconds, stopping the machine before the dough becomes a solid mass.

5 Turn the dough out onto a sheet of aluminum foil, pressing any loose particles into the ball of dough. Form about a 7-inch disk with the dough, wrap, and refrigerate for about 30 minutes, until cold but still pliable.

6 On a lightly floured surface, roll out the dough to an 11-inch circle. Transfer to a baking sheet and trim the edges.

7 To make the filling, combine the cranberries, walnuts, superfine sugar, and brown sugar in a bowl. Toss to distribute the sugar evenly.

8 Spoon the cranberry mixture into the center of the dough round, leaving a 1½-inch border all around the edge. Lift the dough border up over the filling, letting it drape gently over the fruit. Some of the filling will be exposed. Press down on the edges of the dough, snugly securing the sides and the bottom, being careful not to mash the fruit. Gently pinch together the pleats that have formed from the draping.

9 Bake the tart for 15 to 20 minutes, or until the crust is golden. Cool on a wire rack for about 10 minutes. Dust with confectioners' sugar and serve warm, with whipped cream, if desired.

⤞ The tart dough works best when made with very cold butter. This dough recipe makes enough for 2 nine-inch tart shells or 4 four-inch tartlet shells.

Chilled Soup of Santa Rosa Plums Flavored with Vanilla ⤞ Gray Kunz

SERVES 6

PREPARATION TIME: ABOUT 20 MINUTES

COOKING TIME: ABOUT 1 HOUR

CHILLING TIME: AT LEAST 4 HOURS

2½ pounds overripe red plums, preferably Santa Rosa, washed

½ cup plus 1 tablespoon granulated sugar, or to taste

1 vanilla bean, split in half lengthwise

Juice of 1 lemon, or more to taste

10 cups water

Dash of Mirabelle eau-de-vie or other plum-flavored liqueur

1 cup chopped, toasted pistachio nuts (see page 13)

1 pint high-quality vanilla ice cream

This dessert is best made in the summer, when plums are at their most succulent. For fewer calories and no fat, eliminate the ice cream. The idea of serving "soup" for dessert is a delicious one you may not have tried.

1 Assemble *mise en place* trays for this recipe (see page 6).

2 Cut 6 silver dollar-sized slices from the sides of 2 or 3 plums. Chop the remaining plum flesh, discarding the pits.

3 In a medium-sized saucepan, combine the sliced and chopped plums, ½ cup of the sugar, the vanilla bean, lemon juice, and water. Bring to a simmer over medium heat. Reduce the heat to low and simmer, uncovered, for 20 minutes.

4 Using a slotted spoon, carefully transfer 6 plum slices to a plate and sprinkle with the remaining 1 tablespoon of sugar. Set aside. Continue simmering the chopped plum mixture, uncovered, for about 40 minutes more.

5 Strain the chopped plum mixture through a fine sieve into a glass or ceramic bowl, pushing against the solids to extract all the juice. Discard the solids. Taste, and add a little more sugar, if necessary. Cover and refrigerate for about 4 hours, or until well chilled.

6 Just before serving, stir the eau-de-vie or plum liqueur into the soup. Taste, and add lemon juice, if necessary. Ladle the soup into 6 well-chilled, shallow soup bowls.

7 Place the pistachios in a shallow bowl. Scoop out 6 small balls of ice cream and roll each one in the pistachios. Place an ice cream ball in the center of each bowl of soup, lay a sugared plum slice on top, and serve immediately. If not using ice cream, simply garnish the soup with the plum slices.

___

When a recipe calls for overripe plums, select those that feel heavy and juicy and are very "giving" when pressed. Avoid any that are still firm—or that show signs of spoilage.

Chocolate Strudel and Poached Pears with Cinnamon Sauce ❧ Michael Lomonaco

SERVES 6
PREPARATION TIME: ABOUT 45 MINUTES
COOKING AND BAKING TIME: ABOUT 50 MINUTES

___

3 ripe Bosc pears, peeled, cored, and halved lengthwise

1½ cups water

Each component of this dessert can be prepared in advance. The pears can be poached and the strudel rolled so that the dessert can be assembled just before serving.

___

1 Assemble *mise en place* trays for this recipe (see page 6).

2 In a medium-sized, nonreactive saucepan, combine the pears, water, wine, sugar, and cinnamon, and bring to a boil over high heat. Reduce the heat to low and sim-

¾ cup semisweet white wine, such as Muscat de Beaumes-de-Venise or Muscat from Northern Italy

3 tablespoons granulated sugar

1 teaspoon ground cinnamon

6 sheets frozen filo pastry, thawed according to package directions

½ cup unsalted butter, melted

¼ cup chopped walnuts

6 ounces bittersweet chocolate, finely chopped

1 tablespoon unsweetened cocoa powder

Cinnamon Sauce (recipe follows)

6 fresh mint sprigs

mer for 10 to 12 minutes, or until the pears are tender but not soft. Remove from heat and let the pears cool in the liquid.

3 Preheat the oven 375 degrees F.

4 Lay 1 filo sheet on a work surface. Lightly brush it with melted butter, and sprinkle with 1 tablespoon of the walnuts. Lay another filo sheet on top, brush with butter and sprinkle with walnuts. Repeat the layering process with the remaining sheets, leaving the top sheet plain.

5 Sprinkle the chopped chocolate evenly over the top sheet of filo and then sprinkle with the cocoa powder. Starting from a long side, roll up jelly-roll fashion into a log. Brush with the remaining melted butter.

6 Transfer the strudel to a baking sheet. Bake for about 20 minutes, or until golden. Cool on the baking sheet for about 10 minutes.

7 Using a serrated knife, cut the strudel into slices no more than ½ inch thick.

8 Drain the pears well. Cut each half lengthwise from the stem end into thin slices, keeping it intact at the stem end.

9 Spoon the Cinnamon Sauce onto 6 dessert plates. Fan a pear half out on each plate. Place a strudel slice beside each pear. Garnish each plate with a mint sprig and serve.

———————

❧ When working with filo pastry, it is important to keep the sheets you are not using covered with a damp dish towel or cloth. Wrap unused filo well in plastic and foil and freeze.

CINNAMON SAUCE

MAKES ABOUT ¾ CUP

---

1 large egg yolk, at room temperature

2 tablespoons granulated sugar

½ cup milk

¼ teaspoon ground cinnamon

1 In a medium-sized bowl, whisk together the egg yolk, sugar, and cinnamon until smooth.

2 Heat the milk in the top half of a double boiler until scalded (just below a boil). Gradually add the milk to the egg mixture, whisking constantly. Return the mixture to the double boiler and cook over hot water, whisking constantly, for 2 to 3 minutes until thick enough to coat the back of a spoon. Remove the pan from the heat and allow to cool. Use as soon as it's cool, or cover and refrigerate until ready to serve.

Walnut Tart ❧ Carlo Middione

SERVES 6
PREPARATION TIME: ABOUT 30 MINUTES
COOKING TIME: ABOUT 1 HOUR
CHILLING TIME (PASTRY ONLY): ABOUT 1 HOUR

PASTRY:

2 cups all-purpose unbleached flour, or more if necessary

⅓ cup granulated sugar

¼ cup lard or solid vegetable shortening

¼ cup unsalted butter

Grated zest of 1 lemon

1 large egg

3 to 4 large egg yolks

FILLING:

2 cups coarsely chopped walnuts

The key elements here are the walnuts and the mosto cotto, *a jelly-like substance made from wine must. A good substitution for mosto cotto in this recipe is tart, lemony-tasting, red currant jelly.*

---

1 Preheat the oven to 350 degrees F. Assemble *mise en place* trays for this recipe (see page 6).

2 To make the pastry, combine the flour, sugar, lard, butter, and lemon zest in a food processor fitted with the metal blade. Pulse on and off 8 to 10 times, until the mixture resembles coarse crumbs. Add the egg and 3 egg yolks, and process until the dough just comes together. If the dough seems too wet, add additional flour, 1 teaspoon at a time. If the dough is too dry and won't hold together, add 1 more egg yolk.

3 Scrape the dough onto a lightly floured work surface and knead for 1 minute, or until quite soft. Form into a ball, wrap in plastic wrap, and refrigerate for 1 hour.

½ cup raisins

¼ cup finely chopped candied orange peel

1⅓ cups *mosto cotto* or 1 cup red currant jelly

1 large egg, beaten, for egg glaze

■ Special Equipment: Special equipment: 9-inch fluted tart pan with a removable bottom.

4 Meanwhile, make the filling. Stir together the walnuts, raisins, orange peel, and *mosto cotto* or jelly. Set aside.

5 Divide the dough in half. On a lightly floured surface, roll out half the dough to a 12-inch circle. Fit it into a 9-inch fluted tart pan with a removable bottom, leaving about a 1½-inch overhang.

6 Spoon the filling into the tart pan, spreading it evenly.

7 Roll out the remaining piece of dough to a 12-inch circle. Lay the circle on top of the filling. Press the 2 layers of overhanging dough together and then roll up and over to make a raised edge, using your thumb and index finger to flute the edge. Make sure the edge is well sealed.

8 Using a pastry brush, coat the top of the tart with the egg glaze. Insert a small pastry tip into the center of the tart for a steam vent, or cut a cross-hatch in the center of the pastry. Then cut several ½-inch slashes in a decorative pattern over the surface to help steam escape. Set the tart on a baking sheet to catch any juices that escape during baking.

9 Bake for 55 to 60 minutes, or until nicely browned. Transfer to a wire rack to cool for 10 minutes. Remove the tart ring, cut the tart into wedges and serve warm. Or let cool before serving.

❧ To facilitate removing the tart from the pan, place it, while still hot, on a bowl that is smaller than the tart pan, or on a large can. The ring will slip down and the tart will be supported by the metal bottom. If the ring does not slide down of its own accord, apply gentle pressure to the edges to loosen it.

❧ You may be able to buy *mosto cotto* in an Italian market or from a winery. Or, if you live near a winery, you may be able to buy wine must, which is juice freshly squeezed from grapes. If so, make *mosto cotto* by boiling the must in a heavy pan until it reduces to a thick, jelled consistency. Cool and use as you would any jelly.

Vanilla Custard with Maple-Roasted Peanuts ～ Wayne Nish

SERVES 6

PREPARATION TIME: ABOUT 20 MINUTES

COOKING AND BAKING TIME: 35 TO 40 MINUTES

4 cups milk

¾ cup granulated sugar

8 large egg yolks

2 tablespoons pure vanilla extract

⅛ teaspoon salt

1 cup high-quality pure maple syrup

4 ounces maple-roasted peanuts, coarsely chopped

■ Special Equipment: 6 six-ounce ramekins or custard cups

These simple baked custards, with their pure, uncomplicated flavors, are the perfect ending to an elaborate meal.

1 Assemble *mise en place* trays for this recipe (see page 6).

2 In a medium-sized, heavy saucepan, combine the milk and sugar. Cook over low heat, stirring for 5 minutes, or until the sugar is dissolved. Do not allow to boil. Transfer to a large bowl and let cool to room temperature.

3 Whisk the egg yolks, vanilla extract, and salt into the milk mixture. Strain through a fine strainer. Pour the custard into 6 six-ounce shallow ramekins or custard cups.

4 Place the cups in a large, flat roasting pan. Add enough hot water to come about ½ inch up the sides of the cups. Bake for 35 to 40 minutes, or until the custard is barely set. Remove from the oven and allow to cool in the water bath for about 5 minutes before lifting from the roasting pan and cooling completely on the counter.

5 To serve, drizzle about 2½ tablespoons of the maple syrup over each custard and sprinkle each with about 2 tablespoons of the peanuts.

～ The peanuts can be replaced with any glazed, roasted nuts.

～ Place a tea towel or dish towel on the bottom of a roasting pan, under the custard cups, to prevent them from moving around while cooking.

Apricot and Ginger Crisp ❧ Bradley Ogden

SERVES 6

PREPARATION TIME: ABOUT 25 MINUTES

BAKING TIME: 20 TO 30 MINUTES

⅓ cup packed light brown sugar

¾ cup plus 3 tablespoons all-purpose flour

¼ cup grated fresh ginger

1¼ teaspoons ground cinnamon

Grated zest of 1 lemon

5 cups fresh apricot halves (about 2 pounds)

⅔ cup packed dark brown sugar

¼ teaspoon salt

⅛ teaspoon ground ginger

6 tablespoons unsalted butter, cut into 1-inch pieces and chilled

Vanilla ice cream, for serving (optional)

This is a real home-style dessert that is always a hit. You can replace the apricots with ripe peaches or nectarines, depending on what is best in the market.

---

1 Preheat oven to 375 degrees F. Assemble *mise en place* trays for this recipe (see page 6).

2 In a large bowl, combine the light brown sugar, 3 tablespoons of the flour, the grated ginger, 1 teaspoon of the cinnamon, and the lemon zest. Add the apricots and toss gently until lightly coated. Set aside.

3 In another bowl, combine the remaining ¾ cup flour and ¼ teaspoon cinnamon with the dark brown sugar, salt, and ground ginger. Cut in the butter until the mixture resembles coarse meal.

4 Arrange the apricots, cut side down, in a single layer in the bottom of a 9- by 13-inch glass or ceramic baking dish. Sprinkle the topping evenly over the fruit. Bake for 20 to 30 minutes, or until the fruit is soft and the topping is crisp.

5 Serve warm, with ice cream if desired.

Banana-Pecan Strudel with Raisin Brandy Cream ～ Charles Palmer

SERVES 6 (12 STRUDELS)
PREPARATION TIME: ABOUT 20 MINUTES
COOKING AND BAKING TIME: 20 TO 25 MINUTES
SOAKING TIME (RAISINS ONLY): 1 HOUR

¼ cup raisins

½ cup brandy

6 ripe bananas

¾ cup plus 2 tablespoons granulated sugar

1½ cups chopped, toasted pecans (see page 13)

½ cup packed dark brown sugar

18 sheets frozen filo pastry, thawed

¾ cup Clarified Butter (see page 20)

1½ cups heavy cream

Confectioners' sugar, for dusting

An old-fashioned dessert idea is made modern here with an unusual filling.

1 Preheat the broiler. Assemble *mise en place* trays for this recipe (see page 6). Line 2 baking sheets with parchment.

2 Combine the raisins and brandy in a small glass or ceramic bowl and let soak for 1 hour.

3 Meanwhile, peel the bananas and cut in half lengthwise. Cut crosswise into 1-inch pieces. Place the bananas on one of the prepared baking sheets and sprinkle with ½ cup of the granulated sugar. Place under the broiler for about 5 minutes, until the sugar caramelizes, watching carefully to insure that it does not burn. Cool to room temperature. When cool, gently lift the bananas from the baking sheet.

4 Preheat the oven to 350 degrees F.

5 In a bowl, combine the bananas, pecans, ¼ cup of the granulated sugar and the brown sugar. Stir well.

6 Lay 6 sheets of the filo pastry on a work surface. Lightly brush with clarified butter. Lay another filo sheet on top of each and brush with butter. Lay the remaining filo sheets on top. You will have 6 stacks of 3 sheets each. Cut each stack in half crosswise so that you have 12 stacks.

7 Place equal portions of the banana mixture in the center at the short bottom edge of each stack of filo. Fold over the sides and roll into a cylinder.

8 Arrange the strudels on the prepared baking sheets. Bake for 12 minutes, or until golden brown.

9 Meanwhile, in a medium-sized bowl, whip the cream with the remaining 2 tablespoons granulated sugar.

10 Drain the raisins and fold into the whipped cream.

11 Place 2 strudels on each dessert plate. Sprinkle with confectioners' sugar. Place a spoonful of raisin brandy cream at the side, and serve immediately.

❧ Filo dough is available in the freezer section of most supermarkets or specialty food stores.

Baked Apples ❧ Jacques Pépin

SERVES 6

PREPARATION TIME: ABOUT 15 MINUTES

COOKING TIME: ABOUT 1 HOUR

---

6 large, tart apples, such as Russet, Granny Smith, or Pippin, cored

⅓ cup apricot jam

⅓ cup pure maple syrup

3 tablespoons unsalted butter, cut into 6 pieces

A simple dessert straight from the kitchen of "la grand'mère."

1 Preheat the oven to 375 degrees F. Assemble *mise en place* trays for this recipe (see page 6).

2 With the point of a knife, cut an incision about ⅛ inch to ½ inch wide through the skin all around each apple, about a third of the way down from the stem end. As the apples cook, the flesh expands and the tops of the apples will lift up like a lid above this cut. Without this scoring, the apples will burst.

3 Stand the apples upright in a gratin dish or other attractive ovenproof dish. Coat the apples with the apricot jam and maple syrup and dot them with the butter. Bake for 30 minutes.

4 Baste the apples with the cooking juices and bake for 30 to 40 minutes longer, or until the apples are plump, brown, and soft to the touch. Serve warm.

❧ If you prepare the apples early in the day, bake them while you are dining so that they are served hot from the oven.

❧ Delicious served with a slice of pound cake or with sour cream or ice cream.

Pear Clafoutis ❧ Debra Ponzek

SERVES 6

PREPARATION TIME: ABOUT 25 MINUTES

BAKING TIME: ABOUT 40 MINUTES

1 tablespoon unsalted butter, softened

½ cup plus 1 tablespoon granulated sugar

3 large eggs

1 vanilla bean split lengthwise or 2 teaspoons pure vanilla extract

1½ cups heavy cream

1 tablespoon Poire William liqueur (pear liqueur)

6 tablespoons all-purpose flour, sifted

1½ teaspoons ground cinnamon

4 ripe but firm Bartlett or Anjou pears

Although a typically French dessert, usually made with cherries, clafoutis—here made with pears—is a welcome addition to the American table. Easy to prepare, it is delicious warm from the oven.

1 Preheat the oven to 375 degrees F. Assemble *mise en place* trays for this recipe (see page 6). Butter an 11 by 7 by 2-inch rectangular or oval baking dish with 1 tablespoon of the butter. Sprinkle with 1 tablespoon of the sugar.

2 In a large bowl, beat the eggs and the remaining ½ cup of sugar until light yellow and fluffy.

3 Scrape the seeds from the vanilla bean into the eggs or add the extract. Beat in the cream and liqueur. Beat in the flour and cinnamon until well blended. Set aside while you prepare the pears.

4 Peel, quarter, core, and cut the pears lengthwise into ¼-inch thick slices. Arrange the slices in the bottom of the prepared baking dish.

5 Pour the batter over the pears. Bake for 40 minutes, or until puffed up and firm. Remove from the oven and serve immediately, as the clafoutis will quickly deflate.

Warm Chocolate Cake ❧ Alfred Portale

SERVES 6

PREPARATION TIME: ABOUT 30 MINUTES

BAKING TIME: ABOUT 1 HOUR

RESTING TIME: 2 HOURS

1 pound semisweet chocolate, coarsely chopped

3 ounces bittersweet chocolate, coarsely chopped

½ cup plus 2 tablespoons strong brewed coffee

6 large eggs

½ cup plus 2 tablespoons granulated sugar

1 cup heavy cream

Whipped cream or ice cream, for serving (optional)

This is about the best chocolate cake you'll ever eat. You can serve it with whipped cream or, for even more indulgence, toasted almond ice cream.

1 Preheat the oven to 325 degrees F. Assemble *mise en place* trays for this recipe (see page 6). Butter a 10-inch round cake pan. Cut a 10-inch circle of parchment paper and fit it into the bottom of the pan. Lightly butter the parchment paper.

2 In the top half of a double boiler or in a heatproof bowl, combine the chocolates. Set over barely simmering water and allow to melt, stirring frequently. Remove from the heat, stir in the coffee, and mix until smooth. Set aside.

3 In the top half of a double boiler or in a heatproof bowl, combine the eggs and sugar. Set over boiling water and stir constantly until the sugar has dissolved and the mixture is warm. Reduce the heat to a gentle simmer.

4 Using a hand-held mixer set on medium speed, beat the egg mixture for about 5 minutes, or until it forms soft peaks. Remove the top half of the double boiler or the bowl from the heat. Gently fold a third of the beaten eggs into the melted chocolate. Fold in the rest of the egg mixture. Do not overmix; fold just until blended.

5 In a medium bowl, beat the cream until it forms stiff peaks. Gently fold into the chocolate mixture until well blended. Scrape the batter into the prepared pan and smooth the top. Place the pan in a larger pan and add enough hot water to come ½ inch up the sides of the cake pan. Bake for 1 hour.

6 Turn off the oven and open the oven door for 1 minute. Close the door and allow the cake to rest in the oven for 2 hours.

7 Invert the cake onto a serving plate and lift off the pan. Peel off the parchment paper. Serve warm, with whipped cream or ice cream if desired.

Pecan Pie ❧ Wolfgang Puck

SERVES 6

PREPARATION TIME: ABOUT 25 MINUTES

BAKING TIME: ABOUT 45 MINUTES

CHILLING TIME (PASTRY ONLY): 2 HOURS

PIE PASTRY:

1¾ cups all-purpose flour, sifted

1 tablespoon granulated sugar

¼ teaspoon salt

12 tablespoons unsalted butter, cut into 1-inch pieces and chilled

2 large egg yolks

2 to 3 tablespoons heavy cream

FILLING:

1 cup light corn syrup

¾ cup packed light brown sugar

3 large eggs

2 large egg yolks

2 teaspoons pure vanilla extract

2 tablespoons unsalted butter

1½ cups pecan halves

■ Special Equipment: 10-inch fluted tart pan with removable bottom

Wolfgang's classic pecan pie is a perfect dessert to end this slightly Asian meal.

1 Assemble *mise en place* trays for this recipe (see page 6).

2 To make the pie pastry, in a food processor fitted with the metal blade, combine the flour, sugar, salt, and butter. Process until the mixture resembles fine meal.

3 Whisk together the egg yolks and 2 tablespoons cream. With the motor running, slowly add to the flour mixture and process until the dough comes together into a ball. Add additional cream if necessary to make a cohesive dough. Transfer the dough to a lightly floured surface. Pat into a circle about ½ inch thick. Wrap in plastic and refrigerate for 2 hours, or until well chilled.

4 Preheat the oven to 375 degrees F.

5 To make the filling, combine the corn syrup, brown sugar, eggs, egg yolks, and vanilla and whisk well.

6 Heat the butter in a small sauté pan over medium heat for 3 minutes, or until it is browned and gives off a nutty aroma. Immediately stir the butter into the corn syrup mixture.

7 On a lightly floured surface, roll out the dough to a 12-inch circle. Carefully fit it into a 10-inch fluted tart pan with removable bottom and trim off the excess. Set the tart pan in a baking sheet lined with foil.

8 Arrange the pecan halves in the bottom of the pastry shell. Carefully ladle the filling mixture over the pecans. Bake in the lower third of the oven for 40 to 45 minutes, or until a cake tester inserted into the center comes out clean. Transfer to a wire rack to cool to room temperature.

❧ The tart pan is set on a foil-lined baking sheet to catch any sugary overflow from the filling, so as to make cleanup easy.

Sour Cherry Tart ❧ Marta Pulini

SERVES 6

PREPARATION TIME: ABOUT 40 MINUTES

COOKING TIME: ABOUT 1 HOUR AND 25 MINUTES

CHILLING TIME (DOUGH ONLY): AT LEAST 30 MINUTES

DOUGH:

1¾ cups plus 2 tablespoons all-purpose flour

½ cup plus 2 tablespoons granulated sugar

1½ teaspoons baking powder

Grated zest of 1 lemon

1 large egg plus 1 large egg yolk, lightly beaten

9 tablespoons unsalted butter, chilled

*T*he sour cherry tart with its pretty latticed top is an appealing dessert to serve at the end of special meal.

1 Assemble *mise en place* trays for this recipe (see page 6).

2 To make the dough, combine the flour, sugar, baking powder, and lemon zest and mound on a clean work surface. Make a well in the center. Add the beaten egg and butter and, using your fingertips, rub into the flour until the dough just holds together. Form into a ball, wrap in plastic wrap, and refrigerate for at least 30 minutes.

3 Preheat the oven to 375 degrees F. Generously butter a 9-inch fluted tart pan with a removable bottom.

4 To make the filling, combine the cherries, sugar, orange zest, and vanilla bean in a medium-sized saucepan set over low heat. Cook over low heat, stirring frequently, for 35 to 50 minutes, until the mixture resembles chunky preserves (the time depends on the type of cherries). Remove from the heat and allow to cool for 15 minutes. Remove the vanilla bean.

FILLING:

4 cups pitted fresh sour cherries

¾ cup granulated sugar

Grated zest of 1 orange

1 vanilla bean, split

1 tablespoon all-purpose flour

1 large egg yolk beaten with 1 table-spoon milk, for egg wash

■ Special Equipment: 9-inch fluted tart pan with a removable bottom

5 Cut off about a quarter of the dough, rewrap the smaller piece, and refrigerate it. On a lightly floured surface, roll the larger piece of dough to a 12-inch circle. Fit it into the prepared tart pan. Trim the overhanging dough and combine trimmings with reserved dough.

6 Sprinkle the flour over the bottom of the tart shell. Spoon the cherry filling into the shell, smoothing the top.

7 Divide the reserved dough into 8 to 10 pieces and form into long strips by rolling them between the floured palms of your hands. Use the strips to make a widely spaced lattice top, pushing the ends of the ropes into the edges of the bottom shell. Trim off the excess dough.

8 Using a pastry brush, lightly coat the latticework and the edge of the tart with the egg wash. Bake for 30 to 35 minutes, until the crust is golden. Cool for 5 to 10 minutes on a wire rack. Then remove the tart ring, cut the tart into wedges, and serve warm.

———

❧ Sour cherries are in season in midsummer. If you cannot find frozen or dried cherries, use canned. For this recipe, you will need 2 16-ounce cans unsweetened sour cherries packed in water. Drain them well. (Do not use cherry pie filling or sweet cherries!) You can also substitute dried cherries by reconstituting them in warm water for about 30 minutes.

Cranberry-Mango Cobbler with Cinnamon-Pecan Cream ～ Stephan Pyles

SERVES 6

PREPARATION TIME: ABOUT 30 MINUTES

BAKING TIME: ABOUT 1 HOUR

INFUSING AND COOKING TIME (CINNAMON-PECAN CREAM ONLY): ABOUT 50 MINUTES

CRUMB TOPPING:

1 cup all-purpose flour

½ cup granulated sugar

½ cup packed light brown sugar

⅛ teaspoon freshly grated nutmeg

8 tablespoons (1 stick) cold, unsalted butter, cut into ½-inch pieces

COBBLER:

4 cups fresh or frozen cranberries, washed

1 cup plus ⅓ cup granulated sugar

2 cups all-purpose flour

2 teaspoons baking soda

½ teaspoon salt

1 cup (2 sticks) unsalted butter

1 large egg, lightly beaten

1 cup buttermilk

3 ripe mangoes, peeled, seeded, and diced (about 3½ cups)

Cinnamon-Pecan Cream (recipe follows)

■ Special Equipment: candy thermometer

*I*f the end of summer is too early for the usual fall arrival of cranberries, check the freezer section of the supermarket, where cranberries are available all year long.

---

1 Preheat the oven to 350 degrees F. Butter and flour a 9 x 12 x 2-inch baking dish. Assemble *mise en place* trays for this recipe (see page 6).

2 To make the crumb topping, in a medium-sized bowl, combine the flour, granulated sugar, brown sugar, and nutmeg. With your fingers or a pastry blender, quickly blend in the butter until the mixture resembles coarse meal. Set aside.

3 To make the cobbler, in a bowl, combine the cranberries with 1 cup of the granulated sugar and set aside.

4 Sift together the flour, baking soda, and salt. Set aside.

5 In the bowl of an electric mixer, beat the butter and the remaining ⅓ cup sugar at high speed until light and fluffy. Beat in the beaten egg. Finally, stir in the flour mixture and the buttermilk, alternating the dry and liquid ingredients.

6 Spoon the batter into the prepared baking dish and smooth the top.

7 Gently toss the mangoes with the cranberries and spoon the fruit over the batter in an even layer. Sprinkle the reserved crumb topping over the fruit. Bake for 1 hour, or until the topping is crisp and light brown and the center is cooked through.

8 Remove the cobbler from the oven and allow to set for 10 minutes. Cut into squares and serve with the Cinnamon-Pecan Cream.

CINNAMON-PECAN CREAM

2 cups milk

1 vanilla bean, split lengthwise

1 cup chopped toasted pecans

2 cinnamon sticks

6 large egg yolks

⅔ cup granulated sugar

⅔ cup heavy cream, whipped to soft peaks

1 In a large saucepan, combine the milk, vanilla bean, pecans, and cinnamon sticks. Bring to a boil over medium-high heat. Remove from the heat and set aside for 30 minutes to infuse.

2 In a large bowl, using an electric mixer set on high speed, beat the egg yolks and sugar until thick and pale.

3 Return the milk to the heat and bring to a boil. Strain through a fine sieve into the egg mixture, stirring constantly. Return the mixture to the pan and place over simmering water. Cook, stirring frequently, for about 20 minutes, or until the custard has thickened and a candy thermometer inserted into the center registers 180 degrees F.

4 Fill a very large bowl or pan with ice cubes. Set the pan of custard in the ice and stir in the whipped cream just until mixed. Allow to cool, then pour into a bowl, cover and refrigerate until ready to serve.

Chocolate Bread Pudding ❧ Anne Rosenzweig

SERVES 6

PREPARATION TIME: ABOUT 30 MINUTES

BAKING TIME: ABOUT 1 HOUR AND 45 MINUTES

STANDING TIME: AT LEAST 1 HOUR

12 one-inch-thick slices brioche (or other richly flavored egg bread such as challah)

¾ cup unsalted butter, melted

8 ounces bittersweet chocolate, coarsely chopped

3 cups heavy cream

1 cup milk

1 cup granulated sugar

12 large egg yolks

1 teaspoon pure vanilla extract

⅛ teaspoon salt

1 cup heavy cream, softly whipped (optional)

*H*ere is a simply delicious version of an old-fashioned dessert.

---

1 Preheat the oven to 425 degrees F. Assemble *mise en place* trays for this recipe (see page 6).

2 Brush both sides of the bread slices with the melted butter. Place on a baking sheet and toast in the oven for 7 to 10 minutes, or until golden brown. Set aside.

3 Place the chocolate in a medium-sized bowl set over a saucepan of very hot, not simmering, water. The bottom of the bowl should not touch the water. Stir frequently until melted.

4 In a medium-sized saucepan, heat the cream and milk for about 5 minutes, over medium heat to just under a boil. Do not boil. Remove from the heat.

5 In a large bowl, whisk together the sugar and egg yolks until well blended. Gradually whisk the hot cream and milk mixture. Strain through a fine sieve into a bowl and skim off any foam.

6 Whisk the melted chocolate into the yolk mixture. Stir in the vanilla and salt.

7 Arrange the toasted bread in 2 overlapping rows in a 9- by 13-inch baking pan. Pour the chocolate mixture over the bread. Cover with plastic wrap and place a smaller baking pan on top of the bread so that the slices stay submerged. Add weights if necessary. Refrigerate for 1 hour or until the bread is soaked through.

8 Preheat the oven to 325 degrees F.

9 Remove the smaller pan and plastic wrap from the bread pudding. Cover with aluminum foil and punch a few holes in the top to allow the steam to escape. Place in a larger pan and pour in enough water to come ½ inch up the sides of the smaller pan. Bake for about 1 hour and 45 minutes, or until all the liquid has been absorbed and the pudding has a glossy look.

10 Cut the pudding into squares and serve warm with whipped cream, if desired.

Crème Brûlée Le Cirque ✧ Alain Sailhac

SERVES 6

PREPARATION TIME: ABOUT 15 MINUTES

COOKING TIME: ABOUT 35 MINUTES

DRYING TIME (BROWN SUGAR ONLY): 24 HOURS

COOLING TIME: AT LEAST 30 MINUTES

½ cup packed light brown sugar

4 cups heavy cream

1 vanilla bean, split

½ cup plus 2 tablespoons granulated sugar

6 large egg yolks

■ Special Equipment: Shallow 8-ounce oval ramekins

This is the ultimate crème brûlée, the most classic of all French desserts. There are now many Americanized versions, but, in my opinion, this is the one and only, rich and delicious "burnt cream."

1 Spread the brown sugar on a small baking sheet. Place, uncovered, in a dry spot for at least 24 hours, or until the sugar is quite dry. Push through a fine sieve. Set aside.

2 Assemble *mise en place* trays for this recipe (see page 6).

3 Preheat the oven to 350 degrees F.

4 In a medium-sized saucepan, heat the cream and vanilla bean over medium heat for 3 minutes, or until just warm.

5 In a bowl, whisk together the granulated sugar and egg yolks. When well blended, whisk in the cream. Strain through a fine sieve into a bowl.

6 Divide the mixture among 6 eight-ounce shallow oval ramekins. Place in a shallow roasting pan and add enough hot water to come halfway up the side of the ramekins. Bake for about 30 minutes, or until set and a knife inserted in the center comes out clean. The custards will still be soft; do not overbake.

7 Transfer the custards to wire racks to cool for at least 30 minutes.

8 Preheat the broiler.

9 Spoon the brown sugar into a fine sieve and sprinkle evenly over the tops of the custards. Broil for about 15 seconds to melt and burn the sugar topping. Watch carefully to prevent charring. Serve immediately.

↬ Many chefs use a blow torch or a crème brûlée iron to make the brittle burnt sugar topping. Here, the broiler is equally effective because the sugar is already so dry.

Walnut Biscotti ↬ Claudio Scadutto

MAKES ABOUT 6 DOZEN
PREPARATION TIME: ABOUT 20 MINUTES
COOKING TIME: ABOUT 20 MINUTES

3¾ cups all-purpose flour

2 tablespoons baking powder

5 large eggs

1½ cups sugar

1 vanilla bean or 1 teaspoon pure vanilla extract

1½ cups chopped walnuts

1½ cups vegetable oil

*C*risp biscotti are perfect for dunking in a cup of strong, rich espresso. Great keepers, they are a boon to have on hand for unexpected guests.

---

1 Preheat the oven to 350 degrees F. Assemble *mise en place* trays for this recipe (see page 6). Line 2 baking sheets with parchment paper.

2 In a medium-sized bowl, whisk together the flour and baking powder. Set aside.

3 In a large bowl, using an electric mixer set on medium-high speed, beat the eggs and sugar together until light and creamy. Split the vanilla bean, if using, in half and scrape the seeds into the batter. Or add the vanilla extract, if using, and stir to combine. Add the walnuts and stir just to combine.

4 Stir the flour mixture into the batter, alternating it with the oil and mixing gently until incorporated.

5 Scrape about a quarter of the dough into a pastry bag fitted with a #2 plain tip, and pipe long cylinders of dough about 1 inch thick and about the width of the baking sheet onto the prepared sheets, leaving about 2 inches between each one. Refill the pastry bag and repeat with the remaining dough. Bake for 15 minutes, or until golden brown. Remove the baking sheets and leave the oven on.

6 Let the biscotti rest for about 5 minutes. Cut each cylinder on the diagonal into cookies about 3 inches long. The cookies are about ¼ inch thick. Lay the cookies on the baking sheets and bake for 2 to 3 minutes longer. Transfer to wire racks to cool completely.

Grilled Peaches with Blue Cheese and Sweet Balsamic Vinegar Glaze ✤ Chris Schlesinger

SERVES 6

PREPARATION TIME: ABOUT 15 MINUTES

COOKING TIME: ABOUT 40 MINUTES

FAT PER SERVING, WITH BLUE CHEESE: 10 GRAMS

SATURATED FAT: 4.1 GRAMS

CALORIES PER SERVING: 205

CALORIES FROM FAT: 43%

FAT PER SERVING, WITH LOW-FAT SOUR CREAM: 0.3 GRAM

SATURATED FAT: 0.6 GRAM

CALORIES PER SERVING: 161

CALORIES FROM FAT: 33%

1 cup fine-quality balsamic vinegar

2 tablespoons granulated sugar

1 tablespoon coarsely cracked black pepper

This sensual dessert can also be served as an appetizer. If you are counting fat grams closely, eliminate the blue cheese and replace it with a dollop of low-fat sour cream.

1 Assemble *mise en place* trays for this recipe (see page 6).

2 In a small saucepan, combine the vinegar, sugar, and pepper and bring to a boil over medium heat. Reduce the heat and simmer, stirring occasionally, for about 35 minutes, or until reduced by about two thirds and thick enough to coat the back of a spoon. Set the glaze aside.

3 Preheat a charcoal or gas grill or preheat the broiler.

4 Rub the cut surfaces of the peach halves with the oil and grill, cut side down, over medium coals for about 5 minutes, or until just slightly charred. Alternatively, broil 5 to 6 inches from the heat source. Using a pastry brush,

5 peaches, halved and pitted

2 tablespoons olive oil

4 ounces blue cheese, crumbled,
or ¼ cup plus 2 tablespoons low-fat
sour cream

coat the top of each peach with the glaze and grill or
broil for another minute, or until the glaze begins to
caramelize. Remove from the heat.

5 Brush the peaches with the glaze again and cut into
thick slices. Arrange on warm plates and sprinkle with
the blue cheese, or top with the sour cream. Serve
immediately.

Passion Fruit Ice Cream with Raspberry Purée and White Chocolate Sauce ❧ Jimmy Schmidt

SERVES 6

PREPARATION TIME: ABOUT 25 MINUTES

CHILLING AND FREEZING TIME: ABOUT 10 HOURS

ICE CREAM:

2½ cups passion fruit purée

½ cup granulated sugar

8 large egg yolks

1 teaspoon pure vanilla extract

⅛ teaspoon salt

2 cups heavy cream

RASPBERRY PURÉE:

1 pint fresh raspberries

SAUCE:

1 cup half-and-half

1 tablespoon chopped cassia buds
(or 2 three-inch cinnamon sticks,
broken into pieces)

*This dessert is a true indulgence with the tropical per-
fume of the passion fruit enhanced by the rich white
chocolate sauce and delicate raspberry purée—certainly
an exotic end to a most cosmopolitan meal.*

---

1 Assemble *mise en place* trays for this recipe (see page 6).

2 To make the ice cream, in a medium-sized saucepan,
combine the passion fruit purée, sugar, egg yolks, vanilla
extract, and salt. Cook over medium-low heat, stirring
continuously, for 10 minutes, or until the mixture is thick
enough to coat the back of a spoon. Do not allow to boil.

3 Remove from the heat and add the cream. Strain
through a fine sieve into a bowl. Cool until tepid, cover
and refrigerate for at least 2 hours until cold.

4 Pour the passion fruit mixture into an ice cream maker
and process according to the manufacturer's directions.
When frozen, scrape into a freezer container with a lid,
cover, and freeze for at least 8 hours for a firm texture.

5 To make the raspberry purée, put the berries in a
blender or food processor fitted with the metal blade.

3 large egg yolks

2 tablespoons granulated sugar

1 teaspoon pure vanilla extract

⅛ teaspoon salt

5 ounces white chocolate, finely chopped

½ cup heavy cream

6 sprigs fresh mint

■ Special Equipment: ice cream maker

Purée and strain through a fine sieve into a small bowl. Cover and refrigerate.

6 To make the white chocolate sauce, heat the half-and-half in a small saucepan over medium heat until bubbles form around the edges. Do not boil. Remove from the heat and add the cassia. Allow to cool.

7 In a bowl, whisk together the egg yolks, sugar, vanilla, and salt.

8 Strain the half-and-half, return it to the saucepan and heat again until bubbles form around the edges. Remove from the heat and whisk a few tablespoons into the egg mixture. Add the rest of the hot half-and-half to the egg mixture, whisking continuously. Transfer the mixture to the saucepan and cook over medium heat for about 5 minutes, or until thick enough to coat the back of a spoon. Do not boil.

9 Remove the pan from the heat, add the chopped chocolate, and stir continuously until melted. Stir in the cream, and strain through a fine sieve into a bowl. Cool until tepid, cover and refrigerate until ready to use.

10 To serve, spoon a little of the sauce into the center of each of 6 small dessert plates or shallow bowls. Drizzle with the raspberry purée. Place a scoop of ice cream in the center of the sauce. Garnish with the mint sprigs and serve immediately.

<hr />

❧ Passion fruit purée is available in the frozen food section of specialty food stores. It is also sold through restaurant supply companies. According to Chef Schmidt, one fresh passion fruit will yield only about 2 tablespoons of purée, so the frozen is the most economical.

❧ Leftover white chocolate sauce will keep in a tightly sealed jar in the refrigerator for up to 2 days. Leftover ice cream will keep in the freezer for up to 2 weeks.

Baked Peaches with Warm Blueberry-Thyme Sauce ~ Sally Schneider

SERVES 6

PREPARATION TIME: ABOUT 20 MINUTES

BAKING TIME: ABOUT 20 MINUTES

COOKING TIME (SAUCE ONLY): ABOUT 5 MINUTES

FAT PER SERVING: 0

SATURATED FAT: 0

CALORIES PER SERVING: 81

CALORIES FROM FAT: 0%

6 very ripe medium peaches, halved, pitted, and cut into 6 slices each

1 tablespoon fresh lemon juice

¼ cup plus 2 tablespoons granulated sugar

1 vanilla bean

¼ cup plus 1 tablespoon water

Warm Blueberry-Thyme Sauce (recipe follows)

¼ cup plus 2 tablespoons vanilla nonfat yogurt or vanilla nonfat frozen yogurt

Here is the taste of warm peach and blueberry pie without the "no-no" rich pie crust. I promise you won't miss it! But if you want to splurge, serve a few butter cookies with the peaches.

1 Assemble *mise en place* trays for this recipe (see page 6). Preheat the oven to 450 degrees F.

2 Lay the peach slices in a 10-inch glass pie plate or round baking dish and drizzle the lemon juice over the fruit.

3 Put the sugar in a small bowl. Split the vanilla bean in half lengthwise and, using a small paring knife, scrape the seeds into the sugar; reserve the bean. Stir to combine and then sprinkle over the peaches.

4 Cut the vanilla bean into 2-inch pieces. Nestle the pieces among the peaches.

5 Add the water to the dish and bake for 10 minutes. Baste the peaches with the accumulated pan juices and bake for an additional 10 minutes, or until the peaches are very tender and the pan juices are thick and syrupy. Baste the peaches again.

6 Pour the Warm Blueberry-Thyme Sauce into shallow bowls and spoon the peach slices into the center of each. Garnish each with 1 tablespoon yogurt. Serve immediately.

NOTE: The peaches can be baked early in the day and held at room temperature until ready to serve.

Warm Blueberry-Thyme Sauce

MAKES ABOUT 2 CUPS
FAT PER ⅓-CUP SERVING: 0.2 GRAM
SATURATED FAT: 0
CALORIES PER SERVING: 59
PERCENTAGE OF FAT PER SERVING: 4%

3 cups fresh blueberries (about 1 pint)

2 tablespoons honey

2 tablespoons water

2 sprigs fresh thyme

½ vanilla bean, split

In a small saucepan, combine all the ingredients and cook over medium heat for about 5 minutes, or until the berries release their juices but are still whole. Discard the vanilla bean and serve warm.

NOTE: The sauce can be made with blackberries or raspberries. It can be made up to 3 days ahead, covered, and refrigerated. Reheat gently before serving.

Apricots Baked with Kirsch and Vanilla ❧ Sally Schneider

SERVES 6
PREPARATION TIME: ABOUT 10 MINUTES
BAKING TIME: ABOUT 30 MINUTES
FAT PER SERVING: 0.4 GRAM
SATURATED FAT: 0.03 GRAM
CALORIES PER SERVING: 205
CALORIES FROM FAT: 2%

18 ripe apricots, well washed

¼ cup plus 2 tablespoons superfine sugar

1 vanilla bean

½ cup water

2½ tablespoons kirschwasser

You don't need perfect apricots to make this dish—the vanilla sugar and kirsch magically bring out the hidden assets of the fruit. But make sure the apricots are ripe.

1 Assemble *mise en place* trays for this recipe (see page 6). Preheat the oven to 325 degrees F.

2 With a sharp paring knife, make an incision along the natural seam of each apricot, but do not cut all the way around. Gently pry the halves apart, taking care not to separate them completely. Carefully pry out the pits with your fingers and set the apricots aside.

3 Put the sugar in a small bowl. Split the vanilla bean in half lengthwise and, using a small paring knife, scrape the seeds into the sugar; reserve the bean. Stir to com-

bine. Spoon ½ teaspoon into the cavity of each apricot. In a shallow 1½-quart baking dish or a glass pie plate, arrange the apricots cut side up, so they fit snugly.

4 Sprinkle the water, kirsch, and remaining vanilla sugar over the apricots. Cut the vanilla bean into 2-inch pieces and nestle the pieces among the apricots.

5 Bake for 15 minutes. Baste the apricots with the accumulated pan juices and bake for an additional 15 minutes, or until the apricots are tender. Cool to room temperature. Serve at room temperature or chilled.

NOTE: This can be made early in the day and held at room temperature until ready to serve. Or cover and refrigerate if you wish to serve the apricots chilled.

Roasted Caramelized Pears ～ Sally Schneider

SERVES 6
PREPARATION TIME: ABOUT 10 MINUTES
BAKING TIME: ABOUT 45 MINUTES
FAT PER SERVING: 1.5 GRAMS
SATURATED FAT: 0.8 GRAM
CALORIES PER SERVING: 88
CALORIES FROM FAT: 15%

3 medium-sized pears (about 1 pound), peeled, cut lengthwise in half, and cored

⅔ cup sweet dessert wine, such as Muscat de Beaumes-de-Venise, Sauternes, or Barsac

1 vanilla bean

2 teaspoons unsalted butter

1 tablespoon granulated sugar

This rich-tasting dessert is so satisfying, yet it's low in fat and calories. That makes it easy to enjoy without guilt.

1 Assemble *mise en place* trays for this recipe (see page 6). Preheat the oven to 375 degrees F.

2 Arrange the pears cut side up in a 10-inch glass pie plate or baking dish.

3 Put the wine in a small bowl. Split the vanilla bean in half lengthwise and, using a small paring knife, scrape the beans into the wine. Stir to combine and pour over the fruit. (Discard the bean or save it for another use.)

4 Dot the pears with the butter and bake for 20 minutes, basting occasionally with the accumulated pan juices. Turn the pears and sprinkle with the sugar. Bake, basting frequently, for an additional 25 minutes, or until the pears are glazed and golden. If the pan juices evaporate too quickly, add warm water, a tablespoon at a time, to the pan. Cool slightly, then baste once more with the syrup and serve warm.

NOTE: These can be made early in the day, covered, refrigerated, and reheated just before serving. Bring them to room temperature before reheating in a 350-degree-F oven for about 10 minutes.

Plum and Ginger Kuchen ~ Marie Simmons

MAKES ONE 9-INCH CAKE; SERVES 6
PREPARATION TIME: ABOUT 20 MINUTES
BAKING TIME: ABOUT 1 HOUR
FAT PER SERVING: 2.3 GRAMS
SATURATED FAT: 0.6 GRAM
CALORIES PER SERVING: 283
CALORIES FROM FAT: 7%

---

1 pound red plums, washed, halved, pitted, and cut into small pieces

1 cup granulated sugar

1 teaspoon grated fresh ginger

2 large eggs, at room temperature

2 large egg whites, at room temperature

1 teaspoon pure vanilla extract

¾ cup sifted all-purpose flour

¼ cup sifted cornstarch

1 teaspoon baking powder

There is no butter or oil in this old-fashioned fruit dessert. Enjoy it with a scoop of nonfat ice cream or frozen yogurt.

---

1 Assemble *mise en place* trays for this recipe (see page 6). Preheat the oven to 350 degrees F. Lightly spray a 9-inch springform pan with nonstick vegetable spray.

2 In a bowl, combine the plums, ¼ cup of the sugar, and ½ teaspoon of the ginger and toss to combine. Arrange in an even layer in the prepared pan and set aside.

3 In a large bowl, using an electric mixer, beat the eggs, egg whites, and vanilla for about 2 minutes, or until foamy. Gradually add the remaining ¾ cup sugar and beat for about 4 minutes, or until the mixture is pale yellow and thick. Beat in the remaining ½ teaspoon ginger.

4 Sift the flour, cornstarch, and baking powder onto the egg mixture and gently fold in with rubber spatula just until all the flour is incorporated. Carefully spread the batter over the plums.

5 Bake for about 1 hour, or until the top of the cake is browned and the center feels firm to the touch. Cool on a wire rack.

6 When cool, run a small knife around the sides of the pan and remove the rim of the springform pan. Invert the cake onto a serving platter and serve at room temperature.

Dried Fig and Apricot Tart ❧ Marie Simmons

MAKES ONE 9-INCH TART; SERVES 8

PREPARATION TIME: ABOUT 30 MINUTES

COOKING TIME: ABOUT 25 MINUTES

CHILLING TIME: ABOUT 1 HOUR AND 15 MINUTES

BAKING TIME: ABOUT 40 MINUTES

FAT PER SERVING: 12.2 GRAMS

SATURATED FAT: 1.2 GRAMS

CALORIES PER SERVING: 461

CALORIES FROM FAT: 23%

1½ cups diced dried figs

¼ cup diced dried apricots

¼ cup golden raisins

2 cups water

1 cinnamon stick

2 teaspoons pure vanilla extract

2 cups all-purpose flour

¼ cup granulated sugar

1 teaspoon ground cinnamon plus a pinch

½ teaspoon salt

⅓ cup vegetable oil, preferably canola

⅓ cup plus 1 tablespoon 1% milk

1 tablespoon confectioners' sugar

■ Special Equipment: 9-inch tart pan with a removable bottom

To reduce saturated fat, the pastry crust is made with vegetable oil instead of butter. It gets its distinctive, aromatic flavor from cinnamon. This tart is reminiscent of a classic Italian tart called a crostata.

---

1 Assemble *mise en place* trays for this recipe (see page 6).

2 In a medium-sized saucepan, combine the figs, apricots, raisins, water, and cinnamon stick and bring to a boil over medium-high heat. Reduce the temperature to medium and simmer, stirring frequently, for about 25 minutes, or until the fruit is soft and the water is absorbed. (Add more water if it evaporates too quickly during cooking.) The mixture should be very thick. Cool slightly, then remove the cinnamon stick and stir in the vanilla. Spread on a plate and refrigerate for at least 1 hour, or until stiff.

3 In a large bowl, whisk together the flour, sugar, 1 teaspoon of the cinnamon, and the salt. In a glass measuring cup, stir together the oil and ⅓ cup of the milk. Slowly add to the dry ingredients, stirring constantly with a fork. Gather the dough into a disc, wrap in a plastic wrap, and refrigerate for at least 15 minutes, or until cold.

4 Preheat the oven to 425 degrees F.

5 Divide the dough in half. Roll each piece between 2 sheets of wax paper to an 11-inch round. Fit 1 round into a 9-inch tart pan with a removable bottom. Spread the fig mixture over the dough. Top with the remaining round of dough. Trim the edges and crimp the top and bottom crusts together. Using a small sharp knife, cut several steam vents in the top crust. If desired, cut leaves or other design from the scraps of dough and decorate the top crust. Brush the crust with the remaining 1 tablespoon milk.

6 Bake for 15 minutes. Reduce the heat to 350 degrees F and bake for about 35 minutes longer, or until the pastry is lightly browned. Cool completely on a wire rack.

7 Remove the tart ring and place the tart on a serving platter. In a small bowl, combine the confectioners' sugar and pinch of cinnamon. Transfer to a small strainer, sift over the top of the tart, and serve.

Chocolate Mousse ❧ André Soltner

SERVES 6

PREPARATION TIME: ABOUT 45 MINUTES

COOKING TIME: ABOUT 40 MINUTES

CHILLING TIME: AT LEAST 2 HOURS

1¾ cups granulated sugar

2 tablespoons corn syrup

½ cup water

4 large eggs, separated

½ teaspoon cream of tartar

½ teaspoon instant coffee granules

1 teaspoon dark rum

3 tablespoons unsalted butter, melted and cooled

8 ounces bittersweet chocolate, chopped

1 large egg

3 cups heavy cream

- Special Equipment: candy thermometer; pastry bag fitted with a star tip

Here it is—the sublime. Nobody can resist Chef Soltner's chocolate mousse.

---

1 Assemble *mise en place* trays for this recipe (see page 6).

2 Combine ¾ cup of the sugar, 1 tablespoon of the corn syrup, and ¼ cup of the water in a small, heavy saucepan. Bring to a boil over high heat and boil for 15 minutes, or until the syrup reaches 248 degrees F. on a candy thermometer.

3 Just before syrup is ready, using an electric mixer fitted with a wire whisk, whip the 4 egg whites until foamy. Beat in the cream of tartar.

4 Gradually drizzle the hot syrup into the egg whites, beating as you pour. Then continue beating until the mixture has cooled to room temperature and forms stiff peaks. Set aside.

5 Melt the chocolate in the top half of a double boiler set over barely simmering water, stirring occasionally until smooth. Remove from the heat and set aside.

6 Combine the remaining cup of sugar, 1 tablespoon corn syrup, and ¼ cup water in a small heavy saucepan. Bring to a boil over high heat and boil for 15 minutes, or until the syrup reaches 248 degrees F. on a candy thermometer.

7 Just before the syrup is ready, whisk the egg yolks and egg in a large bowl.

8 Gradually drizzle the hot syrup into the beaten yolks, beating as you pour. Then continue beating until the mixture has cooled to room temperature.

9 Dissolve the instant coffee in the rum. Stir into the egg whites and then stir in the melted butter.

10 Fold the melted chocolate into the egg yolk mixture. Gently fold this mixture into the egg whites just until the egg whites are completely incorporated. The egg whites will lighten the mixture; overfolding will cause it to deflate slightly.

11 Whip the cream until stiff and fold into the chocolate mixture. Spoon one cup of mousse into a pastry bag fitted with a star tip and refrigerate. Spoon the remaining mousse into a serving bowl, cover with plastic wrap, and refrigerate for at least 2 hours.

12 When ready to serve, pipe a design on top of the mousse with the reserved mousse in the pastry bag.

Pistachio-Fig Tart ～ Tom Valenti

MAKES ONE 10-INCH TART
PREPARATION TIME: ABOUT 45 MINUTES
COOKING TIME: ABOUT 30 MINUTES
BAKING TIME: ABOUT 30 MINUTES

FILLING:

1¼ pounds dried figs, stems removed

1½ cups granulated sugar

3 tablespoons ground cinnamon

1 tablespoon ground cloves

½ teaspoon ground mace

Pinch of salt

1 teaspoon freshly ground black pepper

1½ cups water

1 cup white wine

PASTRY:

1½ cups plus 3 tablespoons all-purpose flour

1 cup granulated sugar

1 cup finely ground pistachios

2 teaspoons baking powder

Grated zest of 1 lemon

1 cup (2 sticks) plus 2 tablespoons unsalted butter, at room temperature

3 large eggs

1 large egg yolk

1 teaspoon pure vanilla extract

2 tablespoons milk

*T*om told us that, as a boy, he adored Fig Newtons. *When he learned to cook, one of his goals was to make a "grown-up" version of his childhood favorite. This is his delicious tribute to the famous cookie, devised with Paula Smith, the original pastry chef at Alison on Dominick.*

1 Assemble *mise en place* trays for this recipe (see page 6).

2 To make the filling, in a large nonreactive saucepan, combine the figs, sugar, cinnamon, cloves, mace, salt, pepper, water, and wine and bring to a boil over medium-high heat. Reduce the heat and simmer for about 30 minutes, or until the figs are tender and the liquid has reduced to a thick syrup. Set aside to cool to room temperature.

3 In a food processor fitted with the metal blade, purée the figs with their liquid. Transfer to a bowl and set aside.

4 Preheat the oven to 350 degrees F. Lightly oil a 10-inch tart pan with a removable bottom.

5 To make the pastry, in a large bowl, combine the flour, sugar, pistachios, baking powder, and lemon zest. Add the butter and, using an electric mixer set on low speed, mix until blended. Add 2 of the eggs, the egg yolk, and vanilla and beat on medium speed until combined.

6 Spread half the dough in the bottom of the prepared tart pan. Top with the fig mixture, leaving a 1-inch border all around.

7 Place the remaining dough in a pastry bag fitted with a No. 5 plain tip. Pipe a lattice design on top of the tart, allowing the ends to fall over the edges of the pan. Fold the ends under themselves and pat into place so they adhere to the bottom crust.

■ Special Equipment: 10-inch tart pan with removable bottom; pastry bag fitted with No. 5 plain tip

8 In a small bowl, whisk together the milk and the remaining egg. Using a pastry brush, coat the lattice with the egg wash. Bake for about 30 minutes, or until the pastry is golden brown. Cool on a wire rack for about 10 minutes, cut into wedges, and serve warm.

Passion Fruit Club with Strawberries ✒ Jean-Georges Vongerichten

SERVES 6
PREPARATION TIME: ABOUT 35 MINUTES
COOKING TIME: ABOUT 30 MINUTES
RESTING TIME: 1 HOUR

COOKIE TRIANGLES:

4 cups all-purpose flour

¾ cup granulated sugar

1 cup unsalted butter

1 teaspoon pure vanilla extract

2 large eggs

2 tablespoons water

PASSION FRUIT FILLING:

¾ cup milk

⅔ cup passion fruit purée (see note)

1 vanilla bean, split

⅓ cup granulated sugar

2 tablespoons all-purpose flour

1 large egg

2 tablespoons heavy cream, softly whipped

These represent an innovative French chef's exploration of a favorite American sandwich. The exotic flavor of the passion fruit gives an arresting taste to the pastry cream.

1 Assemble *mise en place* trays for this recipe (see page 6).

2 To make the cookies, in a bowl, combine the flour and sugar. Using two kitchen knives, cut in the butter until the mixture resemble coarse meal.

3 In a small bowl, whisk together the vanilla, eggs, and water. Add to the flour mixture and stir to make a stiff dough. Form into a ball, wrap in plastic, and allow to rest for 1 hour at room temperature.

4 Preheat the oven to 350 degrees F. Make a cardboard triangle pattern that is 1½ inches long from apex to base.

5 On a lightly floured surface, roll out the dough to a large circle about ⅛ inch thick.

6 Lay the cardboard pattern on the dough and, using a small sharp knife, cut out 20 or more triangles. (You will need only 18 but make extra to allow for breakage.) Transfer the triangles to an ungreased baking sheet. Bake for about 10 minutes, until very lightly browned. Remove from the oven, lift from the pan, and cool on a wire rack.

18 strawberries, washed, hulled, and halved lengthwise

3 tablespoons confectioners' sugar

7 To make the passion fruit filling, in a medium-sized, heavy-based saucepan, combine the milk, passion fruit purée, and vanilla bean. Bring to a boil over medium heat. Remove from heat.

8 In a medium-sized bowl, whisk together the sugar, flour, and egg. Slowly whisk in the hot milk mixture and then return the mixture to the saucepan. Place over medium heat and bring to a boil, whisking continously. Reduce the heat and cook, whisking continuously, for about 5 minutes until thick. Remove from the heat and allow to cool.

9 Remove the vanilla bean from the cooled pastry cream. Fold in the whipped cream.

10 On a work surface, lay out 6 of the cookie triangles. Place a strawberry half in each corner. Spoon a little passion fruit pastry cream into the center. Top each one with another cookie and repeat the layer with strawberries and pastry cream. Top with the remaining cookies and serve immediately.

NOTE: Passion fruit purée can be difficult to find. Try ordering it from a specialty store or buy some from a local restaurant. (It is easily available to restaurants through wholesalers.) If you cannot find passion fruit purée, substitute peach purée.

❧ If the strawberries are large, you may have to quarter them. In that case, you will need only 9 berries.

❧ To make passion fruit purée yourself, purée the flesh of 12 passion fruits in a food processor fitted with the metal blade. Strain the purée into a nonreactive saucepan and add ½ cup of sugar. Cook, stirring, over medium heat until the sugar dissolves. Increase the heat and bring to a boil. Immediately take the purée from the heat and strain again. Let it cool to room temperature and use it as instructed, or refrigerate it until needed.

Sweet Potato Pie ❧ Brendan Walsh

SERVES 10 TO 12

PREPARATION TIME: ABOUT 1 HOUR

BAKING TIME: ABOUT 1 HOUR 25 MINUTES

CHILLING TIME (PASTRY ONLY): 2 HOURS

PIE PASTRY:

1½ cups all-purpose flour

¼ teaspoon salt

½ cup solid vegetable shortening, chilled

3 to 4 tablespoons ice water

FILLING:

2 pounds sweet potatoes, peeled and cubed

¼ teaspoon salt

2 tablespoons unsalted butter

½ cup honey

¼ cup packed light brown sugar

1 tablespoon dark rum

1 teaspoon ground cinnamon

⅛ teaspoon freshly grated nutmeg

3 large eggs, lightly beaten

½ cup heavy cream, whipped to soft peaks

■ Special Equipment: Special equipment: 9-inch pie plate; pie weights

Borrowing from the cooking of America's South, Chef Walsh prepares Sweet Potato Pie as the perfect ending to a winning meal. Cut this rich pie into thin wedges and serve with a generous scoop of vanilla ice cream alongside, or, if you want more dessert, bake two pies.

---

1 Assemble *mise en place* trays for this recipe (see page 6).

2 To make the pastry, in a medium-sized bowl, combine the flour and salt. With your fingertips or a pastry blender, blend in the shortening until the mixture resembles coarse meal. Add the water, a tablespoon at a time, blending lightly after each addition, until the dough just holds together. Roll the pastry into a ball and flatten slightly. Wrap in plastic wrap and refrigerate for at least 2 hours.

3 Meanwhile, to make the filling, put the sweet potatoes and salt in a saucepan and add enough cold water to cover by several inches. Bring to a boil, lower the heat, and simmer for about 15 minutes, until the potatoes are very tender when pierced with a fork. Drain well.

4 Transfer the drained potatoes to a blender or a food processor fitted with the metal blade. Blend or process until smooth. Transfer the purée to a bowl and allow to cool for 5 minutes.

5 Stir the butter, honey, brown sugar, rum, and spices into the sweet potato purée until well blended. Cover and set aside.

6 Preheat the oven to 425 degrees F.

7 To continue making the pie pastry, roll out the pastry on a lightly floured surface or between 2 sheets of plastic wrap to circle about 12 inches in diameter and ⅛-inch thick. Line a 9-inch pie plate with the pastry so that it overhangs the edges by about 1 inch. Trim the edges and crimp lightly. Prick the bottom of the pastry with a fork.

8 Line the pastry with cooking parchment or aluminum foil and fill with pie weights, dried beans, or rice. Bake for 5 minutes. Remove the weights and parchment and bake for 4 minutes more. The pastry will barely begin to brown. Remove from the oven and cool on a wire rack. Lower the oven temperature to 350 degrees F.

9 Finish making the filling by putting the eggs in the top half of a double boiler over gently simmering water. Using a hand-held electric mixer set on high speed, or a whisk, beat the eggs for 5 minutes, or until very pale and thick. Do not let the water boil or the eggs may scramble.

10 Fold the eggs into the sweet potato purée until well incorporated. Gently fold in the whipped cream.

11 Pour the filling into the partially baked pie shell. Bake for approximately 1 hour and 15 minutes, or until the filling is golden brown on top and set. Transfer to a wire rack and cool before serving.

Lemon Anise Churros ~ David Walzog

SERVES 6
PREPARATION TIME: ABOUT 15 MINUTES
FRYING TIME: ABOUT 20 MINUTES

1¼ cups all-purpose flour

⅛ teaspoon salt

1 cup water

8 tablespoons (1 stick) unsalted butter

2 teaspoons ground star anise

These are David's version of traditional folk fare snacks, with the lemon and anise adding a refreshing lightness. Since these have to be made at the last minute, allow some time between the end of the meal and dessert.

1 Assemble *mise en place* trays for this recipe (see page 6).

2 Sift together the flour and salt into a medium-sized bowl.

3 In a medium-sized saucepan, combine the water, butter, anise, and lemon zest. Bring to a boil over high heat.

Grated zest of 1 lemon

4 large eggs

1 cup granulated sugar

1 cup confectioners' sugar

Vegetable oil, for deep-frying

■ Special Equipment: deep-fat fryer, deep-fry thermometer, pastry bag with a medium star tip

Immediately stir in the flour mixture and cook, beating constantly with a wooden spoon, until the mixture forms a ball and pulls away from the sides of the pan. Remove the pan from the heat.

4 Beat in the eggs, one at a time until they are well incorporated and the batter is smooth.

5 Combine the sugars in a plastic bag and set aside.

6 Spoon the batter into a pastry bag fitted with a medium-sized star tip.

7 Heat the oil in a deep-fat fryer to 375 degrees F. on a deep-fry thermometer. Or pour enough oil into a large heavy pan to reach a depth of 3 inches and heat to 375 degrees F.

8 Pipe the batter into the hot oil in 5- to 6-inch lengths, being careful not to crowd the pan. Fry for about 3 minutes, or until golden brown, turning once with tongs. Remove from the oil with a long-handled slotted spoon or tongs and drain well on paper towels. Continue frying until all the batter is used. Make sure the oil reaches the corrrect frying temperature between batches.

9 While they are still warm, drop the churros into the bag of sugar. Shake the bag to coat the churros generously with sugar. Serve warm.

❧ These are also great breakfast treats served with a steaming cup of Mexican coffee.

Apricot and Cherry Tart ✍ Alice Waters

SERVES 6

PREPARATION TIME: ABOUT 35 MINUTES

BAKING TIME: ABOUT 30 MINUTES

CHILLING TIME (PASTRY ONLY): ABOUT 30
MINUTES

1 ten-inch sheet frozen puff pastry, partially thawed

½ cup crushed amaretti (Italian macaroons)

1 large egg yolk beaten with 2 teaspoons heavy cream, for egg wash

1½ pounds Bing cherries, pitted

1 pound ripe apricots, halved and pitted

1 to 2 tablespoons sugar

3 tablespoons apricot jam

1 teaspoon Kirschwasser, or other eau de vie

Vanilla ice cream, for serving (optional)

The fruit must be absolutely fresh and perfectly ripe to make this tart. Of course you could substitute other deliciously ripe fruit.

1 Preheat the oven to 400 degrees F. Place a baking stone in the bottom of the oven and let it heat for at least 30 minutes. Assemble *mise en place* trays for this recipe (see page 6).

2 On a lightly floured work surface, roll out the puff pastry between 2 sheets of wax paper to a circle about 14 inches in diameter. Carefully fit into a 10-inch fluted tart pan with a removable bottom, and trim the excess pastry. Freeze the tart shell for 30 minutes.

3 Sprinkle the bottom of the tart shell with the amaretti. Using a pastry brush, generously coat the edges of the pastry with the egg wash.

4 Arrange a circle of cherries around the outer edge of the tart, pressing them together as tightly as possible. Arrange a circle of apricot halves, pitted side down, inside the circle of cherries, pressing together as tightly as possible. Continue making circles until the tart is filled. Fill in any holes with remaining cherries and make sure the fruit is tightly packed into the shell. Sprinkle the top with sugar to taste.

5 Bake for 30 minutes, in the bottom third of the oven, until the pastry is golden and the fruit is tender. Transfer to a wire rack to cool slightly.

6 Meanwhile, in a small saucepan, melt apricot jam with the Kirschwasser over low heat. When softened, brush over the top of the warm tart. Cut into wedges and serve warm, with ice cream if desired.

⤳ Baking stones, which can be bought in kitchen shops and houseware stores, intensify the oven heat and help cook the bottom of tarts, breads, pizzas, and other baked goods. Although you can make this recipe without one, the tart may be slightly soft in the middle.

⤳ You can also use unglazed ceramic tiles, also found in most cookware stores, to line the botom of the oven.

Walnut Roll ⤳ Paula Wolfert

MAKES ONE 17-INCH ROLL; SERVES 6 TO 8
PREPARATION TIME: ABOUT 30 MINUTES
BAKING TIME: ABOUT 15 MINUTES
CHILLING TIME: AT LEAST 2 HOURS

CAKE:

2 tablespoons unsalted butter, at room temperature

5 large eggs, separated

½ cup granulated sugar

Pinch of salt

1¼ cups finely ground walnuts (about 5 ounces)

½ teaspoon baking powder

FILLING:

1½ cups ground walnuts (about 6 ounces)

½ cup hot milk

8 tablespoons unsalted butter, at room temperature

⅓ cup granulated sugar

2 tablespoons Cognac

This dessert is rich enough to end any meal in grand style.

1 Assemble *mise en place* trays for this recipe (see page 6).

2 Preheat the oven to 375 degrees F. Using 1 tablespoon of the butter, grease an 11 x 17-inch jelly-roll pan. Line the pan with wax or parchment paper, leaving a 2-inch overhang at each end, and press down on the butter. Using the remaining 1 tablespoon butter, grease the paper.

3 To make the cake, in a large bowl, using an electric mixer set on medium-high speed, beat the egg yolks until foamy. Beat in the sugar and salt until pale and thick. Using a large wire whisk, fold in the nuts and baking powder.

4 In another large bowl, using the mixer set on medium-high speed, beat the egg whites until they hold stiff peaks. Using a spatula, fold the egg whites into the yolk mixture. Spread evenly in the prepared pan.

5 Bake for 15 minutes, or until a cake tester inserted in the center comes out clean. Cool slightly on a rack, cover with a damp kitchen cloth, and refrigerate for 30 minutes.

6 To prepare the filling, put the walnuts in a bowl and pour the milk over them. Allow to cool.

1 cup heavy cream, whipped to soft peaks

About ½ cup confectioners' sugar

■ Special Equipment: 11 x 17-inch jelly roll pan

7 In a large bowl, using an electric mixer set on medium-high speed, cream the butter. Gradually add the sugar and beat until light and fluffy. Beat in the nut mixture and the Cognac. Using a spatula, fold in the whipped cream.

8 Sprinkle the cake with confectioners' sugar. Lay a 20-inch-long sheet of wax paper over the cake. Grip the ends of the jelly-roll pan, holding the wax paper firmly in place, and quickly invert the cake and pan onto a work surface. Remove the pan and peel the paper from the cake. Using a spatula, spread the filling over the cake. Using the second sheet of wax paper to help guide it, roll up the cake like a jelly roll. Cover with foil and refrigerate for at least 1½ hours, or until the filling is set. Just before serving, dust the top of the cake with confectioners' sugar.

NOTE: Use a nut grinder to grind the nuts fine for the cake and the grating blade of a food processor to grind them less fine for the filling.

Glossary

Achiote seeds: Rusty red seeds of the annatto tree. Used ground or whole to impart a rather musky flavor and a red-to-yellow color to foods. Often called annatto in Hispanic markets.

Aïoli: A pungent garlic-flavored mayonnaise commonly used in the Provence region of France.

Al dente: Italian term meaning, literally, "to the tooth." Most often used to describe pasta that has been cooked until it is just tender but still offers some resistance to the tooth when chewed. Can also be used to describe the degree to which certain vegetables should be cooked.

Amaretti: Very light, crisp macaroon-type Italian cookies made with either apricot kernel paste or bitter almond paste.

Amaretto: Almond-flavored liqueur usually made from apricot kernels. Originally, Amaretto di Saronno was imported from Italy, but now it is distilled in the United States.

Anaheim: Long green chile ranging from mild to barely hot and also called *chile verde*. When dried, also known as chile Colorado.

Ancho: Long, dark brown, mildly hot, sweet dried chile, also called *chile negro*. When fresh, its color ranges from dark green to dark red and it is known as poblano. Best toasted before using.

Ancho chile powder: A dark brown, mildly hot, sweet pure chile powder made from ground ancho chiles, or *chiles negros*. Available in Hispanic and other special markets.

Anisette: A sweet, clear, licorice-flavored liqueur made from anise seeds.

Annatto: See Achiote.

Antipasto: An assortment of Italian hors d'oeuvres, served (literally) "before the pasta."

Árbol: Long, thin, bright orange, very hot chile. Used fresh or dried, it is known by the same name.

Arborio rice: Medium-grain, plump, high-starch rice used in Italian cooking, most often to make the traditional risotto. The best is imported from Italy.

Arrowroot: Tasteless, powdery starch derived from a tropical tuber (of the same name), used to thicken sauces, creamy desserts, and pastry fillings, as well as other foods. Arrowroot is used as a flour in some cookies and crackers. It has twice the thickening power of wheat flour.

Arugula: An astringent, fragrant salad green with a sharp, peppery flavor. Also known as rocket and rucola. Highly perishable.

Baba ghanoosh (or ganoush): A Middle Eastern appetizer made from puréed eggplant, sesame seed paste (tahini), olive oil, garlic, and lemon juice.

Balsamella: Italian for the basic French béchamel sauce made by stirring hot milk into a flour-butter roux. Also known as white or cream sauce.

Balsamic vinegar: Italian specialty vinegar that has been produced in Modena for centuries. It is made from the boiled-down must of white grapes. True balsamic vinegar is aged for decades in a succession of different types of wood barrels.

Banana: Mild yellow chile always used fresh. When mature, it turns bright red.

Bard: To tie fat around lean meats, poultry, or game to keep the meat moist during roasting. The fat is removed just before the end of cooking, to allow browning.

Bâton (or bâtonnet): The shape of a vegetable that has been trimmed into a small, thin stick.

Bel Paese: Mild, buttery, semisoft Italian cow's milk cheese produced outside Milan. Literally translated, the name means "beautiful country."

Biscotti: Crisp, twice-baked, not-too-sweet Italian cookie traditionally dipped into strong coffee or dessert wine before being eaten.

Blanc: A liquid preparation used to cook light-colored and certain other vegetables or white offal, to keep them from discoloring. It is usually a mixture of water, lemon juice or vinegar, and flour. Seasoning may be added.

Blanch: To plunge food briefly into boiling water to set color, texture, or both, or to help loosen the skin. Usually, the food is immediately placed in cold or ice water to stop the cooking process.

Blue corn masa: See Masa.

Bok choy: A mild-flavored Chinese cabbage with creamy white stalks and soft green leaves that rather resemble fat celery in shape. Also known as Chinese mustard cabbage. Napa cabbage can be used as a substitute.

Boniato: A white sweet potato-like tuber used extensively in Latin American and Asian cooking. Also called batata or Cuban sweet potato. Available in Latin and Asian markets, as well as some supermarkets.

Bosc pear: A slender, firm-fleshed winter pear with blotchy, yellow-brown skin.

Bouquet garni: A combination of herbs either tied together or wrapped in a cheesecloth bag and used to flavor sauces, stews, soups, and stocks. The classic French combination is parsley, thyme, and bay leaf.

Braise: To, sometimes but not always, brown meat (or vegetables) first, usually in fat, and then to cook slowly, covered, in a small amount of liquid for a long period of time. Primarily done to tenderize inexpensive cuts of meat.

Broccoli rabe: A pungent, firm-stalked, leafy green with broccoli-like flowers, traditionally used in Italian cooking. Also known as broccoli raab or rape.

Bruschetta: Italian bread rubbed with garlic cloves and drizzled with extra-virgin olive oil after being toasted or grilled. Bruschetta is always served warm, and may be topped with an assortment of other ingredients, such as tomatoes and cheese.

Bulgur wheat: Steamed, dried, and crushed wheat berries, used extensively in Middle Eastern cooking. Available in coarse, medium, and fine grinds. Sold in natural food stores, specialty shops, and many supermarkets.

Butterfly: To split an ingredient, such as meat or shrimp, in half down the center without cutting completely through it. The two halves are opened like a book to form a butterfly shape.

Cappuccino: Italian coffee made by topping espresso with hot, frothy, steamed milk. Ground cinnamon or cocoa may be sprinkled on top.

Caramel: The result of melting sugar to a thick, clear, golden-to-light-brown liquid. Depending on what is added to the sugar, caramel can become a sauce, a candy, or a flavoring.

Caramelize: To heat sugar until it becomes syrupy and turns a rich golden to dark brown.

Cassia buds: The bud of cassia is slightly more pungent and bitter than the more familiar Ceylon cinnamon, which can replace it. Cassia buds are sold in specialty and Hispanic markets.

Ceviche (also seviche): A Latin American dish in which very fresh raw seafood is "cooked" by marinating it in citrus juices. The acidic content of the juice serves to solidify the flesh and turn it opaque. Vegetables are often added to the marinade for color and texture.

Chayote: A mild, thin-skinned, pale green squash that can be eaten raw or cooked. It is pear-shaped with a white interior, and is also known as christophene or mirliton.

Chiffonade: A preparation of greens, classically sorrel, chicory, or lettuce, cut into strips of varying degrees of thickness. Easily done by rolling the leaves up cigar fashion and slicing crosswise. Used as a garnish for soups and cold hors d'oeuvres.

Chile in adobo: Canned chiles, usually chipotle chiles, preserved in a tomato-based sauce (see Chipotle).

Chile paste: A strongly seasoned Asian condiment made from fermented beans, chile peppers, and, often, garlic.

Chile powder: A deep red ground seasoning mix combining chiles, herbs, spices, garlic, and salt that may be mild, hot, or in between.

Chiles: Mild to very hot vegetables ranging in color from pale yellow and green to bright red. There are estimated to be more than 500 varieties of chiles grown worldwide. Try to find the type called for in a particular recipe, but if that is impossible, substitute a similar chile—one that is about the same size and has the same degree of heat.

Chinois: A conical strainer with a handle, usually having an extremely fine mesh. Used to strain liquids that must be exceptionally smooth, often by pushing on the solids with a pointed wooden pestle.

Chipotle: Dried smoked jalapeño chile. It is extremely hot and often is prepared in adobo sauce, a mixture of tomatoes, onions, vinegar, and spices. Canned chipotle chiles in adobo sauce are sold in Hispanic and specialty markets.

Chorizo: Flavorful pork sausage seasoned with garlic, onion, chile powder, spices, and vinegar. Used extensively in Hispanic cooking.

Churro: Slightly sweet, doughnut-like Spanish pastry. Usually served as a snack with coffee.

Cilantro: Pungent herb that looks like flat-leaf parsley, used to flavor Asian, Indian, Latin American, and other dishes. The bright green leaves are sometimes referred to as Chinese parsley or fresh coriander. Cilantro is widely available. There is no substitute. Do not use coriander seeds instead!

Clarified butter: Butter that has been heated and skimmed so that all the milk solids are removed, leaving only the clear yellow fat. See page 20 for instructions for clarifying butter.

Confit: Traditionally, a preserved pork, duck, or goose dish whereby the meat is salted and then slowly cooked in its own fat. After cooking, the fat serves as a preservative seal when the mixture is packed into a container and cooled. The term confit is now used by many chefs to describe fruits or vegetables that have been slowly cooked in their own juices, often with herbs added.

Coriander seeds: Yellow-tan seeds with a taste somewhat like an herb-scented lemon. Used in Asian cooking, pickling, and in some baked goods. Coriander seed cannot be used in place of fresh coriander or cilantro.

Corn husks: Dried husks from large ears of corn that are soaked and used as wrappings for tamales. They are not meant to be eaten. Available in Hispanic and specialty markets.

Cornichon: An imported French gherkin made from tiny pickled cucumbers. Very sour and crisp. Often used as a garnish for pâtés or smoked meats.

Couscous: Granular semolina that is a staple of North Africa, particularly Morocco. The term also refers to a dish for which a meat and/or vegetable stew is cooked in the bottom of a couscousière (the special pot used only for this dish) while the couscous it will top steams in the perforated upper half.

Crème fraîche: In France, thickened, unpasteurized cream; in America, pasteurized cream thickened with added fermenting agents. Tastes rather like slightly sweet sour cream.

Cremini mushrooms: Cocoa-colored, firm textured, intensely flavorful cultivated "wild" mushrooms.

Crostini: Thick slices of toasted bread, usually from a rustic peasant loaf.

Deglaze: To add a liquid, usually wine or stock, to the cooking juices and sediment stuck to the bottom of a pan after sautéeing or roasting meats or vegetables. This is heated and the resulting liquid is often used as a base for a sauce to be served with the ingredients cooked in the pan.

Duxelles: A mixture of finely chopped mushrooms, onions, and shallots sautéed in butter until almost paste-like. Herbs can be added for additional flavor. Used as a stuffing or garnish.

Eau de vie: Literally, "water of life" in French, the term refers to a clear, potent spirit distilled from fermented fruit juice.

Emulsify: To slowly whisk together two ingredients (such as oil and vinegar) that would not normally blend easily to create a smooth, thick mixture (such as a salad dressing).

Enchilada: A tortilla that is often dipped in a chile-seasoned sauce and then rolled up or folded over a filling.

Epazote: A wild herb with flat, pointed leaves and a strong, well-defined, pungent taste, used primarily in Mexican cooking. It is often used to flavor beans, as it is said to reduce gas. Also known as wormweed.

Espresso: Strong Italian coffee, usually made by machine. Steam is forced through very finely ground aromatic coffee beans. Espresso can also be made on the stove top with boiling water.

Extra-virgin olive oil: Oil from the cold-pressed first pressing of olives, which yields the purest olive taste. Ranging in color from bright green to pale yellow, it is highly flavored and the most expensive olive oil.

Farfalle: Butterfly- or bow tie-shaped pasta.

Fava beans: Pale, tannish-green, flat pod beans with a tough outer skin that must be removed, usually by blanching, before eating. Used frequently in Mediterranean and Middle Eastern cuisines.

Fennel: A licorice-scented plant having a bulbous base, celery-like ribs, and feathery foliage. Used extensively in Mediterranean cooking for its sweetly aromatic anise flavor.

Feta cheese: A tangy Greek, Bulgarian or Israeli sheep or goat's milk cheese that is cured in a salty brine.

Flageolet: Very small, pale green beans grown in France. Usually purchased dried and available in specialty markets.

Flute: To make a decorative edge on a pie by pressing the dough together between your thumb and index finger.

Fontina: Semisoft, nutty-tasting Italian cow's milk cheese with 45 percent butterfat. The best Fontina is Fontina Val d'Aosta, named for the Alpine region in which it originated.

Fresno chile: Fairly mild, triangular-shaped chile that usually is marketed green, although it can be yellow or red when mature.

Frisée: A tangy, curly-leafed endive relative, often called curly endive. Its pale green leaves are used in salads.

Frittata: Italian omelet in which the flavoring ingredients are mixed into the eggs before they are cooked over low heat.

Gelato: Italian for ice cream or other frozen dishes with the texture of ice cream. Italian gelato is usually denser and less sweet and contains less fat than its American counterpart.

Gnocchi: Light, airy Italian dumplings made from potatoes, farina, or flour and occasionally flavored with cheese, eggs, or spinach. The literal translation is "little lumps."

Gorgonzola: Rich, creamy, blue-veined Italian cow's milk cheese with a strong, musty flavor. Best used as soon as it has been cut from a wheel, since it quickly loses moisture. Named for the town where it was first produced.

Grapeseed oil: Light, almost flavorless oil extracted from grape seeds. Excellent for cooking as it has a high smoking point.

Great northern white beans: Creamy white dried haricot beans, slightly kidney-shaped, that have a mellow, sweet taste when cooked.

Guacamole: Mexican dip or sauce made from mashed avocado flavored with chiles and citrus juice. Tomato, cilantro, garlic, and scallions are frequent additions.

Guajillo: Long, thin, dark red, extremely hot and flavorful dried chile. When fresh, it is called mirasol.

Guava: Sweet, oval tropical fruit usually about 2 inches in diameter. Outer skin may range from yellow to red to nearly black, while the flesh is pale yellow to deep red. Available fresh in green-grocers and some gourmet specialty shops. It is also available as a paste, jam, or sauce in specialty food stores and Hispanic markets.

Guinea hen: A small game bird, a relative of the partridge, thought to have originated in West Africa. Its somewhat gamey, lean, dry meat is usually barded or casseroled to keep it moist.

Habanero: Small, ridged, round, exceedingly hot chile that is related to the scotch bonnet and usually sold when green and immature, but also may be available yellow, orange, or red. This is the hottest chile.

Hand-held immersion blender: A long, portable blender with a blade at the bottom that can be put directly into a saucepan or deep pot to purée sauces, soups, and other mixtures.

Harissa: An extremely hot Tunisian sauce made from chiles, garlic, and spices. Used to flavor stews and soups and, most particularly, as an accompaniment to couscous.

Hoisin sauce: Sweet, slightly spicy Chinese condiment made from soy beans, chile peppers, garlic, and spices. Deep red in color, it is used as an accent for all types of dishes. Available canned or bottled in Asian markets, specialty food stores, and many supermarkets.

Israeli couscous: A toasted wheat pasta larger and softer than traditional couscous. Available at specialty stores.

Jalapeño: Small, triangular-shaped, hot green chile. Can be bright red when mature. Jalapeños are often sold pickled.

Jícama: A large brown-skinned root vegetable with a sweet, crisp white interior, eaten both raw and cooked. Readily available in Hispanic markets and many mainstream supermarkets.

Julienne: Refers to foods, particularly vegetables, that have been cut into uniform thin strips, usually about the size of a matchstick. The vegetable to be julienned is first cut into slices of uniform thickness and then the slices are stacked and cut into even strips. Classically, these strips are one inch long by one quarter inch thick. Usually used as a decorative garnish.

Kalamata olive: A large, purple-black Greek olive cured in a wine or vinegar brine and packed in oil or vinegar.

Kirschwasser: A clear brandy distilled from cherry juice and cherry pits. Also called kirsch.

Le Puy lentils: Dusky green, dried French lentils with the seed coat intact.

Lemon verbena: A potent, slender-leaf herb with a strong lemon flavor. Often used to flavor drinks and sweet and cold dishes.

Lovage: A large celery-like plant whose leaves, stalks, and seeds are used to flavor foods. The seeds are often just called celery seeds. Called céleri bâtard (false celery) in France. Also known as smellage.

Manchego cheese: A mellow, semi-firm Spanish sheep's milk cheese, originally made only with milk from Manchego sheep. Available at fine cheese shops and Spanish markets.

Mandoline: A stainless-steel vegetable slicer composed of a folding stand and two blades. Used to cut vegetables into uniform slices or matchsticks.

Mango: A thick-skinned tropical fruit with a huge seed and succulent, sweet, soft, orange pulp. Mangos may be round, oblong, or kidney-shaped, and range in weight from six ounces to five pounds.

Marsala: A sweet dessert wine.

Masa: Cornmeal dough traditionally used to make tortillas. Masa may be blue or yellow.

Masa harina: Flour made from dried masa.

Mascarpone: Sweet, soft, creamy cow's milk Italian cheese not unlike a very thick, slightly acidic whipped cream.

Maui onions: Sweet, mild, crisp onions grown on Maui in the Hawaiian Islands, in season from April through July. Vidalia and Walla Walla onions can be substituted for Maui onions.

Mesclun: A mixture of very young shoots and leaves of wild plants used for salads. Mesclun also can contain baby lettuces and leafy herbs.

Mexican oregano: An herb from the verbena family with a long, fuzzy, deeply veined leaf. It should not be replaced by the familiar Mediterranean oregano. Look for it in greengrocers, Hispanic markets, and specialty shops.

Mince: To chop very fine.

Mirasol: See Guajillo.

Mortadella: Italian smoked sausage made from ground pork and beef with added cubes of fat and aromatic seasonings.

Mortar: A round, concave container, often made of marble, porcelain, or wood, used to hold foods that are to be hand-ground using a pestle.

Mulato: Long, very dark brown, mildly hot and sweet dried chile. Similar to ancho in use.

Muscovy duck: Domestically raised duck, gamier in flavor than most, almost always served rare as it has a tendency to dry out when cooked.

Must: Freshly pressed grape juice.

New Mexico: Fairly large, red or green, mildly hot chile, used fresh or dried.

Niçoise olive: Very small brownish-black brine-cured French olive often packed in olive oil, and, frequently, herbs.

Nori: Very thin sheets of dried seaweed, ranging from dark green through deep violet to black, generally used to enclose sushi or rice balls, or as a garnish. Available in Asian and specialty markets either toasted or untoasted.

Orzo: Small rice-shaped pasta.

Pancetta: Salt-cured, unsmoked, flavorful Italian bacon, frequently used to season soups, stews, and sauces.

Papaya: A tropical to semi-tropical pear-shaped fruit with greenish-yellow skin and a golden-orange or red-orange interior. Both the juicy, tart-sweet flesh and the spicy black seeds are edible.

Parma ham: see Prosciutto.

Parmigiano-Reggiano: Grainy, hard, dry, pale amber Italian part-skimmed cow's milk cheese with a sharp-sweet taste. Parmigiano-Reggiano is the most eminent of all Parmesan cheeses; its name is always stamped on the rind of cheeses produced in the areas surrounding the Parma and Reggio Emilia regions.

Pasilla: Long, thin, hot dried chile.

Paupiette: A thin slice of meat or fowl covered with a seasoned mixture of meat or vegetables and rolled up and tied. Often covered with a barding of bacon. Usually braised in stock or wine.

Pecorino Romano: Grainy, hard, dry, aged Italian sheep's milk cheese ranging in color from white to soft yellow, with a very pungent flavor. The best known of the pecorino (sheep) cheeses, it is generally grated for use in cooking and can be substituted for grated Parmesan cheese in many recipes; however, less is called for since it has a sharper taste.

Pequín: A tiny, fiery, red chile, that can be used fresh or dried.

Pestle: A utensil used to pound food in a mortar. It can be rounded or pointed depending on the mortar. It is usually made of the same material as the mortar.

Pesto: A Genoan raw sauce traditionally made by grinding herbs in a mortar and pestle. Today, classic pesto is made with fresh basil, garlic, pine nuts, grated Parmesan cheese, and olive oil. Contemporary variations are made from parsley and cilantro, with other nuts and cheeses. Mainly used as a pasta sauce, but may be used to flavor many other dishes, too.

Phyllo (also filo): Tissue paper-thin Greek pastry dough, usually buttered and stacked in layers to enclose sweet or savory mixtures. Available frozen in most supermarkets.

Picholine olive: Long, pointy, pale green brine-cured Provençal olive packed in vinegar or, at times, olive oil.

Pignoli or pine nuts: Small, oval, fatty nuts from the cones of several varieties of pine trees.

Pilaf: A rice or wheat pasta dish in which the rice or pasta is first browned in oil and then cooked in a well-seasoned broth. Often aromatics, herbs, vegetables, or even meats or fish are added. May be either an entrée or side dish.

Poach: To cook food by gently simmering in seasoned liquid.

Poblano: Long, mildly hot, dark green chile. When dried, it is known as ancho.

Poire William: A clear *eau de vie* made from pears. Often sold with a whole pear inside the bottle.

Polenta: Cornmeal that has been cooked in either water or stock and is eaten either as a mush or allowed to firm up and then grilled or fried. Often flavored with cheese. May be served as an entrée or a side dish.

Porcini mushrooms: Meaty wild mushrooms of the Boletus edulis species, ranging in size from less than an ounce to more than a pound. Also known as cèpes, porcini are often sold dried.

Portobello mushrooms: Cremini (see Cremini) mushrooms that are allowed to mature to large open-gill mushrooms with a deep umber, dense, somewhat fibrous flesh.

Poussin: French term for a very young, small chicken weighing about one to one and a half pounds. Also called squab chicken.

Prosciutto: Italian salt-cured and air-dried ham that has been slow-aged for a dense texture and delicate, sweet flavor. Italy's parma ham is the traditional prosciutto.

Provençal: Used to identify food prepared in the style of the dishes of southeastern France, usually incorporating tomatoes, garlic, and olive oil and often anchovies, eggplant, and/or olives as well.

Quenelle: Traditionally, a light dumpling made of seasoned meat, fish, or poultry, molded into a small oval and poached. Also used to describe the oval shape.

Quesadilla: A filled tortilla, folded into a turnover shape and either toasted or fried. Often served as an appetizer.

Quince: A large, yellow, fall fruit with dry, astringent flesh that tastes like a cross between a pear and an apple. It is always eaten cooked.

Quinoa: Ancient, highly nutritional grain from the Andes Mountains in South America that is now being cultivated in small amounts here. Can often be used in recipes calling for other grains. Available in health food stores.

Ragout: A thick, highly seasoned stew.

Ramp: A wild leek that grows in the spring all along the Eastern seaboard and has a strong onion flavor with hints of garlic. Scallions or leeks are sometimes used in place of ramps but lack their distinctive flavor.

Render: To melt animal fat over very low heat to separate the liquid fat from any meat, skin, or tissue particles. Usually, the fat is then strained for clarity.

Rice wine vinegar: A mild Asian vinegar made from fermented rice.

Ricotta: Fresh, creamy Italian cheese made from the whey left from various cheeses. It is pale white, granular, and almost sweet-tasting.

Risotto: A rich, creamy Italian rice dish created by gradually stirring hot liquid into short-grained rice (such as Arborio) that has been sautéed in oil and aromatics.

Roux: A cooked mixture of flour and fat that is blended into liquids to thicken them.

Sachet: See *Bouquet garni*

Saffron: An intensely aromatic spice from the dried stigmas of a small crocus. It is the world's most costly spice, as it takes about 70,000 stigmas to make one pound. It is an integral part of many Mediterranean dishes, imparting a yellow-orange color and a somewhat bitter flavor to paella, bouillabaisse, and risotto milanese, among other foods.

Sambuca: An anise-flavored Italian liqueur, usually served straight up with a few coffee beans floating on the top.

Sashimi-grade tuna: Tuna of the freshest, highest quality, which can be used for sashimi—Japanese sliced raw fish.

Scotch bonnet: A chile related to the habanero but smaller. Sold fresh, in bright colors ranging from green to yellow, orange, and red. Very hot.

Sear: To brown meat or poultry by cooking over (or under) intense heat. This process is used to seal in the juices before longer cooking.

Semolina flour: Coarsely ground durum wheat flour, traditionally used to make pasta.

Serrano: Small, red or green, very hot chile. Always used fresh.

Shiitake mushrooms: Cultivated, full-flavored, dark brown "wild" mushrooms with broad caps ranging from 3 to 10 inches in diameter. Widely available both fresh and dried.

Soba noodles: Japanese noodles made from buckwheat flour. Available in Asian markets and many supermarkets.

Star anise: A dried, star-shaped pod filled with tiny, pungent seeds. The licorice-flavored spice is used mainly in Asian cooking and is most easily found in Asian markets.

Sumac: A reddish-brown, salty-sour powder ground from the berries of one variety of sumac plant. Used extensively in Middle Eastern cooking.

Tabil: A Tunisian seasoning made by pounding garlic, red bell peppers, chile peppers, cilantro, and caraway seeds together. Used to enhance the flavors of soups and stews.

Taco: A tortilla, usually fried, folded over a meat, poultry, or bean filling and garnished with salad-type trimmings.

Tahini: A thick paste made from ground sesame seeds. Used extensively in Middle Eastern cooking.

Tamale: A savory filling encased in dough, wrapped in corn husks, and steamed.

Tamarind: Fruit of the tamarind tree, often used in Indian, African, and Asian cooking to impart a sweet-sour flavor. Sold as a paste, syrup, pulp, powder, or dried bricks.

Tapenade: A Provençal condiment made from olives, capers, and anchovies seasoned with garlic, olive oil, and, sometimes, herbs.

Tarama: Carp or mullet roe, used extensively in Greek cooking. Usually available canned.

Tartare: Coarsely chopped raw meat or fish, seasoned with herbs, salt, and pepper and served uncooked.

Temper: To introduce a small amount of hot liquid into a cold mixture before it is added to a larger amount of hot liquid, to keep the cold mixture from curdling as it is incorporated into the hot. Tempering is a technique often used with egg preparations.

Terrine: A deep, ovenproof dish with slanted sides, handles and a tight-fitting lid. The preparations made in the dish are also called terrines. They may be made from meats, poultry, fish, or vegetables, and are usually highly seasoned and often covered in gelatin or fat.

Tirami-sù: Translated literally, this means "pick me up." It is a rich, traditional dessert made from mascarpone cheese and ladyfingers.

Tomatillo: A light green, plum-sized, astringent fruit covered with a fine, paper-like husk, related to the cape gooseberry. Tomatillos are primarily used either roasted or boiled in Mexican green sauces. Although they are sometimes called Mexican tomatoes, green tomatoes cannot be substituted for them. Tomatillos are widely available in Hispanic markets and many mainstream supermarkets.

Tostada: A crisply fried tortilla; also, a fried tortilla covered with a savory topping.

Tourner: Usually, to trim vegetables into uniform oval shapes, classically with 7 sides, using a small knife. *Tourner* has a number of other French culinary meanings as well, including the folding of croissant dough (see Techniques, page 11).

Truss: To hold meat or poultry in a compact shape by sewing it with a trussing needle threaded with kitchen twine or by tying the meat or poultry with kitchen twine.

Vin santo: Amber-colored, intensely flavored Italian wine used as an apéritif or to accompany desserts. Produced in small quantities in the Chianti vineyards.

Wonton wrappers: Paper-thin dough squares or rounds used in Chinese cooking to enclose savory fillings. These dumplings are then boiled, steamed, or fried. Available in Asian markets, specialty food stores, and some supermarkets.

Yellowfin tuna: A large tuna with pale pink flesh. Often used raw for sushi, sashimi, and tartare.

Index

CONVERSION CHART

WEIGHTS AND MEASURES

1 teaspoon = 5 milliliters
1 tablespoon = 3 teaspoons = 15 milliliters
⅛ cup = 2 tablespoons = 1 fluid ounce = 30 milliliters
¼ cup = 4 tablespons = 2 fluid ounces = 59 milliliters
½ cup = 8 tablespoons = 4 fluid ounces = 118 milliliters
1 cup = 16 tablespoons = 8 fluid ounces = 237 milliliters
1 pint = 2 cups = 16 fluid ounces = 473 milliliters
1 quart = 4 cups = 32 fluid ounces = 946 milliliters (.96 liter)
1 gallon = 4 quarts = 16 cups = 128 fluid ounces = 3.78 liters

1 ounce = 28 grams
¼ pound = 4 ounces = 114 grams
1 pound = 16 ounces = 454 grams
2.2 pounds = 1,000 grams = 1 kilogram